COMPUTER SCIENCE, TECHNOLOGY AND APPLICATIONS

NEW DEVELOPMENTS IN COMPUTER RESEARCH

Computer Science, Technology and Applications

Additional books in this series can be found on Nova's website under the Series tab.

Additional E-books in this series can be found on Nova's website under the E-book tab.

COMPUTER SCIENCE, TECHNOLOGY AND APPLICATIONS

NEW DEVELOPMENTS IN COMPUTER RESEARCH

NIKOS E. MASTORAKIS
EDITOR

Nova Science Publishers, Inc.
New York

Library of Congress Cataloging-in-Publication Data

New developments in computer research / editors, Nikos E. Mastorakis.
p. cm.
Includes index.
ISBN 978-1-61470-321-1 (hardcover)
1. Computer science--Research. I. Mastorakis, Nikos E.
QA76.27.N477 2011
004.072--dc23

2011022210

Published by Nova Science Publishers, Inc. † New York

CONTENTS

PREFACE

This book presents current research in the field of computer science. Topics discussed include reactive diagnosis of active systems; managing IT resources; parallel iterative solvers using programmable devices; current legislation, executive branch initiatives and options for Congress regarding cybersecurity; high-performance reversible and quantum systolic parallel processing; software development for approximate bayesian computation; broadband infrastructure programs in the American Recovery and Reinvestment Act and spectrum policy in the age of broadband

Article 1- Automated diagnosis of discrete-event systems (DESs) is an interdisciplinary task being faced both by the Artificial Intelligence and the Control Theory communities. The authors consider a specific class of asynchronous DESs, called *active systems*, which are modeled as networks of communicating automata. A diagnostic technique for active systems, called reactive diagnosis, based on fragmented temporal observations, is presented. A fragmented observation is perceived one fragment at a time, under uncertain conditions. Each fragment carries some clues on how the system is evolving. Reactive diagnosis is based on three major requirements: *parsimony*, the unavailability of the global model of the system throughout the reasoning process; *reactivity*, the ability to output an updated group of candidate diagnoses at the occurrence of each observation fragment; and *incrementality*, the ability to reason in an incremental way, by exploiting previously generated knowledge-structures when dealing with each new fragment. Parsimony contrasts with the approaches in Control Theory, which need first generating the global model in order to make a diagnosis. Reactivity contrasts with those a posteriori diagnosis of Artificial Intelligence approaches, where the diagnostic task starts when the complete observation of the system has been collected. Experiments show that parsimony and incrementality make the technique workable when dealing with large-scale systems, such as telecommunication and power networks.

Article 2- Cloud computing is an emerging new computing paradigm designed to deliver numerous computing services in ways that have not been experienced before. It is increasingly being viewed as a utility-oriented computing service. There are even speculations that it has the potential to be the 5th utility (after water, electricity, gas and telephony).

Article 3- Virtualization is a technological breakthrough that has brought about innovations and redefined the way the authors look at hardware and software. It has made it possible to consolidate hardware and software resources and benefit users from the individual to large scale enterprises. In this article they discuss how hardware and software resources can be utilized to the highest level of efficiency. The authors provide examples of how PCs and servers can run multiple operating systems simultaneously thus saving costs of hardware, deployment and maintenance. Despite the popularity of virtualization and its broad adoption, many organizations find it difficult to make the most of this technology. They touch on this issue in this article and argue that this situation could potentially push many of those organizations to consider switching to cloud computing, the new computing utility service that is now shaping the global IT landscape.

Article 4- In this paper, the authors aim at increasing the usage of iterative methods in all possible fields by accelerating such solvers using Reconfigurable Hardware. To demonstrate the acceleration of these solvers, they implement the Jacobi solver on different classes of *FPGAs*, such as *Virtex II Pro*, *Altera Stratix* and *Spartan3L*. The design presented is implemented using *Handel-C*, a compiler with hardware output. Obtained results show that reconfigurable hardware is suitable for realizing accelerated versions of such solvers.

Article 5- **Increasing focus on current cyber threats to federal information technology systems, nonfederal critical information infrastructure, and other nonfederal systems has led to numerous legislative cybersecurity proposals and executive branch initiatives.**

The proposed National Defense Authorization Act for Fiscal Year 2010 (NDAA FY20 10) and the Intelligence Authorization Act for Fiscal Year 2010 (IIA FY20 10) both contain provisions that would affect programs and funding for current and future cybersecurity-related programs. In May 2009, the Obama Administration issued its 60-day review of cybersecurity policy, declaring that U.S. information networks would be treated as a strategic national asset.

Article 6- New type of systolic arrays called reversible systolic arrays is introduced. The two-valued quantum systolic architectures' realizations and computations of the new systolic arrays are also introduced. It is shown that the new systolic arrays maintain the high level of regularity while exhibiting the new fundamental bijectivity (i.e., reversibility) and quantum superposition properties. A systolic array is an example of a single-instruction multiple-data (SIMD) machine in which each processing element (PE) performs a single simple operation. Systolic devices provide inexpensive but massive computation power, and are cost-effective, high-performance, and special-purpose systems that have wide range of applications such as in solving several regular and compute-bound problems containing repetitive multiple operations on large arrays of data. Since basic PEs used in the construction of arithmetic systolic arrays are the add-multiply cells, the results introduced in this paper are general and apply to a very wide range of add-multiply-based systolic arrays. Since the reduction of power consumption is a major requirement for the circuit design in future technologies, the new reversible systolic circuits can play an important task in the design of future circuits that consume minimal power and in multi-dimensional quantum signal processing (QSP) applications.

Article 7- This paper introduces a new type of multiple-valued systolic arrays, called multiple-valued reversible systolic arrays, which extends the concept of two-valued reversible systolic arrays that was introduced in the first part of the article. The multiple-valued quantum systolic architectures' computations of the new type of systolic arrays are also introduced. The new multiple-valued systolic arrays maintain the high level of regularity while exhibiting the new fundamental multiple-valued reversibility (equipollent; bijectivity) and multiple-valued quantum superposition properties. Since basic PEs that are used in the construction of arithmetic systolic arrays are the add-multiply cells, the results introduced in this paper are general and apply to a wide range of multiple-valued Galois add-multiply-based systolic arrays. The new reversibility and superposition properties will be essential in performing super-fast arithmetic-intensive computations that are fundamental in several minimal-power consuming future applications such as in multiple-valued multi-dimensional quantum signal processing.

Article 8- Approximate Bayesian computation (ABC) is a recent developed statistical methodology that allows one to apply likelihood-free Bayesian statistics to complex models. This method relies on two main approximations: the use of Monte Carlo simulations, that avoid the need to use explicit likelihood functions; and the use of summary statistics to summarize data, which significantly reduces the amount of data to handle. The first approximation is particularly interesting in that it allows researchers to perform Bayesian inference provided they can generate simulations from the models of interest. Furthermore, one is not bound to a particular model. In fact one can assess the relative fit of different models just by evaluating the fit of the simulated data for all of them. These properties make ABC a powerful tool for statistical inference, which can be applied to many different fields. This method can be particularly attractive for computer scientists since their know-how in software development can be of great value. ABC can also be a very "democratic" method in the sense that, as long as computer packages are available, even researchers with just standard statistical knowledge can perform complex Bayesian inferences.

Article 9- The American Recovery and Reinvestment Act (ARRA, P.L. 111-5) provided $7.2 billion primarily for broadband grant programs to be administered by two separate agencies: the National Telecommunications and Information Administration (NTIA) of the Department of Commerce (DOC) and the Rural Utilities Service (RUS) of the U.S. Department of Agriculture (USDA). Of the $7.2 billion total, the ARRA provided $4.7 billion to establish a Broadband Technology Opportunities Program (BTOP) at NTIA, and $2.5 billion as funding for broadband grant, loan, and loan/grant combination programs at RUS. Broadband grants and loans funded by the ARRA are competitive and applicants must apply directly to NTIA and RUS. The NTIA appropriation also included $350 million for a national broadband inventory map, funding for the Broadband Data Improvement Act (P.L. 110-385), and funding to be transferred to the Federal Communications Commission (FCC) to develop a national broadband plan.

Article 10- The convergence of wireless telecommunications technology with the Internet Protocol (IP) is fostering new generations of mobile technologies. This transformation has created new demands for advanced communications infrastructure and radio frequency spectrum capacity that can support high-speed, content-rich uses. Furthermore, a number of services, in addition to consumer and business communications, rely at least in part on wireless links to broadband backbones. Wireless technologies support public safety communications, sensors, smart grids, medicine and public health, intelligent transportation systems, and many other vital communications.

Versions of these chapters were also published in Volume 18, Issues 1 and 2 of International Journal of Computer Research. They were submitted for appropriate modifications to encourage a wider dissemination of research.

In: New Developments in Computer Research
Editor: Nikos E. Mastorakis
ISBN: 978-1-61470-321-1

REACTIVE DIAGNOSIS OF ACTIVE SYSTEMS

*Gianfranco Lamperti** *and Marina Zanella*
Dipartimento di Ingegneria dell'Informazione
Università di Brescia, Brescia, Italy

ABSTRACT

Automated diagnosis of discrete-event systems (DESs) is an interdisciplinary task being faced both by the Artificial Intelligence and the Control Theory communities. We consider a specific class of asynchronous DESs, called *active systems*, which are modeled as networks of communicating automata. A diagnostic technique for active systems, called reactive diagnosis, based on fragmented temporal observations, is presented. A fragmented observation is perceived one fragment at a time, under uncertain conditions. Each fragment carries some clues on how the system is evolving. Reactive diagnosis is based on three major requirements: *parsimony*, the unavailability of the global model of the system throughout the reasoning process; *reactivity*, the ability to output an updated group of candidate diagnoses at the occurrence of each observation fragment; and *incrementality*, the ability to reason in an incremental way, by exploiting previously generated knowledge-structures when dealing with each new fragment. Parsimony contrasts with the approaches in Control Theory, which need first generating the global model in order to make a diagnosis. Reactivity contrasts with those a posteriori diagnosis of Artificial Intelligence approaches, where the diagnostic task starts when the complete observation of the system has been collected. Experiments show that parsimony and incrementality make the technique workable when dealing with large-scale systems, such as telecommunication and power networks.

Keywords: Diagnosis, Model-based reasoning, Active systems, Monitoring, Uncertainty

1. INTRODUCTION

Automated diagnosis is chronologically one of the first topics that were tackled in Artificial Intelligence. Attention, originally focused on static systems, in the last decade has progressively shifted to dynamic (or time-varying) physical systems [34, 7]. Communicating automata networks are a formalism that can be adopted for the (distributed) specification of

---

* Gianfranco Lamperti lamperti@ing.unibs.it

dynamic systems, where each component is represented by a finite state machine (FSM) that can communicate with other components through links. Since, at some level of abstraction, most real-world systems can be viewed as discrete-event systems (DESs) modeled as networks of communicating automata, and reasoning about such networks is easier than about continuous systems, from the middle '90s the task of diagnosis of DESs has been receiving an increasing interest from both the Artificial Intelligence [15, 25, 29, 10, 18, 26] and the Automatic Control communities [31, 32, 30, 35, 8, 23, 11, 33].

The DESs considered here and in previous works by the authors, called *active systems*, constitute an adaptation of communicating FSMs [5, 6]. In particular, this paper presents a technique for the diagnosis (during monitoring) of DESs endowed with *bounded* links to asynchronously exchange events with each other.

State-of-the-art approaches to automated diagnosis are model-based, that is, they rely on domain-independent reasoning mechanisms that are capable of processing models representing the structure and behavior of the considered physical system. The diagnostic output is a set of candidate diagnoses, with each diagnosis being a set of faults explaining the observation collected during the system operation and provided as input to the task. Diagnosis is either carried out within a monitoring environment, while the system is operating (possibly in a faulty way), or a posteriori, while the system is either out of work or idle. Researchers are in charge of envisaging new models that allow one to represent new systems and/or more realistic observations, and new reasoning processes and architectures as well, so as to (possibly more efficiently) produce sound and complete candidate diagnoses.

In the general case, the specific faults of a DES cannot be inferred without finding out what has happened to the system [24]. This way, the system evolutions complying with the observation, be they called histories [2], situation histories or narratives [4], paths [9], or trajectories [13], become a product of the diagnostic reasoning.

Temporal observations, being inherent to dynamic systems and processes, are endowed not only with a logical content, describing what observable events have been emitted by the system, but also with a temporal content, describing when such events have been emitted. Both (independent) aspects can be modeled either quantitatively or qualitatively, and both of them may be uncertain. The notion of an uncertain observation allows for the modeling of real world observations that are uncertain as to the identity of the observed labels (logical uncertainty) and/or their reciprocal emission order (temporal uncertainty) and/or the identity of the component emitting the label (source uncertainty). A general model for (qualitative uncertain) temporal observations was proposed in [16], and exploited for describing the input of an a posteriori diagnosis task. Such a model consists of a directed acyclic graph where each node contains an uncertain logical content, ranging over a set of qualitative values (labels), and each arc is a temporal precedence relationship, representing a partial emission order. The observation graph implicitly represents all the possible sequences of labels consistent with the temporal observation received over a time interval, where each sequence is a sentence of a regular language [14]. Although the observation graph is intuitive and easy to build from the point of view of the observer, for the sake of efficiency of any further processing it is better to represent a language in the standard way regular languages are represented, that is, by means of a deterministic automaton. This automaton is called *index space* and it is built as the transformation of a nondeterministic automaton, called *prefix space*, drawn from the observation graph. The problem with this construction method arises when the nodes of the observation graph are received and processed one at a time, typically in monitoring-based diagnosis. The need for producing appropriate diagnostic information at each occurring piece of observation, called *observation fragment*, translates to the need for generating a new index space at each new reception. However, a naive approach, that each time makes up the new index space from scratch, would be computationally inadequate. Therefore, a method for the incremental generation of the index space has been proposed [21].

This paper faces the task of monitoring-based diagnosis of active systems by means of a method called reactive diagnosis. The approach is inspired by the *bridged diagnostic method* [18] and by the notion of an uncertain observation [16]. The former deals with monitoring-based diagnosis of polymorphic systems, which are DESs integrating synchronous and asynchronous behavior, that takes into account completely certain observations. The current work, instead, focuses on asynchronous DESs with uncertain temporal observations. No contribution in the literature to monitoring-based diagnosis of DESs considers uncertain temporal observations prior to [20]. The current paper makes a step forward in this direction by providing a comprehensive theoretical framework, by refining the problem-solving method so as to improve its efficiency, and by showing the results of tests run on an implementation of the method itself.

The remainder of the paper is organized as follows. Section 2 introduces a sample application domain that will be exploited in subsequent examples. Section 3 recalls the class of DESs reactive diagnosis is meant to, namely active systems. Section 4 deals with the graph-based representation of the dynamic evolution of active systems. Section 5 presents the notion of a temporal observation and relevant indexing. Section 6 defines the a-posteriori diagnosis problem. The notion of a monitoring-based diagnosis problem is introduced in Section 7. Section 8 proposes a technique for solving a monitoring problem. Section 9 illustrates how to reduce the size of the search. Experimental results based on an implementation of reactive diagnosis are provided in Section 10. Section 11 relates the current approach to further works in the literature. Final remarks and hints for future extensions and refinements are drawn in Section 12.

2. Reference Application Domain

The presentation of the diagnostic technique is supported by several examples that refer to the sample application domain of power networks. The application is simplified so as examples can be conceptually significant yet manageable in size. A power network is composed of transmission lines. Each transmission line is protected by two breakers that are commanded by a protection.

The protection is designed to detect the occurrence of a short circuit on the line based on the continuous measurement of its impedance: when the impedance goes beyond a given threshold, the two breakers are commanded to open, thereby causing the extinction of the short circuit. In a simplified view, the network is represented by a series of lines, each one associated with a protection, as displayed in Figure 1, where lines $l_1 \dots l_4$ are protected by protections $p_1 \dots p_4$, respectively. For instance, p_2 controls l_2 by operating breakers b_{21} and b_{22}. In normal (correct) behavior, both breakers are expected to open when tripped by the protection. However, the protection system may exhibit an abnormal (faulty) behavior, for example, one breaker or both may not open when required.

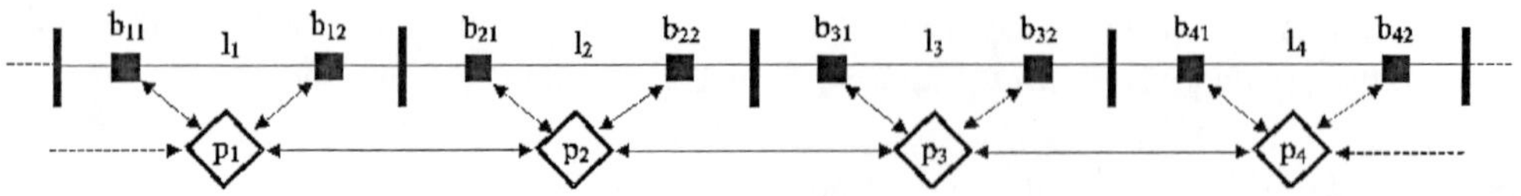

Figure 1. Power transmission network.

In such a case, each faulty breaker informs the protection about its own misbehavior. Then, the protection sends a request of recovery actions to the neighboring protections, which will operate their own breakers appropriately. For example, if p_2 operates b_{21} and b_{22} and the latter is faulty, then p_2 will send a signal to p_3, which is supposed to command b_{32} to open. A recovery action may be faulty on its turn. For example, b_{32} may not open when tripped by p_2, thereby causing a further propagation of the recovery to protection p_4. The protection system is designed to propagate the recovery request until the tripped breaker opens correctly. When the protection system is reacting, a subset of the occurring events are visible to the operator in a control room who is in charge of monitoring the behavior of the network and, possibly, to issue explicit commands so as to minimize the extent of the isolated sub-network. Generally speaking, the localization of the short circuit and the identification of the faulty breakers may be impractical in real contexts, especially when the extent of the isolation spans several lines and the operator is required to take recovery actions within stringent time constraints. On the one hand, there is the problem of observability: the observable events generated during the reaction of the protection system are generally uncertain in nature. On the other, it is impractical for the operator to reason on whatever observation so as to make consistent hypotheses on the behavior of the system and, eventually, to establish the shorted line and the faulty breakers.

3. Active Systems

An active system is a network of *components* that are connected to one another through *links*. Each component is completely modeled by a *communicating automaton* that reacts to events either coming from the external world or from neighboring components through links. Each component is endowed with a set of *input terminals* and a set of *output terminals*. Links connect input terminals to output terminals of different components, thereby supporting the communication between them. A transition from one state to another is triggered by an event ready at an input terminal: such a transition may generate other events at some output terminals of the same component. A transition T of the communicating automaton, from state S to state S', that is triggered by event e at input terminal I, and generates events $e_1, \ldots, e_k$ at output terminals $O_1, \ldots, O_k$, respectively, is denoted by

$$T = S \xrightarrow[(e_1,O_1),\ldots,(e_k,O_k)]{(e,I)} S'. \tag{1}$$

A *standard input* terminal is implicitly assumed, that is meant to receive events from the environment external to the system.

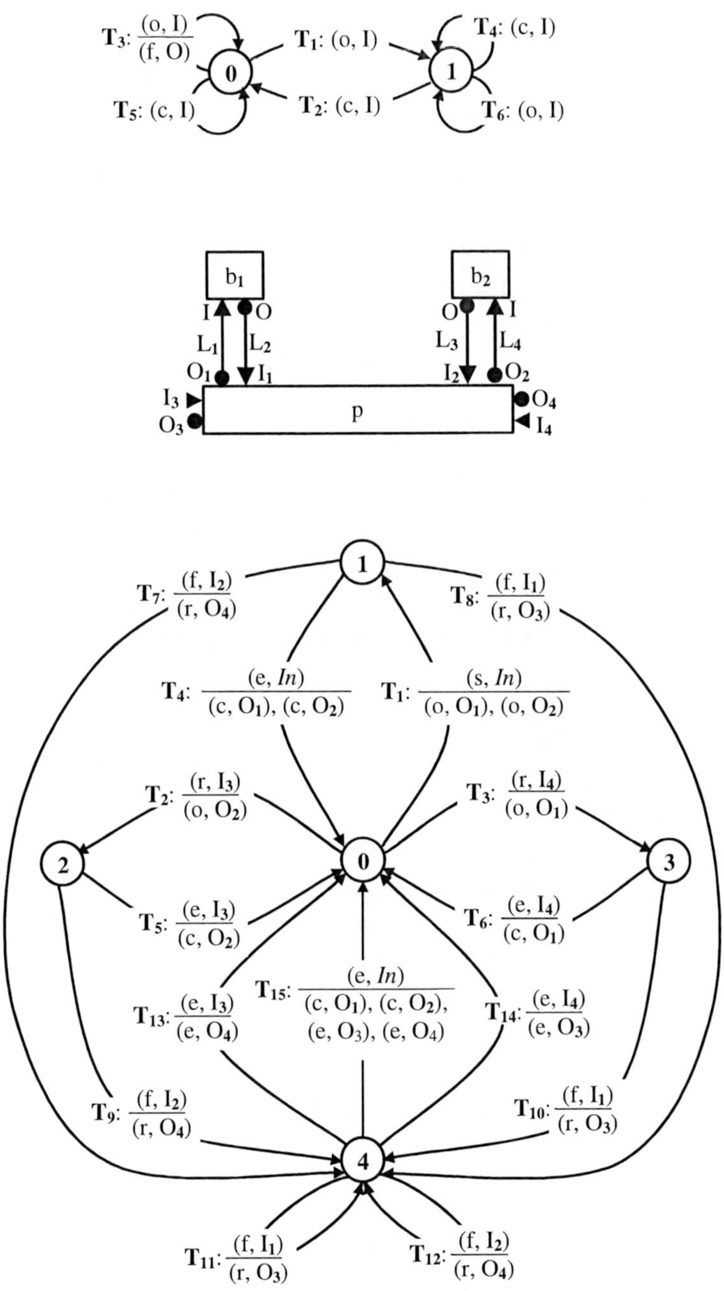

Figure 2. System ψ (center) and models of breaker (top) and protection (bottom).

Example 1. Placed in the center of Figure 2 is the topology of a system ψ, that integrates the three components protecting a generic line, namely protection p and breakers b_1 and b_2. Input and output terminals are denoted by triangles and bullets, respectively. Thus, each breaker is endowed with input terminal I and output terminal O. Terminals I_1, O_1, and I_2, O_2, are meant for p to communicate with b_1 and b_2, respectively. Instead, terminals I_3, O_3, and I_4, O_4, allow the protection to communicate with the adjacent lines on the left and on the right, respectively.[1] The protection is connected with the breakers by means of links L_1 … L_4. System ψ is the abstraction of a sub-part of the protection system. Larger sub-parts of the network may be assembled by connecting instances of ψ together by means of links among protections.

The communicating automaton of breakers is depicted on the top of Figure 2. It involves states 0 (closed) and 1 (open). Transitions between these states are triggered at terminal I by events o and c, namely, T_1 and T_2, respectively. If the breaker is commanded to close when in state 0 or to open when in state 1, then no state change occurs (transitions T_5 and T_6). The possible misbehavior of the breaker is twofold: either it does not open when closed (transition T_3, where event f is output at terminal O) or it does not close when open (transition T_4).

The automaton of the protection is outlined on the bottom of Figure 2. It embodies states 0 … 4 and transitions T_1 … T_{17}. Transition T_1 is triggered by event s (short circuit) at the In standard input terminal, and generates the output event o at both terminals O_1 and O_2 (breakers are commanded to open). Transitions T_2 and T_3 are meant for implementing recovery actions (event r) asked from adjacent lines. Transitions T_7 … T_{12} ask for recovery actions to adjacent lines. Event e denotes the extinction of the short circuit. T_4 moves the protection to its normal state and commands the breakers to close. Instead, transitions T_5 and T_6 move the protection to its normal state based on the notification of short-circuit extinction from the adjacent line that asked for the recovery action: this requires the relevant open breaker to close.

When in state 4, since one or both breakers may have misbehaved, the extinction of the short circuit on the local line requires not only the close command for both breakers but also the notification of the extinction to the adjacent lines so that the breakers involved in the recovery be closed (transition T_{15}).

Transitions T_{13} and T_{14} are triggered by the extinction event sent by an adjacent line: since state 4 denotes a previous request for recovery action from the current protection, such a notification must be forwarded to the relevant adjacent line. Transitions T_{16} and T_{17} consume the extinction event when the protection is in normal state (0).

4. BEHAVIOR

The mode in which a system can behave is constrained by its topology and the models of the components. Additional domain-dependent constraints are possibly given. Interestingly, the whole (possibly unbounded) set of evolutions of a system is confined to a finite automaton representing the *global model* of the system. However, a strong assumption for diagnosis of active systems is the unavailability of the global model since, in real, large-scale applications, the generation of the global model is merely impractical. As such, the global model is intended for formal reasons only. Formally, the graph of the whole set of evolutions of a system Σ, starting from the initial state 0, is called the *behavior space* of Σ, and is indicated by $Bhv(\Sigma, \Sigma_0)$.

Example 2. With reference to system ψ outlined in Figure 2, Figure 3 displays a portion of $Bhv(\psi, \psi_0)$. System states and transitions are represented by (numbered) circles and arrows,

[1] The two adjacent lines are external to system ψ.

respectively. Though not outlined in the figure, each system state is identified by the states of the components and the content of the links. Each arrow is marked by the identifier of the relevant component transition. In particular, state 0 is the initial state of ψ, which is connected with state 1 by an arc marked by transition T_1 of protection p. Based on Example 1, we know that T_1 is triggered by a short circuit on the protected line and generates an opening command to breakers b_1 and b_2 by relevant events at terminals O_1 and O_2 (Figure 2).

A (possibly empty) path between two nodes β and β' of $Bhv(\Sigma, \Sigma_0)$ is a *history segment* of Σ, denoted $\beta \Rightarrow \beta'$. A *history* of Σ is a history segment rooted in the initial state. The (possibly unbounded) sets of history segments and histories are denoted by $\| Bhv^*(\Sigma, \Sigma_0) \|$ and $\| Bhv(\Sigma, \Sigma_0) \|$, respectively.

Example 3. With reference to Figure 3, a possible history is $h = \langle T_1(p), T_1(b_1), T_3(b_2), T_7(p), T_{15}(p), \mathrm{T}_2(\mathrm{b}_1)\rangle$, which corresponds to the following evolution of ψ. $T_1(p)$: Due to the occurrence of a short circuit on the protected line, protection p commands both breakers b_1 and b_2 to open; $T_1(b_1)$: Breaker b_1 opens; $T_3(b_2)$: Breaker b_2 fails to open and notifies p about its misbehavior; $T_7(p)$: Protection p asks a recovery action to the protection apparatus on the right; $T_{15}(p)$: Due to the extinction of the short circuit on the protected line, protection p commands b_1 and b_2 to close, and notifies both adjacent protection apparatus; $T_2(b_1)$: Breaker b_1 closes. In the reaction to the short circuit, the behavior of b_1 is correct, while b_2 is faulty. The extinction of the short circuit is attributable to the recovery action performed by the protection apparatus of one of the right-hand side lines (not necessarily the adjacent one, as a recovery action may be faulty on its turn).

5. Temporal Observation

The history of a system generates towards the external environment a sequence of visible labels, called the *trace* of the history. However, what is actually perceived by the external observer is a *relaxation* of the trace τ, called a *temporal observation*. Formally, let $\mathbf{V}$ be the finite domain of all the observable labels the active system can generate, possibly including the *null* label ε. A temporal observation is a directed acyclic graph (DAG)

$$\mathcal{O} = (\Omega, A) \tag{2}$$

where Ω is the set of nodes, with each $\omega \in \Omega$ being marked with a non-empty subset of labels in $\mathbf{V}$, and $A : \Omega \rightarrow 2^{\Omega}$ is the set of arcs. A '$\angle$' temporal precedence relationship is defined between nodes of the graph. The set of labels marking a node ω is the *extension* of ω, written $\| \omega \|$. $\mathcal{O}$ involves three kinds of uncertainty:

- *Logical uncertainty*: each observable label in the trace τ is perceived as a set of *candidate labels*, possibly including the null label ε. All labels in $\| \omega \|$ but one are *spurious*, with just one being the *actual label*.[2]

[2] If the actual label were ε, then no label was actually generated by the system.

- *Temporal uncertainty*: the absolute temporal ordering of the trace τ is relaxed to partial temporal ordering. If $\omega \angle \omega'$ in $\mathcal{O}$, where l and l' are the actual labels in ω and ω', respectively, then l precedes l' in τ. However, not all precedence relationships between nodes in Ω are known.
- *Source uncertainty*: each observable label may have been generated by different transitions of possibly distinct components.

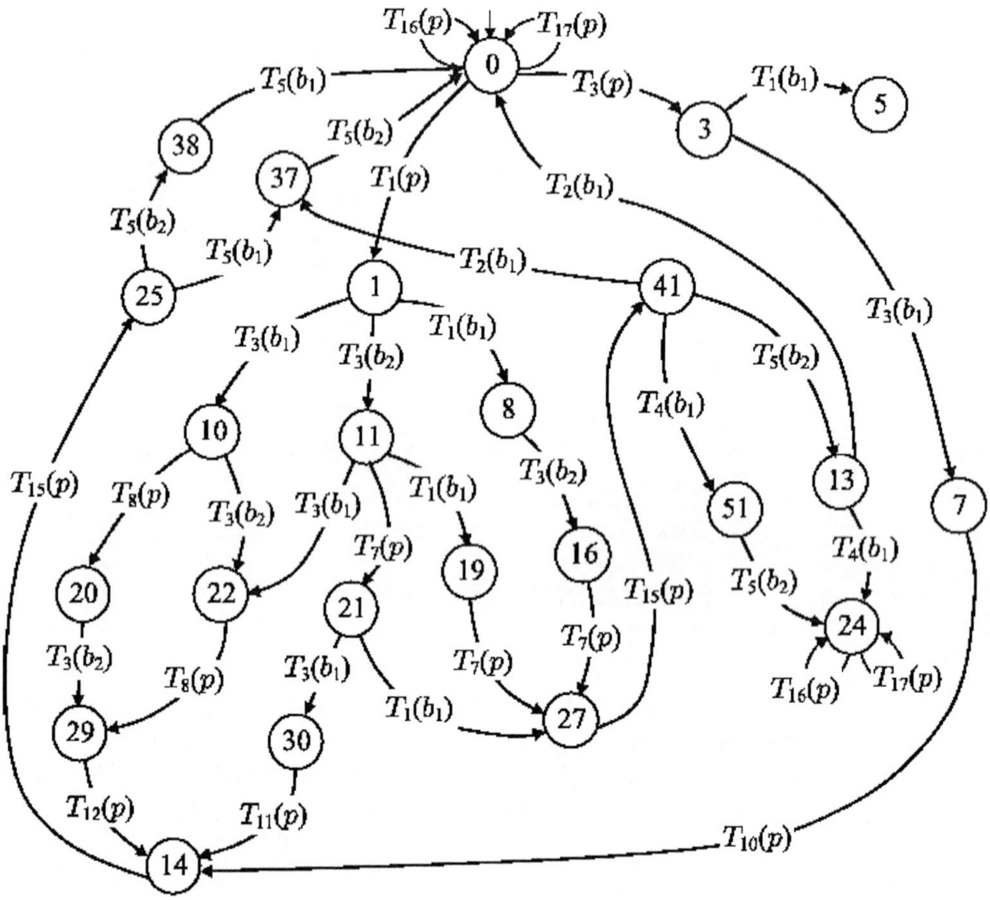

Figure 3. Subspace of $Bhv(\psi, \psi_0)$.

As such, $\mathcal{O}$ implicitly incorporates several *candidate traces*, where each candidate is determined by selecting one label from each node in Ω fulfilling the temporal constraints imposed by the precedence relationships. The set of all the candidate traces of $\mathcal{O}$ is called the *extension* of $\mathcal{O}$, written $\| \mathcal{O} \|$. Among such candidates is (although unknown) the actual trace τ. Like for nodes, all candidate traces but one are spurious.

A temporal observation $\mathcal{O}$ without any logical or temporal uncertainty is a *plain temporal observation*, and can be represented by a sequence of labels, $\mathcal{O} = (l_1, \ldots, l_n)$.

Example 4. Shown in Figure 4 is the graph of a (both logically and temporally uncertain) observation, namely $\mathcal{O}_\psi = (\Omega, A)$, where $\Omega = \{\omega_1, \ldots, \omega_4\}$. Node ω_1 incorporates two

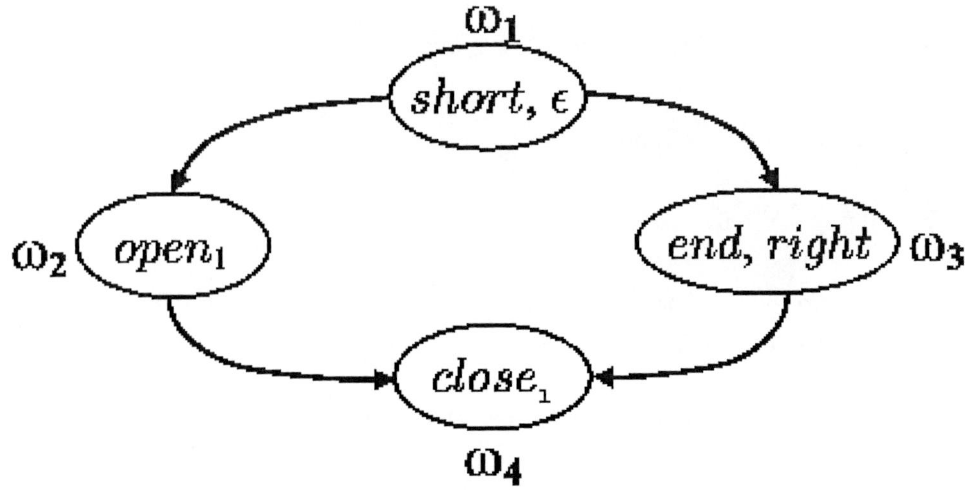

Figure 4. Temporal observation $\mathcal{O}$.

candidate labels, *short* and ε. Then, either ω_2 or ω_3 follows, the former including label $open_1$, the latter including two candidate labels, *end* and *right*. The last generated node is ω_4, with label $close_1$. The observation is logically uncertain since both ω_1 and ω_3 include more than one label, which means that the observer does not know which label was actually generated by the system. For instance, ω_1 points out that the observer does not know whether the system generated label *short* or nothing at all (label ε), that is, what the observer has received may be just pure noise. The extension of the observation, namely $\| \mathcal{O} \|$, includes 8 candidate traces, each of which is obtained by selecting one label for each node without violating the temporal constraints, and then removing the null label ε. For instance, we can pick up labels ε from ω_1, $open_1$ from ω_2, *end* from ω_3, and $close_1$ from ω_4, giving rise to trace $\langle open_1, end, close_1 \rangle$.

Within the diagnostic process it is inconvenient to reason on the temporal observation $\mathcal{O}$ as is, mostly because the explanation-oriented diagnostic reasoning requires some sort of observation- indexing. Such an indexing is more naturally performed based on a surrogate of the observation, namely a deterministic automaton called *index space*. The definition of the latter requires further notions.

Definition 1. (OBSERVATION PREFIX) *Let* $\mathcal{O} = (\Omega, A)$ *be a temporal observation. A* prefix $\mathcal{P}$ *of* $\mathcal{O}$ *is a (possibly empty) subset of* Ω *such that*

$$\forall\, \omega \in \mathcal{P}\, (\nexists\, \omega' \in \mathcal{P}\ (\omega' \prec \omega)). \tag{3}$$

The set of consumed nodes *up to* $\mathcal{P}$ *is*

$$Cons(\mathcal{P}) = \{\omega \mid \omega \in \Omega, \omega' \in \mathcal{P}; \omega \preceq \omega'\}. \tag{4}$$

The set of consumable nodes from $\mathcal{P}$*, called the* frontier *of* $\mathcal{P}$*, is*

$$Front(\mathcal{P}) = \{\omega \mid \omega \in (\Omega - Cons(\mathcal{P})), \forall (\omega' \mapsto \omega) \in A \ (\omega' \in Cons(\mathcal{P}))\}. \tag{5}$$

The composition '$\oplus$' *of $\mathcal{P}$ and a node $\omega \in Front(\mathcal{P})$ is*

$$\mathcal{P} \oplus \omega = (\mathcal{P} \cup \{\omega\}) - \{\omega' \mid \omega' \in \mathcal{P}, \omega' \prec \omega\}. \tag{6}$$

Example 5. Considering the temporal observation $\mathcal{O}$ in Figure 4, a prefix is $\mathcal{P} = \{\omega_2, \omega_3\}$. We have $Cons(\mathcal{P}) = \{\omega_1, \omega_2, \omega_3\}$, $Front(\mathcal{P}) = \{\omega_4\}$, and $\mathcal{P} \oplus \omega_4 = \{\omega_4\}$.

Theorem 1. The frontier of a prefix $\mathcal{P}$ is empty iff the set of consumable nodes of $\mathcal{P}$ equals the set of nodes of the observation graph:

$$Front(\mathcal{P}) = \emptyset \iff Cons(\mathcal{P}) = \Omega. \tag{7}$$

Proof. When $\Omega = \emptyset$ (empty observation), (7) is trivially proven. Thus, we assume $\Omega \neq \emptyset$. Considering $Front(\mathcal{P}) = \emptyset$, based on (5), we have $\{\omega \mid \omega \in (\Omega - Cons(\mathcal{P})), \forall (\omega' \to \omega) \in A \ (\omega' \in Cons(\mathcal{P}))\} = \emptyset$. Assume $Cons(\mathcal{P}) \subset \Omega$. Let $\bar{\omega} \in (\Omega - Cons(\mathcal{P}))$. Three scenarios are possible:

(a) $\forall (\omega' \mapsto \bar{\omega}) \in A \ (\omega' \in Cons(\mathcal{P}))$. In this case, (5) is satisfied for $\omega = \bar{\omega}$, that is, $Front(\mathcal{P}) \neq \emptyset$, a contradiction.

(b) $\nexists \omega' \ (\omega' \mapsto \bar{\omega} \in A)$. Even in this case, (5) is satisfied for $\omega = \bar{\omega}$, as the condition $\forall (\omega' \to \omega) \in A \ (\omega' \in Cons(\mathcal{P}))$ is trivially true. Thus, $Front(\mathcal{P}) \neq \emptyset$, a contradiction.

(c) $\exists (\omega' \mapsto \bar{\omega}) \in A \ (\omega' \notin Cons(\mathcal{P}))$. This scenario makes the universal predicate in (5) false. However, we may choose a different node in $(\Omega - Cons(\mathcal{P}))$, rather than $\bar{\omega}$, specifically one of the ω' satisfying the existential predicate in scenario (c). This way, the above three scenarios are possible for the new node too. In particular, if either (a) or (b) holds, $Front(\mathcal{P}) \neq \emptyset$, a contradiction. If (c) holds, the same considerations are repeated recursively, until either (a) or (b) holds. Since the observation graph is a DAG, such a recursion will end at the either (a) or (b), that is, $Front(\mathcal{P}) \neq \emptyset$, a contradiction.

Thus, $Front(\mathcal{P}) = \emptyset \implies Cons(\mathcal{P}) = \Omega$. Conversely, assume $Cons(\mathcal{P}) = \Omega$ and $Front(\mathcal{P}) \neq \emptyset$. Based on (5), $Front(\mathcal{P})$ includes an ω in $(\Omega - Cons(\mathcal{P})) = \emptyset$, a contradiction. Thus, $Cons(\mathcal{P}) = \Omega \implies Front(\mathcal{P}) = \emptyset$. □

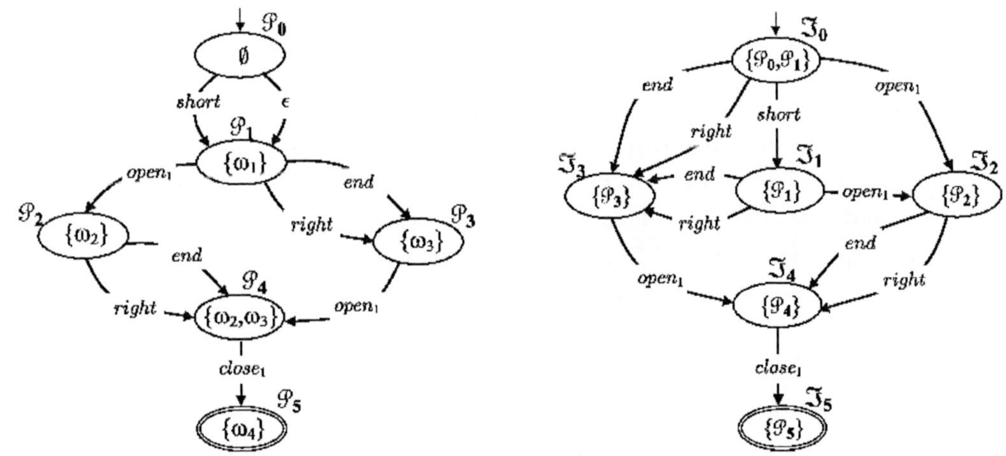

Figure 5. Prefix space $Psp(\mathcal{O}_\psi)$ (left) and index space $Isp(\mathcal{O}_\psi)$ (right).

Definition 2. (PREFIX SPACE) *Let* $\mathcal{O} = (\Omega, A)$ *be a temporal observation. The* prefix space *of* $\mathcal{O}$ *is the nondeterministic automaton*

$$Psp(\mathcal{O}) = (\mathcal{S}^{\mathrm{n}}, \mathcal{L}^{\mathrm{n}}, \mathcal{T}^{\mathrm{n}}, S_0^{\mathrm{n}}, S_{\mathrm{f}}^{\mathrm{n}}) \tag{8}$$

where $\mathcal{S}^{\mathrm{n}}$ *the set of* states:

$$\mathcal{S}^{\mathrm{n}} = \{\mathcal{P} \mid \mathcal{P} \text{ is a prefix for } \mathcal{O}\} \tag{9}$$

$\mathcal{L}^{\mathrm{n}}$ *is the set of* labels:

$$\mathcal{L}^{\mathrm{n}} = \{\ell \mid \ell \in \|\omega\|, \omega \in \Omega\} \tag{10}$$

S_0^{n} *is the* initial state:

$$S_0^{\mathrm{n}} = \emptyset \tag{11}$$

$S_{\mathrm{f}}^{\mathrm{n}}$ *is the* final state:

$$S_{\mathrm{f}}^{\mathrm{n}} = \mathcal{P} \mid \mathcal{P} \in \mathcal{S}^{\mathrm{n}}, Cons(\mathcal{P}) = \Omega \tag{12}$$

and $\mathcal{T}^{\mathrm{n}} : \mathcal{S}^{\mathrm{n}} \times \mathcal{L}^{\mathrm{n}} \mapsto 2^{\mathcal{S}^{\mathrm{n}}}$ *is the* transition function *such that*

$$\mathcal{P} \xrightarrow{\ell} \mathcal{P}' \in \mathcal{T}^{\mathrm{n}} \tag{13}$$

iff the following condition holds:

$$\omega \in Front(\mathcal{P}), \ell \in \|\omega\|, \mathcal{P}' = \mathcal{P} \oplus \omega. \tag{14}$$

Definition 3. (INDEX SPACE) *Let* $\mathcal{O}$ *be a fragmented observation. The* index space *of* $\mathcal{O}$ *is the deterministic automaton*

$$Isp(\mathcal{O}) = (\mathcal{S}, \mathcal{L}, \mathcal{T}, S_0, S_{\mathrm{f}}) \tag{15}$$

equivalent to the prefix space $Psp(\mathcal{O})$. *The* extension *of* $Isp(\mathcal{O})$, *denoted* $\| Isp(\mathcal{O}) \|$, *is the set of sequences of labels generated by paths from the initial state to a final state.*

As proved in [16], the peculiarity of an index space is that $\| Isp(\mathcal{O}) \| = \| \mathcal{O} \|$, that is, each path in the index space, from the initial state to a final state, is a candidate trace of $\mathcal{O}$.

Example 6. Consider the temporal observation $\mathcal{O}_\psi$ in Figure 4. $Isp(\mathcal{O}_\psi)$ is displayed on the right-hand side of Figure 5. This is obtained from $Psp(\mathcal{O}_\psi)$ outlined in the left-hand side of the same figure. Note how (in accordance with the subset-construction algorithm [1] for automaton determinization), each node of $Isp(\mathcal{O}_\psi)$ is identified by a subset of the nodes of $Psp(\mathcal{O}_\psi)$. The extension $\| Isp(\mathcal{O}_\psi) \|$ involves eight temporal sequences (transition paths from 0 to 5). For example, the temporal sequence

$$\Im_0 \xrightarrow{open_1} \Im_2 \xrightarrow{end} \Im_4 \xrightarrow{close_1} \Im_5$$

corresponds to choosing in ω_1, ω_2, ω_3, and ω_4, labels ε, $open_1$, end, and $close_1$, respectively.

Theorem 2. Let $\mathcal{P} \xrightarrow{l} \mathcal{P}'$ be a transition in Psp($\mathcal{O}$). Then,

$$Cons(\mathcal{P}) \subset Cons(\mathcal{P}'). \tag{16}$$

Proof. The proof comes from the definition of the transition function of $Psp(\mathcal{O})$, specifically, from (13) and (14), and the definitions of *Cons* and *Front* in (4) and (5). Since

$$\mathcal{P}' = \mathcal{P} \oplus \omega = (\mathcal{P} \cup \{\omega\}) - \{\omega' \mid \omega' \in \mathcal{P}, \omega' \prec \omega\}, \omega \in Front(\mathcal{P}) \tag{17}$$

$\mathcal{P}'$ will contain node ω that is not contained in $\mathcal{P}'$. On the other hand, the nodes ω' removed from $\mathcal{P}'$ are such that $\omega' \angle \omega$. Thus, based on (4), each ω' is still in $Cons(\mathcal{P}')$, as well as all preceding nodes of ω', namely $Cons(\mathcal{P}') \supset Cons(\mathcal{P})$.

Table 1. Viewer V_ψ (visible transitions only)

Transitions	Observable label
$T_1(p)$	*short*
$T_2(p)$	*left*
$T_3(p)$	*right*
$T_4(p), T_{15}(p)$	*end*
$T_5(p), T_{13}(p)$	*enl*
$T_6(p), T_{14}(p)$	*enr*
$T_1(b_1)$	$open_1$
$T_2(b_1)$	$close_1$
$T_1(b_2)$	$open_2$
$T_2(b_2)$	$close_2$

Corollary 2.1. *Let $\mathcal{P} \xrightarrow{\ell} \mathcal{P}''$ be a transition of Psp($\mathcal{O}$) and $\mathcal{P}'$ a node in the ϵ-closure of $\mathcal{P}''$.* [3] *Then,*

$$Cons(\mathcal{P}) \subset Cons(\mathcal{P}'). \tag{18}$$

6. DIAGNOSIS PROBLEM

In a-posteriori diagnosis of active systems, a diagnosis problem $\wp$ concerns the system model, the observer of the system evolution (viewer), the observation, and the characterization of the faulty behavior (ruler).

Definition 4. (VIEWER) *Let Σ be a system,* **T** *the set of transitions of components in Σ, and* **V** *a domain of labels including the null label ε. A* viewer $\mathcal{V}$ *is a mapping from* **T** *to* **V**. *If* $(T, \varepsilon) \in \mathcal{V}$ *then T* is silent *else T* is visible. *The* product *of a history segment h and a viewer $\mathcal{V}$ is the list of visible labels relevant to transitions in h:*

$$h \boxtimes \mathcal{V} = \langle\, l \mid T \in h, (T, l) \in \mathcal{V}, l \neq \varepsilon \,\rangle \tag{19}$$

Example 7. A viewer $\mathcal{V}_\psi$ for system ψ is defined in Table 1, where transitions associated with the same observable label are grouped together (the missing transitions are assumed to be silent). Since there exist several transitions that are associated with the same label (this occurs for labels *end*, *enl*, *enr*), an observation based on this viewer may be source uncertain. This is the case, for instance, for observation $\mathcal{O}_\psi$ displayed on the left of Figure 4, since node ω_3[3]includes label *end*: given such a label, the observer does not know whether it was generated by either transition T_4 or T_{15} of the protection. Based on Example 3, where $h = \langle T_1(p), T_1(b_1), T_3(b_2), T_7(p), T_{15}(p), T_2(b_1)\rangle$, we have $h \boxtimes \mathcal{V}_\psi = \langle short, open_1, end, close_1\rangle$.

Definition 5. (RULER) *Let T be the set of transitions of components in a system Σ, and* **R** *a domain of labels including the null label ε. A* ruler $\mathcal{R}$ *is a mapping from* **T** *to* **R**. *If* $(T, \varepsilon) \in \mathcal{R}$ *then T is* normal *else T is* faulty. *A* generic diagnosis δ *is a (possibly empty) subset of the non-null labels in* **R**,

$$\delta = \{\varphi_1, \ldots, \varphi_k\} \subseteq (\mathbf{R} - \{\epsilon\}),\ k \geq 0. \tag{20}$$

Table 2. Ruler $\mathcal{R}$ (faulty transitions only)

Transitions	Fault label
$T_1(p)$	sh
$T_3(b_1)$	o_1
$T_4(b_1)$	c_1
$T_3(b_2)$	o_2
$T_4(b_2)$	c_2

The product *of a history segment h and a ruler $\mathcal{R}$ is a generic diagnosis composed of the labels associated with the faulty transitions in h:*

$$h \otimes \mathcal{R} = \{\varphi \mid T \in h, (T, \varphi) \in \mathcal{R}, \varphi \neq \epsilon\}. \tag{21}$$

[3] In a nondeterministic finite automaton, the ε-closure of a state S is the set of states reachable from S by ε-transitions only (including S) [1].

Example 8. Outlined in Table 2 is a ruler $\mathcal{R}_\psi$ for system ψ (normal transitions are omitted). $\mathcal{R}_\psi$ accounts for both the misbehavior of breakers and the occurrence of a short circuit on the protected line. Tracing the latter allows the operator in the control room (see Section 2) to locate the short circuit (this becomes essential when the system under diagnosis encompasses several lines). Based on history $h = \langle T_1(p), T_1(b_1), T_3(b_2), T_7(p), T_{15}(p), T_2(b_1)\rangle$, we have $h \otimes \mathcal{R}_\psi = \{fsh, fo_2\}$: ψ reacts to a short circuit on its protected line and breaker b_2 fails to open.

Definition 6. (DIAGNOSIS PROBLEM) *A* diagnosis problem $\wp$ *for a system* Σ *is a 4-tuple*

$$\wp(\Sigma) = (\Sigma_0, \mathcal{V}, \mathcal{O}, \mathcal{R}) \tag{22}$$

where Σ_0 *is the initial state of C,* $\mathcal{V}$ *a viewer of* Σ, $\mathcal{O}$ *a temporal observation of* Σ, *and* $\mathcal{R}$ *a ruler of* Σ. *The* solution *of* $\wp(\Sigma)$, *written* $\Delta(\wp(\Sigma))$, *consists of a set of candidate diagnoses, with each diagnosis being entailed by a history h in* $Bhv(\Sigma, \Sigma_0)$ *whose trace conforms to* $\mathcal{O}$:

$$\Delta(\wp(\Sigma)) = \{\delta \mid \delta = h \otimes \mathcal{R}, h \in \|Bhv(\Sigma, \Sigma_0)\|, h \boxtimes \mathcal{V} \in \|\mathcal{O}\|\}. \tag{23}$$

The set of candidate diagnoses defined in (23) is sound and complete; in addition, it includes the diagnosis relevant to the actual history of Σ.

Example 9. Let $\wp(\Psi) = (\Psi_0, \mathcal{V}_\psi, \mathcal{O}_\psi, \mathcal{R}_\psi)$, where $\mathcal{O}_\psi$ is shown in Fig. 4, and $\mathcal{V}_\psi$ and $\mathcal{R}_\psi$ in Table 1 and Table 2. Let $h_\psi = \langle T_1(p), T_1(b_1), T_3(b_2), T_7(p), T_{15}(p), T_2(b_1)\rangle$ be the history introduced in Example 3, where $h_\psi \in \|Bhv(\Psi, \Psi_0)\|$. According to Example 7, $h_\psi \boxtimes \mathcal{V}_\psi = \langle short, open_1, end, close_1\rangle$, which, based on Fig. 4, is a candidate trace of $\mathcal{O}_\psi$, that is, $h_\psi \boxtimes \mathcal{V}_\psi \in \|\mathcal{O}_\psi\|$. Since, from Example 8, $\delta_\psi = h_\psi \otimes \mathcal{R}_\psi = \{fsh, fo_2\}$, δ_ψ is a candidate diagnosis of $\wp(\Psi)$.

7. MONITORING PROBLEM

Reactive diagnosis finds out the faults affecting an active system iteratively, once for each considered chunk of observation, as soon as such a chunk has been received. In other words, reactive diagnosis solves a *monitoring problem*. Conceptually, solving a monitoring problem amounts to repeatedly solving a-posteriori diagnosis problems, where the a-posteriori diagnosis problem solved at time $t + 1$ is inherent to the observation considered at time t plus the observation chunk received in the meantime from t to $t + 1$. However, from the operational point of view, the methods for facing the two classes of problems are different since in monitoring-based diagnosis the problem at time $t + 1$ is solved by exploiting the solution of the problem at time t. The uncertain observation taken as input by a monitoring task can still be represented as a DAG. However, this DAG is not given as a whole but, rather, as a list of several *fragments*, where each fragment is composed of one or several nodes along with the relevant temporal constraints (arcs).

Definition 7. (FRAGMENTATION) *Let* $\mathcal{O} = (\Omega, \mathbf{A})$ *be a temporal observation. A* fragmentation $\widehat{\mathcal{O}}$ *of* $\mathcal{O}$ *is a sequence of* fragments,

$$\widehat{\mathcal{O}} = \langle \mathcal{F}_1, \ldots, \mathcal{F}_n \rangle \tag{24}$$

where each fragment $\mathcal{F}_i = (\Omega_i, \mathbf{A}_i)$, $i \in [1 .. n]$, *is such that* $\{\Omega_1, \ldots, \Omega_n,\}$ and $\{\mathbf{A}_1, \ldots, \mathbf{A}_n\}$ *are partitions of* Ω *and* $\mathbf{A}$, *respectively.*

Each fragment $\mathcal{F}_i$ represents a set of observable events received in the current time interval. Each node in Ω_i is an (uncertain) observable event and each arc in $\mathbf{A}_i$ is a temporal precedence relationship (according to the emission order). In particular, $\mathbf{A}_i$ is the minimal set of precedence relationships linking the observable events received in the current interval with each other and with the other events belonging to the observation. In other words, $\mathbf{A}_i$ includes all and only the relationships linking the nodes in Ω_i with their parent nodes.

That given above is the most general definition of a fragmented observation, since it does not constrain the set of parent nodes of a given node in the observation DAG. This means that an event received in the current interval may have one or more parent events (i.e. events that precede it in the emission order) that have not been received yet. To avoid it, we add the following condition, which requires the parents of nodes in the new fragment to be in the fragments received up to now:

$$\forall \omega \mapsto \omega' \in \mathbf{A}_i \left(\omega' \in \Omega_i, \omega \in \bigcup_{j=1}^{i} \Omega_j \right). \tag{25}$$

Each nonempty prefix $\langle \mathcal{F}_1, \ldots, \mathcal{F}_i \rangle$ of $\widehat{\mathcal{O}}$ corresponds to a *temporal sub-observation* $\mathcal{O}_{[i]} = (\Omega_{[i]}, \mathbf{A}_{[i]})$, where

$$\Omega_{[i]} = \bigcup_{j=1}^{i} \Omega_j \qquad \mathbf{A}_{[i]} = \bigcup_{j=1}^{i} \mathbf{A}_j. \tag{26}$$

The *empty* sub-observation is $\mathcal{O}_{[0]} = (\emptyset, \emptyset)$. If $\mathcal{O}$ is known, $\widehat{\mathcal{O}}$ is univocally defined by the sequence of Ω_i, as (25) entails that $\mathbf{A}_i$ necessarily includes all (and only) the arcs entering nodes in Ω_i. For each $i \in [0..\ n]$, we can define a *diagnostic sub-problem*

$$\wp_{[i]}(\Sigma) = (\Sigma_0, \mathcal{V}, \mathcal{O}_{[i]}, \mathcal{R}). \tag{27}$$

Example 10. With reference to Figure 4, a fragmentation of $\mathcal{O}_\psi$ is $\widehat{\mathcal{O}}_\psi = \langle \mathcal{F}_1, \mathcal{F}_2, \mathcal{F}_3, \mathcal{F}_4 \rangle$, where fragments are: $\mathcal{F}_1 = (\{\omega_1\}, \emptyset)$, $\mathcal{F}_2 = (\{\omega_2\}, \{\omega_1 \rightarrow \omega_2\})$, $\mathcal{F}_3 = (\{\omega_3\}, \{\omega_1 \rightarrow \omega_3\})$, and $\mathcal{F}_4 = (\{\omega_4\}, \{\omega_2 \rightarrow \omega_4, \{\omega_3 \rightarrow \omega_4\})$.

Definition 8. (MONITORING PROBLEM) *A* monitoring problem μ *for a system* Σ *is*

$$\mu(\Sigma) = (\Sigma_0, \mathcal{V}, \hat{\mathcal{O}}, \mathcal{R}) \tag{28}$$

where Σ_0 *is the initial state of* Σ, $\mathcal{V}$ *a viewer of* Σ, $\hat{\mathcal{O}} = \langle \mathcal{F}_1, \ldots, \mathcal{F}_n \rangle$ *a fragmented observation of* Σ, *and* $\mathcal{R}$ *a ruler of* Σ. *If* $\hat{\mathcal{O}}$ *is the fragmentation of a plain observation such that each fragment contains just one node, then* $\mu(\Sigma)$ *is a* plain monitoring problem. *The* solution of $\mu(\Sigma)$, *written* $\Delta(\mu(\Sigma))$, *is the list of the solutions of the diagnostic sub-problems* $\wp_{[i]}(\Sigma)$:

$$\Delta(\mu(\Sigma)) = \{\Delta(\wp_{[0]}(\Sigma)), \Delta(\wp_{[1]}(\Sigma)), \ldots, \Delta(\wp_{[n]}(\Sigma))\}. \tag{29}$$

Example 11. Consider the monitoring problem $\mu(\psi) = (\psi_0, \mathcal{V}_\psi, \hat{\mathcal{O}}_\psi, \mathcal{R}_\psi)$, where $\mathcal{V}_\psi$ and $\mathcal{R}_\psi$ are defined in Table 1 and Table 2, respectively, while $\hat{\mathcal{O}}_\psi$ is defined in Example 10. Based on the portion of $Bhv(\psi, \psi_0)$ outlined in Figure 3 and the index space of $\mathcal{O}_\psi$ displayed in Figure. 5, outlined in Figure 6 are the index spaces of the sub-observations of $\mathcal{O}_\psi$, namely, $Isp(\mathcal{O}_{\psi[0]})$, $Isp(\mathcal{O}_{\psi[1]})$, $Isp(\mathcal{O}_{\psi[2]})$, $Isp(\mathcal{O}_{\psi[3]})$, and $Isp(\mathcal{O}_{\psi[4]})$. Let Δ_i, $i \in [0 \,..\, 4]$, denote the solution $\Delta(\wp_{[i]}(\Sigma))$ of the i-th sub-problem of $\wp_{[i]}(\Sigma)$. According to (23), each candidate diagnosis in Δ_i is defined as

$$\delta = h \otimes \mathcal{R}_\psi, \text{ where } h \in \|Bhv(\Psi, \Psi_0)\|, h \boxtimes \mathcal{V}_\psi \in \|\mathcal{O}_{\psi[i]}\|. \tag{30}$$

Considering $i = 0$, since $Isp(\mathcal{O}_{\psi[0]})$ is composed of a unique (both initial and final) state, namely 0, and since there are two silent, normal transitions exiting state 0 of the behavior space, namely $T_{16}(p)$ and $T_{17}(p)$, only the (possibly empty) histories composed of any sequence of such transitions meet (30), therefore $\Delta_0 = \{\emptyset\}$. For $i = 1$, we need considering index space $Isp(\mathcal{O}_{\psi[1]})$. This incorporates two candidate traces, namely $\langle\rangle$ and $\langle$*short*$\rangle$. The former gives rise to the empty diagnosis. Based on Figure 3, the latter matches transition

$$0 \xrightarrow{T_1(p)} 1$$

where $T_1(p)$ is visible via label *short*. Consequently, all the histories obtained by appending to the previous ones such a transition and a tail involving silent transitions only, are consistent with (30). These are the histories ending at either 1, 10, 11, 14, 20, 21, 22, 29, or 30. The relevant solution is therefore $\Delta_1 = \{\emptyset, \{fsh\}, \{fsh, fo_1\}, \{fsh, fo_2\}, \{fsh, fo_1, fo_2\}\}$. For $i = 2$, we focus on index space $Isp(\mathcal{O}_{\psi[2]})$, which involves two candidate traces, $\langle$*short*, $open_1\rangle$ and $\langle open_1\rangle$. The latter does not match any history in Figure 3. The former matches the histories ending at either 8, 16, 19, or 27. These yield the diagnostic set $\Delta_2 = \{\{fsh\}, \{fsh, fo_2\}\}$. Considering index space $Isp(\mathcal{O}_{\psi[3]})$, only two candidate traces match some histories in Figure 3, namely $\langle$*short*, $open_1$, *end*$\rangle$ and $\langle$*right*, $open_1\rangle$. The former matches the histories ending either at 41, 51, 13, or 24. The latter matches only the history ending at 5. Thus, $\Delta_2 = \{\emptyset, \{fsh, fo_2\}, \{fsh, fo_2, fc_1\}\}$. According to $Isp(\mathcal{O}_{\psi[4]}) = Isp(\mathcal{O}_\psi)$, the only candidate trace consistent with the behavior space is $\langle short, open_1, end, close_1\rangle$. This matches the non-empty histories ending either at 37 or 0, which give rise to the singleton $\Delta_4 = \{\{fsh, fo_2\}\}$. Thus, the solution of the monitoring problem is $\Delta(\mu(\psi)) = \langle \Delta_0, \Delta_1, \Delta_2, \Delta_3, \Delta_4\rangle$.

8. SOLVING THE MONITORING PROBLEM

To solve the monitoring problem in Example 11, we tacitly assumed the availability of the relevant behavior space. However, in real application domains, where the active system is large and distributed, this can be regarded as an over-assumption. It is in general infeasible for such systems to generate such a space (the explicit global model), even off-line. Therefore, we need to define a (sound and complete) technique that provides the solution of the problem without any previous generation of the behavior space. Furthermore, we require the technique to generate the index space of each sub-observation incrementally, based on the index space generated for the previous sub-problem. This can be formalized by the following three major requirements.

Requirement 1. (PARSIMONY) The solution of each sub-problem, within the solution of the monitoring problem, shall be generated disregarding the behavior space of the system.

Requirement 2. (REACTIVITY) The solution of each sub-problem, within the solution of the monitoring problem, shall be generated at the occurrence of the relevant fragment.

Requirement 3. (INCREMENTALITY) The generation of the current sub-problem solution shall exploit the reasoning and data structures made up for yielding the previous sub-problem solutions, thereby avoiding starting the diagnostic task from scratch.

During its operation, a system is expected to react to external events and to generate a collection of observable events that are received as a fragmented observation. Solving a monitoring problem $\mu(\Sigma)$ means generating the relevant solution based on each newly generated fragment of observation. In practice, the challenge for the diagnostic technique is to generate each $\Delta(\wp_{[i]}(\Sigma))$ incrementally, based on the previous solution $\Delta(\wp_{[i-1]}(\Sigma))$ and the new fragment $\mathcal{F}_i$, thereby avoiding remaking the entire model-based reasoning rooted in the initial state of the problem.

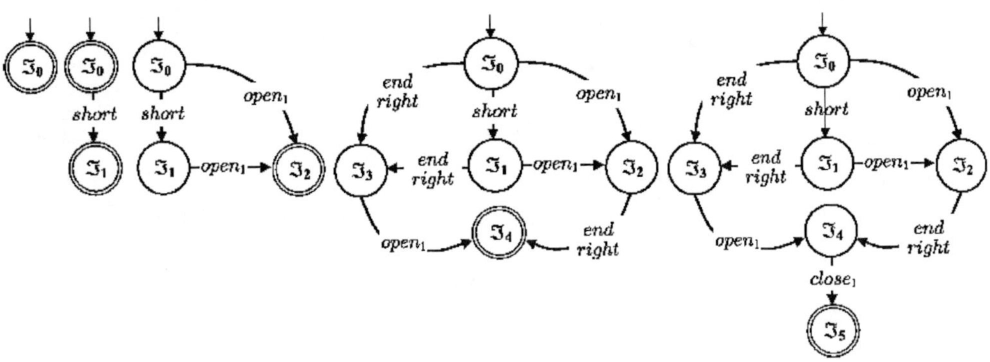

Figure 6. From left to right, $Isp(O_{\psi[0]})$, $Isp(O_{\psi[1]})$, $Isp(O_{\psi[2]})$, $Isp(O_{\psi[3]})$, and $Isp(O_{\psi})$.

The monitoring task needs to know the state reached by the system at the occurrence of each fragment. However, even in case the previous state is univocally known, the current state is bound to be uncertain owing to silent transitions and the uncertain nature of the fragment. On the other hand, the set of possible states at each newly received label is confined within a limited domain, this corresponding to all the states reachable via silent transitions. This domain is a sort of (silent) closure of the current state, which encompasses the part of the behavior that is transparent to the viewer.

Definition 9. (DIAGNOSTIC CLOSURE) *Let $Bhv(\Sigma, \Sigma_0)$ be the behavior space of Σ, with events (which are component transitions) E, states S, and transitions T. Let $\mathcal{V}$ be a viewer and $\mathcal{R}$ a ruler for Σ. Let σ_0 be a state in S. The* diagnostic closure *relevant to* σ_0, $\mathcal{V}$, *and* $\mathcal{R}$ *is a finite deterministic automaton*

$$Dcl(\sigma_0, \mathcal{V}, \mathcal{R}) = (\mathbf{S}, E, \mathbf{T}, S_0, \mathbf{S}_{out}) \tag{31}$$

where $S_0 = (\sigma_0, \mathcal{D}_0)$ is the root, *each state $S \in \mathbf{S}$ is a pair $(\sigma, \mathcal{D})$ where $\sigma \in S$ and*

$$\mathcal{D} = \{\delta \mid \delta = h \otimes \mathcal{R}, h = \sigma_0 \rightsquigarrow \sigma, h \in \|Bhv^*(\Sigma, \Sigma_0)\|, \forall T \in h \ (T \text{ is silent})\} \tag{32}$$

is the diagnostic attribute.[4] *The transition function* $\mathbf{T}$ *is defined as follows:*

$$(\sigma, \mathcal{D}) \xrightarrow{T} (\sigma', \mathcal{D}') \in \mathbf{T} \iff \sigma \xrightarrow{T} \sigma' \in T, T \text{ is silent.} \tag{33}$$

Finally, $\mathbf{S}_{out}$ *is the* leaving set, *so defined:*

$$\mathbf{S}_{out} = \{S \mid S \in \mathbf{S}, S = (\sigma, \mathcal{D}), \sigma \xrightarrow{T} \sigma' \in T, \ T \text{ is visible}\}. \tag{34}$$

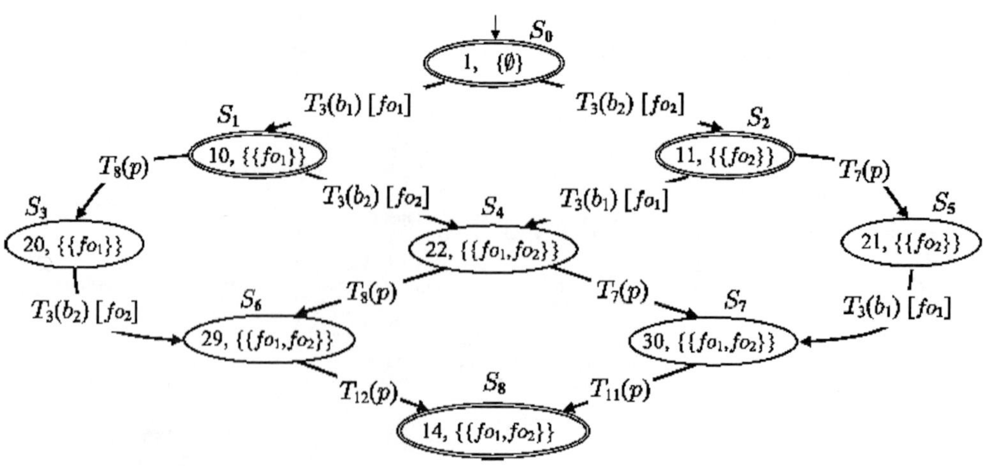

Figure 7. Diagnostic closure $Dcl(1, \mathcal{V}_\psi, \mathcal{R}_\psi)$.

[4] In Section 4, $\| Bhv^*(\Sigma, \Sigma_0) \|$ is defined as the set of history segments within $Bhv(\Sigma, \Sigma_0)$.

Example 12. Consider the portion of $Bhv(\psi,\psi_0)$ in Figure 3, and viewer $\mathcal{V}_\psi$ and ruler $\mathcal{R}_\psi$ in Table 1 and Table 2. The diagnostic closure relevant to state 1 of the behavior space, $Dcl(1, \mathcal{V}_\psi, \mathcal{R}_\psi)$, is depicted in Figure 7 (identifiers of faulty transitions are followed by the fault labels). The initial state is $S_0 = (1, \{\emptyset\})$. For instance, considering state $S_4 = (22, \{\{fo_1, fo_2\}\})$, the diagnostic attribute consists of a single diagnosis $\{fo_1, fo_2\}$, which is entailed by both history segments

$$1 \xrightarrow{T_3(b_1)} 10 \xrightarrow{T_3(b_2)} 22 \text{ and } 1 \xrightarrow{T_3(b_2)} 11 \xrightarrow{T_3(b_1)} 22.$$

The leaving set is $\mathbf{S}_{out} = \{S_0, S_1, S_2, S_3, S_5, S_8\}$, as all these states are left by visible transitions in the behavior space. Incidentally, in Example 12, each diagnostic attribute includes a single diagnosis. Besides, the closure does not involve any cycle. This makes the computation of the closure simple. However, in the general case, such a computation is not as straightforward as that. In fact, the same node in the closure may be reached by several paths. When cycles occur, the number of such paths is unbounded and the diagnostic attribute must account for all such paths. Yielding the closure requires attribute propagation when cycles are detected (see [18] for details).

Definition 10. (MONITOR) *The* monitor *relevant to a system Σ, an initial state Σ_0, a viewer $\mathcal{V}$, and a ruler $\mathcal{R}$, is a graph*

$$Mtr(\Sigma, \Sigma_0, \mathcal{V}, \mathcal{R}) = (\mathcal{N}, \mathcal{L}, \mathcal{A}, N_0) \quad (35)$$

where $\mathcal{N}$ is the set of nodes, $\mathcal{L}$ the set of labels, $\mathcal{A}$ the set of arcs, and $N_0 \in \mathcal{N}$ the initial node. Each node $N \in \mathcal{N}$ is a diagnostic closure

$$N = Dcl(\sigma_0, \mathcal{V}, \mathcal{R}) = (\mathbf{S}, \mathcal{E}, \mathbf{T}, S_0, \mathbf{S}_{out}) \quad (36)$$

where σ_0 is a state of $Bhv(\Sigma, \Sigma_0)$. Let

$$\mathcal{S}_{out} = \bigcup_{N \in \mathcal{N}} \mathbf{S}_{out}(N), \qquad \mathcal{S}_0 = \bigcup_{N \in \mathcal{N}} \{S_0(N)\}, \quad (37)$$

and $\mathbf{V}$ and $\mathbf{R}$ be the domain of labels in $\mathcal{V}$ and $\mathcal{R}$, respectively. Each arc $A \in \mathcal{A}$ is marked by a label in $\mathcal{L} \subseteq \mathcal{S}_{out} \times (\mathbf{V} - \{\epsilon\}) \times \mathbf{R} \times \mathcal{S}_0$. An arc

$$N \xrightarrow{(S,\ell,\varphi,S')} N', \quad (38)$$

where $S = (\sigma, \mathcal{D})$ and $S' = (\sigma', \mathcal{D}')$ are internal nodes of N and N', respectively, is such that:

- *S' is the root of N',*
- *$\sigma \xrightarrow{T} \sigma'$ is a visible transition in $Bhv(\Sigma, \Sigma_0)$,*
- *ℓ is the label associated with T in $\mathcal{V}$, and*
- *φ is the label (possibly ϵ) associated with T in $\mathcal{R}$.*

The root of the diagnostic closure relevant to N_0 is $(\Sigma_0, \mathcal{D}_0)$.

Example 13. Consider the portion of $Bhv(\psi,\psi_0)$ in Figure 3, and viewer $\mathcal{V}_\psi$ and ruler $\mathcal{R}_\psi$ in Table 1 and Table 2. An abstraction of $Mtr(\psi, \psi_0, \mathcal{V}_\psi, \mathcal{R}_\psi)$ (embodying states beyond those in Figure 3) is outlined in Figure 8. Each node of the monitor is depicted as a shaded box encompassing the relevant diagnostic closure. Since each closure is identified by its initial state, we identify each node of the monitor with N_i , where i is the state of $Bhv(\psi,\psi_0)$ relevant to the initial state of the closure. For example, N_1 is the node containing the diagnostic closure shown in Figure 7 (Example 12). Identifiers of component transitions within each diagnostic closure are omitted. Instead, each faulty transition within the closure is marked by the corresponding label in the ruler. Besides, since incidentally each diagnostic attribute is a singleton, it can be identified by the relevant string of ruler labels. For instance, within N_1, state $(14, o_1o_2)$ involves the diagnostic attribute $\mathcal{D} = \{\{o_1, o_2\}\}$, while $(1, \emptyset)$ involves $\mathcal{D} = \{\emptyset\}$. Arcs between nodes of the monitor are only marked by the label of the viewer. Specifically, an arc in (38) is outlined as an arrow from S to S', marked by l.

Definition 11. (LOCAL CANDIDATE SET) *The* local candidate set *of a node $N = (\mathbf{S}, E, \mathbf{T}, S_0, \mathbf{S}_{out})$ in $Mtr(\Sigma, \Sigma_0, \mathcal{V}, \mathcal{R})$ is the union of the candidate attributes of the internal states of N:*

$$\Delta^{loc}(N) = \bigcup_{(\sigma,\mathcal{D})\in \mathbf{S}} \mathcal{D}. \tag{39}$$

Example 14. With reference to Figure 8, the local candidate set of N_1 is $\Delta^{loc}(N_1) = \{\emptyset, \{o_1\}, \{o_2\}, \{o_1,o_2\}\}$, which equals the union of the diagnostic attributes of the nine states involved in the relevant diagnostic closure, namely $Dcl(1, \mathcal{V}_\psi, \mathcal{R}_\psi)$.

The formalization of reactive diagnosis involves two operations on diagnostic sets, namely *diagnostic join* and *diagnostic union*, as detailed below.

Definition 12. (DIAGNOSTIC JOIN) *The* diagnostic join *of two diagnostic sets Δ_1 and Δ_2 is a diagnostic set defined as follows:*

$$\Delta_1 \bowtie \Delta_2 = \{\delta \mid \delta = \delta_1 \cup \delta_2, \delta_1 \in \Delta_1, \delta_2 \in \Delta_2\}. \tag{40}$$

Definition 13. (DIAGNOSTIC UNION) *The* diagnostic union *of a diagnostic set Δ and a label φ, in the domain* **R** *of a ruler, is a diagnostic set defined as follows:*

$$\Delta \uplus \varphi = \begin{cases} \Delta & \text{if } \varphi = \epsilon \\ \{\delta' \mid \delta' = \delta \cup \{\varphi\}, \delta \in \Delta\} & \text{otherwise.} \end{cases} \tag{41}$$

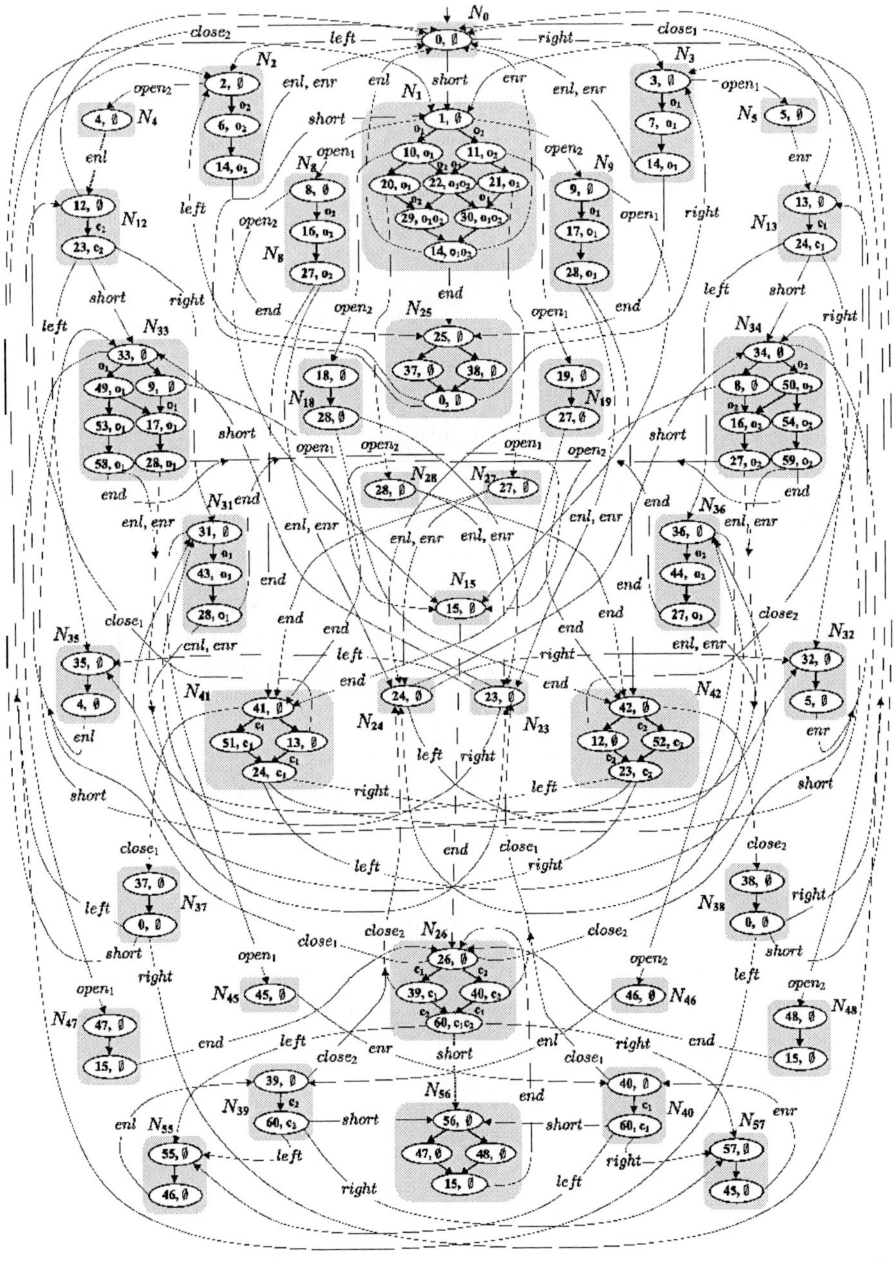

Figure 8. Monitor $Mtr(\psi, \psi_0, \mathcal{V}_\psi, \mathcal{R}_\psi)$.

Theorem 3. The following equivalences hold:

$$\Delta \uplus \epsilon \equiv \Delta \tag{42}$$

$$\Delta \bowtie \{\emptyset\} \equiv \Delta \tag{43}$$

$$\Delta_1 \bowtie \Delta_2 \equiv \Delta_2 \bowtie \Delta_1 \tag{44}$$

$$\Delta_1 \bowtie (\Delta_2 \bowtie \Delta_3) \equiv (\Delta_1 \bowtie \Delta_2) \bowtie \Delta_3 \tag{45}$$

$$\Delta_1 \bowtie (\Delta_2 \cup \Delta_3) \equiv (\Delta_1 \bowtie \Delta_2) \cup (\Delta_1 \bowtie \Delta_3) \tag{46}$$

$$(\Delta_1 \bowtie \Delta_2) \uplus \varphi \equiv (\Delta_1 \uplus \varphi) \bowtie (\Delta_2 \uplus \varphi) \tag{47}$$

$$(\Delta_1 \bowtie \Delta_2) \uplus \varphi \equiv \Delta_1 \bowtie (\Delta_2 \uplus \varphi) \tag{48}$$

$$(\Delta_1 \cup \Delta_2) \uplus \varphi \equiv (\Delta_1 \uplus \varphi) \cup (\Delta_2 \uplus \varphi). \tag{49}$$

Proof. Equations (42) and (43) derive immediately from the definitions. (44) is supported by the commutative property of union:

$$\begin{aligned} \Delta_1 \bowtie \Delta_2 &= \{\delta \mid \delta = \delta_1 \cup \delta_2, \delta_1 \in \Delta_1, \delta_2 \in \Delta_2\} \\ &= \{\delta \mid \delta = \delta_2 \cup \delta_1, \delta_2 \in \Delta_2, \delta_1 \in \Delta_1\} = \Delta_2 \bowtie \Delta_1. \end{aligned}$$

Equation (45) is grounded on the associative property of union:

$$\begin{aligned} (\Delta_1 \bowtie \Delta_2) \bowtie \Delta_3 &= \{\delta \mid \delta = \delta_{12} \cup \delta_3, \delta_{12} \in (\Delta_1 \bowtie \Delta_2), \delta_3 \in \Delta_3\} \\ &= \{\delta \mid \delta = \delta_{12} \cup \delta_3, \delta_{12} \in \{\delta \mid \delta = \delta_1 \cup \delta_2, \delta_1 \in \Delta_1, \delta_2 \in \Delta_2\}, \delta_3 \in \Delta_3\} \\ &= \{\delta \mid \delta = \delta_1 \cup \delta_2 \cup \delta_3, \delta_1 \in \Delta_1, \delta_2 \in \Delta_2, \delta_3 \in \Delta_3\}. \end{aligned} \tag{50}$$

$$\begin{aligned} \Delta_1 \bowtie (\Delta_2 \bowtie \Delta_3) &= \{\delta \mid \delta = \delta_1 \cup \delta_{23}, \delta_1 \in \Delta_1, \delta_{23} \in (\Delta_2 \bowtie \Delta_3)\} \\ &= \{\delta \mid \delta = \delta_1 \cup \delta_{23}, \delta_1 \in \Delta_1, \delta_{23} \in \{\delta \mid \delta = \delta_2 \cup \delta_3, \delta_2 \in \Delta_2, \delta_3 \in \Delta_3\}\} \\ &= \{\delta \mid \delta = \delta_1 \cup \delta_2 \cup \delta_3, \delta_1 \in \Delta_1, \delta_2 \in \Delta_2, \delta_3 \in \Delta_3\}. \end{aligned} \tag{51}$$

The equivalence is based on the equality of the two sides (50) and (51). Equation (46) can be derived as follows:

$$\begin{aligned} \Delta_1 \bowtie (\Delta_2 \cup \Delta_3) &= \{\delta \mid \delta = \delta_1 \cup \delta_{23}, \delta_1 \in \Delta_1, \delta_{23} \in (\Delta_2 \cup \Delta_3)\} \\ &= \{\delta \mid \delta = \delta_1 \cup \delta_2, \delta_1 \in \Delta_1, \delta_2 \in \Delta_2\} \cup \{\delta \mid \delta = \delta_1 \cup \delta_3, \delta_1 \in \Delta_1, \delta_3 \in \Delta_3\} \\ &= (\Delta_1 \bowtie \Delta_2) \cup (\Delta_1 \bowtie \Delta_3). \end{aligned}$$

Equation (47) can be immediately proved when $\varphi = \varepsilon$:

$$\begin{aligned} (\Delta_1 \bowtie \Delta_2) \uplus \epsilon &= \Delta_1 \bowtie \Delta_2 \\ (\Delta_1 \uplus \epsilon) \bowtie (\Delta_2 \uplus \epsilon) &= \Delta_1 \bowtie \Delta_2. \end{aligned}$$

when $\varphi \neq \varepsilon$, we have the following:

$$\begin{aligned} (\Delta_1 \uplus \varphi) \bowtie (\Delta_2 \uplus \varphi) &= \{\delta' \mid \delta' = \delta_1' \cup \delta_2', \delta_1' \in \Delta_1 \uplus \varphi, \delta_2' \in \Delta_2 \uplus \varphi\} \\ &= \{\delta' \mid \delta' = (\delta_1 \cup \{\varphi\}) \cup (\delta_2 \cup \{\varphi\}), \delta_1 \in \Delta_1, \delta_2 \in \Delta_2\} \\ &= \{\delta' \mid \delta' = \delta_1 \cup \delta_2 \cup \{\varphi\}, \delta_1 \in \Delta_1, \delta_2 \in \Delta_2\}. \end{aligned} \tag{52}$$

$$\begin{aligned} (\Delta_1 \bowtie \Delta_2) \uplus \varphi &= \{\delta' \mid \delta' = \delta \cup \{\varphi\}, \delta = \delta_1 \cup \delta_2, \delta_1 \in \Delta_1, \delta_2 \in \Delta_2\} \\ &= \{\delta' \mid \delta' = \delta_1 \cup \delta_2 \cup \{\varphi\}, \delta_1 \in \Delta_1, \delta_2 \in \Delta_2\}. \end{aligned} \tag{53}$$

The equivalence is based on the equality of the two sides (52) and (53). Equation (48) can be immediately proved when $\varphi = \varepsilon$:

$$(\Delta_1 \bowtie \Delta_2) \uplus \epsilon = \Delta_1 \bowtie \Delta_2$$
$$\Delta_1 \bowtie (\Delta_2 \uplus \epsilon) = \Delta_1 \bowtie \Delta_2.$$

When $\varphi \neq \varepsilon$, we have the following:

$$\begin{aligned}\Delta_1 \bowtie (\Delta_2 \uplus \varphi) &= \Delta_1 \bowtie \{\delta'_2 \mid \delta'_2 = \delta_2 \cup \{\varphi\}, \delta_2 \in \Delta_2\} \\ &= \{\delta' \mid \delta' = \delta_1 \cup \delta'_2, \delta_1 \in \Delta_1, \delta'_2 = \delta_2 \cup \{\varphi\}, \delta_2 \in \Delta_2\} \\ &= \{\delta' \mid \delta' = \delta_1 \cup \delta_2 \cup \{\varphi\}, \delta_1 \in \Delta_1, \delta_2 \in \Delta_2\} \\ &= (\Delta_1 \bowtie \Delta_2) \uplus \varphi \text{ (owing to (53))}.\end{aligned}$$

Finally, Equation (49) is trivially proved when $\varphi = \varepsilon$:

$$(\Delta_1 \cup \Delta_2) \uplus \epsilon = \Delta_1 \cup \Delta_2$$
$$(\Delta_1 \uplus \epsilon) \cup (\Delta_2 \uplus \epsilon) = \Delta_1 \cup \Delta_2.$$

When $\varphi \neq \varepsilon$, we have the following:

$$(\Delta_1 \uplus \varphi) \cup (\Delta_2 \uplus \varphi) = \{\delta'_1 \mid \delta'_1 = \delta_1 \cup \{\varphi\}, \delta_1 \in \Delta_1\} \cup \{\delta'_2 \mid \delta'_2 = \delta_2 \cup \{\varphi\}, \delta_2 \in \Delta_2\}. \tag{54}$$

$$\begin{aligned}(\Delta_1 \cup \Delta_2) \uplus \varphi &= \{\delta' \mid \delta' = \delta \cup \{\varphi\}, \delta \in (\Delta_1 \cup \Delta_2)\} \\ &= \{\delta'_1 \mid \delta'_1 = \delta_1 \cup \{\varphi\}, \delta_1 \in \Delta_1\} \cup \{\delta'_2 \mid \delta'_2 = \delta_2 \cup \{\varphi\}, \delta_2 \in \Delta_2\}.\end{aligned} \tag{55}$$

The equivalence is based on the equality of the two sides (54) and (55). This concludes the proof of Theorem 3.

The notion of a monitor allows us to trace the state of the system based on a given fragmented observation, so as to eventually output the solution of the monitoring problem. However, such a state is uncertain for three reasons: (*i*) the uncertain nature of the fragment, (*ii*) the unobservability of the transitions within nodes of the monitor, and (*iii*) the nondeterministic nature of the monitor, where different arcs leaving the same node can be marked by the same observable label.

The formalization of the trace of the system is given first for a plain monitoring problem[5]. Then, it is generalized to whatever monitoring problem.

Definition 14. (MONITORING STATE) *Let* $\mu(\Sigma) = (\Sigma_0, \mathcal{V}, \widehat{\mho}, \mathcal{R})$ *be a plain monitoring problem and* $Mtr(\Sigma, \Sigma_0, \mathcal{V}, \mathcal{R}) = (\mathcal{N}, \mathcal{L}, \mathcal{A}, N_0)$ *a relevant monitor.* A context χ *is a pair* (N, Δ), *where* $N \in \mathcal{N}$ *and* Δ *is a diagnostic set.* A monitoring state $\mathcal{M} = \{\chi_1, \ldots, \chi_n\}$ *is a set of contexts.*

[5] According to Definition 8, a plain monitoring problem involves the fragmentation of a plain observation, with each fragment comprising one observation-node only.

Definition 15. (PLAIN TRAJECTORY) *Let* $\mathcal{O} = (l_1, \ldots, l_n)$ *be the plain observation relevant to the fragmented observation* $\widehat{\mathcal{O}}$ *(see Definition 14). The* plain trajectory *of* $\mu\,(\Sigma)$ *is a sequence of monitoring states*

$$Trj(\mu(\Sigma)) = \langle \mathcal{M}_0, \mathcal{M}_1, \ldots, \mathcal{M}_n \rangle \tag{56}$$

defined as follows:

- $\mathcal{M}_0 = \{(N_0, \{\emptyset\})\}$;
- $\forall i \in [1..n]$, $\mathcal{M}_i$ *is the minimal (even empty) set of contexts* $\chi' = (N', \Delta')$ *such that:*

$$\chi \in \mathcal{M}_{i-1},\ \chi = (N, \Delta), \tag{57}$$

$$S = (\sigma, \mathcal{D}) \text{ is a state in the leaving set } \mathrm{S}_{\mathrm{out}} \text{ of } N, \tag{58}$$

$$N \xrightarrow{(S, \ell_i, \varphi, S_0(N'))} N' \in \mathcal{L}, \tag{59}$$

$$\Delta' \supseteq (\mathcal{D} \bowtie \Delta) \uplus \varphi. \tag{60}$$

Example 15. Let $\mu'(\psi) = (\psi_0, \mathcal{V}_\psi, \widehat{\mathcal{O}}'_\psi, \mathcal{R}_\psi)$, where $\mathcal{V}_\psi$ and $\mathcal{R}_\psi$ are in Table 1 and Table 2, respectively, and $\mathcal{O}'_\psi = \langle short, open_1, end, close_1 \rangle$. Consider $Mtr(\psi, \psi_0, \mathcal{V}_\psi, \mathcal{R}_\psi)$ displayed in Figure 8. The plain trajectory $Trj(\wp'(\psi)) = \langle \mathcal{M}_0, \mathcal{M}_1, \mathcal{M}_2, \mathcal{M}_3, \mathcal{M}_4 \rangle$ is generated as follows. $\mathcal{M}_0 = (N_0, \{\emptyset\})$. To compute $\mathcal{M}_1$ we consider the arc leaving state $(0, \{\emptyset\})$ in N_0 and entering state $(1, \{\emptyset\})$ in N_1, according to (59),

$$N_0 \xrightarrow{((0,\{\emptyset\}), short, fsh, (1,\{\emptyset\}))} N_1$$

Based on (60), the diagnostic set associated with N_1 is $(\{\emptyset\} \bowtie \{\emptyset\}) \uplus fsh = \{\{fsh\}\}$. Thus, $\mathcal{M}_1 = \{(N_1, \{\{fsh\}\})\}$. To compute monitoring state $\mathcal{M}_2$ we need to instantiate (59) three times:

$$N_1 \xrightarrow{((1,\{\emptyset\}), open_1, \epsilon, (8,\{\emptyset\}))} N_8$$

$$N_1 \xrightarrow{((11,\{\{fo_2\}\}), open_1, \epsilon, (19,\{\emptyset\}))} N_{19}$$

$$N_1 \xrightarrow{((21,\{\{fo_2\}\}), open_1, \epsilon, (27,\{\emptyset\}))} N_{27}.$$

Similarly, (60) is to be instantiated three times: $(\{\emptyset\} \bowtie \{\{fsh\}\}) \uplus \varepsilon = \{\{fsh\}\}$, $(\{\{fo_2\}\} \bowtie \{\{fsh\}\}) \uplus \varepsilon = \{\{fsh, fo_2\}\}$, and $(\{\{fo_2\}\} \bowtie \{\{fsh\}\}) \uplus \varepsilon = \{\{fsh, fo_2\}\}$. The second monitoring state will be $\mathcal{M}_2 = \{(N_8, \{\{fsh\}\}), (N_{19}, \{\{fsh, fo_2\}\}), (N_{27}, \{\{fsh, fo_2\}\})\}$. To determine $\mathcal{M}_3$, (57) will involve the contexts in $\mathcal{M}_2$. For each of them, (59) becomes

$$N_8 \xrightarrow{((27,\{\{fo_2\}\}),end,\epsilon,(41,\{\emptyset\}))} N_{41}$$

$$N_{19} \xrightarrow{((27,\{\emptyset\}),end,\epsilon,(41,\{\emptyset\}))} N_{41}$$

$$N_{27} \xrightarrow{((27,\{\emptyset\}),end,\epsilon,(41,\{\emptyset\}))} N_{41}.$$

The instantiation of (60) yields the same diagnostic set, $(\{\{fo_2\}\} \bowtie \{\{fsh\}\}) \uplus \varepsilon = \{\emptyset\} \bowtie \{\{fsh, fo_2\}\}) \uplus \varepsilon = \{\{fsh, fo_2\}\}$. Thus, $\mathcal{M}_3 = \{(N_{41}, \{\{fsh, fo_2\}\})\}$. To compute $\mathcal{M}_4$, we instantiate (59) by

$$N_{41} \xrightarrow{((41,\{\emptyset\}),close_1,\epsilon,(37,\{\emptyset\}))} N_{37}$$

$$N_{41} \xrightarrow{((13,\{\emptyset\}),close_1,\epsilon,(0,\{\emptyset\}))} N_0.$$

(60) is to be instantiated twice by the same expression: $(\{\emptyset\} \bowtie \{\{fsh,fo_2\}\}) \uplus \varepsilon = \{\{fsh,fo_2\}\})$. Hence, $\mathcal{M}_4 = \{(N_{37}, \{\{fsh, fo_2\}\}), (N_0, \{\{fsh, fo_2\}\})\}$.

Definition 16. (REACTIVE SEQUENCE) *Let $\mu(\Sigma) = (\Sigma_0, \mathcal{V}, \mathcal{O}, \mathcal{R})$ be a plain monitoring problem, $\mathcal{O} = \langle \ell_1, \ldots, \ell_n \rangle$, $Mtr(\Sigma, \Sigma_0, \mathcal{V}, \mathcal{R}) = (\mathcal{N}, \mathcal{L}, \mathcal{A}, N_0)$ the monitor, and $Trj(\mu(\Sigma)) = \langle \mathcal{M}_0, \mathcal{M}_1, \ldots, \mathcal{M}_n \rangle$ the relevant plain trajectory. The* reactive sequence *of $\mu(\Sigma)$ is a sequence of diagnostic sets*

$$React(\mu(\Sigma)) = \langle \Delta_0, \Delta_1, \ldots, \Delta_n \rangle \tag{61}$$

defined as follows:

$$\forall i \in [0..n] \left(\Delta_i = \bigcup_{(N,\Delta) \in \mathcal{M}_i} (\Delta^{\mathrm{loc}}(N) \bowtie \Delta) \right). \tag{62}$$

Example 16. Consider the monitoring problem $\mu'(\psi)$ in Example 15, and the monitor in Figure 8. The reactive sequence $React(\mu'(\psi)) = (\Delta_0, \Delta_1, \Delta_2, \Delta_3, \Delta_4)$ is determined as follows:

$$\Delta_0 = \Delta^{\mathrm{loc}}(N_0) \bowtie \{\emptyset\} = \{\emptyset\} \bowtie \{\emptyset\} = \{\emptyset\}.$$

$$\Delta_1 = \Delta^{\mathrm{loc}}(N_1) \bowtie \{\{fsh\}\} = \{\{fsh\}, \{fsh, o_1\}, \{fsh, fo_2\}, \{fsh, fo_1, fo_2\}\}.$$

$$\Delta_2 = \Delta^{\mathrm{loc}}(N_8) \bowtie \{\{fsh\}\} \cup \Delta^{\mathrm{loc}}(N_{19}) \bowtie \{\{fsh, fo_2\}\} \cup \Delta^{\mathrm{loc}}(N_{27}) \bowtie \{\{fsh, fo_2\}\}$$
$$= \{\{fsh\}, \{fsh, fo_2\}\}.$$

$$\Delta_3 = \Delta^{\mathrm{loc}}(N_{41}) \bowtie \{\{fsh, fo_2\}\} = \{\{fsh, fo_2\}, \{fsh, fo_2, fc_1\}\}.$$

$$\Delta_4 = \Delta^{\mathrm{loc}}(N_{37}) \bowtie \{\{fsh, fo_2\}\} \cup \Delta^{\mathrm{loc}}(N_0) \bowtie \{\{fsh, fo_2\}\} = \{\{fsh, fo_2\}\}.$$

The diagnostic set reduces to diagnosis $\{fsh, fo_2\}$ at the occurrence of the last fragment.

The notions of plain trajectory and reactive sequence have been introduced based on plain observations. On the other hand, reactive diagnosis is meant for solving monitoring problems with uncertain (general) fragmented observations. We know that a fragmented observation is a DAG from which an index space can be generated, as shown in Section 7.

Since each state of the index space corresponds to several possible ways in which observable labels may have been generated by the system evolution, in fact, several plain observations, the computation of the reactive sequence in the general case requires associating each state $\Im$ of the index space with the set of monitoring states that are consistent with all the plain observations up to $\Im$. Hence, reactive diagnosis requires a decoration of the index space.

Definition 17. (DECORATION) *Let* $\mu(\Sigma) = (\Sigma_0, \mathcal{V}, \widehat{\mathcal{O}}, \mathcal{R})$ *be a monitoring problem. The* decoration *of the index space* $Isp(\mathcal{O})$ *based on* $\mu(\Sigma)$ *is an automaton* $Isp^*(\mathcal{O})$ *isomorphic to* $Isp(\mathcal{O})$, *where each state* $\Im$ *is marked by a monitoring attribute*

$$\mathcal{M} = \bigcup_{\mathcal{O}' \in \|\Im\|} \mathcal{M}_k \tag{63}$$

where $\| \Im \|$ *denotes the set of plain observations up to* $\Im$ *in* $Isp(\mathcal{O})$, $\mathcal{O}' = \langle l_1, \ldots, l_k \rangle$, $\mu'(\Sigma) = (\Sigma_0, \mathcal{V}, \widehat{\mathcal{O}}', \mathcal{R})$, $Trj(\mu'(\Sigma)) = \langle \mathcal{M}_0, \mathcal{M}_1, \ldots, \mathcal{M}_k \rangle$.

Example 17. Consider the index space $Isp(\mathcal{O}_\psi)$ in Figure 4, and the monitor in Figure 8. We have to mark each state of $Isp(\mathcal{O}_\psi)$ with the relevant monitoring attribute, as specified in (63). That is, for each $i \in [0 .. 5]$, we have to decorate state i with monitoring attribute $\mathcal{M}(\Im_i)$. The latter is the aggregation of the last monitoring states of the plain trajectories relevant to the prefix of the candidate traces ending at $\Im_i$ in $Isp(\mathcal{O}_\psi)$. To this end, we may reuse some of the results computed in Example 15, specifically, $\mathcal{M}(\Im_0) = \mathcal{M}_0 = \{(N_0, \{\varnothing\})\}$ and $\mathcal{M}(\Im_1) = \mathcal{M}_1 = \{(N_1, \{\{fsh\}\})\}$. To yield $\mathcal{M}(\Im_2)$ we need considering the two candidate traces ending at 2, namely $\langle short, open_1 \rangle$ and $\langle open_1 \rangle$. The former leads to the set of contexts $\mathcal{M}_2$ already computed in Example 15. The latter leads to the empty set, as no arc marked by $open_1$ leaves node N_0 in the monitor. Thus, $\mathcal{M}(\Im_2) = \mathcal{M}_2 = \{(N_8, \{\{fsh\}\}), (N_{19}, \{\{fsh, fo_2\}\}), (N_{27}, \{\{fsh, fo_2\}\})\}$. The computation of $\mathcal{M}(\Im_3)$ requires considering the four candidate traces ending at 3, namely $\langle end \rangle$, $\langle right \rangle$, $\langle short, end \rangle$, and $\langle short, right \rangle$. However, the first and the last of them yield empty monitoring states (because such plain observations do not match any path in the monitor). Plain observation $\langle right \rangle$ leads to monitoring state $\{(N_3, \{\varnothing\})\}$, while $\langle short, end \rangle$ leads to a monitoring state that can be computed starting from $\mathcal{M}(\Im_1)$ and considering the following label *end*, that is, the monitor arc

$$N_1 \xrightarrow{((14,\{\{fo_1,fo_2\}\}),end,\epsilon,(25,\{\emptyset\}))} N_{25}.$$

Based on (60), the associated monitoring attribute is $(\{\{fo_1, fo_2\}\} \bowtie \{\{fsh\}\} \uplus \varepsilon = \{\{fsh, fo_1, fo_2\}\}$. Hence, $\mathcal{M}(\Im_3) = \{(N_3, \{\varnothing\}), (N_{25}, \{\{fsh, fo_1, fo_2\}\})\}$. Computing $\mathcal{M}(\Im_4)$ would, in principle, require considering the eight plain observations up to $\Im_4$. However, only two of them matches the monitor graph, namely $\langle right, open_1 \rangle$ and $\langle short, open_1, end \rangle$. The former leads to monitoring state $\{(N_5, \{\varnothing\})\}$, while the latter is $\mathcal{M}_3$, already computed in Example 15. Thus, $\mathcal{M}(\Im_4) = \mathcal{M}_3 = \{(N_5, \{\varnothing\}), (N_{41}, \{\{fsh, fo_2\}\})\}$. Considering $\mathcal{M}(\Im_5)$, there is only one candidate trace matching the monitor, $\langle short, open_1, end, close_1 \rangle$, this being the plain observation $\mathcal{O}'_\psi$ defined in Example 15, hence, $\mathcal{M}(\Im_5) = \mathcal{M}_4 = \{(N_{37}, \{\{fsh, fo_2\}\}), (N_0, \{\{fsh, fo_2\}\})\}$.

Based on the concept of index-space decoration, both notions of plain trajectory and reactive sequence can be straightforwardly extended to monitoring problems involving general fragmented observations.

Definition 18. (TRAJECTORY) *Let* $\mu(\Sigma)$ *be a monitoring problem involving a fragmented observation* $\mathcal{O} = \langle \mathcal{F}_1, \ldots, \mathcal{F}_n \rangle$. *Let* $Isp^*(\mathcal{O}_{[i]})$ *be the decorated index space relevant to the sub-observation* $\mathcal{O}_{[i]}$, $i \in [0 .. n]$, *with set of final states. The* trajectory *of* $\mu(\Sigma)$ *is the sequence of monitoring states*

$$Trj(\mu(\Sigma)) = \langle \mathcal{M}_0, \mathcal{M}_1, \ldots, \mathcal{M}_n \rangle, \ \forall i \in [0..n] \left(\mathcal{M}_i = \bigcup_{(\Im, \mathcal{M}) \in \mathcal{S}^*_{f_i}} \mathcal{M} \right). \tag{64}$$

The definition of the reactive sequence does not change, apart from replacing the plain observation with the fragmented observation and the plain trajectory with a trajectory.

Example 18. Consider the monitoring problem $\mu(\psi)$ of Example 9. The index space $Isp(\mathcal{O}_\psi)$ of the relevant observation is displayed in Figure 4 and has been decorated in Example 17. $Trj(\mu(\psi)) = \langle \mathcal{M}'_0, \mathcal{M}'_1, \mathcal{M}'_2, \mathcal{M}'_3, \mathcal{M}'_4 \rangle$ is determined, based on (64) and on the index spaces of the sub- observations in Figure 6, as follows:

$$\begin{aligned}
\mathcal{M}'_0 &= \mathcal{M}(\Im_0) = \{(N_0, \{\emptyset\})\}. \\
\mathcal{M}'_1 &= \mathcal{M}(\Im_0) \cup \mathcal{M}(\Im_1) = \{(N_0, \{\emptyset\}), (N_1, \{\{fsh\}\})\}. \\
\mathcal{M}'_2 &= \mathcal{M}(\Im_2) = \{(N_8, \{\{fsh\}\}), (N_{19}, \{\{fsh, fo_2\}\}), (N_{27}, \{\{fsh, fo_2\}\})\}. \\
\mathcal{M}'_3 &= \mathcal{M}(\Im_4) = \{(N_5, \{\emptyset\}), (N_{41}, \{\{fsh, fo_2\}\})\}. \\
\mathcal{M}'_4 &= \mathcal{M}(\Im_5) = \{(N_{37}, \{\{fsh, fo_2\}\}), (N_0, \{\{fsh, fo_2\}\})\}.
\end{aligned}$$

The reactive sequence $React(\mu(\psi)) = \langle \Delta'_0, \Delta'_1, \Delta'_2, \Delta'_3, \Delta'_4 \rangle$ is generated based on (62) as follows:

$$\begin{aligned}
\Delta'_0 &= \Delta^{loc}(N_0) \bowtie \{\emptyset\} = \{\emptyset\}. \\
\Delta'_1 &= \Delta^{loc}(N_0) \bowtie \{\emptyset\} \cup \Delta^{loc}(N_1) \bowtie \{\{fsh\}\} = \{\emptyset, \{fsh\}, \{fsh, fo_1\}, \{fsh, fo_2\}, \{fsh, fo_1, fo_2\}\}. \\
\Delta'_2 &= \Delta^{loc}(N_8) \bowtie \{\{fsh\}\} \cup \Delta^{loc}(N_{19}) \bowtie \{\{fsh, fo_2\}\} \cup \Delta^{loc}(N_{27}) \bowtie \{\{fsh, fo_2\}\} \\
&= \{\{fsh\}, \{fsh, fo_2\}\}. \\
\Delta'_3 &= \Delta^{loc}(N_5) \bowtie \{\emptyset\} \cup \Delta^{loc}(N_{41}) \bowtie \{\{fsh, fo_2\}\} = \{\emptyset, \{fsh, fo_2\}, \{fsh, fo_2, fc_1\}\}. \\
\Delta'_4 &= \Delta^{loc}(N_{37}) \bowtie \{\{fsh, fo_2\}\} \cup \Delta^{loc}(N_0) \bowtie \{\{fsh, fo_2\}\} = \{\{fsh, fo_2\}\}.
\end{aligned}$$

Note how $React(\mu(\psi))$ is the solution $\Delta(\mu(\psi))$ determined in Example 11 based on the behavior space $Bhv(\psi, \psi_0)$. This equality is not at all incidental, as asserted by the following theorem of equivalence, which states the soundness and completeness of the monitoring-problem solving method proposed in the current section.

Theorem 4. Let $\mu(\Sigma)$ be a monitoring problem. Then,

$$React(\mu(\Sigma)) = \Delta(\mu(\Sigma)). \tag{65}$$

Proof. The proof is supported by Lemma 4.1, which is a restriction of Theorem 4 to a plain diagnosis problem. This lemma is in its turn supported by Lemmas 4.2 and 4.3.

Lemma 4.1. Equation (65) holds when $\wp(\Sigma) = (\Sigma_0, \mathcal{V}, \mathcal{O}, \mathcal{R})$ is a plain diagnosis problem.

Proof of Lemma 4.1. Since the problem is plain, the observation is a sequence of labels in $\mathcal{V}$, namely $\mathcal{O} = \langle l_1, \ldots, l_n \rangle$. Let $React(\mu(\Sigma)) = \langle \Delta_0, \Delta_1, \ldots, \Delta_n \rangle$ and $\Delta(\mu(\Sigma)) = \langle \Delta(\wp_{[0]}(\Sigma)), \Delta(\wp_{[1]}(\Sigma)), \ldots, \Delta(\wp_{[n]}(\Sigma)) \rangle$. We have to show the equality of the two sequences. First we prove

$$\Delta(\wp_{[0]}(\Sigma)) = \Delta_0. \tag{66}$$

Since $\wp_{[0]}(\Sigma) = (\Sigma_0, \mathcal{V}, \langle\rangle, \mathcal{R})$ and $\| Isp(\langle\rangle) \| = \{\langle\rangle\}$, based on (23) and (27),

$$\Delta(\wp_{[0]}(\Sigma)) = \{\delta \mid \delta = h \otimes \mathcal{R}, h \in \|Bhv(\Sigma, \Sigma_0)\|, h \boxtimes \mathcal{V} = \langle\rangle\}. \tag{67}$$

Thus, the histories h are silent. On the other hand, based on Definition 16, the first element of the reactive sequence is

$$\Delta_0 = \bigcup_{(N,\Delta) \in \{(N_0, \{\emptyset\})\}} (\Delta^{\text{loc}}(N) \bowtie \Delta) = \Delta^{\text{loc}}(N_0) \bowtie \{\emptyset\} = \Delta^{\text{loc}}(N_0). \tag{68}$$

Let $N_0 = (\mathbf{S}, \boldsymbol{E}, \mathbf{T}, S_0, \mathbf{S}_{\text{out}})$, where $S_0 = (\Sigma_0, \mathcal{D}_0)$. From Definition 11, we have

$$\Delta^{\text{loc}}(N_0) = \bigcup_{(\sigma, \mathcal{D}) \in \mathbf{S}} \mathcal{D} \tag{69}$$

where, based on (32), the diagnostic attribute is

$$\mathcal{D} = \{\delta \mid \delta = h \otimes \mathcal{R}, h = \Sigma_0 \rightsquigarrow \sigma, h \in \|Bhv^*(\Sigma, \Sigma_0)\|, \forall T \in h \, (T \text{ is silent})\}. \tag{70}$$

Since in (70) history segments h are rooted in Σ_0, they are in fact histories and the last condition may be reformulated as $h \in \| Bhv(\Sigma, \Sigma_0) \|$, where h is silent. Thus,

$$\Delta_0 = \Delta^{loc}(N_0) = \{\delta \mid \delta = h \otimes \mathcal{R}, h \in \|Bhv(\Sigma, \Sigma_0)\|, h \text{ is silent}\}. \tag{71}$$

By comparing (67) and (71) makes (66) proved.

Let $Trj^*(\wp(\Sigma))$ denote the *connected trajectory* of $\wp(\Sigma)$, the graph obtained by connecting the elements of the monitoring states in $Trj^*(\wp(\Sigma))$ by means of the relevant arcs of the monitor. Specifically, considering (59), an arc from $S \in \mathbf{S}_{out}(N)$ to $S_0(N')$ will be inserted and marked by the corresponding visible transition T defined in point (2) of Definition 10. This way, $Trj^*(\wp(\Sigma))$ can be viewed as a directed (and connected) graph rooted in the initial state of node N_0 relevant to $\mathcal{M}_0$.

Lemma 4.2. Let S_0 be the root of node N_0 in the monitoring state $\mathcal{M}_0$. Let S_i be a state of a node $N_i \in \mathcal{M}_i$. Then, each path $S_0 \Rightarrow S_i$ in $Trj^*(\wp(\Sigma))$ is a history h such that $h \in \| Bhv(\Sigma, \Sigma_0) \|$ and $h \boxtimes \mathcal{V} = \langle l_1,\ldots,l_i \rangle$., and vice versa.

Lemma 4.3. Let (N, Δ) be a context in a monitoring state $\mathcal{M}$ in $Trj(\wp(\Sigma))$. Then, Δ is the set of candidate diagnoses relevant to the histories in $Trj^*(\wp(\Sigma))$ ending at root S_0 of N.

Proof of Lemma 4.3. The proof is by induction on the nodes (in the monitoring states) that are involved in the histories ending at the root of N. The basis considers (the only) node N_0 in $\mathcal{M}_0$, where $\Delta = \{\varnothing\}$. Due to the emptiness of the histories ending at the root of N_0, the relevant set of candidate diagnoses is in fact empty. In the induction step we show that, if Lemma 4.3 holds for a context $(N, \Delta) \in \mathcal{M}_i$, $i \in [0 \,..\, n-1]$, then it holds as well for the successive node $(N', \Delta') \in \mathcal{M}_{i+1}$. In fact, based on (59) and (60), we have

$$\Delta' = \{(\mathcal{D} \bowtie \Delta) \uplus \varphi \mid (N, \Delta) \in \mathcal{M}_i, S = (\sigma, \mathcal{D}), S \in \mathbf{S}_{out}(N), N \xrightarrow{(S, \ell_{i+1}, \varphi, S_0(N'))} N' \in \mathcal{L}\} \tag{72}$$

where, based on Definition 12 and Equation (32), and, as Δ is the set of candidate diagnoses relevant to the histories in $Trj^*(\wp(\Sigma))$ that end at the root of N (induction hypothesis), $\mathcal{D} \bowtie \Delta$ is in fact the set of diagnoses relevant to the histories ending in $S \in \mathbf{S}_{out}(N)$. Hence, based on Definition 13, $(\mathcal{D} \bowtie \Delta) \uplus \varphi$ is the set of diagnoses relevant to the histories ending at the root of N'. This proves the induction step and concludes the proof of Lemma 4.3.

Based on Lemma 4.3, $\forall i \in [1 \,..\, n]$, we can now prove

$$\Delta(\wp_{[i]}(\Sigma)) = \Delta_i. \tag{73}$$

Based on (62), we have

$$\Delta_i = \bigcup_{(N,\Delta) \in \mathcal{M}_i} (\Delta^{loc}(N) \bowtie \Delta) \tag{74}$$

where according to (39)

$$\Delta^{\mathrm{loc}}(N) = \bigcup_{(\sigma,\mathcal{D})\in \mathrm{S}} \mathcal{D}, \tag{75}$$

with S being the set of internal states of *N*. Based on (44) and (46) , we have

$$\Delta^{\mathrm{loc}}(N) \bowtie \Delta = \Delta \bowtie \Delta^{\mathrm{loc}}(N) = \Delta \bowtie \bigcup_{(\sigma,\mathcal{D})\in \mathrm{S}} \mathcal{D} = (\Delta \bowtie \mathcal{D}_1) \cup \cdots \cup (\Delta \bowtie \mathcal{D}_k) \tag{76}$$

where $\mathcal{D}_1, \ldots, \mathcal{D}_k$ are the diagnostic attributes of states in *S*. In other words, owing to Lemma 4.3, $\Delta^{\mathrm{loc}}(N) \bowtie \Delta$ is the set of the candidate diagnoses relevant to the histories ending at any internal state of *N*. Moving this result to (74), we conclude that Δ_i is the set of candidate diagnoses relevant to histories ending in any state of any node *N* where $(N, \Delta) \in \mathcal{M}_i$. Hence, (73) holds. This concludes the proof of Lemma 4.1.

Based on Lemma 4.1, we now prove (65) in the general case. First notice how (66) still holds in the general case. Besides, according to (64), in the generalized trajectory, for each $i \in [1 \,..\, n]$ we have

$$\mathcal{M}_i = \bigcup_{(\mathfrak{I},\mathcal{M})\in \mathcal{S}^*_{f_i}} \mathcal{M} \tag{77}$$

where $\mathcal{M}$ is the monitoring attribute associated with a final state $\mathfrak{I}$ of the decorated index space $Isp^*(\mathcal{O}_{[i]})$. According to (63), $\mathcal{M}$ is the union of the last monitoring states of each trajectory $Trj(\wp_i^j(\Sigma))$, where $\wp_i^j(\Sigma)$ is the plain diagnosis problem involving the *j*-th plain observation $O_i^j \in \| Isp(\mathcal{O}_{[i]}) \|$. Assuming *m* to be the cardinality of $\| Isp(\mathcal{O}_{[i]}) \|$, (77) can be rewritten as

$$\mathcal{M}_i = \bigcup_{j=1}^{m} \mathcal{M}_i^j \tag{78}$$

Based on (62), the *i*-th element of the reactive sequence is

$$\Delta_i = \bigcup_{(N,\Delta)\in \mathcal{M}_i} \left(\Delta^{\mathrm{loc}}(N) \bowtie \Delta\right) \tag{79}$$

which, based on (78) and Lemma 4.1, can be rewritten as

$$\Delta_i = \bigcup_{j=1}^{m} \left(\bigcup_{(N,\Delta) \in \mathcal{M}_i^j} (\Delta^{\text{loc}}(N) \bowtie \Delta) \right) = \bigcup_{j=1}^{m} \Delta(\wp_i^j(\Sigma)). \tag{80}$$

On the other hand, as by definition the solution $\Delta(\wp_{[i]}(\Sigma))$ is

$$\Delta(\wp_{[i]}(\Sigma)) = \{\delta \mid \delta = h \otimes \mathcal{R}, h \in \|Bhv(\Sigma, \Sigma_0)\|, h \boxtimes \mathcal{V} \in \|Isp(\mathcal{O}_{[i]}\|\}, \tag{81}$$

such a solution can be rephrased as the union of the solutions relevant to each plain problem:

$$\Delta(\wp_{[i]}(\Sigma)) = \bigcup_{j=1}^{m} \{\delta \mid \delta = h \otimes \mathcal{R}, h \in \|Bhv(\Sigma, \Sigma_0)\|, h \boxtimes \mathcal{V} = \mathcal{O}_i^j\} \tag{82}$$

In other terms,

$$\Delta(\wp_{[i]}(\Sigma)) = \bigcup_{j=1}^{m} \Delta(\wp_i^j(\Sigma)). \tag{83}$$

Comparing (80) and (83) brings us to the conclusion

$$\Delta(\wp_{[i]}(\Sigma)) = \Delta_i \tag{84}$$

which terminates the proof of Theorem 4. □

At the beginning of this section we required the monitoring problem to be solved without the availability of the global system model, in other words, the possibility of constructing the monitor without the behavior space. To be convinced of the feasibility of this approach, it suffices noticing that each node of the monitor (a diagnostic closure) is in fact a piece of reconstructed behavior decorated with diagnostic information. Besides, each node can be generated on demand, that is, whenever the new observation fragment leads to a system state (the root of the diagnostic closure) not considered already. On the one hand, the monitor is generated incrementally starting from the initial node (created before the reception of the first observation fragment). On the other, the construction of a new node essentially follows the same algorithm presented in [3] for reconstructing the system behavior relevant to an a-posteriori diagnosis problem, with three differences: (*i*) the generation of the monitor is based on a (fragmented) temporal observation, (*ii*) only the silent part of the behavior rooted in the initial state of the node is created, and (*iii*) the piece of system behavior is then decorated by diagnostic information (as detailed in [18]). In particular, following the same technique of behavior reconstruction presented in [3], point (*ii*) can be performed without the previous generation of the behavior space.

9. Optimization

In order to meet optimization criteria, the actual algorithms may operate on a surrogate of the index space. The opportunity for optimization raises from evidence that, generally speaking, only a sub-graph of the index space is relevant to the computation of the diagnostic-problem solution. In fact, the reactive sequence $React(\wp(\Sigma))$ depends upon the trajectory $Trj(\wp(\Sigma))$.

According to (64), $Trj(\wp(\Sigma))$ is a sequence of monitoring states $\mathcal{M}_i$ that depend on the final states of the decorated index space $Isp^*(\mathcal{O}_{[i]})$. This property raises two peculiarities:

(a) A node $\Im^*$ of $Isp^*(\mathcal{O}_{[i]})$ may be decorated with the empty set, $\Im^* = (\Im, \emptyset)$, meaning that each sequence of observable labels up to in $Isp(\mathcal{O}_{[i]})$ is inconsistent with the relevant monitor;

(b) An arc $\Im_1^* \xrightarrow{l} \Im_2^*$ in $Isp^*(\mathcal{O}_{[i]})$ may be inconsistent with all the monitoring states in the decoration of $\Im_1^*$, even though the decoration of $\Im_2^*$ is not empty.

These possibilities shall not come as a surprise if we recall that the index space is a surrogate of the observation, this being uncertain both logically and temporally. Consequently, not all of the candidate traces in the index space are in general consistent with the system and, therefore, with the monitor.

Note how condition (*a*) entails condition (*b*) to hold for every arc entering $\Im^*$. More precisely, $\Im^*$ is empty-decorated iff all entering arcs fall in condition (*b*). On the other hand, condition (*b*) may hold for one or several arcs entering $\Im^*$ without the latter being empty-decorated.

When condition (*b*) holds for an arc, the latter can be removed from the index space without any effect on the solution of the problem. The same applies to a node in condition (*a*): it can be removed along with all its exiting (dangling) arcs, preserving the soundness and completeness of the diagnostic technique (see Theorem 5).

Example 19. Consider the index space $Isp(\mathcal{O}_\psi)$ in Figure 5 and the relevant decoration computed in Example 17. Based on the monitor displayed in Figure 8, although each node of $Isp^*(\mathcal{O}_\psi)$ is not empty-decorated (no node in condition (*a*)), some of the arcs are in condition (*b*), precisely,

$$\Im_0 \xrightarrow{end} \Im_3, \Im_0 \xrightarrow{open_1} \Im_2, \Im_1 \xrightarrow{right} \Im_3, \text{ and } \Im_2 \xrightarrow{right} \Im_4$$

which can thus be removed.

Definition 19. (Indexing) *Let $Mtr(\Sigma, \Sigma_0, \mathcal{V}, \mathcal{R})$ be the monitor of the diagnosis problem $\wp(\Sigma) = (\Sigma_0, \mathcal{V}, \mathcal{O}, \mathcal{R})$. The* indexing *$Ind(\mathcal{O})$ of observation $\mathcal{O}$ is the sub-graph of $Isp(\mathcal{O})$ obtained by the following rules:*

- *A node $\Im \in Isp(\mathcal{O})$ is removed if $(\Im, \emptyset) \in Isp^*(\mathcal{O})$;*
- *An arc is removed if it enters or leaves a node fulfilling the previous condition;*
- *An arc $\Im \xrightarrow{\ell} \Im'$ is removed if $(\Im, \mathcal{M}) \in Isp^*(\mathcal{O})$ and no arc marked by ℓ leaves any of the monitor nodes relevant to $\mathcal{M}$.*

If an arc or node is removed from $Isp(\mathcal{O})$ then it is *inconsistent* else it is *consistent*. The notion of consistency and inconsistency can be generalized to a DAG, say *G*, whose arcs are marked by visible labels. We define a pruning function, *Prun*(*G*), that returns the sub-graph of *G* that is consistent with the monitor. Clearly,

$$Prun(Isp(\mathcal{O})) = Ind(\mathcal{O}). \tag{85}$$

The notion of decorated index space (Definition 17) can be applied to indexings too.

Theorem 5. Theorem 4 still holds when, in Definition 18 of trajectory, the decorated index space $Isp^*(\mathcal{O}_{[i]})$ is replaced by the decorated indexing $Ind^*(\mathcal{O}_{[i]})$.

Proof. The proof is based on the property that the reactive sequence $React(\mu(\Sigma))$ depends upon the (generalized) trajectory $Trj(\mu(\Sigma))$. According to (64), each monitoring state $\mathcal{M}_i$ of the trajectory, $i \in [0 .. n]$, is the aggregation of the decorations associated with the final states of $Isp^*(\mathcal{O}_{[i]})$. Thus, it suffices to show that:

(*a*) Each final state $\Im \in Isp(\mathcal{O}_{[i]})$ such that $(\Im, \mathcal{M}) \in Isp^*(\mathcal{O}_{[i]})$, $\mathcal{M} \neq \emptyset$, is still retained as a final state in $Ind(\mathcal{O}_{[i]})$, with the same decoration as in $Ind^*(\mathcal{O}_{[i]})$;

(*b*) $Ind(\mathcal{O}_{[i]})$ does not include any final state which is not in $Isp(\mathcal{O}_{[i]})$.

Based on Definition 19, point (*b*) comes directly from the fact that states can only be removed. Thus, the only possibility to have a different final state in $Ind(\mathcal{O}_{[i]})$ would be by transforming a non-final state $\Im \in Isp(\mathcal{O}_{[i]})$ into a final one, but this cannot occur as the set of paths up to $\Im$ in $Ind(\mathcal{O}_{[i]})$ can only be reduced by pruning. As to point (*a*), a final state $\Im \in Isp(\mathcal{O}_{[i]})$ with non-empty decoration ($\mathcal{M} \neq \emptyset$) cannot become non-final after pruning because is still entered by a consistent arc (otherwise it would be empty-decorated, a contradiction of $\mathcal{M} \neq \emptyset$). This allows $\Im$ to be connected with the root by means of a candidate trace, which makes $\Im$ final. Finally, we have to show that each final node $(\Im, \mathcal{M}) \in Ind^*(\mathcal{O}_{[i]})$ keeps the same decoration, that is, $(\Im, \mathcal{M}) \in Isp^*(\mathcal{O}_{[i]})$. In fact, according to Definition 17, the decoration of $\Im$ depends on the last element $\mathcal{M}_k$ of the plain trajectories relevant to paths up to $\Im$. According to Definition 15, each element $\mathcal{M}_i$ of the trajectory is inductively defined in terms of $\mathcal{M}_{i-1}$, starting from $\mathcal{M}_0 = \{(N_0, \{\emptyset\})\}$. Specifically, (59) requires that there exists a context $(N, \Delta) \in \mathcal{M}_{i-1}$ and an arc in the monitor leaving *N* marked by label l_i. If such an arc, although being in $Isp^*(\mathcal{O}_{[i]})$, does not exist in the monitor, it does not contribute to the computation of $\mathcal{M}_i$. In this case, the arc is inconsistent and its removal does not change the decoration of $\mathfrak{I}$. Since the root cannot change its decoration, by induction, all nodes in the path will retain their decoration after the removal of the inconsistent arcs. □

10. EXPERIMENTATION

A suite of algorithms substantiating reactive diagnosis have been specified in pseudo-code. These algorithms have been implemented in the C language under Linux operating system. In order to assess the practical value of the algorithms, a number of experiments of different sizes were run. These aimed to answer the following questions:

- *Is the incremental generation of the index space worthwhile?*
- *Is reactive diagnosis more efficient than a posteriori diagnosis?*
- *What about space allocation?*

Considering the first question, the efficiency of the incremental generation of the index space was checked on a fragmented observation composed of 600 fragments, relevant to a system of 600 components. Specifically, the observation involves the short circuits of 200 lines and the opening of relevant breakers. The results are displayed in Figure 9, where the x-axis and y-axis indicate the number of fragments of each sub-observation and the time (in seconds) to generate the index space either incrementally (plain curve) or from scratch (dotted curve), respectively. Note how the incremental generation is more efficient than the generation from scratch.

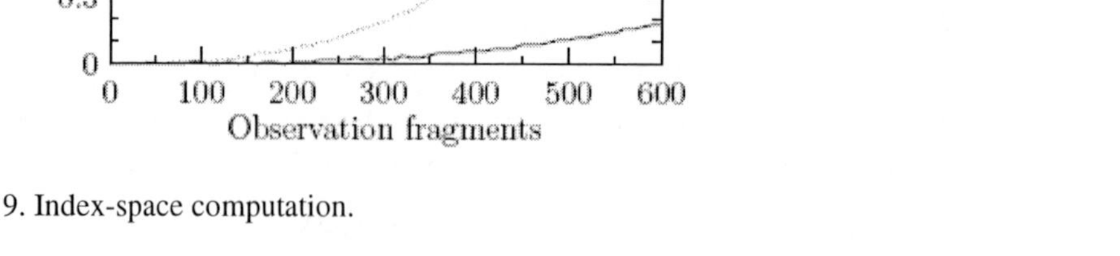

Figure 9. Index-space computation.

To answer the second question, we defined three diagnosis problems, each characterized by a different sort of observation, namely, linear, temporally-uncertain, and logically-uncertain, respectively, and a given number of fragments (60, 18, and 40). Then we considered all the subproblems of these three problems and compared reactive diagnosis with a posteriori diagnosis for all of them. The results are displayed in Figure 10, 11, and 12, respectively. On the left of each figure, both the time response of a posteriori diagnosis (dotted curve) and that of reactive diagnosis (plain curve) are displayed. The latter is also detailed (on a different time scale) on the right of each figure.

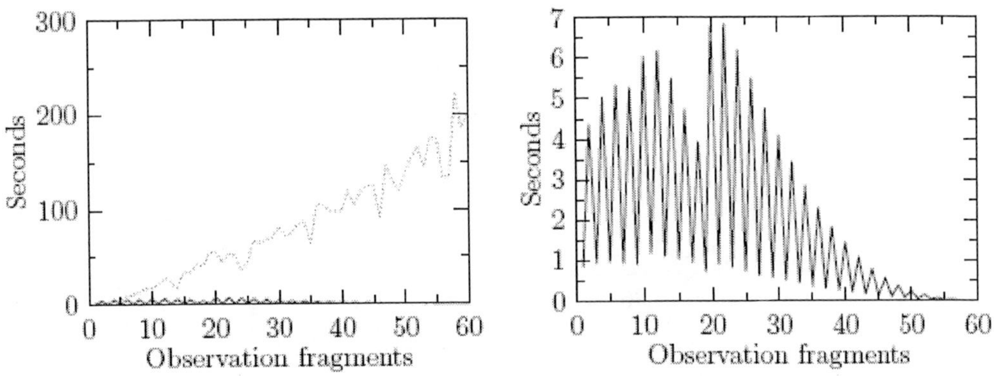

Figure 10. Diagnosis with linear observation.

Figure 10 shows the results for the problems with linear observation, where the system involves 90 components. Note how the response time of a posteriori diagnosis is practically linear with the length of the observation (number of fragments). By contrast, the response of reactive diagnosis is much faster, close to zero when approaching the completion of the observation. For example, for 60 fragments, a posteriori diagnosis needs more than three minutes to provide the solution, while reactive diagnosis needs only 0.01 seconds.

The results relevant to problems with temporally-uncertain observation are outlined in Figure 11, where a system of 27 components and an observation with 18 fragments are considered. In this case, the response time of a posteriori diagnosis has a sudden change after the sixteenth fragment. Reactive diagnosis is faster, even though not so as with linear observation.

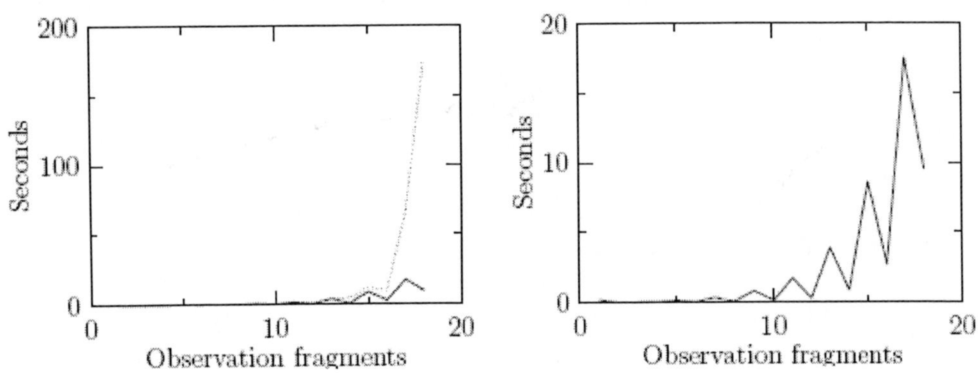

Figure 11. Diagnosis with temporally-uncertain observation.

Figure 12 shows the results for problems involving logically-uncertain observations, where the logical content of each node embodies three labels, while the system embodies 60 components. Note how the curves are very similar to those in Figure 10, with a posteriori diagnosis being essentially linear, while the response is similar to that of Figure 10.

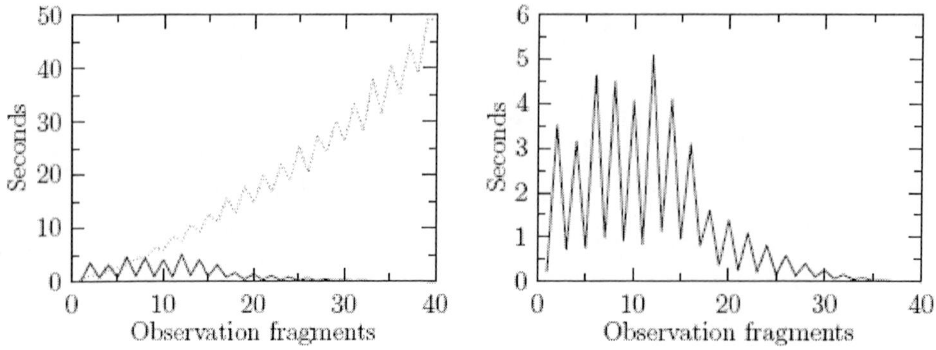

Figure 12. Diagnosis with logically-uncertain observation.

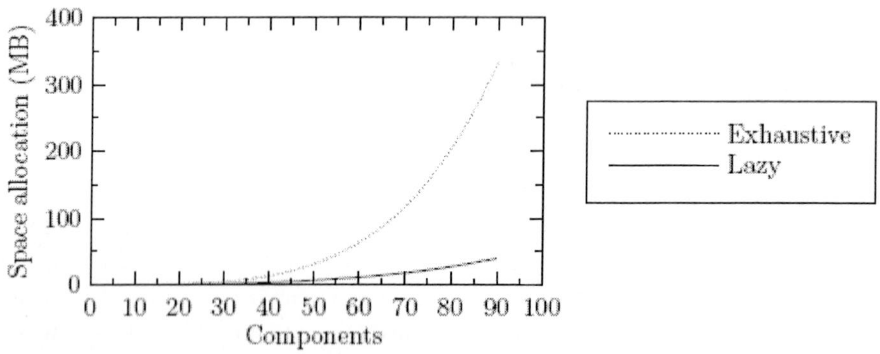

Figure 13. Space allocation for monitor construction.

Finally, as to the third question, experiments indicate that reactive diagnosis requires a considerable amount of working memory when the system grows in number of components, especially when diagnosis problems involving observations with high temporal-uncertainty are considered. However, among other things, what makes the technique workable is the lazy generation of the monitor: nodes of the monitor are only created when they are actually needed to the diagnostic engine. Displayed in Figure 13 are the experimental results relevant to the construction of the monitor. The x-axis indicates the complexity of the system (number of components). The y-axis indicates the corresponding size of the monitor (MBytes). Specifically, the dotted curve is relevant to the exhaustive generation of the monitor. The plain curve, instead, indicates the size of the part of the monitor actually generated by reactive diagnosis for specific diagnosis problems. Note how laziness allows the diagnostic engine to save a considerable amount of memory.

11. DISCUSSION

This paper deals with monitoring-based diagnosis of DESs, a task that is also considered by the diagnoser approach [31, 32] and its extension [29], by the decentralized protocol approach [11, 12], the bridged diagnostic method [18], and the incremental decentralized diagnosis approach [26]. However, out of these contributions, only a previous work by the authors [18] and the incremental decentralized diagnosis approach [26] fulfill the three requirements for reactive diagnosis, namely parsimony, reactivity and incrementality (Section 8, page 17). All the cited contributions, although exploiting compositional modeling and basically using the same modeling primitives, that is, FSMs for describing the complete behavior of each component, as the current work, differ from it in several aspects.

First, they differ in the class of considered systems: [31, 32] deal with synchronous DESs, [29] with timed asynchronous DESs (and is oriented to telecommunication networks), while [18, 26] consider systems integrating both synchronous and asynchronous behavior. Reactive diagnosis, instead, copes with untimed asynchronous DESs, where a system transition amounts to a component transition, triggered by a single event, and wherein there may be delays between the time an event is received by a component and the time it is consumed. Every such system may follow behavioral silent cycles over time, which is not the case for the diagnoser approach, its extension, and the decentralized protocol approach.

Second, the essential novelty of this paper lies in applying monitoring-based diagnosis to uncertain observations. In [29] the observation is a completely certain stream of time-stamped alarms and represents time constraints explicitly. A certain plain observation is considered in [31, 32, 27, 18]. In [26] the system observation consists of a set of certain plain observations, with each plain observation being inherent to a single component, plus a set of temporal constraints that can lead to envisage a partial order of the observable events generated by each considered (sub)system. Reactive diagnosis, instead, takes as input a sequence of observation fragments, where each fragment may be logically and/or temporally and/or source uncertain.

Third, the definition of a diagnosis problem in the current paper differs from [18] as well as from all the works on monitoring by other authors since it includes the notions of a ruler and a viewer [19], which decouple the (behavioral) models of system components from the descriptions of their observability and abnormality properties. In the model-based diagnosis literature, only a more limited separation from observability properties can be found: in [10] each specific diagnosis problem assigns the same observability to all the instances of the same component type, whereas in the active system approach each instance can be endowed with distinct properties. As to the separation from abnormality properties, this is an exclusive feature of the active system approach.

Finally, the method for carrying out monitoring-based diagnosis supported by the concepts defined in the present paper adapts the diagnostic algorithm in [18], and it is different from the algorithms of the other approaches. According to the method previously proposed by the authors [18], at each step, the reasoning engine starts from the current system state and finds out all possible evolutions (sequences of transitions) that comply with the given certain observable event, thus reaching the next system state, the diagnostic closure of which is thereafter reconstructed. Since there may be several evolutions complying with the same observable event, each estimated system state belongs to a hyperstate possibly consisting of several diagnostic closures, the same as in reactive diagnosis. However, since in the bridge diagnostic method the observation is a plain one, no observation management is needed. The first attempts to perform observation management by updating a deterministic automaton, the index space, in one shot, at the arrival of each observation fragment, appeared in [21]. This algorithm has then been extended beyond the diagnosis domain, resulting in a general-purpose algorithm for incremental determinization of finite automata [22]. The dynamic optimization of the index space is instead a novelty of the present paper.

In the following, some recent approaches to monitoring-based diagnosis of DESs by other authors are briefly compared with the current work in order to detail some of the differences highlighted above, and to isolate further differences and similarities.

11.1. Decentralized Protocol Approach

The *decentralized protocol approach* [11, 12] adopts the same modeling abstraction as the diagnoser approach [31, 32], from which it stems.

The diagnoser approach distinguishes *on-line* activities, which are carried out while monitoring the system, and *off-line* ones, which are accomplished beforehand once and for all. Diagnosis is performed on-line whereas the verification of the diagnosability properties of the system and the automatic generation of the data structure, called *diagnoser*, that will be exploited on-line are accomplished off-line. The diagnoser is derived from the behavioral model of the whole system, called system model, which is both assumed not to incorporate silent cycles and to generate a live language. These two assumptions together guarantee that a failure event is, sooner or later, followed by an observable event. The generation of the diagnoser, which is a deterministic, completely observable FSM, starts from a known initial state, which is assumed to be normal. The purpose of the diagnoser is to infer about past occurrences of failures, based on observed events. Monitoring the DES amounts to following on-line a path in the diagnoser, a transition each time an event is observed. If a sequence of events has already been observed, then, following the (only) path marked by this sequence of events, a node is reached which contains all the possible current states of the DES, where each state is associated with a set of faults. Each state in the node is reachable in the system model by means of a sequence of transitions producing the given observation, while its corresponding set of faults contains all the faults occurred along that sequence, that is, the set of faults is a candidate diagnosis. Thus, each node of the diagnoser contains all the relevant candidate diagnoses.

Coming back to the decentralized protocol approach, the term ‘decentralized’ addresses a processing architecture consisting of several separate local sites, each monitoring the same given system and communicating information to a coordinator that is responsible for diagnosing the failures occurred in the system itself. The main aim of the approach is to limit the amount of data exchanged among the workstations. The decentralized protocol approach can generate a complete (and sound) set of candidate diagnoses only if there is a set of (categories of) observable events that makes the system diagnosable according to the definition of diagnosability given in the diagnoser approach. This quite differentiates the work from the approach presented in this paper, which (after the active system approach in general) guarantees the (soundness and) completeness of results independently of the diagnosability properties of the systems to diagnose.

In the decentralized protocol approach, the set of observable events is decomposed into several subsets, so that the system is not diagnosable with respect to any of them. Each subset contains the categories of events observable by a distinct local site. A local site monitors the whole system based on its set of observable events, by exploiting the global diagnoser of the whole system corresponding to this set, where the diagnoser is built by means of the diagnoser approach.

The need for several distinct global diagnosers (one for each site) significantly reduces the advantages of compositional modeling and makes the approach not applicable in practice to large systems, since the diagnoser generation runs into significant computational difficulties, as pointed out in [28, 27]. Moreover, the generation of the system model is another major difference of all the approaches that exploit diagnosers 'a la Sampath et al.' with respect to the reactive diagnosis approach. In other words, the decentralized protocol approach does not fulfill the parsimony requirement, while it meets the reactivity and incrementality requirements.

In the decentralized protocol approach what is actually decentralized is the observation: each local site makes a diagnosis based on its partial observation, which is a totally temporally ordered sequence of precise messages. The expressive power of the notion of an observation adopted by the reactive diagnosis approach allows one to represent a decentralized observation (its observation graph is disconnected), which is realistic since distinct types of (physical) events are sent to the observer(s) by means of distinct communication channels, and removes the simplifying assumption made by the decentralized protocol approach that each connected portion of the observation graph is necessarily totally temporally ordered and logically certain. However, the approach described in the current paper cannot cope with overlapping observations, a topic which has been dealt with in [17].

The local sites of the decentralized architecture are allowed to report to the coordinator a concise processed version of their results, according to a communication protocol. The challenge is to enable the coordinator, which is assumed not to be provided with any model of the system, to 'perform as well' as the (centralized) diagnoser corresponding to the whole set of observable events, that is, the set with respect to which the system is diagnosable. The centralized diagnoser is capable of detecting the occurrence of every fault in a diagnosable system within a finite number of events. Then, in the intentions of the authors of the decentralized protocol approach, the decentralized architecture should be able to do the same, even if, maybe, with different delay values. The challenge, which has been faced both in case the information transmitted by the local sites are received by the coordinator in the order they are sent and in case they are received with a bounded temporal error, has been won even if not in the general case but, rather, under a set of assumptions concerning the diagnosers exploited by the local sites.

11.2. Extended Diagnoser Approach

In [29], a work rooted in [28], the diagnoser approach [31, 32] is adapted to deal with telecommunication networks. Like the diagnoser approach, a behavioral model of the system is produced off-line and transformed into an *extended diagnoser*, an automaton against which each observed event is matched on-line in order to output the current set of candidate diagnoses. Therefore, the extended diagnoser approach fulfills the reactivity and incrementality requirements. The adopted compositional model of the system is quite similar to that of the reactive diagnosis approach and different from the diagnoser approach since connections between components are modeled as affected by delays. In the extended diagnoser approach all faults are transient and specific modeling primitives have been introduced so as to relax the hypothesis of permanent failures made by the diagnoser approach. In particular, non instantaneous connections and internal events have been introduced, which are unobservable events used to model non instantaneous changes of states. Instead, the active system approach, generally speaking, makes no assumption as to the nature of faults, and the management is uniform for all of them.

A limitation addressed by [29] is the incompleteness of the output of the diagnoser approach when a system is taken into account that is not diagnosable (according to the definitions of diagnosability and I-diagnosability provided by the diagnoser approach). The price paid in [29] for achieving the completeness of candidate diagnoses is the nondeterminism of the extended diagnoser vs. the determinism of the original diagnoser, in other words, there may be several distinct edges leaving a state of the extended diagnoser marked by the same observable event. This means that a nondeterministic search is performed on-line when matching the observation against the extended diagnoser. A nondeterministic search is performed on-line also by reactive diagnosis, which itself, as already remarked, guarantees the completeness of candidate diagnoses.

The extended diagnoser approach deals with explicit temporal information, which is completely missing both in the original diagnoser approach and in the reactive diagnosis approach (as well as in the active system approach in general). In particular, it integrates temporal constraints concerning emission and transmission delays on connections.

The extended diagnoser approach does not fulfill the parsimony requirement although the authors of [29] are aware of the computational difficulties of the diagnoser approach, deriving from the need for generating the whole system model. Thus, they propose to take advantage of the regular structure of the system both in modeling and in the diagnostic task by exploiting a generic model of a subsystem, from which a *generic* (extended) diagnoser is drawn. The latter, in fact, provides diagnoses inherent to all the distinct instances of a modeled subsystem (called generic component) and, in addition, it produces the diagnostic output in a concise way by exploiting set-theoretic operators. All these advantages, however, can be obtained when a system consists of several topologically identical subsystems not interacting with each other, as the telecommunication network at hand, but does not solve the problem of scalability in the general case, wherein the interaction between subsystems has to be managed as well as the consistency of candidate diagnoses in case there are components shared by two or more subsystems. Moreover, even in case the system can be viewed as an assembly of topologically identical non-interacting subsystems, the issue of scalability shifts from the system to the subsystem, which may itself be too large for the generation of its generic model, or, still more, for drawing the generic diagnoser from the generic model. In fact, given the same initial system model, the corresponding extended diagnoser is larger than the diagnoser of the original diagnoser approach.

The algorithm for building such an extended diagnoser is not modular while all algorithms proposed in the active system approach for behavior reconstruction, which are exploited by reactive diagnosis when building each diagnostic closure, are modular.

11.3. Incremental Decentralized Diagnosis Approach

The *incremental decentralized diagnosis approach* [26], a work rooted in [27], performs a sort of generalized monitoring that produces the histories of the system at hand by taking into account a packet of messages at each step. A packet encompasses all the messages received by the (only) supervision center within the time span of a so-called *temporal window*, and consists of several sequences of messages, with each sequence being ordered according to the emission time and pertaining to a single system component. Possibly available additional information about the 'channels' that convey messages from the system to the supervision center, such as their maximum propagation delay and their possible synchronization, can be exploited as constraints among the received messages, so as to create a partial temporal order among the messages relevant to a (sub)system. However, the only sort of uncertainty affecting the observation is the temporal one: unlike the approach in the current paper, neither logical nor source uncertainty are coped with.

Like the reactive diagnosis approach, there is a current set of already computed diagnoses at every moment and a new set of diagnoses is produced at each step based on the newly acquired packet of messages by updating the data structures produced in the previous step. This is why the approach is qualified as 'incremental' and, as stated, both approaches share the incrementality principle. Moreover, the 'decentralized' qualifier means that the method, like reactive diagnosis, does not need generating the global behavioral model of the system to be diagnosed, that is, both approaches fulfill the parsimony requirement.

Both the incremental decentralized diagnoser approach and reactive diagnosis deal with faults that can be either persistent or transient. The former, however, makes a simplifying assumption which is not made by reactive diagnosis: the set of all the (either internal or external) input events of a component is disjoint from the set of output events of the same component.

Another modeling difference between the incremental decentralized diagnosis approach and reactive diagnosis is inherent to links between components, called communication channels in [26]. As anticipated in Section 11, [26] considers both synchronous and asynchronous DESs, however, only synchronous communication between components is a modeling primitive. In case the communication channel between two given components is not instantaneous (that is, the emission and the reception of a message do not occur at the same time) or not reliable (that is, if transmitted events may be lost), such a channel is modeled as an additional component that communicates with the two given ones (sending/receiving events to/from it) by means of synchronous (instantaneous) links. On the one hand, treating uniformly components and links enables the technique to merge histories of components/(sub)systems by means of a synchronous composition operation. On the other, this choice is disadvantageous from the problem-size viewpoint. In fact, the number of automaton states (and therefore the space) needed for representing, for instance, the behavior of a simple FIFO buffer is exponential in its capacity. Moreover, as a consequence of representing uniformly links and components and of performing synchronous composition, the behavior of each component/link is represented as an automaton where each state is endowed with an additional empty (auto)transition. This makes the size of the problem still larger, while not enlarging the class of DESs representable by the incremental decentralized diagnosis approach with respect to the reactive diagnosis approach since, in principle, also the latter allows the modeler to represent the normal and faulty behavior of any kind of links by means of the modeling primitives of components.

Thus, in matter of communication between components, we can conclude that the incremental decentralized diagnoser approach is oriented towards systems either endowed with synchronous links only or with asynchronous links too, provided their capacity is quite limited.

In the incremental decentralized diagnosis approach the diagnosis of a (sub)system, where a subsystem is a generic subset of system components, is a set of paths that explain the observed behavior, where each path belongs to the synchronized product of the automata representing the behaviors of all the involved components. However, a concise view of the state and the history of the system is provided, which is based on a partial order reduction method.

The rationale is that, if two failures are independent, in case they both occur, it is irrelevant to know the temporal order of their occurrences. A dependence relation is defined, which partitions the behavior of the (sub)system into classes of paths, called traces. Any path belonging to a trace can represent the trace itself: in the reduced diagnosis representation a path p from each trace is chosen. All the other paths belonging to the same trace can be obtained starting from p by repeatedly swapping the order of any two adjacent independent transitions.

The exploitation of a partial order reduction method for representing system evolutions is a very good idea of the incremental decentralized diagnosis approach. Such an idea produces gains in efficiency when evolutions are merged, therefore it could be beneficial for reactive diagnosis too. For each temporal window, the incremental decentralized diagnosis approach computes a (concise representation of the) diagnosis for each subsystem and then it builds a global diagnosis of the system by merging the subsystem diagnoses. A strategy is adopted that dynamically recognizes an efficient way to apply the merging operation based on the observation of the current temporal window.

The purpose of the strategy is to detect and compute subsystem diagnoses that claim no interaction with other subsystems (they are called independent diagnoses). If an independent diagnosis is detected, it is useless to merge it. Dependent diagnoses instead are iteratively merged two-by-two until a single independent diagnosis is obtained. The most-interacting evolutions are merged first since, the more constrained the interaction, the more likely that the size of the resulting automaton is smaller. Therefore, the global diagnosis is totally represented by a set of independent diagnoses, with each diagnosis being based on a subsystem disjoint from the others. In the worst case, there is only one independent diagnosis. The authors of the incremental decentralized diagnoser approach remark (and the specific experiments they present confirm) that 'independent diagnoses exist because a failure does not usually propagate its consequences on all the components of a system'. However, this claim is questionable because: .i/ one should consider the propagation of the consequences not only of failures but also of normal behavior since also the normal behavior of the whole system (or of part of it) has to be reconstructed in case it is compatible with the observation, and (ii) in physical devices that do not consist of the interconnection of identical modules according to a repetitive structure, all components are usually involved in the system operation.

Anyway, the choice made by the incremental decentralized diagnoser approach to represent a global diagnosis as a set of independent diagnoses is meaningful and, notwithstanding the overhead needed to determine the interactions between subsystem paths, the strategy is timesaving when independent diagnoses actually exist. In other words, such a choice is oriented towards either highly concurrent devices that exhibit a strong independence of the parts in both normal and faulty behavior (i.e. lack of exchanged events), and/or to devices that have been designed so as to confine the consequences of faults to small subsystems and where the faulty behavior of each subsystem is quite different from normal behavior.

The main difference between the incremental decentralized diagnosis approach and reactive diagnosis is that the latter provides a general working framework for performing monitoring- based diagnosis, while the former proposes a task definition and a task implementation that are valid only under some assumptions (and, in the general case, one cannot check whether such assumptions hold given the observation).

The incremental decentralized diagnosis approach, in fact, discusses two mutually exclusive incremental algorithms. The first one is run under the assumption that the received messages are exactly those emitted by the system in the considered temporal window. The technique is the same as that adopted for a posteriori diagnosis, with the only difference that, at each time step, the construction of the histories starts from several initial states rather than one, where such states are the final states of the current global diagnoses. However, no means is provided to check whether the assumption holds given the received messages, that is, the choice of the temporal window is still an open problem.

If the above assumption is relaxed, that is, if the sequence of messages emitted within a temporal window may be randomly split into successive observation packets, the second algorithm will be performed. According to this algorithm, an extended set of global candidate diagnoses is produced, which summarizes both the trajectories that explain the events observed in the considered window and some trajectories that explain also a set of hypothetical unreceived events supposed to have been emitted but not yet received by the observer.

Possible wrong hypotheses made during the computation of the successive extended diagnoses are removed with the help of the diagnoses of the last window, when no more messages are expected. The main problem still to be solved here at any step is how to hypothesize unreceived messages so as not to miss any history of the considered system.

CONCLUSION

In the literature, the approaches to monitoring-based diagnosis of DESs can be accommodated at the two extremes of a spectrum, depending on when the computation load is faced, either off- line or on-line. On the one extreme is the *diagnoser* approach [31, 32] and it extension [29] and derivation [11]: they perform an off-line compilation of the distributed component models into a diagnoser, against which each observable event generated by the system is matched on-line in constant time. As such, the diagnoser is a data structure that enables solving any diagnosis problem sharing a given initial state of the system.

On the other extreme of the spectrum is a former work by the authors [18], the *incremental decentralized diagnoser approach* [26], and *reactive diagnosis*, the approach presented in this paper: they process the observable events on-line so as to reconstruct, in an incremental way, what has happened to the system. Such approaches produce data-structures specialized by the actual problem (the initial state of the system and, in particular, its observation).

Both classes of approaches suffer from limitations: intractability of off-line processing for the former, non-deterministic on-line search for the latter. The approaches in the latter class adopt several strategies to reduce on-line computation time: partial order reduction in [26], pruning in the current work. The degree and the sort of uncertainty affecting the observation deeply influences the size of the search space. The incremental decentralized diagnoser approach and reactive diagnosis mainly differentiate from each other for the type of uncertainty in observations. In fact, in this paper, attention is focused on uncertain observation management in monitoring-based diagnosis (while the previous work on the same task accounted for certain observations only [18]).

Both the observation graph and the index space are modeling primitives for uncertain temporal observations. Whereas the former (a DAG) is the front-end representation, suitable for modeling an observation while being received over a time interval, the latter (a deterministic automaton) is a back-end representation, suitable for model-based problem-solving, so as to reduce on-line search.

Experimental results have shown that reactive diagnosis brings a significant reduction of the computation time with respect to the other viable method of constructing the index space anew, at each step, based on the whole observation received so far. A further reduction of the processing time has been obtained by dynamically exploiting the reconstruction of the behavior of the system to prune the index space in case one or more sequences of labels, although complying with the observation, are physically impossible. These computational savings are meaningful whenever a processing step has to be performed after each observation fragment is received, as is when the tasks of supervision and dynamic diagnosis (and state estimation, in general) are considered. Chances are that other approaches to model-based reasoning on DESs can exploit this result, since the proposed algorithm relies on the model of a DES observation, which is, to a large extent, independent of the model adopted for the DES. Also, the new algorithm for the incremental generation of the index space is a contribution to automata theory, by enabling, under classified conditions, to make the *subset-construction algorithm* [1] incremental [22].

Moreover, the notion of an index space brings the advantage of adopting for observations the same formalism traditionally exploited for component models of DESs, whether synchronous or asynchronous. Actually, in the literature, each reasoning step performed on the behavior of DESs translates to the composition of two or more automata. Now that the awareness has grown that DES observations can be represented as automata themselves [13], the (only) operation that is needed for carrying out several model-based tasks is the synchronization between automata, where observations are handled exactly as the other models. Besides, the index space, since adhering to the standard formal representation of regular languages, could be adopted as an interchange format of uncertain observations among distinct application contexts.

In between the two ends of the spectrum is an unexplored zone for future research, approaches that give up constant on-line processing time to increase scalability, approaches that can trade-off off-line and on-line computation, on-line approaches that can (maybe adaptively) trade-off space and time since, based on our experimental results, the increase of space occupation is more critical than the increase of processing time. For instance, in reactive diagnosis, one can save all the silent closures produced so far, or, in order to reduce space occupation at the expenses of time, save a concise processed form of the silent closures, or, from step to step, keep only the silent closures inherent to the final states of the decorated index space and possibly a selection of the others, and so on. Moreover, some silent closures (typically, those inherent to the most frequent system states) could be generated off-line. Adopting a modular computation both for the construction of silent closures and for observation management might help increase efficiency. All these are directions for further stimulating investigation.

REFERENCES

[1] Aho, M.S. Lam, R. Sethi, and J.D. Ullman. *Compilers – Principles, Techniques, and Tools.* Addison-Wesley, Reading, MA, second edition, 2006.

[2] P. Baroni, G. Lamperti, P. Pogliano, and M. Zanella. Diagnosis of large active systems. *Artificial Intelligence*, 110(1): 135–183, 1999.

[3] P. Baroni, G. Lamperti, P. Pogliano, and M. Zanella. Diagnosis of a class of distributed discrete-event systems. IEEE Transactions on Systems, Man, and Cybernetics - Part A: *Systems and Humans*, 30(6):731–752, 2000.

[4] Barral, S. McIlraith, and T.C. Son. Formulating diagnostic problem solving using an action language with narratives and sensing. In *Seventh International Conference on Knowledge Representation and Reasoning – KR '2000*, pages 311–322, Breckenridge, Colorado, 2000. Morgan Kaufmann, S. Francisco, CA.

[5] G.V. Bochmann. Finite state description of communication protocols. *Computer Networks*, 2:361–372, 1978.

[6] Brand and P. Zafiropulo. On communicating finite-state machines. *Journal of ACM*, 30(2):323–342, 1983.

[7] V. Brusoni, L. Console, P. Terenziani, and D. Theseider Dupré. A spectrum of definitions for temporal model-based diagnosis. *Artificial Intelligence*, 102(1):39–80, 1998.

[8] C.G. Cassandras and S. Lafortune. *Introduction to Discrete Event Systems,* volume 11 of The Kluwer International Series in Discrete Event Dynamic Systems. Kluwer Academic Publisher, Boston, MA, 1999.

[9] L. Console, C. Picardi, and M. Ribaudo. Diagnosis and diagnosability using PEPA. In *Fourteenth European Conference on Artificial Intelligence - ECAI'2000*, pages 131–135, Berlin, D, 2000. IOS Press, Amsterdam, NL.

[10] L. Console, C. Picardi, and M. Ribaudo. Process algebras for systems diagnosis. *Artificial Intelligence*, 142(1): 19–51, 2002.

[11] R. Debouk, S. Lafortune, and D. Teneketzis. Coordinated decentralized protocols for failure diagnosis of discrete-event systems. *Journal of Discrete Event Dynamic Systems: Theory and Applications*, 10:33–86, 2000.

[12] R. Debouk, S. Lafortune, and D. Teneketzis. A diagnostic protocol for discrete-event systems with decentralized information. In E*leventh International Workshop on Principles of Diagnosis - DX'00,* pages 41–48, Morelia, MX, 2000.

[13] Grastien, M.O. Cordier, and C. Largouët. Incremental diagnosis of discrete-event systems. In *Sixteenth International Workshop on Principles of Diagnosis – DX'05*, pages 119–124, Monterey, CA, 2005.

[14] J.E. Hopcroft, R. Motwani, and J.D. Ullman. *Introduction to Automata Theory, Languages, and Computation.* Addison-Wesley, Reading, MA, third edition, 2006.

[15] G. Lamperti and P. Pogliano. Event-based reasoning for short circuit diagnosis in power transmission networks. In *Fifteenth International Joint Conference on Artificial Intelligence – IJCAI'97,* pages 446–451, Nagoya, J, 1997. Morgan Kaufmann, S. Francisco, CA.

[16] G. Lamperti and M. Zanella. Diagnosis of discrete-event systems from uncertain temporal observations. *Artificial Intelligence*, 137(1–2):91–163, 2002.

[17] G. Lamperti and M. Zanella. *Diagnosis of Active Systems – Principles and Techniques,* volume 741 of The Kluwer International Series in Engineering and Computer Science. Kluwer Academic Publisher, Dordrecht, NL, 2003.

[18] G. Lamperti and M. Zanella. A bridged diagnostic method for the monitoring of polymorphic discrete-event systems. *IEEE Transactions on Systems, Man, and Cybernetics - Part B: Cybernetics*, 34(5):2222–2244, 2004.

[19] G. Lamperti and M. Zanella. Diagnosis of discrete-event systems by separation of concerns, knowledge compilation, and reuse. In *Sixteenth European Conference on Artificial Intelligence – ECAI'2004*, pages 838–842, Valencia, E, 2004.

[20] G. Lamperti and M. Zanella. Monitoring and diagnosis of discrete-event systems with uncertain symptoms. In *Sixteenth International Workshop on Principles of Diagnosis – DX'05,* pages 145–150, Monterey, CA, 2005.

[21]] G. Lamperti and M. *Zanella. Incremental indexing of temporal observations in diagnosis of active systems. In Seventeenth International Workshop on Principles of Diagnosis – DX'06*, pages 147–154, Peñaranda de Duero, E, 2006.

[22] G. Lamperti, M. Zanella, G. Chiodi, and L. Chiodi. Incremental determinization of finite automata in model-based diagnosis of active systems. In I. Lovrek, R.J. Howlett, and L.C. Jain, editors, *Knowledge-Based Intelligent Information and Engineering Systems,* volume 5177 of LNAI, pages 3 62–374. Springer, 2008.

[23] J. Lunze. Diagnosis of quantized systems based on a timed discrete-event model. *IEEE Transactions on Systems, Man, and Cybernetics – Part A: Systems and Humans,* 30(3):322– 335, 2000.

[24] S.A. McIlraith. Explanatory diagnosis: conjecturing actions to explain observations. In *Sixth International Conference on Principles of Knowledge Representation and Reasoning - KR'98*, pages 167–177, Trento, I, 1998. Morgan Kaufmann, S. Francisco, CA.

[25] Y. Pencolé. Decentralized diagnoser approach: application to telecommunication networks. In *Eleventh International Workshop on Principles of Diagnosis – DX'00,* pages 185–192, Morelia, MX, 2000.

[26] Y. Pencolé and M.O. Cordier. A formal framework for the decentralized diagnosis of large scale discrete event systems and its application to telecommunication networks. *Artificial Intelligence*, 164:121–170, 2005.

[27] Y. Pencolé, M.O. Cordier, and L. Rozé. Incremental decentralized diagnosis approach for the supervision of a telecommunication network. In *Twelfth International Workshop on Principles of Diagnosis – DX'01,* pages 151–158, San Sicario, I, 2001.

[28] L. Rozé. Supervision of telecommunication network: a diagnoser approach. In *Eighth International Workshop on Principles of Diagnosis – DX'97,* pages 103–111, Mont St. Michel, F, 1997.

[29] L. Rozé and M.O. Cordier. Diagnosing discrete-event systems: extending the 'diagnoser approach' to deal with telecommunication networks. *Journal of Discrete Event Dynamic Systems: Theory and Application,* 12:43–81, 2002.

[30] M. Sampath, S. Lafortune, and D.C. Teneketzis. Active diagnosis of discrete-event systems. *IEEE Transactions on Automatic Control*, 43(7):908–929, 1998.

[31] M. Sampath, R. Sengupta, S. Lafortune, K. Sinnamohideen, and D.C. Teneketzis. Diagnosability of discrete-event systems. *IEEE Transactions on Automatic Control,* 40(9): 1555– 1575, 1995.

[32] M. Sampath, R. Sengupta, S. Lafortune, K. Sinnamohideen, and D.C. Teneketzis. Failure diagnosis using discrete-event models. *IEEE Transactions on Control Systems Technology*, 4(2):105–124, 1996.

[33] G. Schullerus and V. Krebs. Diagnosis of a class of discrete-event systems based on parameter estimation of a modular algebraic model. In *Twelfth International Workshop on Principles of Diagnosis – DX'01,* pages 189–196, San Sicario, I, 2001.

[34] P. Struss. Fundamentals of model-based diagnosis of dynamic systems. In *Fifteenth International Joint Conference on Artificial Intelligence – IJCAI'97*, pages 480–485, Nagoya, J, 1997. Morgan Kaufmann, S. Francisco, CA.

[35] S.H. Zad, R.H. Kwong, and W.M. Wonham. Fault diagnosis in timed discrete-event systems. In *38th IEEE Conference on Decision and Control – CDC'99*, pages 1756–1761, Pheonix, AZ, 1999. IEEE, Piscataway, NJ.

In: New Developments in Computer Research
Editor: Nikos E. Mastorakis

ISBN: 978-1-61470-321-1

WHAT CAN CLOUD COMPUTING OFFER TO SCIENTIFIC RESEARCH?

Nabil Sultan*
Faculty of Sciences and Social Sciences,
Liverpool Hope University, UK

ABSTRACT

Cloud computing is an emerging new computing paradigm designed to deliver numerous computing services in ways that have not been experienced before. It is increasingly being viewed as a utility-oriented computing service. There are even speculations that it has the potential to be the 5th utility (after water, electricity, gas and telephony).

This computing service is underpinned by a number of existing technologies such as the Internet, virtualization, grid computing and Web services. The flexibility of this computing service approach and its provision in a pay-as-you-go way have opened many possibilities for organizations, of all types, that did not exist before. Among those organizations are those engaged in scientific research. A number of cloud computing services are now emerging to cater for the scientific community, with a potential to bring substantial cost-saving and efficiency advantages.

This chapter will highlight those issues and also analyze some of the limitations that are currently associated with this computing service modality.

Keywords: Cloud Computing, Web Services, Virtualization, Virtual Machines (VMs), Grid Computing, High Performance Computing (HPC), Small and Medium Enterprises (SMEs)

---

* Dr. Nabil Sultan graduated from the University of Liverpool with a PhD in Management in 1992 and in 1996 he received his MSc in Information Systems from the same university. After a two-year working period for the United Nations Development Program (UNDP) as Program Officer he moved on to work as a lecturer in IT and Business for the University of Liverpool's Center for Continuing Education until 1998 and since 1999 as Senior Lecturer and Program Director for Liverpool Hope University's Faculty of Sciences and Social Sciences where he developed many successful modules and programs. Dr. Sultan has many published works in IT and management. E-mail: sultann@hope.ac.uk

INTRODUCTION

The provision of software as a service (SaaS) is not a new computing practice. In fact, it predates the emergence of computers themselves. In the 1930s some companies (such as IBM) specialized in producing electric accounting machines based on punch-cards and were able to offer data processing services (e.g., payrolls) to organizations. Providers of such services operated many 'service bureaus' where customers would bring their data for processing in return for a fee. Organizations that were unable to purchase those data processing equipment found it economically viable to pay for those services. Then came mainframe computers in the 1950s and 1960s which continued this practice that became known as 'timesharing'. Organizations that were unable to afford buying mainframes computers would rent the data processing functionality of those machines from a number of providers. Connection to mainframes was achieved through a normal telephone line connecting those massive machines and 'teletypes', replaced afterwards with better visual display machines, at the clients' end. Then came personal computers which effectively killed timesharing due to the affordability of personal computers and also the flexibility of the software used on them. Campbell-Kelly (2009) argues that the very things that killed the timesharing industry in the 1980s have reversed, in that computing infrastructure has become increasingly complex and expensive to maintain due, for example, to issues relating to security and constant software upgrades thus making cloud computing a more economically viable alternative. One analyst called cloud computing 'Timesharing 2.0' in reference to the old practice of buying computing resources on demand (Campbell, 2009).

However, despite the popularity of personal computers, a form of utility computing still existed. Many software providers, known as Application Service Providers (ASPs), emerged in the 1990s to provide organizations with software as a service via the medium, this time, of the Internet. These early attempts at "utility computing" did not prove to be popular. There were two main reasons for this. Firstly, most of the software offered by those providers was proprietary, which meant organizations using this type of service cannot change providers very easily, i.e., they were vendor-locked. Secondly, lack of sufficient bandwidth was another problem. During the 1990s broadband was neither cheap nor plentiful enough to deliver computing services with the required speed and reliability (Carr, 2009). Then came Web services (especially those based on the XML-based SOAP message protocol) that promised to deliver highly portable software remotely, through the medium of the Internet, without any ties to any platform (i.e., operating systems) or programming languages. Web services heralded a new era of 'software as a service' (SaaS).

The idea of delivering software remotely took a new turn with the emergence of cloud computing. Not only can software be consumed remotely, it can also be consumed as and when needed through a pay-as-you-go cost structure. Cloud computing also promises many other exciting possibilities where other computing-related functionality can be consumed remotely as and when needed, thanks to other relatively new technologies such as virtualization and grid computing.

Virtualization is a technology that masks the physical characteristics of computing resources (e.g., a PC, a Server) in order to simplify the way in which other systems, applications, or end users interact with them. For example, a PC running Windows can use virtualization to enable another operating system (e.g., Linux) to run besides Windows. Furthermore, the technology also enables single physical resources (e.g., a server, an operating system, an application, or storage device) to appear as multiple logical resources.

Grid computing involves the use of software to combine the computational power of many computers, connected in a grid, in order to solve a single problem, often one that requires a great deal of computer processing power. Furthermore, grid computing also uses software that can divide and farm out pieces of a program to as many as several thousand computers. Grid technology, therefore, can be thought of as the technology that enables the establishment of network-distributed parallel processing and distributed and large-scale cluster computing.

Both virtualization and grid computing technologies have become two fundamental building blocs of cloud computing.

Cloud Computing: Definition

A Web search for cloud computing is likely to reveal a stream of definitions. There seems to be no common standard or definition for cloud computing (Voas and Zhang, 2009; Grossman, 2009). A study conducted by McKinsey (the global management consulting firm) found 22 definitions for cloud computing. A more commonly used definition describes it as clusters of distributed computers (largely vast datacenters and server farms) which provide on-demand resources and services over a networked medium (usually the Internet). The term "cloud" was probably inspired by cloud illustrations depicting the Internet which are often found in many computing textbooks and journals.

In order to understand what cloud computing is all about it is perhaps useful to have an idea of the type of services it offers for consumers. The following is a list of the three main types of services offered by cloud computing (Sultan, 2010):

- Infrastructure as a Service (IaaS): Products offered via this mode include the remote delivery (through the Internet) of a full computer infrastructure (e.g., virtual computers, servers, storage devices, etc.);
- Platform as a Service (PaaS): To understand this cloud computing layer, one needs to remember the traditional computing model where each application managed locally required hardware, an operating system, a database, middleware, Web servers, and other software. One also needs to remember the team of network, database and system management experts that are needed to keep everything up and running. With cloud computing, these services are now provided remotely by cloud providers under this layer;
- Software as a Service (Saas): Under this layer, applications are delivered through the medium of the Internet as a service. Instead of installing and maintaining software, you simply access it via the Internet, freeing yourself from complex software and hardware management. This type of cloud service offers a complete application functionality that ranges from productivity (e.g., office-type) applications to programs such as those for Customer Relationship Management (CRM) or Enterprise Resource Management (ERM).

Despite the flexibility of cloud computing, it should not be assumed that cloud products offered by any of the above services are likely to work out-of-the-box (i.e., they are not purely plug-and-play). In some cases they might. Messaging and collaboration cloud products such as Google Apps are perhaps examples of those out-of-the-box products, even though they still require some level of configuration nevertheless. Some degree of development (i.e., programming) will be required through the use of the cloud providers' APIs (application programming interfaces). These are the programming instructions created and offered by the cloud service providers to those who want to access the functionality of their products.

Currently, some of those APIs are proprietary. This is an issue which will be explored later when examining some of the limitations and concerns of cloud computing.

However, the notion of providing a wide array of computing-related services on the fly on a pay-as-you-go basis opens many opportunities for the providers of those services to exploit this expanding market which (according to Merrill Lynch) is worth 100 billion US dollars (Buyya, Yeo and Venugopal, 2009). At the same time, it increases the options available to policy makers entrusted with the job of ensuring the efficient functioning of their organization's IT resources. On that basis, cloud computing probably represents a paradigm shift in the way IT, in its all aspects, is being viewed by commoditizing it in a manner that was not possible before (Sultan, 2010).

PUBLIC, PRIVATE AND HYBRID CLOUDS

Cloud services, such as those listed above, are known as public clouds when offered by commercial cloud providers. This is to distinguish them from private clouds, also known as internal or corporate clouds, where the cloud infrastructure (e.g., datacenters, servers, etc.) and services are provided, housed and maintained internally by the users themselves. This is an example of organizations becoming themselves the providers and consumers of cloud services. This approach, which might provide organizations with total security and control of their own resources, actually defeats the whole utility-oriented purpose of cloud computing which is supposed to guarantee choice, flexibility and cost-effectiveness. In fact, it is doubtful if this type of arrangement has anything to do with cloud computing as a concept which is largely utility-based. A number of public cloud providers are now coming up with solutions which incorporate elements of both private and public clouds that might be classified as "hybrid clouds". For example, companies such as Amazon have very recently launched a service known as Virtual Private Cloud (VPC) designed to address this issue of security and control which seems to be one of the concerns of large organizations. Amazon's VPC allows organizations to connect their existing legacy infrastructures to Amazon's clouds via a Virtual Private Network (VPN) connection [1]. This means that Amazon's cloud customers can create their own Amazon isolated resources, i.e., virtual private clouds (VPCs) within Amazon's cloud infrastructure and then connect those resources directly to their network servers using industry-standard encrypted IPsec VPN connections. In doing so, these customers will be able to extend their existing security and management policies within their IT infrastructures to their VPCs as if they were running locally.

---

[1] A virtual private network (VPN) is a private network that provides remote access to its resources through a public telecommunication infrastructure, such as the Internet.

Public Cloud Services for HPC

There are many public cloud computing services on offer. Many of those serve a variety of tasks such as enabling users to: create hundreds, even thousands, of virtual machines (e.g., servers) at the click of button; acquire unlimited space to save their data; access the required amount of software functionality for office-related tasks (e.g., word processing, spreadsheets, etc.) and business-related operations (e.g., CRM). If fact, there is now a potential to create one's entire IT infrastructure in the cloud. A Californian startup company by the name of 3Tera has developed software, named AppLogic, that can automate the creation of complex corporate systems. The software provides a simple graphical user interface which a designer can use to drag and drop icons representing traditional components (e.g., databases, routers, firewalls, cables, etc.) onto a page in a Web browser. When the designer has the arrangement in place, he or she can then click a button and the software creates the virtual IT infrastructure in a matter of minutes (Carr, 2009).

Cloud computing for high performance computing (HPC) has not been on the priority list of many cloud providers. However, this attitude is now changing as cloud providers have begun to realize the business potential of this area of computing. Currently, there are few cloud providers that can declare themselves as having cloud solutions for HPC. However, two cloud providers, namely Amazon and Microsoft, have two cloud platforms that have the potential to provide the high performance computing required by the scientific community. The first product is Elastic Compute Cloud (EC2) from Amazon and the second is Azure from Microsoft. Amazon's EC2 is part of Amazon Web Services (AWS). It offers s a simple web service interface that allows users to request, monitor, and manage any number of virtual machine (VM) instances running on physical compute nodes in their datacenters. The system therefore enables users to scale capacity, both up and down, as their computing requirements change. Compute nodes are organized into CPU capacity (several CPUs), RAM, and local storage. The user can programmatically start and stop compute node instances to deal with increasing or decreasing demand. EC2 is now increasingly been targeted by the scientific community for HPC purposes and is proving to be useful (see The MathWorks, 2008; Rehr et al., 2008).

Azure is a complex beast. It has three components: Windows Azure, SQL Azure and Azure AppFabric (formerly known as .Net Services). Windows Azure is designed to provide developers with on-demand compute and storage to host, scale, and manage Internet or cloud applications. SQL Azure is developed to extend the capabilities of SQL Server, Microsoft's database managing system (DBMS), into the cloud as a Web-based distributed relational database. AppFabric is a set of integrated technologies designed to help developers connect applications and services between Windows Azure and on-premises deployments (see Foley, 2009; Bailey, 2009). Microsoft is devoting increasing sources behind this platform such as adding more datacenters. This has made Azure attractive for some HPC projects as demonstrated by some of Microsoft's case studies (Microsoft, 2009a).

An increasing number of small HPC providers are now migrating some of their services to the cloud. For example, Silicon Graphics International (SGI), an HPC solution provider, recently launched a cloud-based platform named 'Cyclone'. Cyclone is expected to, initially, support five technical domains: computational fluid dynamics, finite element analysis, computational chemistry and materials, computational biology, and ontologies (Leung, 2010).

Another small HPC solution provider to enter the cloud market is Penguin Computing with its Penguin on Demand (POD). POD, according to Penguin Computing, is a high-performance, scalable, on-demand HPC as a Service solution with high-density compute nodes and high-speed storage that offers users a persistent, load on demand, virtualized compute environment (Penguin Computing, 2010).

It is likely that more cloud providers will be moving into this computing area in the future as more people from the scientific community begin to look at this computing service for solutions to their problems.

ECONOMICS, FLEXIBILITY AND GREEN CREDENTIALS

Economics, simplification and convenience of the way computing-related services are delivered seem to be among the main drivers of cloud computing (Erdogmus, 2009). Many people see huge potential of the technology in reducing the cost of IT to organizations and freeing them from the expense and hassle of having to install and maintain applications locally (Leavitt, 2009). Providing IT services in the cloud shifts much of this expense to a pay-as-you-go model and consequently offers significant cost advantages according to one view (Lin, Fu, Zhu and Dasmalchi, 2009). Furthermore, a great proportion of the costs of running an IT infrastructure comes from electricity consumption which is needed to run hardware (e.g., PCs, servers, switches, backup drives) and cooling which is needed to reduce the heating generated by the hardware. Cloud computing is likely to reduce expenditure in this area and also reduce labor-related costs, as less people (e.g., technicians) than before will be required to run a cloud-based IT infrastructure.

The cost advantage of cloud computing is not just related to how much cloud users can save by not buying and installing hardware and software and using less power. Users of cloud computing are more likely to significantly reduce their carbon footprint. Research suggests that ICT is already responsible for 2 percent of global carbon emissions, and that its relative share will increase further. In the UK, for example, increasingly stringent regulations (such as the Carbon Reduction commitment and EU Energy Using Products Directive) are likely to put pressure on organizations and educational establishments to make ICT more sustainable (James and Hopkinsons, 2009). In an environment where there is increasing concern about institutions' carbon footprint and energy costs, virtualized services (such as those offered by cloud computing) may become especially appealing (Katz, 2008).

THE GROWING APPEAL OF CLOUD COMPUTING FOR HPC

Until recently, high performance computing has not been a good candidate for cloud computing due to a number of factors such as its requirement for tight integration between server nodes via low-latency interconnects and high-speed networking (Shainer et al 2010). For example, the performance overhead associated with host virtualization, a prerequisite technology for migrating local applications to the cloud, quickly erodes application scalability and efficiency in an HPC context which often involves sending messages back and forth many times per second, a process that is likely to increase the possibility of latency (Niccolai,

2009). However, new virtualization solutions that use KVM (kernel-based virtual machine) and XEN hypervisors[2] have managed to solve the performance issue by reducing the virtualization management overhead through enabling native performance capabilities from the VMs and by allowing direct access from the VMs to the network. High-speed networking is also an important factor in HPC which requires fast communication between clusters of servers and storage (Shainer et al., 2010). With the ability of more cloud vendors to provide faster speed and networking connections, this issue has become less of a problem for HPC.

Hence, a number of scientific and research communities have begun to look at the possibility of using cloud computing in order to take advantage of its economic and efficiency benefits. The experience of the Medical College of Wisconsin Biotechnology and Bioengineering Center in Milwaukee in the USA is one example. Scientists at this institute are making protein research (a very expensive undertaking) more accessible to scientists worldwide, thanks largely to renting the massive processing power that is available on Amazon's powerful cloud-based servers.

One of the major challenges for many laboratories setting up proteomics programs has been the need to obtain and maintain a computational infrastructure required for analyzing a vast flow of proteomics data generated by mass spectrometry instruments used in determining the elemental composition as well as chemical structure of a molecule. Cloud computing provided that ability at a very competitive cost. This meant that many more users could set up and customize their own systems and investigators could analyze their data in greater depth than was previously attainable, thus making it possible for them to learn more about the systems they are studying (La Susa, 2009; Halligan et al., 2008).

Major cloud computing providers such as IBM and Google are also actively promoting cloud computing as tools for aiding research. In 2007 Google and IBM announced a cloud computing university initiative designed to improve computer science students' knowledge of highly parallel computing practices in order to address the emerging paradigm of large-scale distributed computing. In 2009 the National Science Foundation (NSF) awarded nearly US$ 5 million in grants to fourteen universities through its Cluster Exploratory (CLuE) program to help facilitate their participation in the IBM/Google initiative. The initiative's goal was to provide the computing infrastructure for leading-edge research projects that could help promote better understanding of our planet, bodies and many other issues.

A number of other US government departments are also beginning to explore the merits of cloud computing for scientific purposes. Two of those come to mind: the Department of Energy (DOE) and NASA, the American space agency. The DOE has embarked on a US$ 32 million cloud infrastructure project aimed at exploring the ability of cloud computing to provide a cost-effective and energy-efficient computing service for scientists to accelerate discoveries in a variety of disciplines, including analysis of scientific data sets in biology, climate change and physics. The DOE's centers at the Argonne Leadership Computing Facility (ALCF) in Illinois and the National Energy Research Scientific Computing Center (NERSC) in California are hoping to be able to determine how much of DOE's mid-range computing needs could and should run in a cloud environment and what hardware and

[2] A hypervisor is a virtual machine monitor (VMM) that allows multiple operating systems to run concurrently on a host computer.

software features are needed for science clouds. Due to the exploratory nature of this project, it was named 'Magellan', in honor of the Portuguese explorer who led the first effort to sail around the globe and for whom the 'clouds of Magellan' – two small galaxies in the southern sky – were named. Pete Beckman, director of Argonne's Leadership Computing Facility and project lead, said "We know that the model works well for business applications, and we are working to make it equally effective for science." (Argonne National Laboratory, 2009a).

Another interesting cloud-based HPC solution developed by the US DOE at its Argonne National Laboratory[3] is called 'Nimbus' (a Latin word for 'cloud' or 'rain storm'). Nimbus is an open source cloud software infrastructure that allows users to deploy clusters of appliances (i.e., VMs) on remote resources, similar to Amazon's EC2 (see Argonne National Laboratory, 2009b; Keahey, Tsugawa, Matsunaga and Fortes, 2009). The advantages of using cloud computing for scientific purposes were illustrated recently by researchers working on the STAR nuclear physics experiment at Brookhaven National Laboratory's Relativistic Heavy-Ion Collider. The researchers needed simulation results to present at the Quark Matter physics conference but found it difficult to do so as all the computational resources at their disposal were either committed to other tasks or did not support the environment needed for STAR computations. However, the STAR researchers were finally able to use the Nimbus platform in order to dynamically provision virtual clusters on commercial cloud computers and run the additional computations.

Jerome Lauret, software and computing project leader for the STAR project, commented:

> 'The benefits of virtualization were clear to us early on....We can configure the virtual machine image exactly to our needs and have a fully validated experimental software stack ready for use. The image can then be overlaid on top of remote resources using infrastructure such as Nimbus'. (Argonne National Laboratory, 2009b)

He added that with cloud computing 'a 100-node STAR cluster can be online in minutes [whereas] Grid resources available at sites not expressly dedicated to STAR can take months to configure' (Ibid.)

The STAR scientists initially developed and deployed their VMs on a small Nimbus cloud configured at the University of Chicago. Then they used the Nimbus Context Broker[4] to configure the customized cloud into grid clusters which served as a platform for remote job submissions using existing grid tools. However, these resources soon proved insufficient to support STAR production runs.

In order to meet these needs, the Argonne Nimbus team turned to Amazon EC2 for help. The team developed a Nimbus gateway which allowed them to move easily between the small Nimbus cloud and Amazon EC2.

Kate Keahey, the lead member of the Nimbus project, commented:

---

[3] The Argonne National Laboratory is operated by the University of Chicago for the United States Department of Energy (DOE).

[4] This Context Broker is a service that allows users to coordinate large virtual cluster launches automatically and repeatedly. It is used to deploy 'one-click' virtual clusters that function right after launch as opposed to launching a set of unconnected' VMs which most VM-on-demand services provide. It also provides a facility to 'personalize' VMs (e.g., enable access policies).

> 'In the early days, the gateway served as a protocol adapter as well...But eventually we found it easier to simply adapt Nimbus to be protocol-interoperable with EC2 so that the scientists could move their virtual machines between the University of Chicago cloud and Amazon easily' (Ibid.)

Generating the needed results for the Quark Matter conference at the last minute proved the viability of using cloud resources for scientific purposes, according to Kate Keahey. She elaborated:

> 'One day a provider could be running STAR images, and the next day it could be climate calculations in entirely different images, with little or no effort...With Nimbus, a virtual cluster can be online in minutes." (Ibid.)

The Nimbus cloud is available to all members of the scientific community who want to run their applications in the cloud. To gain access to Nimbus, scientists are required to provide a justification, i.e., a few sentences explaining their science project.

NASA, the US space agency, is also moving towards cloud computing in a big way. It has recently contracted Parabon Computation, a grid computing software company, to deliver a platform that lets NASA scientists and engineers develop and run modeling and simulation applications as a service via a standard Web browser. For example, complex climate models can be constructed that can predict what would happen to global temperatures over the next hundred years if humans double carbon dioxide emissions. According to Michael Seablom, head of the software integration and visualization office at NASA's Goddard Space Flight Center in Maryland:

> 'Trying to get the models running is difficult and it costs us a lot of money here because we have to help groups build the system on their local machine.....The problem with that is if you're a graduate student, you could spend months just trying to get the model running and verify that it's working correctly.' (Brodkin, 2010).

Although the system will initially run climate models, it can be used for many types of scientific research. NASA is also developing its own cloud platform named 'Nebula'. Nebula is a self-service platform built from open source software. It is intended to provide high capacity computing, storage, and network connectivity for NASA's research. Chris Kemp, Chief Information Officer of NASA Ames Research Center, commented that Nebula has been designed to automatically increase the computing power and storage available to science- and data-oriented web applications as demand rises (Miller, 2009).

Interestingly, Nebula's datacenter is housed in an out-door 40-feet mobile shipping container built by Verari Systems and equipped with Cisco tools. This new approach of building datacenters is intended to be a fast and more energy-efficient way of meeting cloud providers' computing and storage requirements (Ibid.).

Nebula is using the open source 'Eucalyptus' software which was developed at the University of California at Santa Barbara. The current interface to Eucalyptus is compatible with Amazon's EC2 interface, thus making it possible for AWS-compatible tools to work with Nebula; a case of promoting inter-cloud operability.

A number of HPC solution providers have begun to take their businesses to the cloud in order to take advantage of the growing demand for cloud-based solutions from the scientific community. Companies such as SGI (with its Cyclone platform) and Penguin Computing (with its Penguin Computing on Demand), as mentioned earlier, are just two simple examples.

Cloud Problems: Should Users Worry?

Cloud computing, as indicated above, is an emerging computing service paradigm. Like other new services of this scale and complexity, there are bound to be fears, uncertainties and concerns about the technology's maturity. The most important of those concerns can be identified as those relating to control, vendor-lock, performance, latency, security, privacy and reliability.

In some cases, there is an outright rejection of this model. Richard Stallman, creator of the GNU operating system and founder of the Free Software Foundation, described cloud computing as a 'trap' aimed at forcing people to buy into locked, proprietary systems that are likely to prove costly in the future. He once told the Guardian: 'It's stupidity. It's worse than stupidity: it's a marketing hype campaign". This view was also echoed by Larry Ellison, the founder of Oracle, who criticized the 'rash' to cloud computing at one time as 'fashion-driven' and "complete gibberish" and commented that it would be hard to make money in this technology which he saw as 'lacking a clear business model' (Johnson, 2008; Hasson, 2008).

IT managers are likely to be wary of surrendering control of their resources to outside providers who can change the underlying technology without customers' consent. Issues relating to performance and latency (evidenced by the temporary run-outs of capacity by some providers) are also cited as problematic.

Furthermore, there are also valid security and privacy concerns. A recent survey of chief information officers and IT executives by IDC (International Data Corporation) rated security as their main cloud computing concern and almost 75 percent of respondents said that they were worried about security. Recently, the Electronic Privacy Information Center (a not-for-profit organization), has filed a complaint with the US Federal Trade Commission (FTC) about the security standards of Google's cloud computing, arguing that Google does not encrypt information held on its servers (Marshall, 2009). Moreover, various governments, such as those in the European Union (EU), have privacy regulations that prohibit the transmission of some types of personal data outside the EU. This issue prompted companies such as Amazon and others to develop offerings using storage facilities located in the EU.

Organizations are likely to adopt a careful approach to cloud computing. A survey by EDUCAUSE [5] involving 372 of its member institutions revealed that a great proportion of the respondents with use cases that involved cloud-based services reported that data privacy risks and data security risks were among their top barriers to overcome (Goldstein, 2009).

Another concern is vendor-lock and failures. Currently, many cloud providers offer their services through proprietary APIs. Portability is likely to be increasingly important as the number of cloud providers increases. One solution would be to base those APIs on open source message standards such as SOAP or REST. In some situations this is already happening. For example, Amazon is making its S3 (simple storage service) cloud available

[5] EDUCAUSE is a US-based non-profit organization whose mission is to promote the intelligent use of information technology in order to advance higher education.

through both SOAP and REST and Microsoft ensured that its Azure cloud also supports those two open source standards. The need for inter-cloud interoperability was highlighted by Vint Cerf, a co-designer of the Internet's TCP/IP, who likened the current lack of cloud communication standards to that of computer networks in the early 1970s (Krill, 2010). However, there are currently efforts by some organizations such as the Cloud Computing Interoperability Forum to address this issue (Grossman, 2009).

Furthermore, failure of a cloud provider that owns datacenters can have serious repercussions for end users who trusted their data with such a provider. This issue may force potential cloud users to go for well established and large companies that are likely to be around for many years to come.

Lastly, reliability can also be a serious problem for cloud users. Salesforce.com, for example, left customers without service for six hours in February 2008 while Amazon's S3 and EC2 suffered a three-hour outage in the same month a few days later and an eight-hour outage in July of the same year by S3 (Leavitt, 2009). In early 2009, Google's Gmail (its Webmail service) went down for three hours, thus preventing its 113 million users from accessing their emails or the documents which they store online as "Google Docs" (Naughton, 2009). Vendors often provide service credits for outages. However, those credits, according to a director of a US market research firm, are "cold comfort for sales opportunities missed and executives cut off from business information" (Leavitt, 2009).

Cloud computing may not be suitable for all organizations. For example, for large companies, the loss of service as a result of cloud glitches would be a major concern, particularly if it impacts on their customers and results in substantial loss of sale opportunities and customer dissatisfaction. The issue of reliability with relation to cloud services will continue to be a problem. Similar glitches that befell the cloud services of Amazon and Google are likely to surface again as the number of cloud providers and users increase. However, for small companies struggling to survive the current global economic downturn and cash-strapped educational establishments, often used to similar glitches caused by their old in-house systems, cloud computing is likely to remain an attractive option due to its cost structure and flexibility.

Furthermore, evidence is also emerging to suggest that even large companies, contrary to conventional wisdom, are actually embracing cloud services. A recent report by Forrester (the independent technology and market research company), based upon a survey of small and large enterprises located in North America and Europe, revealed that large firms were more interested than small firms in leveraging IaaS external cloud capability (Golden, 2009).

For organizations involved in scientific research, most of the above concerns may not be as important to them as they might be to those who provide services to consumers e.g., e-commerce companies. For example, the loss of a few hours of services may not be as dramatic for an organization conducting a research experiment as it would be for an online auction or an online chain of retailers. Furthermore, issues of privacy and data protection are likely to be of less concern or indeed relevance, especially if research organizations only use an IaaS cloud for high speed compute operations. So, while the aforementioned cloud drawbacks will remain of concern to many organizations contemplating using cloud computing, their current advantages are likely to outweigh their potential disadvantages for the scientific community. On that basis, one could deduce that cloud computing's market share of HPC is more likely to continue rising in the years to come. Indeed, there are speculations that cloud computing's share of the computing service industry as a whole will increase. In fact, there is an increasingly perceived vision that this computing service will one day be the 5th utility, after water, electricity, gas and telephony (Buyya et al., 2009).

CONCLUSION

Cloud computing is an emerging computing paradigm which promises to provide opportunities for delivering a variety of computing services in a way that has not been experienced before. Until recently, HPC was considered not suitable for cloud computing due to the performance overhead associated with virtualization which can impact on HPC's requirement for tight integration between server nodes via low-latency interconnects. However, these issues have been overcome by virtualization solutions that use new hypervisors such as KVM and XEN. Furthermore, the economic, and indeed the green credentials, of cloud computing have made this computing service an attractive and viable option. To demonstrate the growing popularity of cloud computing for HPC a number of examples were provided in this article of research organizations that decided to go the cloud way.

Despite its growing popularity, there are still some concerns relating to this computing service such as security, outages and vendor-locking. Given the nascent nature of this technology, this is not surprising. However, there are currently efforts being made to address some of those issues. Furthermore, some organizations are more likely to cope with the consequences of those concerns than others. This article has argued that, given the attractive attributes of cloud computing with relation to 'economy' and 'efficiency', some organizations such as small businesses, academic institutes and those involved in scientific research might find that cloud computing's potential disadvantages are more likely to be outweighed by their current advantages.

This article gives a broad idea of how cloud computing has managed to attract the attention of members of the scientific community. A detailed analysis of the costs and benefits of cloud computing for a sample of HPC projects would give clear evidence of the merits or demerits of cloud computing for research and scientific projects. This issue will provide a good focus point for a future study of this type.

REFERENCES

Argonne National Laboratory (2009a), 'DOE to explore scientific cloud computing at Argonne, Lawrence Berkeley national laboratories', http://www.anl.gov/Media_Center/News/2009/news091014a.html (Accessed on: 24 January 2010).

Argonne National Laboratory (2009b), 'Nimbus and cloud computing meet STAR production demands', http://www.hpcwire.com/offthewire/Nimbus-and-Cloud-Computing-Meet-STAR-Production-Demands-42354742.html?viewAll=y (Accessed on: 5 April, 2010).

Bailey, D (2009), "Does Azure have the allure to drive enterprises into the cloud?", *Computing*, http://www.computing.co.uk/computing/analysis/2246131/azure-cure-enterprises-current (Accessed on: 14 March, 2010).

Brodkin, J (2010), 'NASA building cloud service for climate modeling', *Computer World*, http://www.computerworld.com/s/article/9150381/NASA_building_cloud_service_for_climate_modeling?source=rss_software (Accessed on: 4 April, 2010).

Buyya, R., Yeo, C. S. and Venugopal, S. (2009), 'Market-Oriented Cloud Computing: Vision, Hype, and Reality of Delivering IT Services as Computing Utilities', *The 10 th IEEE International Conference on High Performance Computing and Communications*, pp 5-13.

Buyya et al (2009), 'Cloud computing and emerging IT platforms: Vision, hype, and reality for delivering computing as the 5th utility', *Future Generation Computer Systems*, Vol. 25, No. 6, pp. 599-616.

Campbell-Kelly, M (2009), 'The Rise, Fall, and Resurrection of Software as a Service', *Communications of the ACM*, Vol. 52, No. 6.

Campbell, S (2009), 'Timesharing 2.0', *HPCwire,* http://www.hpcwire.com/specialfeatures/cloud_computing/features/Timesharing-20-66169142.html (Accessed on: 5 April, 2010).

Carr, N (2009), *The Big Switch: Re-Wiring the World, from Edison to Google*, New York and London: W. W. Norton.

Erdogmus, H (2009), "Cloud Computing: Does Nirvana Hide behind the Nebula?," *IEEE Software*, vol. 26, no. 2, pp. 4-6.

European Commission (2005), *The New SME Definition: User Guide and Model Declaration*, Enterprise and Industry Publications.

Foley, M. J. (2009), 'Three new codenames and how they fit into Microsoft's cloud vision', *zdnet*, http://blogs.zdnet.com/microsoft/?p=4582 (Accessed on: 15 December 2009).

Golden, B (2009), 'Forrester Bucks Conventional Wisdom on Cloud Computing', *CIO*, http://www.cio.com/article/496213/Forrester_Bucks_Conventional_Wisdom_on_Cloud_Computing (Accessed on: 1 August 2009).

Goldstein, P (2009), 'Alternative IT Sourcing Strategies: From the Campus to the Cloud', *EDUCAUSE Center for Applied Research,* http://net.educause.edu/ir/library/pdf/EKF/EKF0905.pdf.

Grossman, R (2009), 'The Case for Cloud Computing', *IT Professional*, Vol. 11, No. 2, pp. 23-27,

Halligan et al (2008), 'Low Cost, Scalable Proteomics Data Analysis Using Amazon's Cloud Computing Services and Open Source Search Algorithms', *Journal of Proteome Research*, Vol. 8, PT. 6, pp. 3148-3153.

Hasson, J (2008), 'Cloud computing is for the birds', *FierceCIO*, http://www.fiercecio.com/story/cloud-computing-birds/2008-10-11 (Accessed on: 5 July, 2009.

James, P and Hopkinsons, L (2009), 'Sustainable ICT in Further and Higher Education: Final Report', A Report for Joint Information Services Committee (JISC).

Johnson, B (2008), "Cloud computing is a trap, warns GNU founder Richard Stallman", *The Guardian*, http://www.guardian.co.uk/technology/2008/sep/29/cloud.computing.richard.stallman (Accessed on: 5 July 2009).

Katz, R. N (2008), 'The Gathering Cloud: Is this the End of the Middle?', in Katz, R. N (ed.), *The Tower and the Cloud: Higher Education in the Age of Cloud Computing*, EDUCAUSE.

Keahey, K., Tsugawa, M., Matsunaga, A and Fortes, J (2009), 'Sky Computing', *IEEE Computer Society*, September/October.

Krill, P (2010), 'Cerf urges standards for cloud computing', *Info World*, http://www.infoworld.com/d/cloud-computing/cerf-urges-standards-cloud-computing-817 (Accessed on: 5 April, 2010).

La Susa, E (2009), 'Cloud computing brings cost of protein research down to Earth", *Eureka Alert!*, http://www.eurekalert.org/pub_releases/2009-04/mcow-ccb040909.php (Accessed on: 31 July 2009).

Leavitt, N (2009), 'Is Cloud Computing Really Ready for Prime Time?', *Computer*, Vol. 42, No. 1, pp. 15-20.

Leung, L (2010), 'Scientists Offered Free Access to Azure Cloud', *Data Center Knowledge*, http://www.datacenterknowledge.com/archives/2010/02/05/scientists-offered-free-access-to-azure-cloud/ (Accessed on: 6 April, 2010).

Lin, G., Fu, D., Zhu, J. and Dasmalchi, G (2009), 'Cloud Computing: IT as a Service', *IT Professional*, vol. 11, no. 2, pp. 10-13.

Marshall, R (2009), "Privacy group slams Google's cloud services", *V3* (formerly *vnunet*), http://www.v3.co.uk/articles/print/2238733 (Accessed on: 20 July 2009).

MathWorks (2008), 'Parallel Computing with MATLAB on Amazon Elastic Compute Cloud', *Math Works*, http://www.mathworks.com/products/techkitpdfs/91593v00.pdf (Accessed on: 6 April, 2010).

Microsoft (2009a), 'Microsoft Case Studies: RiskMetrics', http://www.microsoft.com/casestudies/Case_Study_Detail.aspx?CaseStudyID=4000005921 (Accessed on: 8 April, 2010).

Microsoft (2009b), 'SME role for cloud computing', http://www.microsoft.com/uk/smallbusiness/sbnews/growing-a-small-business/SME-role-for-cloud-computing-19227631.mspx (Accessed on: 18 July 2009).

Miller, R (2009), 'NASA's Nebula: The Cloud in a Container', Data Center Knowledge, http://www.datacenterknowledge.com/archives/2009/12/02/nasas-nebula-the-cloud-in-a-container/ (Accessed on: 4 April, 2010).

Naughton, J (2009), 'There's silver lining to Google's cloud computing glitch', *The Observer*, http://www.guardian.co.uk/technology/2009/mar/01/gmail-outage-cloud-computing (Accessed on 21 July 2009).

Niccolai, J (2009), 'Penguin puts high-performance computing in the cloud', *Info World*, http://www.infoworld.com/d/cloud-computing/penguin-puts-high-performance-computing-in-cloud-282.

Penguin (2010), 'Penguin Computing on Demand', http://www.penguincomputing.com/POD/Summary.

Rehr, J. J et al (2008), 'Scientific Computing in the Cloud', http://arxiv.org/ftp/arxiv/papers/0901/0901.0029.pdf (Accessed on: 10 April, 2010).

Shainer, G et al (2010), 'Cloud Computing Will Usher in a New Era of Science Discovery', *HPC Wire*, http://www.hpcwire.com/specialfeatures/cloud_computing/features/Cloud-Computing-Will-Usher-in-a-New-Era-of-Science-Discovery-82710127.html (Accessed on: 10 April, 2010).

Sultan, N (2010), 'Cloud Computing for Education: A New dawn?', *International Journal of Information Management*, Vol. 30, No. 2.

Voas, J and Zhang, J (2009), 'Cloud Computing: New Wine or Just a New Bottle?', *IT Professional*, vol. 11, no. 2, pp. 15-17.

In: New Developments in Computer Research
Editor: Nikos E. Mastorakis
ISBN: 978-1-61470-321-1

MANAGING IT RESOURCES THE SMART WAY: THE CASE FOR VIRTUALIZATION

Nabil A. Sultan* and Saad Salim
Faculty of Sciences and Social Sciences,
Liverpool Hope University, UK

ABSTRACT

Virtualization is a technological breakthrough that has brought about innovations and redefined the way we look at hardware and software. It has made it possible to consolidate hardware and software resources and benefit users from the individual to large scale enterprises. In this article we discuss how hardware and software resources can be utilized to the highest level of efficiency. We provide examples of how PCs and servers can run multiple operating systems simultaneously thus saving costs of hardware, deployment and maintenance. Despite the popularity of virtualization and its broad adoption, many organizations find it difficult to make the most of this technology. We touch on this issue in this article and argue that this situation could potentially push many of those organizations to consider switching to cloud computing, the new computing utility service that is now shaping the global IT landscape.

Keywords: Virtualization, Virtual Machines (VMs), Virtual Servers, Cloud Computing

1. DEFINING VIRTUALIZATION

The term virtualization has been around for quite some time. However, its popularity over the last few years is in part due to the potential benefits it brings such as lower costs, consolidation of infrastructure, more control over security and management simplification. One of the main reasons virtualization was slow to take off in the past is because the idea was ahead of the technology in some ways at that time. In the last 10-15 years, a modern, state of the art processor's context switches per unit of time count has risen by a huge factor of at least 1,000. Also the system processor speed has increased by a factor of at least 100. Nowadays, the manufacturing process is changing every day. The number of transistors on a chip, per cubic inch on a silicon wafer has increased by a factor of at least 130. This in turn

* E-mail: sultann@hope.ac.uk

has allowed us to perform 90,000 context switches at a much less cost of 10 percent of the microprocessor's clock. This has enabled flexibility in design and speed that was unthinkable 10-15 years ago and so ensured new designs and ideas can now be incorporated into virtualized networks and systems (Bee Limited).

Apart from simplifying IT infrastructures, virtualization can also help companies lower their costs and make the management of their IT resources much more efficient. All these factors are contributing to the popularity of virtualization among companies and it is also getting popular among home-based users who are adopting it to utilize their home-based systems to their fullest potential.

Virtualization is fairly well-established and expanding technology and its adoption is growing. According to Barb Goldworm, president of Focus Consulting, about 75 percent of large enterprises use virtualization to some extent, even though most of those have virtualized only about 10 percent of their servers (Shavit, 2008).

Virtualization can be described as an approach to pooling and sharing technology resources to ensure supply can readily meet business demands. With servers, storage, or networks, virtualization is used to take a single physical asset and make it operate as if it were many separate, smaller assets. This process improves asset utilization and efficiency, and decreases costs by reducing the need for physical assets. Additionally, with storage or networks, virtualization is used to combine multiple assets and present them to servers and applications as if they were a single, larger asset. This dramatically simplifies server and application architecture and reduces costs.

2. History of Virtualization

Before we go into the details of current virtualization technologies, it is useful to take a step back into history to discover the beginning of virtualization. This concept is not something that appeared recently but its roots can be traced back in history to the mainframe environment where it was introduced.

The conception of 'virtual memory' dates back to the 1950s when a group of researchers at the University of Manchester introduced automatic page replacement [1] in the Atlas system which was then a transistorized mainframe computer. At that time, this concept of paging was well understood. However, this group devised a system to automate the process of paging which stores and moves the data in memory; thus creating the first working prototype of virtual memory.

Virtualization was first developed in the 1960s in order to partition large, mainframe hardware for better hardware utilization. The term virtual machine (VM) dates back to that era. IBM became the pioneer of VM systems when it introduced the System/360 (model 67) in 1967 with integrated virtual memory. This model also introduced the concept of a self-virtualizing processor instruction set which was perfected in later models. VM capability was to allow a single processor machine to host several operating systems. In essence, VM and Mainframe hardware worked together so that more than one copy of an operating system can co-exist with its own protected instructions.

[1] Page replacement is a method of moving program instructions in and out of memory to ensure efficient use of memory resources.

IBM also developed the concept of time-sharing [2] with its M44/44X project in the 1960s. This was an experimental project designed to explore paging, the VM concept, and computer performance measurement. The main IBM system for this project was the IBM 7044 (M44) combined with a VM image of the 7044 (44X). In time, this project led to VM/timesharing systems, including IBM's VM/370.

The emergence of virtual storage (also known as virtual memory) took application programs to the next level, by making them less complex to develop. Virtual storage is a process that increases the actual amount of memory available to a computer by allocating it space on that computer's hard disk. This was an advantage due to the fact that at that time hardware resources (especially memory) were extremely expensive. This form of virtualization was popular in the research and commercial sectors, but this trend only lasted until the 1970s. The time frame between 1980s and part of 1990s witnessed the disappearance of virtualization as low-cost minicomputers and personal computers came on the market.

In the late 1990s, the world saw the re-emergence of this technology, triggered by a sudden increase of the number of servers used throughout the enterprise which created a major issue of hardware redundancy. This redundancy was due to the conflict between the software installed on servers which necessitated acquiring and assigning servers with specific tasks in order to avoid that conflict. This resulted in servers only using a fraction of their resources. Organizations soon realized that this large abundance of servers had a high maintenance cost, especially when those servers were not being utilized to their full capability. This issue increased the appeal of virtualization (Campbell and Jeronimo, 2006).

3. Virtualization Architecture

Prior to virtualization, each computer system had a single operating system. Software and hardware were tightly coupled (i.e., closely associated) running on the same machine. Most of these systems were not utilizing their full potential (VMware). Virtualization provided hardware-independence for operating systems and applications by running them in virtual environments with their own set of instructions. To virtualize a given computer, a piece of software needs to be installed. This piece of software is often referred to as "hypervisor" or a "virtual machine monitor". After this software is installed, an individual VM can be run on the same hardware with its own operating system and set of other applications. On x86 platforms there are two approaches to achieve virtualization: bare-metal and hosted. Sometimes these types are referred to as Type-1 and Type-2 hypervisors respectively (see National Instruments, 2009; Siebert, 2009).

3.1. Hosted Architecture

"Hosted" means that an operating system must first be installed on a server before the virtualization layer is installed; similar to an application that can only be installed on a machine if that machine has an operating system (see figure 1 below). A hosted approach

---

[2] Time-sharing refers to the ability of a computer processor to share its processing time when executing multiple tasks so that each task thinks that it has the processor's full attention to itself.

provides partitioning services on top of a standard operating system and supports the broadest range of hardware configurations (Siebert, 2009).

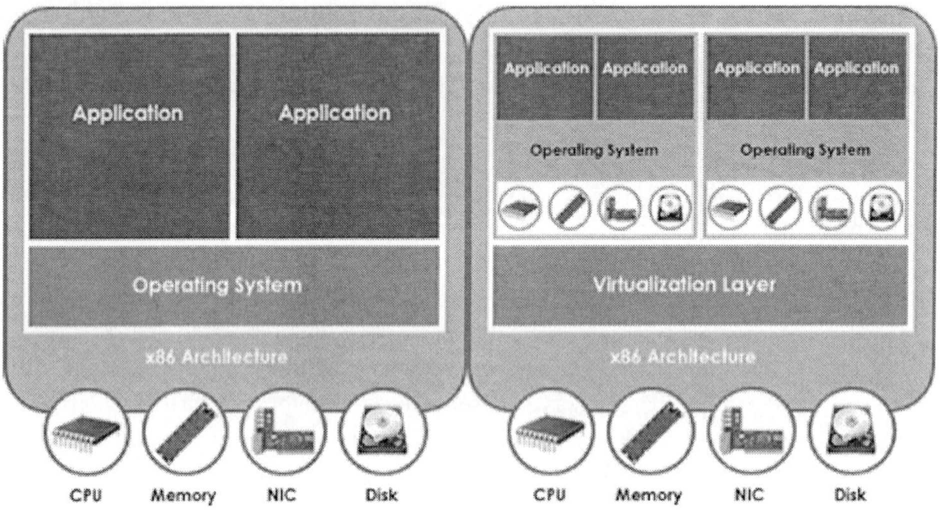

Figure 1. Hosted Architecture (Adapted from: Siebert, 2009).

In the hosted virtualization architecture, each VM (i.e., guest operating system) normally has access to a limited number of I/O devices. The host operating system retains ownership of the physical I/O devices connected to a given computer, and the hypervisor provides an emulated view of the actual hardware (when possible) to each VM. Because the hypervisor has no knowledge of most non-generic I/O devices (e.g., PCI data acquisition cards), it does not present these emulated devices to VMs. Only generic devices like network interface cards and CD-ROM drives are emulated. However, many hosted virtualization solutions (e.g., VMware Workstation [3]) support 'passthrough' functionality for USB ports. This feature allows users to access USB devices from individual VMs directly, thus providing for limited I/O capabilities beyond the emulated devices mentioned above.

In fact, several software components work together to make I/O possible in a hosted virtualization architecture. For example, the VMware Workstation product directs I/O requests from the VMs through a low-level hypervisor component, then through a driver (e.g., VMX), and finally to a user-level application component called VMApp. In the end, the VMApp component passes I/O requests through the host operating system. The most important thing to remember is that I/O requests are ultimately passed through the host OS in this virtualization architecture as depicted in figure 2 (National Instruments, 2009).

Benefits and Drawbacks

The benefit of choosing the hosted virtualization route is that it is easy to setup; installation and configuration are comparable to installing a regular application on an operating system. For example, VMware workstation software can be installed in a short

[3] VMware Workstation is a virtual machine software suite for x86 and x86-64 computers from VMware. The software suite allows users to set up multiple x86 and x86-64 virtual computers and to use one or more of these virtual computers simultaneously with one host operating system.

amount of time under a Windows operating system. After installation, a user can create multiple VMs that run different operating systems, all on the same physical computer.

The drawback for the above hosted virtualization approach, as mentioned above, is that this form of virtualization is not capable of emulating non-generic PCI I/O devices (e.g., data acquisition cards). The other main drawback would be that all the I/O requests have to go through the hosted operating system from VMs which will cause performance degradation. A further drawback of this approach is its lack of support to run a real-time OS inside a VM deterministically when using hosted virtualization (Ibid).

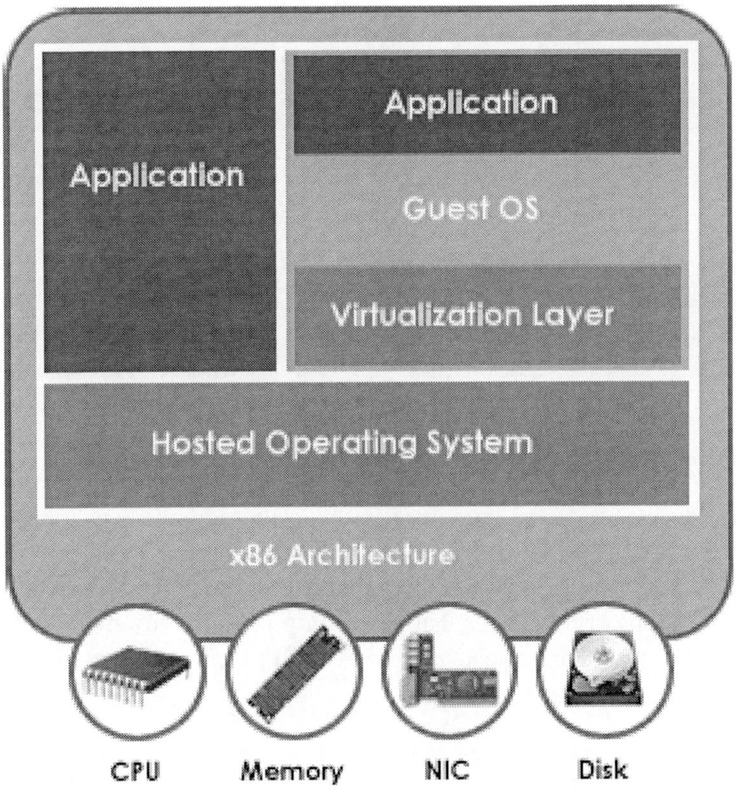

Figure 2. I/O Access (Adapted from: National Instruments, 2009).

This approach gives the flexibility to create an environment in which different operating systems can co-exist on one machine, whereby some of those operating system can be dedicated for software development as test bed and others can be setup in such a way that old (i.e., legacy) applications can exist that are not used very often (Ibid).

3.2. Bare-Metal Architecture

Bare-metal means that the virtualization layer (i.e., hypervisor) is installed directly onto a server without the need for a traditional operating system like Windows or Linux to be installed first (hence the "bare metal" name). Since this method enables the hypervisor to have direct access to the server's hardware resources, it is more efficient than a hosted architectures, thus enabling greater scalability, robustness and performance.

The hypervisor emulates computer hardware by allowing multiple operating systems to run on a single physical host computer (see figure 3). Each operating system appears to have the host's processor, memory, and other resources all to itself. However, the hypervisor is actually controlling the host processor and resources and allocates the necessary resources to each operating system, making sure that the operating systems cannot disrupt each other (Siebert, 2009).

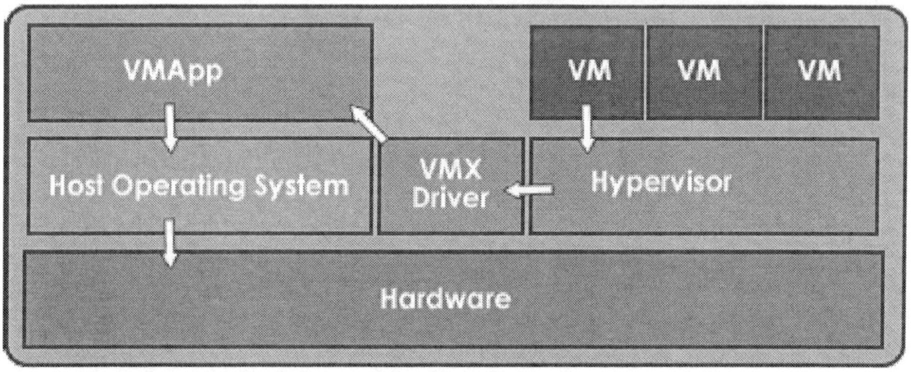

Figure 3. Bare-metal Architecture (Adapted from: Siebert, 2009).

One of the advantages of the bare-metal virtualization architecture is that it provides a number of options to access I/O devices from VMs. This system works differently from the hosted approach where the VM has to go through the host operating system for I/O access. In this architecture, the hypervisor layer that sits on top of the hardware is using a low-level driver to help all VMs to communicate directly for I/O access and is emulating these shared drives to all guest VMs (see figure 4).

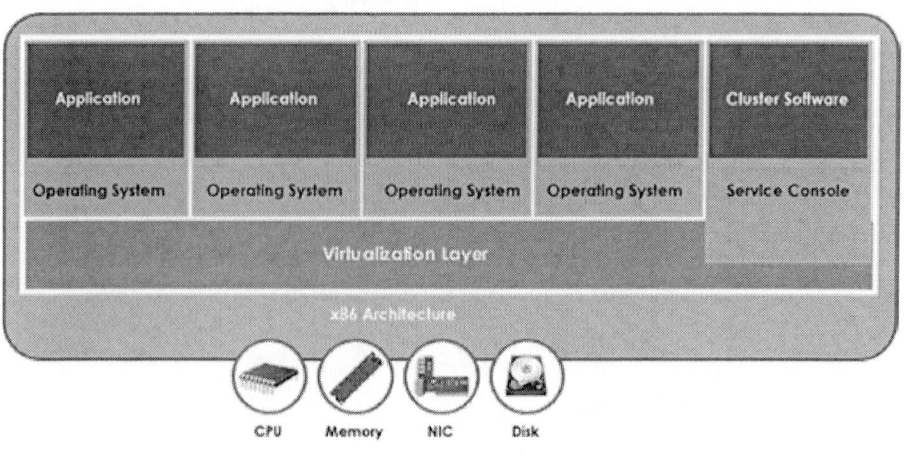

Figure 4. Using a low-level driver to help VMs communicate with I/O devices (Adapted from: National Instruments, 2009).

Bare-Metal virtualization architecture can also achieve I/O access by assigning an individual device to a specific VM. This process (see figure 5) is known as partitioning and can improve I/O performance by carefully distributing the resources among the VMs according to their specific roles. Since partitioned PCI [4] devices can be accessed straight from their VMs this arrangement will cause less stress on the hypervisor (Ibid).

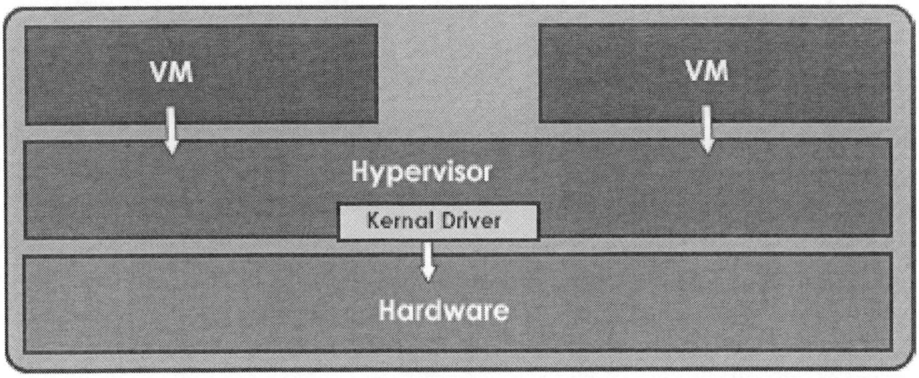

Figure 5. Partitioning I/O devices (Adapted from: National Instruments, 2009).

Benefits and Drawbacks

In addition to the improved I/O performance gained by partitioning devices such as PCI data acquisition cards between individual VMs, the bare-metal virtualization architecture also has the benefit of supporting real-time operating systems. Since this architecture does not rely on an underlying host operating system, bare-metal hypervisors can implement features to bound interrupt latency and enable deterministic performance. This means that engineers using this virtualization architecture can run real-time and general purpose operating systems in parallel on the same processing hardware.

However, this form of virtualization does have some drawbacks. For example, drivers needed to support various hardware platforms must be included in the hypervisor in addition to drivers for devices that will be shared amongst VMs. Furthermore, since bare-metal hypervisors are not installed on top of a host OS, they are often more difficult to install and configure than when using a hosted solution (National Instruments, 2009).

Due to their low-level nature and the I/O access they provide, bare-metal hypervisors are ideal for deployed applications that use multiple operating systems. For example, applications that must provide real-time data processing and provide access to general purpose OS services (such as a graphical user interface) can benefit from bare-metal virtualization (Ibid).

4. VIRTUALIZATION FAMILY

There are many forms of virtualization in the world of computing. Server virtualization is by far the most commonly used and understood form of virtualization. Apart from that, there

---

[4] Peripheral Component Interconnect i.e., the personal computer bus.

are storage virtualization (used for data storage), Network virtualization (used for sharing network devices) and application virtualization (used to share software applications):

4.1. Server Virtualization

Server virtualization is one of the most successful forms of virtualization today. Three main vendors (e.g., Citrix, VMware and Microsoft) seem to be the leading vendors in this area (Ruest and Ruest, 2009). Citrix, that was once the "lone wolf" of application virtualization, now also owns the world's most-used cloud vendor software: Xen (the basis for its commercial Xen Server). Amazon uses Xen for its Elastic Compute Cloud (EC2) services as well as Rackspace, Carpathia, SoftLayer and 1and1 for their cloud offerings. On the corporate side, Xen is also used by companies such as Bechtel, SAP and TESCO. VMware, on the other hand, dominates the server virtualization market. Its domination does not seem to stop with its commercial product e.g., vSphere. It also dominates the desktop-level virtualization market and perhaps even the free server virtualization market with its VMware Server product, thanks to its innovations, strategic partnerships and rock-solid products. Microsoft came up with the only non-Linux hypervisor, namely Hyper-V, to compete in a tight server virtualization market that VMware currently dominates. Microsoft seems to provide attractive licensing for its Hyper-V product and also the operating systems that live on it (Hess, 2010).

Server virtualization is often called full virtualization. There are three methods that can be used to create virtual servers: full virtualization, paravirtualization and Operating System-level virtualization. All three methods share a few common traits. The physical server is called the host or host server. The virtual servers are called guests or guest servers. The virtual servers behave like physical machines. Each method (see below) uses a different approach to allocate physical server resources to virtual server needs (Vugt, 2006; Damiani, Ardagna and El loini, 2008):

- In a full virtualization environment, the virtualization software emulates a complete machine, including all the hardware resources. The operating system running in a full virtualization environment can communicate with the virtual hardware directly and it is not aware that it is running in a virtual environment. This is done through the hypervisor software. The hypervisor has its own processing needs which means that the physical server has to reserve some processing power and resources in order to run the hypervisor application. This issue can have an impact on the overall server performance and therefore slow down other applications.
- Conversely, in a paravirtualization environment, the operating system in the VM cannot access the hardware directly. It needs an application programming interface (API) to be able to do that and therefore has to be modified by the hypervisor. One of the main advantages of working in this environment is that there is no requirement to create virtual drivers for all the hardware and, on that basis, it offers a better performance than full virtualization.

- The operating system-level virtualization approach works differently compared to the other two. In operating system-level virtualization, the physical server is virtualized at the operating system level, enabling multiple isolated and secure virtualized servers to run on a single physical server. This method does not require a hypervisor to work. The virtualization capability here is part of the host operating system and performs all the functions of a fully virtualized hypervisor. The biggest drawback of this approach is that all the guest virtualized servers must run the same operating system. In this setup, each virtual server is independent from all the others. Due to this constraint, this system is called a homogeneous environment.

4.2. Storage Virtualization

Storage vendors have been offering high-performance storage solutions to their customers for quite some time now. Consider the assembly of multiple physical disk drives, or spindles, which are presented as a single entity to the host machine and operating system. This is an example of storage virtualization because all the drives operate and interact as a single logical drive.

The true storage tier and its components were further masked by the introduction and adoption of Storage Area Network (SAN) technologies. Without any change to the operating system code responsible for managing storage subsystems, IT organizations are now sharing storage components between multiple servers. Even though each server thinks it has its own dedicated physical storage, storage administrators have simply carved out a virtual quantity of drive space and presented it to the hosts for use as one entity.

More advanced technologies have begun to hit the market taking storage virtualization to the next level. Products now exist that are capable of migrating storage in real time from one storage platform to another in the background based on rules and policies without any interruption or impact to the host. Furthermore, there are also software products that trap and emulate native SCSI [5] commands and translate them to other storage instructions in the background, thus making it possible for a disk array to look like a suite of tape drives and tape libraries to backup software and operating systems without any modifications (Dittner and Rule, 2007).

4.3. Network Virtualization

To share a network interface among a set of VMs, the hypervisor must accomplish two key tasks. First, the hypervisor must provide shared access to the network interface. This means that the VMs' outgoing network traffic must be multiplexed together before being sent over the network; similarly, incoming network traffic must be demultiplexed before being delivered to the appropriate VMs. Second, the hypervisor must protect the VMs from each

[5] SCSI stands for '*Small Computer System Interface*' and is pronounced "skuzzy". It is a standard for connecting a wide range of peripheral devices such as scanners, hard disk drives, CD-ROM drives etc.

other. This means that no VM can be allowed to transfer data into or out of another VM's memory. Just like storage vendors, manufacturers of network hardware have been in the virtualization arena for quite some time but have not been recognized as virtualization vendors (Ibid). For example, consider network virtualization using VLAN (Virtual Local Area Network), Virtual IP and VPN (Virtual Private Network):

- *VLAN:* This is a group of network stations and devices. A switch can be partitioned into multiple VLANs. Although the VLANs are in the same switch, they are isolated. That is, they have their own broadcast domains and the computers in VLANs are restricted to communication with the computers within the same VLAN. Different VLANs cannot communicate without the use of a router and network layer addresses. VLANs are especially useful in creating workgroups where users share the same resources, such as databases and disk storage (Wong and Yeung, 2009).
- *Virtual IP:* Virtual IP, also called a circuitless or loopback interface, is a powerful function that has multiple uses. It provides a way to assign one or more addresses to the system without the need of binding the address to a physical interface. This can be used when one needs to run multiple occurrences of a web server bound to different addresses or if one needs to run other services that need to bind to default ports (IBM).
- *VPN:* A Virtual Private Network (VPN) is a connection that allows one's computer to access a computer on a remote network. This form of connection usually takes place over the Internet which is highly insecure. However, a VPN creates a secure tunnel through an insecure medium such as the Internet by using a specialized piece of software in order to connect to a remote network.

4.4. Application Virtualization

Application virtualization is a new approach to software management that improves portability, manageability and compatibility of applications by encapsulating them from the underlying operating system on which they are executed. For example, a fully virtualized application is not installed in the traditional sense even though it is still executed as if it is. The application is fooled at runtime into believing that it is directly interfacing with the original operating system and all the resources managed by it, when in fact it is not.

There are some benefits of moving to application virtualization as it eliminates applications' conflicts by using correct version files and registry settings without intervention by the operating system. It also reduces installation rollout times by instantly deploying prepackaged applications locally or over the network, and supports deployment of multiple versions of an application running on the same machine (Dittner and Rule, 2007).

5. Advantages of Virtualization

Virtualization has many advantages and there are many good reasons to use this technology. For example, virtualization can:

- provide organizations with the capabilities to have one physical server appearing as several servers, each serving different purposes, which helps avoid hardware over-provisioning and reduce the need for more office space.
- help organizations save money in the long run because it can drastically reduce energy consumption that would have arisen from having too many machines, thus making virtualization environmentally friendly.
- improve efficiency by simplifying administration tasks. For example, in a virtualized environment (VE), if there is need to deploy a server on a different machine, the only task that is needed is to copy the installation of the virtualized environment to another computer (Georgieva, 2009).

6. Disadvantages of Virtualization

Like many other technologies, virtualization has some drawbacks. The following list briefly explains those issues (Pietroforte, 2008):

- Magnified physical failures could result from using virtualization. For example, if you have 10 virtual servers running on a single server and that server goes down then the services from all 10 servers will be lost.
- Virtualization demands powerful machines to run multiple virtual environments. Lower spec servers will degrade performance. Even if the machines on which the virtualized operating systems and virtualized applications are run are powerful enough, performance issues are still possible. Unfortunately, it is hard to predict if a particular application is likely to run as normal when virtualized. In this case a thorough testing of this application within the virtualized solution becomes a necessity.
- Managing a virtualized environment requires a new set of skills which are needed to handle the complexity of multiple virtual servers sharing one machine. Finding the root cause of a problem in this virtualized environment can sometimes be a daunting task.

7. Virtualization and Cloud Computing

Virtualization is increasingly becoming one of the important building blocks of cloud computing. Cloud computing is an emerging computing service paradigm which provides (usually over the medium of the Internet) on demand computing services to organizations. The type of services provided by cloud computing can be listed in three main categories, as explained below (Sultan, 2010):

- Infrastructure as a Service (IaaS): Products offered via this mode include the remote delivery (through the Internet) of a full computer infrastructure (e.g., virtual computers, servers, storage devices etc.).

- Platform as a Service (PaaS): services provided by the traditional computing model which involved teams of network, database, and system management experts to keep everything up and running. (e.g., operating systems, databases, middleware, Web servers and other software) are now provided remotely by cloud providers under this layer.
- Software as a Service (SaaS): Under this layer applications are delivered through the medium of the Internet as a service. Instead of installing and maintaining software, one can simply access it via the Internet; thus freeing oneself from complex software and hardware management. This type of cloud service offers a complete application functionality that ranges from productivity applications (e.g., word processing, spreadsheets etc.) to programs such as those for Customer Relationship Management (CRM) or Enterprise-Resource Management (ERM).

Cloud services offered by companies such as Amazon, Google and Saleforce.com are known as public clouds. This is to distinguish them from private clouds, also known as internal or corporate clouds, where the cloud infrastructure (e.g., datacenters, servers, etc.) and services are provided, housed and maintained internally by the users themselves. A number of public cloud providers are now coming up with solutions which incorporate elements of both private and public clouds that might be classified as "hybrid clouds". For example, companies such as Amazon have very recently launched a service known as Virtual Private Cloud (VPC) designed to address issues of security and control which seem to be one of the concerns of large organizations that contemplate using cloud computing. Amazon's VPC allows organizations to connect their existing legacy infrastructures to Amazon's clouds via a Virtual Private Network (VPN) connection. This means that Amazon's cloud customers can create their own Amazon isolated resources (i.e., virtual private clouds) within Amazon's cloud infrastructure and then connect those resources directly to their network servers using industry-standard encrypted IPsec VPN connections. In doing so, these customers will be able to extend their existing security and management policies within their IT infrastructure to their VPCs as if they were running within their own infrastructures. By combining elements of private and public clouds in a hybrid solution, companies will have the private advantages of greater control, enhanced security and resiliency in combination with the cost flexibility provided by public clouds (Brookbanks, 2010).

Organizations that adopted x86 virtualization in the past focused on server consolidation, and have benefited from cost savings and increased flexibility as a consequence. Some of these organizations are now looking forward to use virtualization through cloud computing, the next big trend on the horizon (Stratus Technologies, 2009).

The cloud concept takes virtualization a step further by enabling users of IT resources to avoid having to invest in dedicated infrastructures. In this scenario, IT costs become a variable operational expense for organizations due to the scalable nature of cloud computing use. By adopting this model, organizations are able allow capacity to scale up and down dynamically and immediately in a manner that advances how virtualization is used today (Ibid).

At a fundamental level, the value proposition promised by cloud computing remains much the same as that derived from virtualization in terms of reducing expenses and improving agility to meet changing business needs. However, while virtualization solutions are a known quantity and deployed in real-world IT environments, cloud computing is still developing. In reports published in 2009 by Forrester Research (the independent technology and market research company), it was estimated that 54 percent of enterprises had implemented x86 server virtualization or planned to do so within the next 12 months while 53 percent of small and medium businesses (SMBs) had already implemented x86 server virtualization or planned to do so within the next 12 months. In the cloud computing area, Forrester found 5 percent of enterprises had already implemented pay-per-use-hosting of virtual servers, with 3 percent more intending to use cloud computing for this purpose within the next 12 months. Among the SMBs polled, 2 percent had already implemented pay-per-use-hosting of virtual servers (Ibid).

However, despite broad adoption of virtualization, many firms still struggle with the technical and organizational changes which the technology brings. Some of the major challenges experienced by those firms include getting managers interested, motivating application owners to move to VMs and restructuring their teams to achieve maximum efficiency in a virtualized environment (Schreck and Dines, 2009). Furthermore, research suggests that two thirds of virtual servers are only running production-level applications due to the fact that many organizations remain cautious about virtualizing their critical applications (Woo and Chen, 2009).

These factors and the flexibility of scalability and on-demand cost structure provided by cloud computing could play an important role in the future in persuading many organizations to rely on this new computing 'utility' for some or most of their IT requirements.

Conclusion

Contrary to common perceptions, the idea of virtualization is not new. It dates back to as early as the 1950s and the 1960s. One of the main reasons for not taking off in the way it did in the last decade or so is because the idea of virtualization was ahead of the technology that existed at that time. Rapid developments in microprocessor technology during the last 15 years have created flexibility in design and speed that was unthinkable before and so enabled new designs and ideas to be incorporated into virtualized networks and systems.

The idea of virtualization received a major boost during the late 1990s triggered by a sudden increase in the number of servers used by organizations which created a major issue of hardware redundancy that had a huge maintenance cost. This was the turning point in the life of this technology which has witnessed great advances since then.

Virtualization technology is enabling many organizations to make optimal use of their IT resources and consequently lower the management costs of those resources. It has effectively changed the way organizations have traditionally viewed their IT resources. IT resources are no longer viewed as static infrastructural entities but rather as scalable and flexible organizational resources that can be used more innovatively (thanks to virtualization technology) in order to derive maximum benefits for their owners.

However, virtualization (like any other innovative technology) has its own learning curve. Many organizations (and other stakeholders) still struggle with the technical and organizational changes which this technology brings despite the fact that an increasing number of organizations have adopted some aspects of it in one form or another. Despite the importance of this issue, it may not be a problem for long. Virtualization is now emerging as one of the main building blocks of cloud computing, the new and fast-developing on-demand computing service utility. This new development, once again, is likely to change how organizations choose to manage their own IT resources.

REFERENCES

Bee Limited. *Virtualization and the past.* Retrieved on 8 May 2010 from: http://www.beeltd.com/a-reason-for-virtualization/.

Brookbanks, M. (2010, May 20). More clouds coming, *IT Now* (A British Computer Society magazine), pp16-17.

Campbell, S and Jeronimo, M. (2006). *Virtualization White Paper - An introduction to virtualization.* Retrieved on 8 May 2010 from: http://www.dabcc.com/downloadfile.aspx?id=455.

Damiani, E., Ardagna, C. A. and El loini, N (2008). *Open Source Systems Security Certification.* Springer.

Dittner, R and Rule. D. (2007). *The best damn server virtualization book period Including Vmware, Xen, and Microsoft Virtual Server*, Syngress.

Georgieva, T. (2009). *Advantages of Virtualization - Virtualization Solutions Can Bring Lots of Benefits to an Enterprise.* Retrieved on 21 May 2010 from: http://computersoftware.suite101.com/article.cfm/advantages_of_virtualization.

Hess, K. (2010). *Top 10 Virtualization Technology Companies.* Retrieved on 24 May 2010 from:http://www.serverwatch.com/article.php/3877576/Top-10-Virtualization-Technology-Companies.htm.

IBM. *Routing with virtual IP.* Retrieved on 4 May 2010 from: http://publib.boulder.ibm.com/infocenter/iseries/v5r3/index.jsp?topic=/rzajw/rzajwviproute.htm.

National Instruments. (2009). *Virtualization Technology Under the Hood.* Retrieved on 4 May 2010 from: http://zone.ni.com/devzone/cda/tut/p/id/8709.

Pietroforte , M. (2008). *Seven disadvantages of server virtualization.* Retrieved on 21 May 2010 from: http://4sysops.com/archives/seven-disadvantages-of-server-virtualization/.

Ruest, N and Ruest, D. (2009). *Virtualization: A Beginner's Guide*, McGraw-Hill Osborne.

Schreck, G and Dines. R. A. (2009). *Best Practices: Aligning Your Infrastructure And Operations Department Around Virtualization.* Retrieved on 9 May 2010 from: http://www.stratus.com/whitep/documents/ServerVirtualizationandCloudComputing.pdf.

Shavit, Y. (2008). *Advantages and disadvantages of server virtualization.* Retrieved on 4 May 2010 from: http://searchsystemschannel.techtarget.com/generic/0,295582,sid99_gci1307133,00.html.

Siebert, E. (2009). *What is virtualization?.* Retrieved on 8 May 2010 from: http://itknowledgeexchange.techtarget.com/virtualization-pro/what-is-virtualization/.

Stratus Technologies. (2009). *Server Virtualization and Cloud Computing: Four Hidden Impacts on Uptime and Availability*, (white paper). Retrieved on 9 May 2010 from: http://www.stratus.com/whitep/documents/ServerVirtualizationandCloudComputing.pdf.

Sultan, N. (2010). Cloud computing for education: A new dawn?, *International Journal of Information Management*, 30 (2), pp. 109-116.

VMware. *Virtualization Overview*. Retrieved on 4 May 2010 from: http://www.nitro.ca/images/pdf/virtualization.pdf.

Vugt, S (2006*). The Definitive Guide to SUSE Linux Enterprise Server*, Apress.

Wong, A and Yeung, A. (2009). *Network Infrastructure Security*, Springer.

Woo, B and Chen, G. (2009). *The Future of Virtualization*. Retrieved on 9 May 2010 from: http://idcdocserv.com/826.

* *Dr. Nabil Ahmed Sultan* graduated from the University of Liverpool with a PhD in Management in 1992 and in 1996 he received his MSc in Information Systems from the same university. After a two-year working period for the United Nations Development Program (UNDP) as Program Officer he moved on to work as a lecturer in IT and Business for the University of Liverpool's Center for Continuing Education until 1998 and since 1999 as Senior Lecturer and Program Director for Liverpool Hope University's Faculty of Business and Computer Science where he developed many successful modules and programs. Dr. Sultan has many published works in IT and management.

Saad Salim received his early graduate education in Information Technology from Pakistan. In 2006 he graduated with an MSc in Computer Science from Liverpool Hope University in the UK and in 2009 he received his International MBA degree from the same university. He worked for a software company in Pakistan as Development Manager and for a British company that specializes in providing IT solutions for education as Web Consultant and Developer for 18 months. He currently works for Liverpool Hope University as IT Research and Support Specialist.

In: New Developments in Computer Research
Editor: Nikos E. Mastorakis
ISBN: 978-1-61470-321-1

PARALLEL ITERATIVE SOLVERS USING PROGRAMMABLE DEVICES

***Safaa Kasbah*[1] *and Issam Damaj*[*2]**
[1]Foundation Program, Dhofar University, Oman
[2]Division of Sciences and Engineering,
American University of Kuwait, Safat, Kuwait

ABSTRACT

In this paper, we aim at increasing the usage of iterative methods in all possible fields by accelerating such solvers using Reconfigurable Hardware. To demonstrate the acceleration of these solvers, we implement the Jacobi solver on different classes of *FPGAs*, such as *Virtex II Pro*, *Altera Stratix* and *Spartan3L*. The design presented is implemented using *Handel-C*, a compiler with hardware output. Obtained results show that reconfigurable hardware is suitable for realizing accelerated versions of such solvers.

1. INTRODUCTION

Physical, chemical and biological phenomena are modeled using Partial Differential Equations (*PDEs*). Interpreting and solving *PDEs* is the key for understanding the behavior of the modeled system. The broad field of modeling real systems has drawn the researchers' attention for designing efficient algorithms for solving *PDEs*. The two basic approaches for finding the solution of the modeled system are the Direct and the Iterative Methods. In Direct Methods, the exact solution of the system is found by using finite number of operations. In Iterative Methods, an approximate guess of the solution to the *PDE* is made; then this guess is used in the second iteration to generate another approximate solution with a higher accuracy than the initial guess [1]. Iterative Methods are more powerful than Direct methods and thus are the methods of choice for solving nowadays modeled systems. Examples of Iterative Methods are: Multigrid, Successive Over Relaxation, Gauss-Seidel, and Jacobi.

Researchers have benefited from the continuous advances in hardware devices and software tools to accelerate the computation of complex mathematical problems [2]. At early stages, algorithms were designed and implemented to run on a general purpose processor

---

[*]Contact Author: Division of Sciences and Engineering, American University of Kuwait, P.O. Box 3323, Safat, Kuwait 13034, idamaj@auk.edu.kw

(software). Techniques for optimizing and parallelizing the algorithm, when possible, were then devised to achieve better performance. As applications are getting more complicated, the performance provided by processors degenerates. A better performance can be achieved using a dedicated hardware where the algorithm is digitally mapped onto a silicon chip. Though it provides better performance than traditional processors, customized hardware lacks flexibility. In the last decade, a new computing paradigm, Reconfigurable Computing (*RC*), has emerged [3]. *RC* overcomes the limitations of the processor and the *IC* technology. *RC* benefits from the flexibility offered by software and the performance offered by hardware [3-5]. *RC* has successfully accelerated a wide variety of applications including cryptography and signal processing [6]. This requires a reconfigurable hardware, such as Field Programmable Gate Array (*FPGA*), and a software design environment that aids in the creation of configurations for the reconfigurable hardware [3].

In this paper, we aim at increasing the usage of iterative methods in all possible fields by accelerating such solvers using Reconfigurable Hardware. To demonstrate the acceleration of these solvers, we implement the Jacobi solver on different classes of *FPGAs*, such as *Virtex II Pro*, *Altera Stratix* and *Spartan3L*. The design presented is implemented using *Handel-C*, a compiler with hardware output. Obtained results show that reconfigurable hardware is suitable for realizing accelerated versions of such solvers.

2. Reconfigurable Computing

Today, it has become possible to benefit from the advantages of both software and hardware with the presence of the Reconfigurable Computing paradigm [3]. Actually, the first idea to fill the gap between the two computing approaches, hardware and software, goes back to the 1960s when Gerald Estrin proposed the concept of *RC* [7].

The basic idea of Reconfigurable Computing is the "*ability to perform certain computations in hardware to increase the performance, while retaining much of the flexibility of a software solution*" [3].

The realization of the *RC* paradigm is made possible by the presence of programmable hardware such as large scale Complex Programmable Logic Device (*CPLD*) and Field Programmable Gate Array *(FPGA)* chips [8]. Reconfigurable computing involves the modification of the logic within the programmable device to suite the application at hand.

2.1. Hardware Compilation

There are certain procedures to be followed before implementing a design on an *FPGA*. First, the user should prepare his/her design by using either a schema editor or by using one of the Hardware Description Languages (*HDLs*) such as *VHDL* (Very high scale integrated circuit Hardware Description Language) and *Verilog*. With schema editors, the designer draws his/her design by choosing from the variety of available components (multiplexers, adders, resistors, ..) and connects them by drawing wires between them. A number of companies supply schema editors where the designer can drag and drop symbols into a design, and clearly annotate each component [9].

Schematic design is considered simple and easy for relatively small designs. However, the emergence of big and complex designs has substantially decreased the popularity of schematic design while increasing the popularity of *HDL* design. Using an *HDL*, the designer has the choice of designing either the structure or the behavior of his/ her design. Both *VHDL* and *Verilog* support structural and behavioral descriptions of the design at different levels of abstractions. A *VHDL* behavioral and structural model of a half adder is shown in Figure 2. In structural design, a detailed description of the system's components, sub-components and their interconnects are specified. The system will appear as a collection of gates and interconnects [9]. Though it has a great advantage of having an optimized design, structural presentation becomes hard, as the complexity of the system increases. In behavioral design, the system is considered as a black box with inputs and outputs only, without paying attention to its internal structure. In other words, the system is described in terms of how it behaves rather than in terms of its components and the interconnection between them.

Though it requires more effort, structural representation is more advantageous than the behavioral representation in the sense that the designer can specify the information at the gate-level allowing optimal use of the chip area [10]. It is possible to have more than one structural representation for the same behavioral program.

Noting that modern chips are too complex to be designed using the schematic approach, we will choose the *HDL* instead of the schematic approach to describe our designs.

Whether the designer uses a schematic editor or an *HDL*, the design is fed to an Electronic Design Automation (*EDA*) tool to be translated to a netlist. The netlist can then be fitted on the *FPGA* using a process called place and route, usually completed by the *FPGA* vendors' tools. Then the user has to validate the place and route results by timing analysis, simulation and other verification methodologies. Once the validation process is complete, the binary file generated is used to (re)configure the *FPGA* device. More about this process is found in the coming sections.

Implementing a logic design on an *FPGA* is depicted in Figure 1:

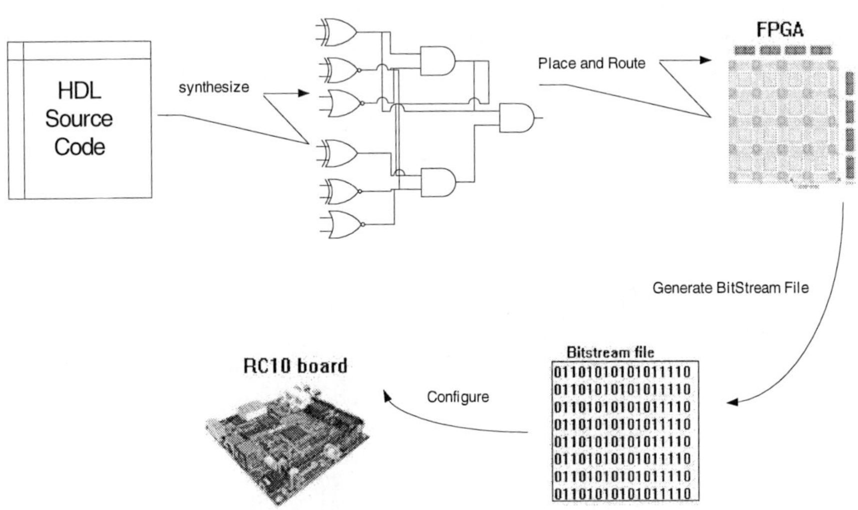

Figure 1. FPGA design flow.

The above process consumes a remarkable amount of time; this is due to the design that the user should provide using *HDL,* most probably *VHDL* or *Verilog*. The complexity of designing in *HDL*; which has been compared to the equivalent of assembly language; is overcome by raising the abstraction level of the design; this move is achieved by a number of companies such as *Agility*, *Cadence* and *Synopsys*. These companies are offering higher level languages with concurrency models to allow faster design cycles for *FPGA*s than using traditional *HDLs*. Examples of higher level languages are *Handel-C*, *SystemC*, and *Superlog* [9] [11].

2.2. Handel-C Language

Handel-C is a high level language for the implementation of algorithms on hardware. It compiles program written in a C-like syntax with additional constructs for exploiting parallelism [9]. The *Handel-C* compiler comes packaged with the *Agility DK Design Suite* which also includes functions and memory controller for accessing the external memory on the *FPGA*. A big advantage, compared to other C to *FPGA* tools, is that *Handel-C* targets hardware directly, and provides a few hardware optimizing features [12]. In contrast to other *HDLs*, such as *VHDL, Handel-C* does not support gate-level optimization. As a result, a *Handel-C* design uses more resources on an *FPGA* than a *VHDL* design and usually takes more time to execute. In the following subsections, we describe Handel-C features' that we have used in our design [12] [13].

2.2.1. Types and Type Operator

Almost all ANSI-C types are supported in Handel-C with the exception of float and double. Yet, floating point arithmetic can still be performed using the floating point library provided by *Agility*. Also, Handel-C supports all ANSI-C storage class specifiers and type qualifiers expect volatile and register which have no meaning in hardware. Handel-C offers additional types for creating hardware components such as memory, ports, buses and wires. Handel-C variables can only be initialized if they are global or if declared as static or const. Handel-C types are not limited to width since when targeting hardware, there is no need to be tied to a certain width. Variables can be of different widths, thus minimizing the hardware usage.

2.2.2. Par Statement

The notion of time in *Handel-C* is fundamental. Each assignment happens in exactly one clock cycle, everything else is "free" [12].

An essential feature in *Handel-C* is the '*par'* construct which executes instructions in parallel.

2.2.3. Handel-C Targets

Handel-C supports two targets. The first is a simulator that allows development and testing of code without the need to use hardware, P1 in Figure 2. The second is the synthesis of a netlist for input to place and route tools which are provided by the *FPGA*'s vendors, P2 in Figure 2.

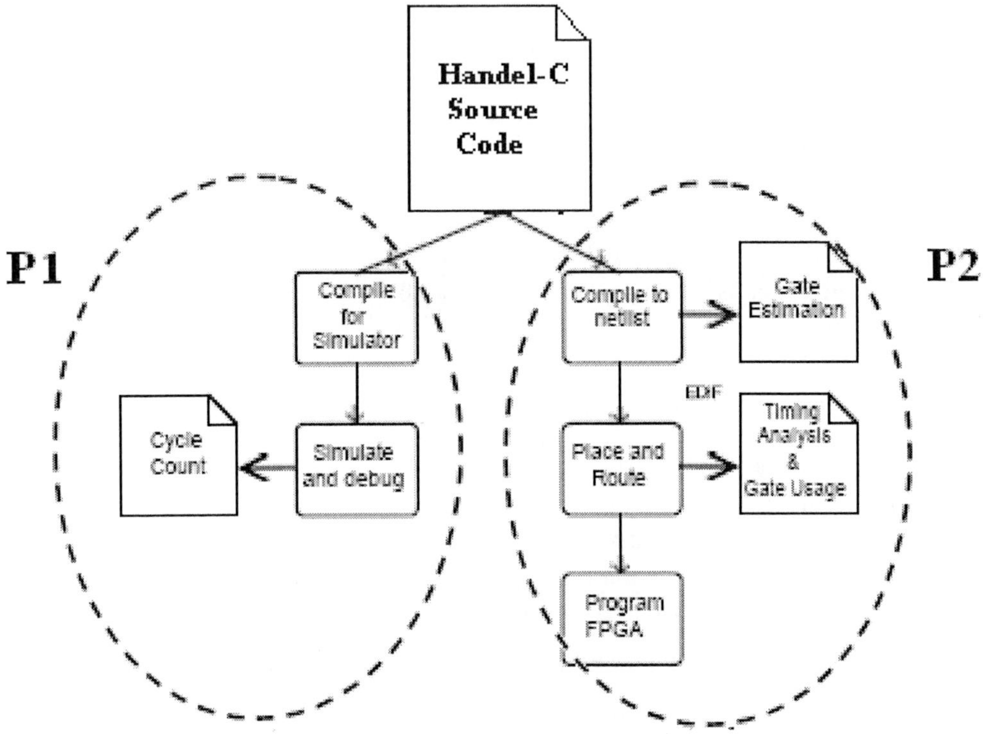

Figure 2. Handel-C targets.

The remaining of this section describes the phases involved in P2, as it is clear from P1 that we can test and debug our design when compiled for simulation.

The flow of the second target involves the following steps:

Compile to netlist: The input to this phase is the source code. A synthesis engine, usually provided by the *FPGA* vendor, translates the original behavioral design into gates and flip flops. The resultant file is called the *netlist*. Generally, the *netlist* is in the Electronic Design Interchange Format (*EDIF*) format. An estimate of the logic utilization can be obtained from this phase.

Place and Route (PAR): The input to this phase is the *EDIF* file generated from the previous phase; i.e. after synthesis. All the gates and flip flops in the netlist are physically placed and mapped to the *FPGA* resources. The *FPGA* vendor tool should be used to place and route the design. All design information regarding timing, chip area and resources utilization are generated and controlled for optimization at this phase.

Programming and configuring the FPGA: After synthesis and place and route, a binary file will be ready to be downloaded into the *FPGA* chip [14] [15].

3. ITERATIVE METHODS

A large number of physical phenomena can be expressed as systems of linear equations. The two basic approaches for finding the solution of the modeled system are the Direct and the Iterative Methods. In Direct Methods, the exact solution of the system is found by using finite number of operations. In Iterative Methods, an approximate guess of the solution to the *PDE* is made; then this guess is used in the second iteration to generate another approximate solution with a higher accuracy than the initial guess [1]. Iterative Methods are more powerful than Direct methods and thus are the methods of choice for solving nowadays modeled systems. Examples of Iterative Methods are: Multigrid, Successive Over Relaxation, Gauss-Seidel, and Jacobi.

The well-known iterative methods are: Multigrid, Successive Over Relaxation, Gauss-Seidel, and Jacobi. In this paper, we have chosen the Jacobi to study the feasibility of accelerating iterative methods using reconfigurable hardware.

3.1. Description of the Jacobi Algorithm

The Jacobi Method is considered to be as the simplest iterative method for solving a linear system. As it is the case with the other iterative methods (Gauss-Seidel, SOR and Multigrid), the Jacobi technique starts with an initial estimate for the true solution and at each step, the current approximate solution is used to produce a better approximation for the true solution. This iterates continues until the approximate solution is sufficiently close to the true solution. Unlike Gauss-Seidel and SOR strategies where the update of the $(i+1)^{th}$ element depends on the update of the ith element, the Jacobi's strategy is updating all the elements at the same time [16].

Given the linear system of equations:

$$A\Phi = b$$

where A can be split into three matrices: the diagonal (D), an upper triangular (U) and a lower triangular (L); having D the diagonal part of A, $-U$ the upper part of A, and $-L$ the lower part of A

A can be written as: $A = D - L - U$

Therefore:

$$(D - L - U)\Phi = b$$

can be rewritten as:

$$D\Phi = (L+U)\Phi + b \quad \text{and} \quad \Phi = D^{-1}(L+U)\Phi + D^{-1}b$$

This leads to the iterative Jacobi technique:

$$\Phi^{(k)} = D^{-1}(L+U)\Phi^{(k-1)} + D^{-1}b \quad \text{where } k = 1,2,...$$

The convergence of the Jacobi technique is guaranteed if the matrix A is diagonally dominant; i.e., in every row of the matrix, the magnitude of the diagonal entry in that row is larger than the sum of the magnitude of all the other entries in that row [16].

4. HARDWARE IMPLEMENTATION OF JACOBI

We used Handel-C, a higher-level hardware design tool to design the Jacobi method. Handel-C comes packaged with DK Design Suite from *Agility*. It allows the designer to focus more on the specification of the algorithm rather than adopting a structural approach to coding [12]. Handel-C syntax is similar to the ANSI-C with additional extensions for expressing parallelism [12]. One of the most important features in Handel-C which is used in our implementation is the 'par' construct that allows statements in a block to be executed in parallel and in the same clock cycle.

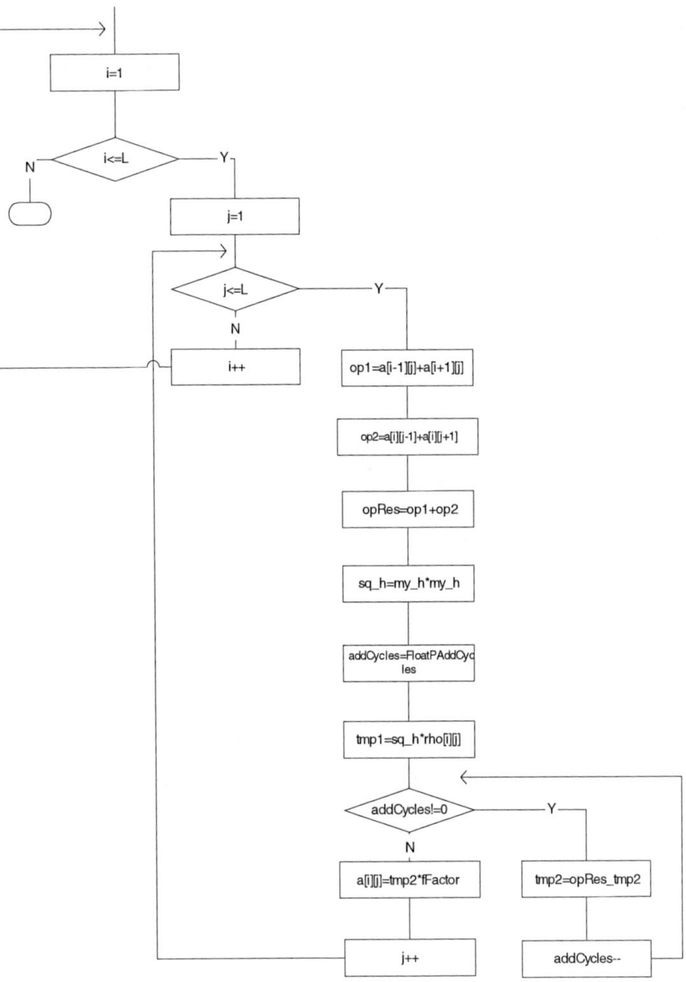

Figure 3. Jacobi flowchart, sequential version.

Our design has been tested using the Handel-C simulator; afterwards, we have targeted a Xilinx Virtex II Pro FPGA, an Altera Stratix FPGA, and Spartan3L which is embedded in an RC10 FPGA-based system from *Agility*. We have used the proprietary software provided by the devices vendors' to synthesize, place and route, and analyze the design [12], [17], [18]

In Figure 3 and Figure 4, we present a parallel and a sequential version of SOR. In the first version, we used the 'par' construct whenever it was possible to execute more than one instruction in parallel and in the same clock cycle without affecting the logic of the source code. The dots in the combined flowchart/concurrent process model which is shown in Figure 3 represent replicated instances. Figure 4 shows a traditional way of sequentially executing instructions on a general purpose processor. Executing instructions in parallel have shown a substantial improvement in the execution of the algorithm.

To handle floating point arithmetic operations which are essential in finding the solution to PDE using iterative methods, we used the Pipelined Floating Point Library provided by *Agility* [12]. However, an unresolved bug in the current version of the DK simulator limited the usage of the floating point operations to four in the design. The only possible way to avoid this failure was to convert/Unpack the floating point numbers to integers and perform integer arithmetic on the obtained unpacked numbers. Though it costs more logic to be generated, the integer operations on the unpacked floating point numbers have a minor effect on the total number of the design's clock cycles.

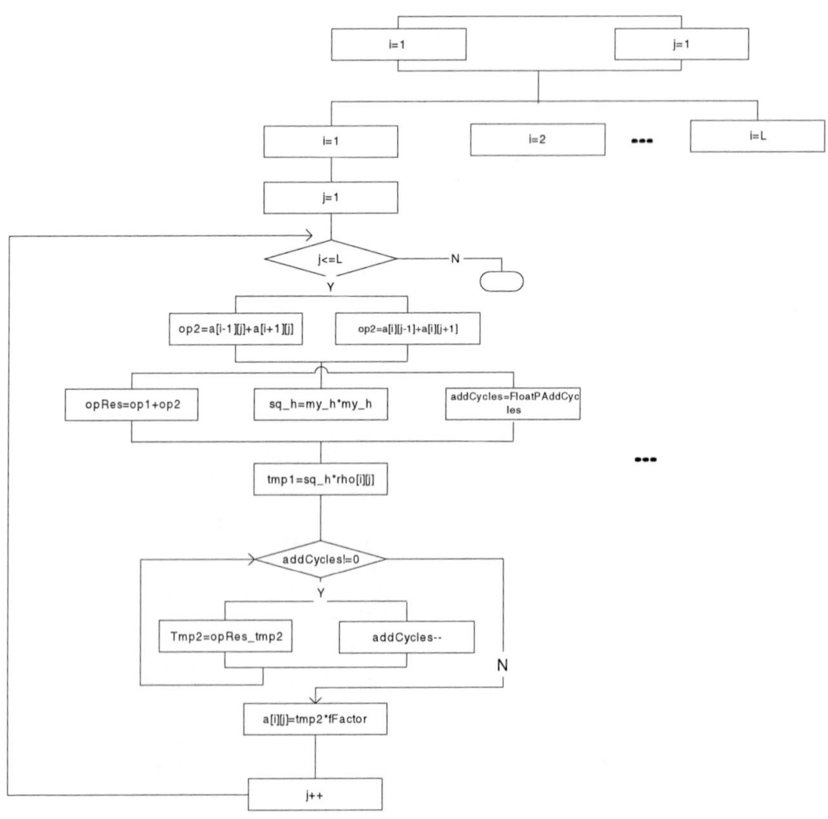

Figure 4. Jacobi parallel version, showing the combined flowchart/concurrent process model. The dots represent replicated instances.

5. EXPERIMENTAL RESULTS

There are two criteria on which our obtained results are based on:

- *Speed of convergence:* the time it takes the Jacobi method to find the solution to the *PDE* in hand. In another word, it is the time needed to execute the Jacobi algorithm. In hardware implementation, the speed of convergence is measured using the clock cycles of the design divided by the frequency at which the design operates at. The first parameter is found using the simulator while the second is found using the timing analysis report which is generated using the *FPGA* vendor's tool.
- *Chip-area:* this performance criterion measures the number of occupied slices on the *FPGA* on which the design is implemented. The number of occupied slices is generated using the *FPGA* vendor's place and route tool.

We use the *FPGA* vendor's tools (*DK Design Suite*, *Xilinx ISE 8.1i* and *Quartus II 5.1*) to analyze and report the performance results of each *FPGA*. The software version was written in C++, compiled using *Microsoft Visual Studio .Net* and running on a Pentium (M) processor 2.0 GHz, 1.99 GB of *RAM*.

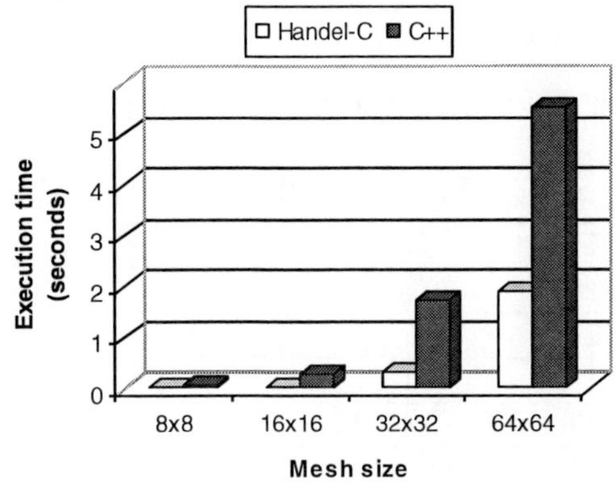

Figure 5(a). Jacobi execution time results in both versions *Handel-C* and *C++*.

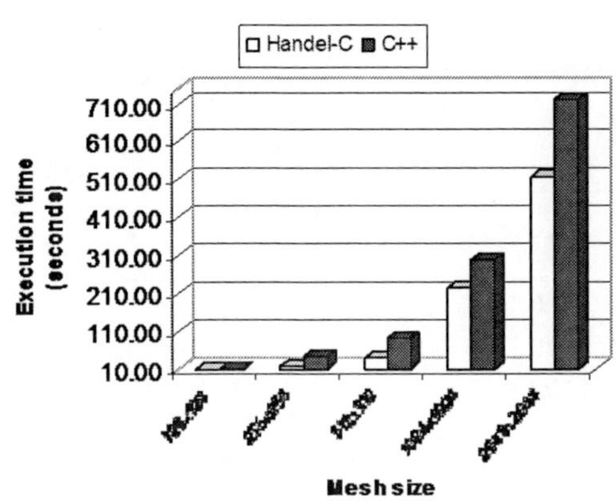

Figure 5(b). Jacobi execution time results in both versions *Handel-C* and *C++*.

The execution time of Jacobi in hardware (*Handel-C*) and in software (*C++*) is shown in Figure 5 for different problem sizes. As the Figure shows, a significant improvement in the execution time of the hardware implementation of the algorithm over the software implementation. The acceleration of the Jacobi algorithm is directly presented in the following table. The Handel-C code was synthesized for *Xilinx Virtex II Pro* (*2vp7ff672-1*), *Altera Stratix* (*ep1s10f484C5*), and *Spartan3L* (*3s15001fg320-4*) which is embedded on *RC10* board from *Agility.* Tables 2, 3 and 4 report the obtained synthesis results.

Table 1. Design Speedup: Execution Time (C++) / Execution Time (Handel-C)

Mesh Size	Speedup
8x8	223.8095
16x16	56.2
32x32	5.676667
64x64	2.89267
128x128	1.409887
256x256	2.287887
512x512	2.386364
1024x1024	0.753898
2024x2024	1.391351

Table 2. *Virtex II Pro* Synthesis Results

Mesh Size	Number of Occupied Slices	Total equivalent gate count
8x8	146	3,229
16x16	159	3,397
32x32	299	5,090
64x64	380	7,849
128x128	499	11,897
256x256	839	17,864
512x512	1286	23,649
1024x1024	1890	31,327
2048x2048	3198	35,839

Table 3. *RC10 Spartan3L* Synthesis Results

Mesh Size	Number of Occupied Slices	Total equivalent gate count
8x8	416	356,109
16x16	599	357,631
32x32	7326	359,989
64x64	9010	342,768
128x128	1198	389,999
256x256	1665	397,987
512x512	2810	498,030

Table 4. Altera Stratix Synthesis Results

Mesh Size	Total Logic Elements	Logic element usage by number of LUT inputs	Total Registers
8x8	610	354	189
16x16	709	401	232
32x32	880	556	300
64x64	1001	681	385
128x128	1286	801	390
256x256	1590	950	476
512x512	2589	1,101	560
1024x1024	3342	1,499	689
2048x2048	3927	1,941	819

CONCLUSION

In this paper, we aim at increasing the usage of iterative methods in all possible fields by accelerating such solvers using Reconfigurable Hardware. To demonstrate the acceleration of these solvers, we implemented the Jacobi solver on different classes of *FPGAs*, such as *Virtex II Pro*, *Altera Stratix* and *Spartan3L*. The design presented was coded and implemented using *Handel-C*, a compiler with hardware output. The design was then mapped onto high-performance *FPGAs*: *Virtex II Pro*, *Altera Stratix*, and *Spartan3L* which is embedded in the *RC10* board from *Agility*. We used the *FPGAs* vendor's tool to analyze the performance of our hardware implementation. For testing purposes, we designed a software version of the algorithm and compiled it using *Microsoft Visual Studio .Net*.

The synthesis results obtained show that it is feasible to implement iterative methods on reconfigurable hardware. The software implementation results were compared to the hardware implementation results. The obtained timing results show that hardware implementation of the Jacobi algorithm outperforms the software implementation. Thus, iterative methods can be accelerated using reconfigurable hardware. The Jacobi's speedup can be further accelerated by designing a pipelined version of the algorithm. Its efficiency can be further improved by moving from Handel-C to a lower level HDL such as VHDL. Also, we consider accelerating complicated iterative solvers, such as, generalized minimal residual method (GMRES), and biconjugate gradient method BiCG, by implementing them on reconfigurable hardware devices.

REFERENCES

[1] D. Young: *Iterative Methods for Solving Partial Difference Equations of Elliptic Type*. Ph.D. thesis, Harvard University 1950.

[2] D. Bailey, and J.M. Borwein. Future Prospects for Computer-assisted Mathematics. *Canadian Mathematical Society Notes*, 37(8), 2-6, 2005.

[3] K. Compton and S. Hauck. Reconfigurable Computing: A Survey of Systems and Software. In: *ACM Computing Surveys*. 34(2), 171-210, 2002.

[4] R. Enzler, *The Current Status of Reconfigurable Computing*, Technical Report, Electronics Lab., Swiss Federal Institute of Technology (ETH) Zurich, 1999.

[5] Y. Li, T. Callahan, E. Darnell, R. Harr, U. Kurkure, J. and Stockwood, Hardware-Software Co-Design of Embedded Reconfigurable Architectures. In 37th Design Automation Conference, Los Angeles, CA, pp. 507-512, 2000.

[6] A. J. Elbirt and C. Paar. An FPGA Implementation and Performance Evaluation of the Serpent Block Cipher. *ACM/SIGDA International Symposium on FPGAs*, pp. 33-40, 2000.

[7] F. Vahid, and T. Givargis. *Embedded systems design: a unified hardware/software introduction.* New York: Wiley; 2002.

[8] T.J. Todman, G.A. Constantinides, S.J.E. Wilton, O. Mencer, W. Luk, and P.Y.K. Cheung. Reconfigurable computing: architectures and design methods. IEE Proceedings - Computers and Digital Techniques, vol. 152, no. 2, pp. 193-197. 2005.

[9] J. Turely. How Chips are Designed. Prentice Hall; 2003, Professional TechnicalReference:http://www.phptr.com/articles/article.asp?p=31679andseqNum=2andrl=

[10] S. K. Valentina, Designing A Digital System with VHDL, *Academic Open Internet Journal,* vol. 11, 2004.

[11] D. Pellerin, and S. Thibault: *Practical FPGA programming in C.* Upper Saddle River, N.J. : Prentice Hall Professional Technical Reference 2005.

[12] Agility, http://www.agilityds.com. 2008.

[13] C. Peter .Overview: Hardware Compilation and the Handel-C language. Oxford University Computing Laboratory, 2000

[14] http://web.comlab.ox.uk/oucl/work/christian .peter/overview_handelc.html.

[15] J. Cong. FPGAs Synthesis and Reconfigurable Computing. University of California, Los Angeles, 1997: http://www.ucop.edu/research/micro/96_97/96_176.pdf

[16] J. Shewel: A Hardware / Software Co-Design System using Configurable Computing Technology, 1998. http://ipdps.cc.gatech.edu/1998/it/schewel.pdf.

[17] D. P. Bertsekas and J.N. Tsitsiklis, "Some aspects of parallel and distributed iterative algorithms -- a survey," Automatica, vol. 27, no. 1, pp. 3--21, 1991.

[18] Altera Inc., www.altera.com. 2008.

[19] Xilinx , http://www.xilinx.com, 2008.

In: New Developments in Computer Research
Editor: Nikos E. Mastorakis

ISBN: 978-1-61470-321-1

CYBERSECURITY: CURRENT LEGISLATION, EXECUTIVE BRANCH INITIATIVES, AND OPTIONS FOR CONGRESS*

Catherine A. The ohary and John Rollins

ABSTRACT

Increasing focus on current cyber threats to federal information technology systems, nonfederal critical information infrastructure, and other nonfederal systems has led to numerous legislative cybersecurity proposals and executive branch initiatives.

The proposed National Defense Authorization Act for Fiscal Year 2010 (NDAA FY20 10) and the Intelligence Authorization Act for Fiscal Year 2010 (IIA FY20 10) both contain provisions that would affect programs and funding for current and future cybersecurity-related programs. In May 2009, the Obama Administration issued its 60-day review of cybersecurity policy, declaring that U.S. information networks would be treated as a strategic national asset.

There is no single congressional committee or executive agency with primary responsibility over all aspects of cybersecurity; each entity involved pursues cybersecurity from a limited vantage point dictated by committee jurisdiction. Many different initiatives exist, but because of fragmentation of missions and responsibilities, "stove-piping," and a lack of mutual awareness between stakeholders, it is difficult to ascertain where there may be programmatic overlap or gaps in cybersecurity policy.

Drawing from common themes found in the Comprehensive National Cybersecurity Initiative (CNCI), a study by the Center for Strategic and International Studies (CSIS) Commission for the 44th Presidency, and the proposed near-term action plan from the President's recent Cyberspace Policy Review, this report identifies priority areas in cybersecurity for policy consideration.

The report then lists and synopsizes current legislation that has been developed to address various aspects of the cybersecurity problem. It then lists the current status of the legislation and compares legislation with existing executive branch initiatives. Finally, analysis of information contained in executive branch initiatives and congressional legislation is used to offer cybersecurity-related considerations for Congress.

---

* This is an edited, reformatted and augmented version of CRS Report R40836, dated September 30, 2009.

INTRODUCTION

Comprehensively addressing national cybersecurity-related issues is a difficult task because of a number of technical and policy considerations. A persistent set of issues has stymied significant progress in detecting and deterring existing threats and implementing effective safeguard measures [1]. Issues that appear to continually challenge U.S. cybersecurity efforts include:

- uncertainty of the geographic location of the perpetrators of cyber attacks;
- the evolving integration of mobile technology devices into critical information infrastructure;
- the introduction of new vulnerabilities to the nation's infrastructure from increasingly sophisticated threats;
- a poorly coordinated federal-private sector approach to addressing emerging risks; and
- legal ambiguities with respect to U.S. response and offensive actions.

While the ever-changing nature of modern technological devices is often noted as a complicating factor in securing the nation's telecommunications and cyber infrastructure, many security observers suggest that an equally daunting group of strategy and policy challenges must be addressed if the United States is to continue to rely on technology as a major component of societal activities. Since 2008, a number of strategy and policy proposals have been offered that may assist in addressing the appropriate balance of relying on emerging technology and network- centric governance while safeguarding critical infrastructure and control systems, as well as privacy and civil liberty considerations.

Recent events such as the April 2007 cyber attacks on Estonia and cyber attacks during the 2008 Georgian incursion have served to increase awareness that cybersecurity is not just about protecting computers, but also has implications for U.S. national security and economic wellbeing. The Obama Administration declared that U.S. critical information infrastructures are a strategic national asset in a May 29, 2009, speech by the President [2] Recognizing the importance of cyberspace over the past few years, both the legislative and executive branches of government have developed cybersecurity legislation and related initiatives, respectively. However, just as there is no single congressional committee that can claim primary jurisdiction over cyberspace, neither is there a single executive agency or department with sole cybersecurity responsibility or commensurate authorities. As the President stated, "No single official oversees cybersecurity policy across the federal government, and no single agency has the responsibility or authority to match the scope and scale of the challenge. Indeed, when it comes to cybersecurity, federal agencies have overlapping missions and don't coordinate and communicate nearly as well as they should—with each other or with the private sector."[3]

Cybersecurity is a cross-cutting field that affects many government and non-governmental stakeholders. As such, one of the most basic concerns, but most difficult to address, is that the term itself can carry different connotations for the various entities. For example, the U.S. military views cyberspace as a warfighting domain as well as a force enabler, enhancing troops' ability to operate in real-time and with improved situational awareness. For the Department of Defense, cybersecurity takes on an offensive or defensive national security role. For other government stakeholders, cybersecurity means information security, or securing the information that resides on cyber infrastructure such as telecommunications networks, or the processes these networks enable. And for some, cybersecurity means protecting the information infrastructure from a physical or electronic attack.

Research Methodology

For purposes of this report, cybersecurity is broadly defined as the protection of critical information infrastructure and its processes and content. This report does not discuss reorganizing the executive branch to better address cybersecurity-related issues, nor does it discuss the military's role in securing federal cyber networks. The report presents the emerging issues in cybersecurity as identified by the Comprehensive National Cybersecurity Initiative (CNCI), the Center for Strategic and International Studies (CSIS) Report to the 44th President, and the Obama Administration's 60-day policy review report, and groups common themes into broad subject areas. These issues are compared to the current statutory framework, new legislative efforts in the 111th Congress, and executive branch initiatives to identify commonalities and possible gaps.

Federal executive branch programs, strategy documents, and reports have been analyzed to illustrate the government's response to emerging challenges in cybersecurity. It should be noted that some of the apparent gaps discovered may actually be addressed by existing classified programs, which cannot be discussed in this unclassified report.

Difficulties in Addressing Cybersecurity Issues

Conceptual and definitional differences among agencies make a unified government strategic approach to cybersecurity a difficult challenge to coordinate. For the Department of Defense, cybersecurity is both the protection of its own networks, processes and content—sometimes referred to as "information assurance"—as well as enabling the freedom of movement to fight and win battles in cyberspace. This approach differs from that of the Department of Homeland Security (DHS), which is tasked to coordinate cybersecurity between the rest of the federal government and the private sector. DHS 's task is complicated, as cyberspace technology and processes are largely owned and operated by the private sector, and as the authority of the federal government to exert control over cybersecurity activities may be limited. Some point to the 2003 National Strategy to Secure Cyberspace as a framework for organizing and prioritizing federal cybersecurity efforts, including the private sector. However, others note that this document fails to take into account the rapid rate of change in technologies or fails to offer a comprehensive strategy for combating current threats and anticipating future threats.

At the operational level, some security observers are concerned about the federal government's present ability to first detect and then respond in a coordinated way to a cyber incident of major significance. Agencies may have their own response plans, procedures, and responsible entities that vastly differ from those of other cooperating agencies. The Cyber Incident Annex to the National Response Plan of December 2004 describes many different authorities and policy documents to guide a response, as well as many different organizations that must communicate effectively in the event of a crisis. Multiple federal information systems enterprise networks make a concerted strategic approach to network security even more difficult, in that each has its own authentication procedures and security standards.

Another cybersecurity difficulty for the government is balancing the protection of civil liberties and individual privacy protections with the desire for comprehensive security of networks and information. It is difficult to secure information infrastructures and their content without tradeoffs between security and the freedoms associated with the Internet. Many concerned about civil liberties fear that the executive branch will use its national security powers and national defense mandate as justification for encroaching on privacy without adequate oversight. Others regard security measures, such as network traffic monitoring, as a violation of the Universal Declaration of Human Rights, which states that "no one shall be subjected to arbitrary interference with his privacy, family, home or correspondence." [4] Complicating the issue is a lack of consensus on the definition of "privacy" in the context of the Internet, and a lack of consensus on what sort of government resolution may be necessary as a network security measure.

Recent Initiatives Addressing U.S. Cybersecurity Concerns

Since 2008, numerous executive branch, legislative, and think tank recommendations and proposals have been offered to address various aspects of ongoing and emerging cybersecurity issues. The Comprehensive National Cybersecurity Initiative (CNCI), the Center for Strategic and International Studies (CSIS) Commission on Cybersecurity for the 44th Presidency, [5] and the White House 60-Day Cyberspace Policy Review (commonly referred to as the 60-Day Cyber Security Review) [6] are the most current attempts to frame the issue and are often referred to when discussions arise regarding how best to identify challenges and implement changes to the current U.S. approach to cybersecurity.

The Comprehensive National Cybersecurity Initiative

In January 2008, the Bush Administration initiated the Comprehensive National Cybersecurity Initiative (CNCI) in an effort to make the United States more secure against cyber threats. The Homeland Security Presidential Directive 23 and National Security Presidential Directive 54 establishing the CNCI are classified, although some details of the initiative have been made public through departmental press releases, speeches by executive branch leaders, and analysis offered by individuals who follow cybersecurity- and terrorism-related issues.

Reportedly, the CNCI "establishes the policy, strategy, and guidelines to secure federal systems." [7] The CNCI also delineates "an approach that anticipates future cyber threats and technologies, and requires the federal government to integrate many of its technical and organizational capabilities to better address sophisticated threats and vulnerabilities." [8] Rather than serving as an overarching national strategy document with specific instructions for federal agency implementation activities, the CNCI is seen as a plan of action for programs and initiatives to be addressed at the operational and tactical level. Given the classified nature of the presidential directives and the secrecy accompanying department and agency activities related to this issues, few details are known about CNCI-related federal government implementation efforts. According to one media account, Steven Chabinsky, Deputy Director of the Joint Interagency Cyber Task Force for the Office of the Director of National Intelligence, stated at an information technology security conference that there are 12 objectives supporting the initiative's goal of comprehensively addressing the nation's cyber security concerns [9] These include the following:

1. Move toward managing a single federal enterprise network (an integrated communications system architecture for the federal government with common security standards across the network).
2. Deploy intrinsic detection systems.
3. Develop and deploy intrusion prevention tools.
4. Review and potentially redirect research and funding.
5. Connect current government cyber operations centers.
6. Develop a government-wide cyber intelligence plan.
7. Increase the security of classified networks.
8. Expand cyber education.
9. Define enduring leap-ahead technologies (investing in high-risk, high-reward research and development to ensure transformational change).
10. Define enduring deterrent technologies and programs.
11. Develop multi-pronged approaches to supply chain risk management (potential tampering within the production line and the risk associated with computer products and parts made outside the United States).
12. Define the role of cybersecurity in private sector domains.

Commission on Cybersecurity for the 44th Presidency

A Cybersecurity Commission (the Commission) organized by the Center for Strategic and International Studies (CSIS) was formed in 2008 to provide advice to the new Administration on the creation and maintenance of a comprehensive cybersecurity strategy. In a December 2008 report, the Commission provided findings and recommendations to secure cyberspace during the 44th presidency and to help inform policymaking. The following actions were proposed in the report as areas requiring priority attention:

- create a comprehensive national cybersecurity strategy;
- lead from the White House;
- reinvent public-private partnership;
- regulate cyberspace;
- authenticate digital identities;
- modernize legal authorities;
- use acquisitions to improve security;
- build capabilities through research training and education.

Obama Administration 60-Day Cyberspace Policy Review

On May 29, 2009, President Obama issued the results of the Administration's 60-Day Cyberspace Policy Review (60-day review). Following the issuance of the CNCI, the review's goal was to assess U.S. policies and organizational structures for cybersecurity. In order to develop a strategic framework to ensure that the U.S. government's initiatives are appropriately integrated, resourced, and coordinated, the following near-term action plan issues were noted in the 60-day review:

- Appoint a cybersecurity official to coordinate interagency strategy and policy.
- Prepare and update national strategy to secure the information and communications infrastructure.
- Designate cybersecurity as one of the President's key management priorities and establish performance metrics.
- Designate a privacy and civil liberties official in the NSC cybersecurity directorate.
- Convene appropriate interagency mechanisms to conduct legal analysis of priority cybersecurity issues [10]
- Initiate a national cybersecurity public awareness and education campaign.
- Develop U.S. government positions for an international cybersecurity policy framework.
- Prepare a cybersecurity incident response plan.
- Develop a framework for research and development strategies that focus on "game-changing" technologies that enhance security.
- Build a cybersecurity-based identity management vision and strategy that addresses privacy and civil liberties interests.

Common Themes of Recent Cybersecurity Initiatives

Some common themes begin to emerge from the initiatives and recommendations suggested in CNCI, the CSIS report, and the 60-day review. These themes are broadly captured under the following headings:

National cybersecurity strategy—conceptualizing a current comprehensive approach toward a government-wide cybersecurity solution, outlining ends, ways, and means along with a prioritization of effort.

Executive branch organization—reorganizing existing executive branch structures, or standing up new entities to coordinate cybersecurity throughout the interagency process.

Congressional oversight concerns—identifying committee jurisdictions to oversee budgetary priorities and goals for cybersecurity programs.

Establish/update legal authorities—expanding and/or clarifying roles and responsibilities of cybersecurity stakeholders.

Privacy and civil liberties—maintaining privacy and freedom of speech protections on the Internet while devising cybersecurity procedures.

Awareness, research, education, and training—developing a workforce to meet cybersecurity goals, raising citizenry awareness of cybersecurity best practices, and developing more secure technologies.

Outreach, collaboration, and policy formation—working across government and with the private sector to share information on threats and other data, and to develop shared approaches to securing cyberspace.

These broad themes are used to compare current policy and legislative proposals with executive branch initiatives. A description of selected executive branch initiatives is followed by a comparison matrix that illustrates trends in cybersecurity efforts.

Representative Sampling of Preexisting Executive Branch Programs and Initiatives

Upon release of the Administration's 60-day review, President Obama announced the creation of a new cabinet-level position to coordinate cybersecurity strategy and policy across the federal government. This new "Cyber Coordinator," sometimes referred to as a "Cyber Czar," is to report to the National Security Advisor and the Director of the National Economic Council. As of September 2009, the position has not been filled.

Programs in several departments address various aspects of cybersecurity within their respective areas of responsibility. While every department and agency has an individual and collective role in securing federal cyber enterprises, some organizations have appeared to have greater authority and capability than others. A few of the departments and their accompanying responsibilities are noted below.

The Department of Commerce's National Institute of Standards and Technology (NIST) has primary responsibility for reducing cyber vulnerabilities in the electrical grid. In the Energy Independence and Security Act of 2007 (EISA; P.L. 110-139), Congress directed NIST to lead the Department of Energy and other agencies in ensuring an interoperable, secure, and open energy infrastructure that will enable all electric resources to contribute to an efficient and reliable electricity network. Specifically, EISA gave NIST "primary responsibility to coordinate development of a framework that includes protocols and model standards for information management to achieve interoperability of smart grid devices and systems." Cybersecurity and associated standards are being addressed as part of this Smart Grid Interoperability Framework that is under development [11]. NIST is also tasked to promote the development of key security standards and guidelines to support the implementation of and compliance with the Federal Information Security Management Act of 2002 (FISMA; P.L. 107-347) [12]

The Department of Health and Human Services (HHS) has recently adopted new interoperability standards for health care information technology. HHS is responsible for implementing privacy and security standards for electronic personal health information [13].

The Department of Homeland Security (DHS) leads the cybersecurity coordination for nonmilitary departments and agencies in the federal government. The National Cyber

Security Directorate works with private industry on a voluntary basis to promote safe cybersecurity practices. DHS is also home to the National Cyber Security Center, a clearinghouse whose mission is to coordinate information from all agencies to help secure cyber networks and systems, foster collaboration, and improve situational awareness.

The Department of Defense (DOD) has a number of programs designed to address vulnerabilities and threats to its own networks. Secretary Gates recently announced the creation of a new sub- unified command under the U.S. Strategic Command, to be called U.S. Cyber Command (CYBERCOM). This new command is to coordinate a unified approach to defending and securing military cyber networks. The December 2006 National Military Strategy for Cyberspace Operations (NMS-CO) guides computer network attack and defense principles. The Defense Industrial Base (DIB) initiative provides a vehicle through which DOD and industry partners can better share information on cyber threats and defense practices. DOD also has established a Cybercrime Center (DC3) that assists in criminal, counterintelligence, counterterrorism, and fraud investigations by the Defense Criminal Investigative Organizations (DCIOs) and DOD counterintelligence activities. In addition to setting forensics standards, it provides training and testing laboratories for protection of defense information systems.

Common themes often noted by many cybersecurity experts underscore a lack of transparency and dearth of defined departmental roles and responsibilities in addressing cyber-related issues from a comprehensive national approach. Such concerns often assert that a continuation of addressing cyber incidents as a myopic individual agency responsibility will eventually lead to increased systemic national vulnerabilities and put the nation at greater risk. It is argued by some that a more strategic approach to detecting, identifying, mitigating, and responding to future cyber incidences may strengthen both the individual agency and the whole-of-government approach to securing the technologies that underpin every aspect of modern society.

Comparison Matrix

The following table is designed to assist in identifying emerging cybersecurity themes contained within previously enumerated respective executive branch activities, including both Administration-led initiatives, federal agency programs, statutes, and proposed legislation. While the issue contained in the applicable legislation and executive branch initiatives do not always perfectly align (based on the number of issues addressed and the degree of specificity), Table 1 notes corresponding legislation proposed in both the 111th Congress and the 110th Congress to relevant existing statutory frameworks. Finally, current appropriations bills are shown to illustrate congressional spending priorities. Overview lists and summaries of the cybersecurity-related legislation are found in the Appendix.

A common theme emerging from a review of the current proposals is the need for a current comprehensive national cybersecurity strategy. The most recent strategy, the 2003 National Strategy to Secure Cyberspace, outlined a unified, whole-of-government approach to dealing with cybersecurity [14]. Some say that the 2003 policy has not kept pace with the rapidly evolving technologies and threats in cyberspace, and have called upon the Administration to craft [15] a new national cybersecurity strategy with the assistance of Congress. Others say it is not a comprehensive strategy but is instead a set of recommendations, much like the CSIS Commission report. The Administration's 60-day review's near-term action plan calls for preparing and updating a new national strategy for securing communications and information infrastructure.

Table 1. Comparison of Emerging Cybersecurity Themes

Emerging Issues	Executive Branch Activity	111th Congress	110th Congress	Statutory Framework
National Cybersecurity Strategy	CNCI; 60-Day Review; 2003 NSSC; NMS-CO	S. 773		44 U.S.C. § 3541; 18 U.S.C. § 1030
Executive Branch Organization	Cyber Coordinator; CYBERCOM; DHS NCC, NCSD	H.R. 1174; H.R. 1910; S. 921; H.R. 2165; H.R. 2195; S. 778;		
Congressional Oversight Concerns		S. 1494; S. 1438		
Establish/Update Legal Authorities		S. 773; S. 946		
Privacy and Civil Liberties	HHS Rules	H.R. 1		42 USC § 201; 18 U.S.C. §1030
Awareness, Research, Education, Training	DOD Cybercrime Center; DHS NCC	H.R. 2200; H.R. 2454; S. 177; S. 1391; H.R. 2647; H.R. 2892; H.R. 266; H.R. 1	H.R. 1; H.R. 4986; H.R. 2764; H.R. 2638	
Outreach, Collaboration and Policy Formation	Cyber Coordinator; DIB Initiative; NIST standards	S. 1436; H.R. 2020; H.R. 1	H.R. 6	
Appropriations		H.R. 3293; H.R. 2892	H.J.Res. 20	

From the table, the legislative branch appears to share this concern; legislation proposed in S. 733 calls upon the President to present a national strategy within one year of the bill's enactment. This bill would also create a national advisory panel to oversee implementation of the strategic plan and to periodically advise the president on the need for revising the strategy. Some have criticized the provision, which would give the President emergency control over public and private networks in the event of a crisis, and have argued that the bill is vague in addressing civil liberties protections. As this legislation is marked up, alternative proposals may be considered.

Another area of interest is executive branch organization. As the federal government continues to organize to defend its strategic cyber assets, some Members of Congress have proposed legislation that would create new offices or positions, or give greater authority and direction to existing positions. It is unclear how proposals such as S. 778 to establish the

Office of the National Cybersecurity Advisor within the Executive Office of the President fits with the administration's recently proposed Cyber Coordinator, a cabinet position that will report to both the National Security Advisor and the Director of the National Economic Council [16].

Privacy and civil liberties concerns appear to be lacking in recent congressional proposals. However, there are Internet privacy and non-disclosure policies written into statutory frameworks that may not specifically address cybersecurity, such as the Health Insurance Portability and Accountability Act (HIPAA; P.L. 104-191) and personal health care information safeguards, or the Gramm-Leach-Bliley Act (P.L. 106-102) and financial information for corporations or individuals. Civil liberties is an area of concern for both Congress and privacy advocates, but does not appear to be an immediate priority reflected in legislative action to date. This may suggest to some that existing programs have emphasized securing networks before tackling the attendant issues such as freedom of speech, privacy, and civil liberty protections as they pertain to the Internet.

Upon review of the legislation contained in Table 1, another common area of focus appears to be addressing issues related to workforce development, outreach, and collaboration-based initiatives. The proposed S. 733 in its initial version contained provisions for presidential cybersecurity authorities. Rewrites of this legislation reportedly may revise this provision [17]. Such activities could be replaced or supplemented with the inclusion of additional focus on the training, education, and research aspects of cybersecurity.

CONSIDERATIONS AND OPTIONS FOR CONGRESS

Questions of resources and appropriate organizational structures appear to dominate legislative and executive branch efforts and proposals for federal cybersecurity programs. However, the lack of a current and clearly articulated national strategy remains a concern to some. Without an overall government strategy and underlying policies to outline cybersecurity priorities, goals, and how to achieve them, executive organization and program funding may be a muddled process. Congress may consider drafting legislation that would outline a strategic security framework and priority areas for the Obama Administration to address. With the advent of a new strategy, Congress may then wish to review the authorization and appropriations legislation for cybersecurity related programs for possible mission duplication and adherence to strategic goals.

Reportedly, the Homeland Security and Governmental Affairs Committee, recognizing calls for lawmakers to combine efforts, is to work with the Armed Services, Commerce, Intelligence and Judiciary panels to craft comprehensive cybersecurity legislation. [18].

In addition to the options and recommendations contained in the legislative proposals, CNCI, White House 60-Day Cyber Security Review, and the Commission on Cybersecurity for the 44th Presidency reports, Congress may wish to consider other options when addressing current and emerging cyber risks to the nation. Additional options may include the following:

- Drafting legislation, strategy, and policies that take into account rapidly changing telecommunications and Internet-based technologies.
- Ensuring risk reduction education and training is a core component for all federal government employee performance assessments, with an advanced course provided to individuals who spend a majority of their work time undertaking technology-related activities.
- Requiring the National Intelligence Council to produce classified and unclassified annual reports addressing current and emerging cyber-related based threats.
- Requiring the Department of Homeland Security annually to produce cybersecurity risk assessments for all nonfederal government entities with security responsibilities. The assessments could address issues relating to current and emerging threats, current best security practices, and mitigation and remediation recommendations, as well as provide a venue for the recipients of this report to submit threat information and requests for assistance to the Department.
- Legislatively defining U.S. cyber offensive and defensive responsibilities and authorities.
- Establishing a permanent Congressional Commission or Task Force that would assess and report to Congress successes and ongoing challenges in U.S. cybersecurity programs and activities.
- Drafting legislation to mandate privacy and freedom of speech protections to be incorporated into a national strategy.
- Assessing current congressional committee jurisdiction.

APPENDIX. CYBERSECURITY-RELATED LEGISLATION IN THE 111TH AND 110TH CONGRESSES

This appendix provides an overview list of legislative proposals in the 111th Congress, followed by a brief summary of the related section. Following this is an overview list of legislation that was proposed in the 110th Congress, indicating legislative initiatives extending back into the previous Administration. The final section of the appendix summarizes existing statutory foundations in cybersecurity. These lists are not exhaustive, but rather are designed to give a representative overview of cybersecurity related activities in the federal government and to assist in identifying priority areas where legislation may be necessary.

This information is current as of September 28, 2009. For the most up-to-date information, please consult the Legislative Information System (LIS) at http://www.congress.gov/.

Overview list of Bills in the 111th Congress that Address a Cybersecurity-Related Issue

Directly Tied to Cybersecurity

S. 1438 Fostering a Global Response to Cyber Attacks Act (referred to Senate committee).

H.R. 266 Cybersecurity Education Enhancement Act of 2009 (referred to House subcommittee)—expansion of professional cybersecurity education programs.

S. 778 To establish, within the Executive Office of the President, the Office of the National Cybersecurity Advisor (referred to Senate committee).

S. 773 Cybersecurity Act of 2009 (referred to Senate committee).

Cybersecurity Components as Part of Broader Legislation

H.R. 2195 To amend the Federal Power Act to provide additional authorities to adequately protect the critical electric infrastructure against cyber attack, and for other purposes (referred to House subcommittee)—protection of electric infrastructure from cyber attack.

H.R. 2165 Bulk Power System Protection Act of 2009 (referred to House committee)—to amend Part II of the Federal Power Act to address known cybersecurity threats to the reliability of the bulk power system, and to provide emergency authority to address future cybersecurity threats to the reliability of the bulk power system.

S. 921 United States Information and Communications Enhancement Act of 2009 (referred to Senate committee)—creation of the National Office for Cyberspace.

H.R. 2868 Chemical Facility Anti-Terrorism Act of 2009 (referred to House committee)— several sections mention cybersecurity in connection with overall security for chemical facilities.

S. 1494 Intelligence Authorization Act for Fiscal Year 2010 (passed/agreed to in Senate)—has an extensive and detailed section (340) on cybersecurity oversight.

H.R. 1910 Chief Technology Officer Act of 2009 (referred to House subcommittee)—to create the Office of the Chief Technology Officer within the Executive Office of the President.

Tied via Appropriations or Authorization

H.R. 2892 Department of Homeland Security Appropriations Act, 2010 (awaiting conference)—"$1,700,000 shall be for the Center for Counterterrorism and Cyber Crime."

H.R. 2647 National Defense Authorization Act for Fiscal Year 2010 (awaiting conference)— civilian cybersecurity training authorization, creation of Joint Program Office for Cyber Operations Capabilities.

S. 1391 Department of Defense Authorization Act for Fiscal Year 2010 (awaiting conference)—civilian cybersecurity training authorization.

Peripheral Cybersecurity Related or Mentions

P.L. 111-5 (H.R. 1) American Recovery and Reinvestment Act, 2009—under Title XXX Health Information Technology and Quality, section 13001 directs privacy standards for electronic health information.

Title VI directs the Commerce Department and the Federal Communications Commission (FCC) to institute and expand the "broadband technologies and opportunities program."

S. 177 Strengthening Our Economy Through Small Business Innovation Act of 2009 (referred to Senate committee)—cybersecurity mentioned as a research priority for small businesses.

H.R. 1131 Community Protection and Response Act of 2009 (referred to House subcommittee)—includes a cyber attack in the listing of major disaster.

H.R. 1174 FEMA Independence Act of 2009 (referred to House subcommittee)—an Assistant Secretary for Cybersecurity is mentioned for an independent FEMA.

H.R. 2454 American Clean Energy and Security Act of 2009 (placed on calendar in Senate)— cybersecurity mentioned as a concern.

H.R. 2200 Transportation Security Administration Authorization Act (referred to Senate committee after being received from House)—mentions a cyber attack as a security concern.

S. 1436 Energy and Water Development and Related Agencies Appropriations Act, 2010 (placed on Calendar in Senate)—for the "purpose of forming and governing a national energy sector cyber organization that have the knowledge and capacity to focus cybersecurity research and development and to identify and disseminate best practices; organize the collection, analysis and dissemination of infrastructure vulnerabilities and threats; work cooperatively with the Department of Energy and other federal agencies to identify areas where federal agencies with jurisdiction may best support efforts to enhance security of the bulk power electric grid."

H.R. 3293 Departments of Labor, Health and Human Services, and Education, and Related Agencies Appropriations Act, 2010 (placed on calendar in Senate)—provides $607,482,000 for the public health and social services emergency fund "to support activities related to countering potential biological, nuclear, radiological, chemical, and cybersecurity threats to civilian populations."

Details on Bills in the 111th Congress that Address a Cybersecurity Related Issue

H.R. 2892 Department of Homeland Security Appropriations Act, 2010

Status of bill: Awaiting conference.

See under: Title III—Protection, Preparedness, Response, and Recovery; infrastructure protection and information security.

See under: Title III—Protection, Preparedness, Response, and Recovery; Federal Emergency Management Agency; State and local programs; item 12 (B).

Summary: The bill would allocate $1,700,000 for the Center for Counterterrorism and Cyber Crime, located in Norwich University, Northfield, Vermont.

H.R. 2454 American Clean Energy and Security Act of 2009

Status of bill: Placed on Calendar in Senate.

See under: Section 216 A—Transmission Planning. Subsection on "objectives" (1), under "Federal Policy" (a).

Summary: One of the objectives of the mentioned "federal policy" is to provide cybersecurity for the regional electrical grid.

H.R. 3293 Departments of Labor, Health and Human Services, and Education, and Related Agencies Appropriations Act, 2010

Status of bill: Placed on Calendar in Senate.

See under: Title II—Office of the Secretary, public health and social services emergency fund.

Summary: Provides $607,482,000 for the public health and social services emergency fund to support activities related to countering potential threats to civilian populations, among them, cybersecurity related threats. Cybersecurity threats are mentioned together with biological, nuclear, radiological, and chemical threats.

S. 1436 Energy and Water Development and Related Agencies Appropriations Act, 2010

Status of bill: Placed on Calendar in Senate.

See under: Title III—Department of Energy; Energy Programs; Electricity Delivery and Energy Reliability.

Summary: The section would allocate funding for the Department of Energy as it relates to electricity delivery and energy reliability. As part of the funding the Secretary must establish an "independent national energy sector cyber security organization to institute research, development and deployment priorities, including policies and protocol to ensure the effective deployment of tested and validated technology and software controls to protect the bulk power electric grid and integration of smart grid technology to enhance the security of the electricity grid."

H.R. 2200 Transportation Security Administration Authorization Act

Status of bill: Referred to Senate Committee after being received from House.

See under: Title I—Authorization of Appropriations; Section 102. Risk-Based System for Allocation of Resources; Assessment and Prioritization of Risks.

Summary: The section would require TSA to implement a system of risk-based allocation of resources and provide a report that includes "a summary that ranks the risks within and across transportation modes, including vulnerability of a cyber attack."

H.R. 1910 Chief Technology Officer Act of 2009

Status of bill: Introduced in House—referred to House Subcommittee on Information Policy, Consensus, and National Archives.

See under: Section 2—Office of the Chief Technology Officer; Policy Planning, Analysis and Advice.

Summary: The bill would create the office of the Chief Technology Officer within the Executive Office of the President. Section 2 would require the Chief Technology Officer to assess the impact of information technology and networked information technology systems and applications on cybersecurity and personal privacy and advise the President on steps necessary to mitigate and manage security and privacy risks.

Beyond this specific cybersecurity concern, the CTO would also be responsible for "fact-gathering, analysis, and assessment of the federal government's information technology infrastructures, information technology strategy, and use of information technology." Other responsibilities would be ensuring "the security and privacy of the federal information technology infrastructure and networks" and "coordinating closely with other federal departments and agencies having responsibilities regarding security and privacy of the infrastructure and networks."

H.R. 1174 FEMA Independence Act of 2009

Status of bill: Introduced in House—referred to House Subcommittee on Emergency Communications, Preparedness, and Response.

See under: Title V—Other Offices and Functions; Section 514.

Summary: The section would create an "Assistant Secretary for Cybersecurity and Communications" as part of an independent FEMA.

H.R. 1131 Community Protection and Response Act of 2009

Status of bill: Introduced in House—referred to House Subcommittee on Early Childhood, Elementary, and Secondary Education.

See under: Section 3—Definition of Major Disaster.

Summary: The section would amend the Disaster Relief and Emergency Assistance Act to improve federal response efforts after a terrorist strike or other major disaster affecting homeland security. In the section for the definition of a major disaster it would include cyber attack on computer systems as one of the possibilities under "terrorist attack."

S. 177 Strengthening Our Economy Through Small Business Innovation Act of 2009

Status of bill: Introduced in Senate—referred to Senate Committee on Small Business and Entrepreneurship.

See under: Section 6—Inclusion of Energy, Security, Transportation, And Water Related Research In The List of Topics Deserving Special Consideration As SBIR Research Topics.

Summary: The bill would extend allocation of funds for research programs related to the Small Business Innovation Research program. Section 6 includes cybersecurity as one of the topics of interest, in particular the research by the National Academy of Sciences relating to cybersecurity.

S. 1391 Department of Defense Authorization Act for Fiscal Year 2010

Status of bill: Awaiting conference.

See under: Title IX—Department of Defense Organization and Management; Subtitle D—Other Matters; Section 932—Instruction of Private Sector Employees in Cyber Security Courses of the Defense Cyber Investigations Training Academy.

Summary: The bill provides authority for the Secretary of Defense to permit private sector employees to enroll in and receive instruction at the Defense Cyber Investigations Training Academy. No more than 200 full-time student positions may be filled at any one time by private sector employees enrolled under this section. Eligible private sector employees will be those engaged in providing significant defense related support to the Department of Defense or other federal agencies or those whose work product is relevant to national security policy or strategy.

In addition to the above section (932)—section 1222 "Report on Cuba and Cuba's Relations With Other Countries" includes "the status and extent of Cuba's cyberwarfare program" as one of the seven subjects to be addressed by the report on Cuba required from the Director of National Intelligence.

H.R. 2647 National Defense Authorization Act for Fiscal Year 2010

Status of bill: Awaiting conference.

See under: Title IX—Department of Defense Organization and Management; Subtitle D—Other Matters; Section 932—Instruction of Private Sector Employees in Cyber Security Courses of the Defense Cyber Investigations Training Academy.

Summary: The bill provides authority for the Secretary of Defense to permit private sector employees to enroll in and receive instruction at the Defense Cyber Investigations Training Academy. No more than 200 full-time student positions may be filled at any one time by private sector employees enrolled under this section. Eligible private sector employees will be those engaged in providing significant defense related support to the Department of Defense or other federal agencies or those whose work product is relevant to national security policy or strategy.

In addition to the above section (932)—section 1222 "Report on Cuba and Cuba's Relations With Other Countries" includes "the status and extent of Cuba's cyberwarfare program" as one of the seven subjects to be addressed by the report required from the Director of National Intelligence on Cuba.

S. 1494 Intelligence Authorization Act for Fiscal Year 2010

Status of bill: Passed/agreed to in Senate.

See under: Title III—General Intelligence Community Matters; Subtitle D—Congressional Oversight, Plans, and Reports; Section 340 – Cybersecurity Oversight.

Summary: Section 340 would improve congressional oversight of federal cybersecurity programs. S. 1494 would require that the President inform Congress about every cybersecurity program currently in operation and every new program created thereafter. The program notification must include some type of certification on the legality of the program as well as an assessment on the program's privacy impact.

H.R. 2868 Chemical Facility Anti-Terrorism Act of 2009

Status of bill: Introduced in House—referred to House Committee on the Judiciary.

See under: Title XXI – Regulations of Security Practices at Chemical Facilities; Section 2101— Definitions.

Summary: The bill defines "chemical facility security performance standards" as including the deterrence of cyber sabotage, "including by preventing unauthorized onsite or remote access to critical process controls." Later in the bill, cybersecurity is mentioned several times alongside physical security as seemingly equally important for the overall security of chemical facilities.

S. 921 United States Information and Communications Enhancement Act of 2009

Status of bill: Introduced in Senate—referred to Senate Committee on Homeland Security and Governmental Affairs.

See under: Subchapter II—Information Security; Subsection 3552—National Office for Cyberspace.

Summary: S. 921 would establish the National Office for Cyberspace within the Executive Office of the President. The Director of the National Office for Cyberspace is tasked with developing and implementing a comprehensive national cyberspace strategy. The Office would play a crucial role in deterring cyber attacks and defending the cyber critical infrastructure.

H.R. 2165 Bulk Power System Protection Act of 2009

Status of bill: Introduced in House—referred to House Committee on Energy and Commerce.

See under: Section 3—Protection of Bulk Power System From Cybersecurity Threats.

Summary: The bill seeks to amend Part II of the Federal Power Act in order to address cybersecurity threats to the reliability of the bulk power system. In addition, the Federal Energy Regulatory Commission would be authorized to respond in cases of imminent cyber security threats. The section also emphasizes ensuring that the Commission protects cybersecurity-related information.

H.R. 2195 To amend the Federal Power Act to provide additional authorities to adequately protect the critical electric infrastructure against cyber attack, and for other purposes

Status of bill: Introduced in House—referred to House Subcommittee on Emerging Threats, Cybersecurity, and Science and Technology.

See under: Section 224—Critical Infrastructure; Part B—Assessment, Report, and Determination.

Summary: The bill attempts to improve the cybersecurity of the critical electric infrastructure through added powers and responsibilities for the Secretary of Homeland Security as well as the Federal Energy Regulatory Commission. Beyond assessing the cyber threats to the critical electric infrastructure, the Secretary of Homeland Security would be required to initiate several interim measures to protect the system from cyber attack. The Secretary of Homeland Security would then produce periodic assessments on the vulnerabilities and threats to the critical electric infrastructure and provide those to Congress as well as to the Federal Energy Regulatory Commission.

S. 773 Cybersecurity Act of 2009

Status of bill: Introduced in Senate—referred to Senate Committee on Commerce, Science, and Transportation.

See under: Section 3—Cybersecurity Advisory Panel.

Summary: Section 3 would instruct the President to designate a Cybersecurity Advisory Panel.

See under: Section 4—Real-Time Cybersecurity Dashboard.

Summary: Section 4 would require the Secretary of Commerce to implement a system to provide dynamic and real-time cybersecurity status and vulnerability information for all federal government information systems and networks managed by the Department of Commerce.

See under: Section 5—State and Regional Cybersecurity Enhancement Program; Part A— Creation and Support of Cybersecurity Centers.

Summary: The section would require the Secretary of Commerce to provide assistance for the creation and support of Regional Cybersecurity Centers in order to promote and implement cybersecurity standards at the state and regional levels.

See under: Section 6—NIST Standards Development and Compliance.

Summary: The section would require the National Institute of Standards and Technology to establish measurable security cybersecurity standards for all federal government, government contractor, or grantee critical infrastructure information systems and networks in the following areas: cybersecurity metrics research, security controls, and software security.

See under: Section 7—Licensing and Certification of Cybersecurity Professionals.

Summary: The section would require the Secretary of Commerce to develop and integrate a national licensing, certification, and periodic recertification program for cybersecurity professionals.

See under: Section 11—Federal Cybersecurity Research and Development.

Summary: The section would require the Director of the National Science Foundation to give priority to computer, information science, and engineering research to ensure support is provided to meet cybersecurity challenges.

See under: Section 1 8—Cybersecurity Responsibilities and Authority.

Summary: The section would require the President to develop and implement a comprehensive national cybersecurity strategy that includes such thigs as a long-term plan of the nation's cybersecurity future as well as a Quadrennial Cyber Review.

S. 778 To establish, within the Executive Office of the President, the Office of the National Cybersecurity Advisor

Status of bill: Introduced in Senate—referred to Senate Committee on Homeland Security and Governmental Affairs.

See under: Section 1—Office of the National Cybersecurity Advisor.

Summary: The bill would establish an Office of the National Cybersecurity Advisor within the Executive Office of the President. The position would serve the President as the principal advisor for all cybersecurity related matters.

H.R. 266 Cybersecurity Education Enhancement Act of 2009

Status of bill: Introduced in House—referred to the Subcommittee on Higher Education, Lifelong Learning, and Competitiveness.

See under: Section 2—Department of Homeland Security Cybersecurity Training Programs and Equipment.

Summary: The bill would authorize the Secretary of Homeland Security to establish a program to award grants to institutions of higher education for the establishment or expansion of cybersecurity professional development programs.

S. 1438 Fostering a Global Response to Cyber Attacks Act

Status of bill: Introduced in Senate—referred to Senate Committee on Foreign Relations. See under: Section 4—Report On Improving Cybersecurity.

Summary: The bill expresses the interest of Congress is improving the nation's cybersecurity overall. Section 4 would require the Secretary of State to submit to the Senate and House a report describing "any actions taken by the United States to work with the governments of foreign countries to improve cybersecurity."

Procurement

Title XLI—Procurement (in thousands of dollars)

Under "Procurement—Defense Wide": Major Equipment DISA #027—Cyber Security Initiative $18,188.

Under "Operational Systems Development" for the Navy: # 030 1372N Cyber Security Initiative GDIP unknown amount (classified).

Under "Research, Development, Test & Evaluation, Air Force": Cybersecurity for control networks research $4,000.

Under "Operational Systems Development"—Airforce: #0305 103F Cybersecurity initiative $2,065.

Under "RDT&E" Defense-wide: # 0305 103E Cybersecurity initiative $30,400.

Under "Operational Systems Development" Defense-wide: # 0301371 G Cybersecurity initiative CCP unknown amount (classified).

Under "Operational Systems Development" Defense-wide: # 030 1372L Cybersecurity initiative GDIP unknown amount (classified).

Under "Operational Systems Development" Defense-wide: # 0305 103D8Z Cybersecurity initiative $993.

Under "Operational Systems Development" Defense-wide: # 0305 103G Cybersecurity initiative unknown amount (classified).

Under "Operational Systems Development" Defense-wide: # 0305103K Cybersecurity initiative $10,080.

Title XLVI—Department of Energy National Security Programs Under "Cyber security": $122,511.

Overview of Bills in the 110th Congress that Address(ed) a Cybersecurity-Related Issue

Passed Bills—Public Law

P.L. 110-5 (H.J.Res. 20) Revised Continuing Appropriations Resolution, 2007. Provides $43,075,000 for "cybersecurity" activities for DOE.

P.L. 110-53 (H.R. 1) Implementing Recommendations of the 9/11 Commission Act of 2007. Creates an Under Secretary responsible for overseeing critical infrastructure protection, cybersecurity, and other related programs of the Department.

Also, creates R&D program that can "research technologies that mitigate damages in the event of a cyber attack."

P.L. 110-139 (H.R. 6) Energy Independence and Security Act of 2007. Mandates that the "smart grid" must incorporate "full cybersecurity."

P.L. 110-18 1 (H.R. 4986) National Defense Authorization Act for Fiscal Year 2008. Indicates that the annual report on the military power of the People's Republic of China must include "developments in China's asymmetric capabilities, including efforts to acquire, develop, and deploy cyberwarfare capabilities."

Section 1814 requires the Secretary of Defense to prepare a plan for response to natural disasters and terrorist events—including a "cyber attack" as one of the scenarios that must be included in the plans.

Section 3123 includes cybersecurity threats as part of the "plan for addressing security risks posed to nuclear weapons complex."

P.L. 110-161 (H.R. 2764) Consolidated Appropriations Act, 2008. Includes $143,539,000 in FBI salaries and expenses to "address emerging threats in counterterrorism and cybersecurity."

P.L. 110-329 (H.R. 2638) Consolidated Security, Disaster Assistance, and Continuing Appropriations Act, 2009. Provides the Department of Homeland Security with $806,913,000 for "necessary expenses for infrastructure protection and information security programs and activities" including $3,500,000 for State and local cybersecurity training; and $4,000,000 for the Power and Cyber Systems Protection, Analysis, and Testing Program at the Idaho National Laboratory.

Bills That Did Not Become Law

H.R. 263 Cybersecurity Education Enhancement Act of 2008. Would have directed the Secretary of Homeland Security, acting through the Assistant Secretary of Cybersecurity, to establish a program awarding competitive grants to institutions of higher education for (1) cybersecurity professional development programs, (2) associate degree programs in cybersecurity, and (3) the purchase of equipment to provide training in cybersecurity for professional development and degree programs. (CRS summary)

Final status: Reported by the Committee on Homeland Security.

H.R. 4791 Federal Agency Data Protection Act. In section 4, under the "authority of Director of Office of Management and Budget to establish information security policies and procedures," it would have required agencies comply with a "minimally acceptable system configuration requirements consistent with best practices, including checklists developed under section 8(c) of the Cyber Security Research and Development Act (P.L. 107-305; 116 Stat. 2378) by the Director of the National Institute of Standards and Technology."

Final status: Referred to Senate Committee after being Received from House.

H.R. 5959 Intelligence Authorization Act for Fiscal Year 2009. Bill called for the President to create a "comprehensive national cybersecurity initiative advisory panel" that would be composed of representatives of Congress, the executive branch, and the private sector to report on information security for the federal government, critical infrastructure, among other issues.

Final status: Placed on Calendar in Senate.

H.R. 7007 National Commission on American Cybersecurity Act of 2008. The bill would have established the "American Cybersecurity Commission" to investigate the current threats to the cybersecurity of American business and infrastructure from foreign entities. The commission would have focused on "strategy for American business, national infrastructure, and United States Government non-military and non-national security related computer systems."

Final status: Introduced in House.

Summary List of Statutory Foundations for Cybersecurity Legislation

44 U.S.C. § 3541 Federal Information Security Management Act of 2002

Status of bill: P.L. 107-347 on December 17, 2002.

See under: Title III of the E-Government Act of 2002.

Summary: Contains standards for securing information and information systems within federal agencies, and requires compliance reports be submitted to the Office of Management and Budget (OMB).

18 U.S.C. § 2510 Electronic Communications Privacy Act of 1986

Status of bill: P.L. 99-508 100 Stat. 1848, October 21, 1986.

See under: Titles I and II of the ECPA.

Summary: Title I of the ECPA protects wire, oral, and electronic communications while in transit. It sets down requirements for search warrants that are more stringent than in other settings. Title II of the ECPA, the Stored Communications Act (SCA) protects communication held in electronic storage, most notably messages stored on computers.

18 U.S.C. § 1030 Computer Fraud and Abuse Act of 1984

Status of bill: P.L. 98-473, 98 Stat. 2190 on October 12, 1984.

Summary: Defines criminality of security breaches and unauthorized access to data on federal computer systems and certain financial institutions.

42 USC § 201 The Health Insurance Portability and Accountability Act of 1996 (HIPAA)

Status of bill: P.L. 104-191, 110 Stat. 1936.

See under: 45CFR1 64.501—Privacy rule.

Summary: Protects the privacy of individually identifiable health information in computerized insurance records.

15 U.S.C. § 6801 Financial Services Modernization Act of 1999 (Gramm-Leach-Bliley)

Status of bill: P.L. 106-102, 113 Stat. 1338, enacted November 12, 1999.

See under: Disclosure of Nonpublic Personal Information (Financial Privacy Rule).

Summary: Requires financial institutions to provide consumers with a privacy notice at the time the consumer relationship is established and annually thereafter. The privacy notice must explain the information collected about the consumer, where that information is shared, how that information is used, how that information is protected, and the option to opt-out of sharing with third-party companies.

REFERENCES

[1] For background in cyber vulnerabilities, see archived CRS Report RL33123, *Terrorist Capabilities for Cyberattack*: *Overview and Policy Issues*, by John Rollins and Clay Wilson

[2] White House Office of the Press Secretary, "Remarks by the President on Securing our Nation's Cyber Infrastructure," press release, May 29, 2009, http://www.whitehouse.gov/the_press_office/Remarks-by-the-Presidenton-Securing-Our-Nations-Cyber-Infrastructure/.

[3] Ibid.

[4] Article 12 of the Universal Declaration of Human Rights, accessed at http://www.un.org/en/documents/udhr/.

[5] CSIS Commission on Cybersecurity for the 44th Presidency, Securing Cyberspace for the 44th Presidency, December 2008, http://www.csis.org/tech/cyber/.

[6] The White House, Cyberspace Policy Review, May 29, 2009, http://www.whitehouse.gov/assets/documents/ Cyberspace_Policy_Review_final.pdf.

[7] Department of Homeland Security, Fact Sheet: DHS End-of-Year Accomplishments, December 18, 2008, http://www.dhs.gov/xnews/releases/pr_1229609413187.shtm.
[8] Department of Homeland Security, Department Responsibilities: Maximize Use of Science, Technology and Innovation, http://www.dhs.gov/xabout/gc_12446599 18636.shtm.
[9] Jill R. Aitoro, "National Cyber Security Initiative will have a dozen parts," *NextGov,* August 1, 2008.
[10] For additional information and analysis regarding potential legal considerations of cybersecurity related issues, see CRS Report R40427, Comprehensive National Cybersecurity Initiative: Legal Authorities and Policy Considerations, by John Rollins and Anna C. Henning
[11] Testimony of Cita M. Furlani, Director Information Technology Laboratory, National Institute of Standards and Technology, United States Department of Commerce, Before the House Committee on Homeland Security Subcommittee on Emerging Threats, Cybersecurity, and Science and Technology, United States House of Representatives July 21, 2009.
[12] See CRS Report RL32357, Computer Security: A Summary of Selected Federal Laws, *Executive Orders, and Presidential Directives*, by John D. Moteff.
[13] See CRS Report RS20934, *A Brief Summary of the HIPAA Medical Privacy Rule*, by Gina Stevens.
[14] George W. Bush, The National Strategy to Secure Cyberspace, (Washington, D.C.: The White House, February 2003) http://www.dhs.gov/xlibrary/assets/National_ Cyberspace_Strategy.pdf.
[15] Declan McCullagh, "Bill would give president emergency control of Internet," CNet News, August 28, 2009, pp. http://news.cnet.com/8301-13578_3-10320096-38.html.
[16] White House Office of the Press Secretary, "Remarks by the President on Securing our Nation's Cyber Infrastructure," press release, May 29, 2009, http://www.whitehouse. gov/the_press_office/Remarks-by-the-Presidenton-Securing-Our-Nations-Cyber-Infrastructure/.
[17] David Sessions, "Cybersecurity Bill Gives President Broad Powers Over Internet," PoliticsDaily, August 31, 2009, http://www.politicsdaily.com/2009/08/31/ cybersecurity-bill-gives-president-broad-powers-over-internet/.
[18] Gautham Nagesh, "Lawmakers join forces on cybersecurity legislation," September 14, 2009, p. http://www.nextgov.com/nextgov/ng_20090914_5789.php?oref=topstory.

In: New Developments in Computer Research
Editor: Nikos E. Mastorakis
ISBN: 978-1-61470-321-1

HIGH-PERFORMANCE REVERSIBLE AND QUANTUM SYSTOLIC PARALLEL PROCESSING, PART I: TWO-VALUED IMPLEMENTATIONS

Anas N. Al-Rabadi*

Department of Computer Engineering, The University of Jordan, Jordan
Office of Graduate Studies and Research (OGSR), Portland State University, US

ABSTRACT

New type of systolic arrays called reversible systolic arrays is introduced. The two-valued quantum systolic architectures' realizations and computations of the new systolic arrays are also introduced. It is shown that the new systolic arrays maintain the high level of regularity while exhibiting the new fundamental bijectivity (i.e., reversibility) and quantum superposition properties. A systolic array is an example of a single-instruction multiple-data (SIMD) machine in which each processing element (PE) performs a single simple operation. Systolic devices provide inexpensive but massive computation power, and are cost-effective, high-performance, and special-purpose systems that have wide range of applications such as in solving several regular and compute-bound problems containing repetitive multiple operations on large arrays of data. Since basic PEs used in the construction of arithmetic systolic arrays are the add-multiply cells, the results introduced in this paper are general and apply to a very wide range of add-multiply-based systolic arrays. Since the reduction of power consumption is a major requirement for the circuit design in future technologies, the new reversible systolic circuits can play an important task in the design of future circuits that consume minimal power and in multi-dimensional quantum signal processing (QSP) applications.

1. INTRODUCTION

Due to the anticipated failure of Moore's law around the year 2020, quantum computing will hopefully play an increasingly crucial role in building more compact and less power consuming computers [1,3,12]. Due to this fact, and because all quantum computer gates should be reversible [1,12], reversible computing will have an increasingly more existence in the future design of regular, compact, and universal circuits. As was proven in [11], it is a necessary (but not sufficient) condition for not dissipating power in any physical circuit that

* Email: alrabadi@yahoo.com

all system circuits must be built using fully reversible logical components. For this reason, different technologies have been studied to implement reversible logic in hardware like adiabatic CMOS [15], optical [13], and quantum [12].

In circuit design, simple and regular interconnections lead to cheap implementations and high densities, and higher density implies both higher performance and lower overhead for support components [8], where it has been shown that multi-dimensional (MD) pipelining plus multi-processing at each stage of a pipeline can lead to the best possible computing performance [8,9]. Systolic systems provide inexpensive and massive computation power, and provide a model of computation which captures the concepts of pipelining, parallelism, and interconnection structures which has been implemented in wide range of applications [6,7,8,9,10,16], and provide a model of computation for studying parallel algorithms for VLSI that takes into account the issues of I/O, control, and inter-processor communication. In a systolic system, MD pipelining can overlap I/O with computation to ensure high throughput with no extra control logic is required [8,9]. In systolic circuits, communication paths inherently require more space and energy than processing elements (PEs) do, and communication among processors is performed through fixed data paths, where these paths have simple and regular geometries. It has been shown that data flow patterns in systolic systems are fundamental in matrix computations [9]: e.g., the two-way flow on the linearly connected network is common to both matrix-vector multiplication and the solution of triangular linear systems, and the three-way flow on the hexagonally mesh-connected network is common to both matrix multiplication and the LU-decomposition.

The main contribution of this paper is the new design method to implement 2-valued logic functions bijectively through the realization of 2-valued reversible functional expansions using reversible systolic arrays and the corresponding quantum systolic arrays as illustrated in Figure 1. The new reversible logic synthesis method possesses high-level of regularity in addition to the preservation of the reversibility property. In addition to the reversibility (bijectivity) property, the extension of the new reversible systolic arrays to the quantum domain will result in the emergence of the quantum superposition property which is responsible for the exponential speedups of the computational processes in the quantum domain [12]. One of the advantages for the use of new families of quantum systolic circuits is their potential utilization in low-power circuit designs for digital signal processing applications in analogy to the role of classical systolic circuits in non-adiabatic VLSI circuits, where also the use of quantum circuit technology speeds up the computational process due to the existence of the quantum computational parallelism.

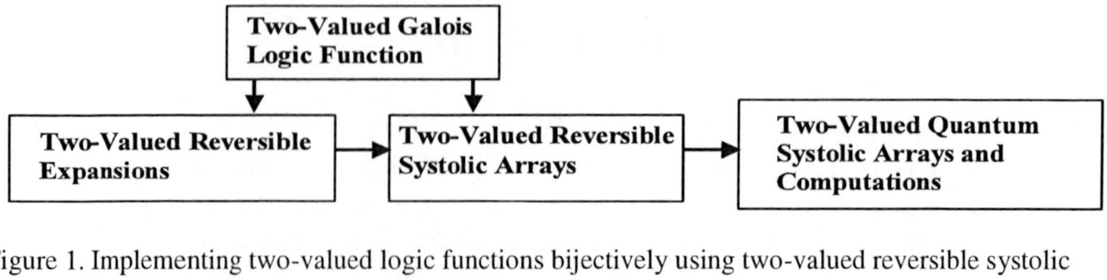

Figure 1. Implementing two-valued logic functions bijectively using two-valued reversible systolic arrays and their corresponding two-valued quantum systolic arrays.

Basic background on systolic arrays is given in Section 2. Reversible logic is presented in Section 3. The new two-valued reversible systolic arrays are introduced in Section 4.

Quantum realizations and computations of the new two-valued reversible systolic architectures are introduced in Section 5. Conclusions and future work are presented in Section 6.

2. Systolic Arrays

Systolic arrays are examples of single-instruction multiple-data (SIMD) machines consisting of a set of interconnected processing elements (PEs) in which a PE is only capable of performing a single simple operation [9]. In a systolic computing system, data flows from the host through the array in a rhythmic fashion and computations are synchronized by a global clock signal where data items are pumped out from a memory [8,9]. In systolic arrays, the function of the processor is analogous to that of the heart; every processor (i.e., processing element (PE)) regularly pumps data in and out, each time it is performing a short computation, so that regular data flow is kept up in the network [8,9].

The power behind the systolic arrays comes from the way in which the data flows between the processing elements. Typically a systolic array is capable of performing a single operation such as matrix multiplication or inversion. They are thus special purpose machines used to solve many regular problems containing repetitive operations on large arrays of data and are used mainly in dedicated equipment and not in general purpose computers.

Properly designed parallel structures that need to communicate *only* with their nearest neighbors will gain the most from very-large-scale-integration (VLSI) technologies, because valuable time is usually lost when modules that are far apart must communicate. Because simple, regular communication and control structures have substantial advantages over complicated ones in design and implementation, cells in a systolic system are typically interconnected to form a systolic array or a systolic tree. Information in a systolic system flows between cells in a pipelined fashion, and communication with the outside world occurs only at the "boundary" cells; only those cells on the array boundaries may be I/O ports for the system. The basic function of a systolic array is achieved by replacing a single PE with an array of PEs, and a higher computation throughput can be achieved without increasing the memory bandwidth [9]. As mentioned previously, the function of the memory is analogous to that of the heart; it pulses data from memory through the array of PEs. The central point of this approach is to ensure that once a data item is brought out from the memory it can be used effectively at each cell it passes, and this is possible in a wide class of compute-bound computations where multiple operations are performed on each data item in a repetitive manner. The gain in processing speed in MOPS (millions of operations per second) can be justified with the fact that the number of pipeline stages has been increased n-times (equals n-PEs). Other advantages of systolic arrays include modular expansionability, simple and regular data and control flows, use of simple and uniform cells, elimination of global broadcasting, limited fan-in, and fast response time. The I/O remains the bottleneck in systolic systems where the major problem with a systolic array is in its I/O barrier, and the globally structured systolic array can speedup the computations only if the I/O bandwidth is high [8,9].

Linearly connected, orthogonally connected, and hexagonally connected PEs are examples of mesh-connected systolic arrays [8]. Various systolic configurations have been shown along with their potential usage in performing computations [8,9]: 1D linear arrays are suitable for convolution, FIR filtering and discrete Fourier transform (DFT); 2D square arrays are suitable for dynamic programming and graph algorithms; 2D hexagonal arrays are suitable for matrix arithmetic and DFT; Trees are suitable for search algorithms; and triangular arrays are suitable for inversion of triangular matrix and formal language recognition.

2a. Band Matrix – Band Matrix Multiplication Systolic Array

Band matrices are important since several scientific and engineering computations involve such matrices, and since a dense matrix can be viewed as a band matrix having the maximum-possible bandwidth. Each pulsation of a systolic array consists of the following operations [9]: (1) *shift* and (2) *multiply* and *add*. Basic processing cells that are used in the construction of systolic arithmetic arrays are the add-multiply cells. This kind of cells has three inputs $\{a, b, c\}$ and three outputs $\{a = a, b = b, d = c + a * b\}$. One can assume *six interface registers* are attached at the I/O ports of a processing cell. All registers are clocked for synchronous transfer of data among adjacent cells. The add-multiply operation is needed in performing the inner product of two vectors, matrix-matrix multiplication, matrix inversion, and LU decomposition of a dense matrix. Hexagonally connected processors (i.e., processing elements (PEs)) can optimally perform matrix multiplication [9]. In a hexagonal systolic array, three data streams flow through the array in a pipelined fashion. One can follow the operation of the 2D hexagonal systolic array by studying the data flow by moving transparencies of the band matrices over the network (cf. Figure 2). The multiplication of two band matrices [***A***] and [***B***], [***A***] · [***B***] = [***C***], and the associated definition of bandwidth is shown as follows [9]:

$$\begin{bmatrix} a_{11} & a_{12} & 0 & 0 & 0 \\ a_{21} & a_{22} & a_{23} & 0 & 0 \\ a_{31} & a_{32} & a_{33} & a_{34} & 0 \\ 0 & a_{42} & a_{43} & a_{44} & a_{45} \\ 0 & 0 & a_{53} & a_{54} & a_{55} \end{bmatrix} \cdot \begin{bmatrix} b_{11} & b_{12} & b_{13} & 0 & 0 \\ b_{21} & b_{22} & b_{23} & b_{24} & 0 \\ 0 & b_{32} & b_{33} & b_{34} & b_{35} \\ 0 & 0 & b_{43} & b_{44} & b_{45} \\ 0 & 0 & 0 & b_{54} & b_{55} \end{bmatrix} = \begin{bmatrix} c_{11} & c_{12} & c_{13} & c_{14} & 0 \\ c_{21} & c_{22} & c_{23} & c_{24} & c_{25} \\ c_{31} & c_{32} & c_{33} & c_{34} & c_{35} \\ c_{41} & c_{42} & c_{43} & c_{44} & c_{45} \\ 0 & c_{52} & c_{53} & c_{54} & c_{55} \end{bmatrix}$$

Band_1 Band_2 Band_3

where bandwidth$_1$: $w_1 = 3 + 2 - 1 = 4$, bandwidth$_2$: $w_2 = 2 + 3 - 1 = 4$, and bandwidth$_3$: $w_3 = w_1 + w_2 - 1 = 4 + 4 - 1 = 7$. Figure 2 shows the two-dimensional (2D) hexagonal systolic array [9] that implements the operation of multiplying two band matrices [***A***] and [***B***].

Each data level in the three data flow streams in Figure 2 is called a *wave front*, the initial values of the input [***C***] array elements (from the lower side in Figure 2) are all zeros, and the final (resulting) values of the output [***C***] array elements (from the upper side in Figure 2) are obtained as follows:

$c_{11} = a_{11}b_{11} + a_{12}b_{21}$, $c_{21} = a_{21}b_{11} + a_{22}b_{21}$, $c_{31} = a_{31}b_{11} + a_{32}b_{21}$, $c_{41} = a_{42}b_{21}$, $c_{51} = 0$, $c_{12} = a_{11}b_{12} + a_{12}b_{22}$, $c_{22} = a_{21}b_{12} + a_{22}b_{22} + a_{23}b_{32}$, $c_{32} = a_{31}b_{12} + a_{32}b_{22} + a_{33}b_{32}$, $c_{42} = a_{42}b_{22} + a_{43}b_{32}$, $c_{52} = a_{53}b_{32}$, $c_{13} = a_{11}b_{13} + a_{12}b_{23}$, $c_{23} = a_{21}b_{13} + a_{22}b_{23} + a_{23}b_{33}$, $c_{33} = a_{31}b_{13} + a_{32}b_{23} + a_{33}b_{33} + a_{34}b_{43}$, $c_{43} = a_{42}b_{23} + a_{43}b_{33} + a_{44}b_{43}$, $c_{53} = a_{53}b_{33} + a_{54}b_{43}$, $c_{14} = a_{12}b_{24}$, $c_{24} = a_{22}b_{24} + a_{23}b_{34}$, $c_{34} = a_{32}b_{24} + a_{33}b_{34} + a_{34}b_{44}$, $c_{44} = a_{42}b_{24} + a_{43}b_{34} + a_{44}b_{44} + a_{45}b_{54}$, $c_{54} = a_{53}b_{34} + a_{54}b_{44} + a_{55}b_{54}$, $c_{15} = 0$, $c_{25} = a_{23}b_{35}$, $c_{35} = a_{33}b_{35} + a_{34}b_{45}$, $c_{45} = a_{43}b_{35} + a_{44}b_{45} + a_{45}b_{55}$, $c_{55} = a_{53}b_{35} + a_{54}b_{45} + a_{55}b_{55}$.

The topological distribution of the processing elements (PEs) in the systolic structure, shown in Figure 2, is obtained as follows: # PEs in top-left = $w_1 = 4$, # PEs in top-right = $w_2 = 4$, # PEs in bottom = $w_3 = 7$, and the total # PEs = $4 \cdot 4 = 16$.

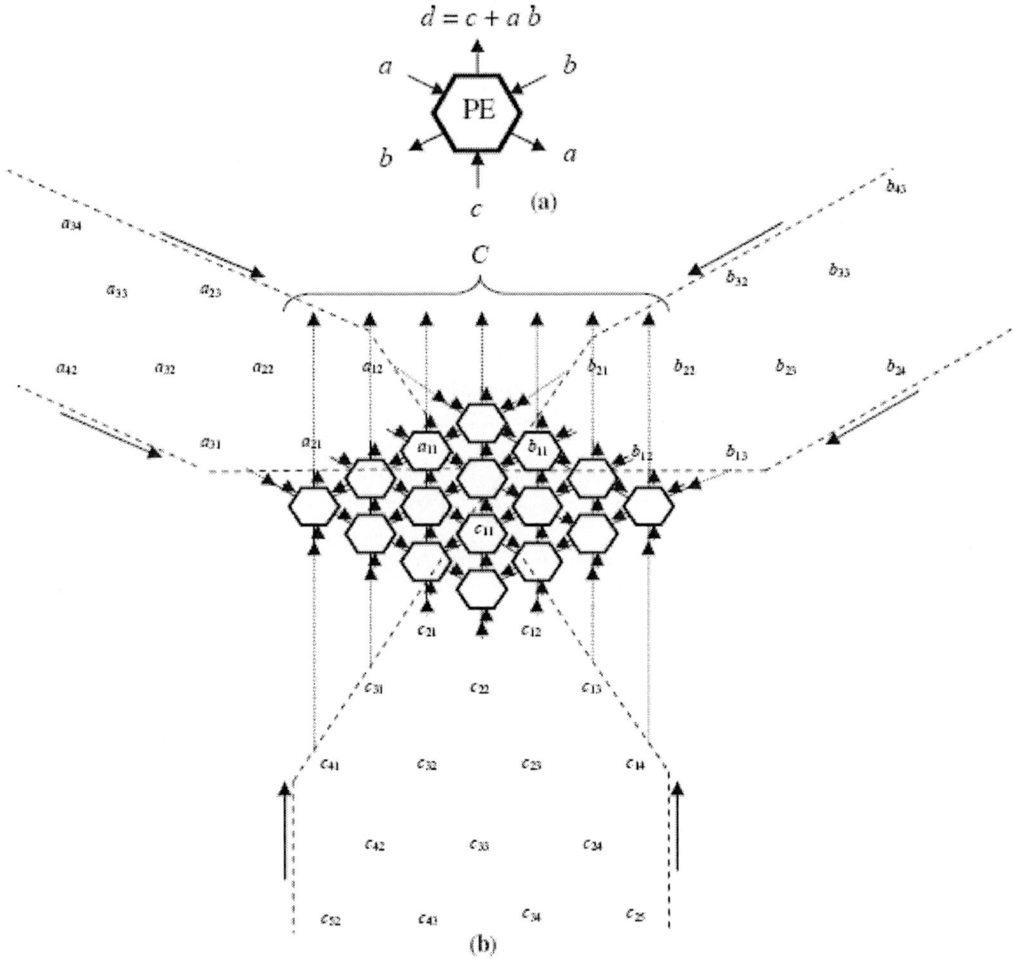

Figure 2. Two-dimensional (2D) hexagonal systolic array: (a) Kung cell, and (b) Kung systolic array.

2b. Toeplitz Matrix – Vector Multiplication (Linear Convolution) Systolic Array

The convolution problem can be viewed as a matrix-vector multiplication where the matrix is a triangular Toeplitz matrix. As an example of the linear convolution, let $u(n)$ and $w(n)$ be causal sequences and each is of finite length N, then the linear convolution of $u(n)$ and $w(n)$ is a causal sequence computed as:

$$y(n) = u(n) * w(n) = \sum_{k=0}^{N-1} u(k)w(n-k), \quad n = 0,1,2,\ldots,(2N-2).$$

The linear convolution of two vectors { $\vec{a} = \{a_0, a_1, a_2, a_3, a_4\}, \vec{x} = \{x_0, x_1, x_2, x_3, x_4\}$ } can be represented in a matrix form called Toeplitz matrix as $\begin{bmatrix} a_0 & 0 & 0 & 0 & 0 \\ a_1 & a_0 & 0 & 0 & 0 \\ a_2 & a_1 & a_0 & 0 & 0 \\ a_3 & a_2 & a_1 & a_0 & 0 \\ a_4 & a_3 & a_2 & a_1 & a_0 \end{bmatrix} \begin{bmatrix} x_0 \\ x_1 \\ x_2 \\ x_3 \\ x_4 \end{bmatrix} = \begin{bmatrix} b_0 \\ b_1 \\ b_2 \\ b_3 \\ b_4 \end{bmatrix}$. As can be seen, a Toeplitz matrix [**T**] is a matrix that has constant elements along the main diagonal and the sub-diagonals. Such matrices describe the input-output transformations of one-dimensional linear shift invariant (LSI) systems and correlation matrices of stationary sequences.

Example 1. Let $u(n) = \{u_0, u_1, u_2, u_3\}$, $w(n) = \{w_0, w_1, w_2, w_3\}$, $\therefore N = 4 \Rightarrow n = 0, 1, 2, 3, 4, 5, 2 \cdot 4 - 2 = 6$, then the linear convolution of $u(n)$ and $w(n)$ is as follows:

$$y(0) = \sum_{k=0}^{3} u(k)w(0-k) = u(0)w(0), \quad y(1) = \sum_{k=0}^{3} u(k)w(1-k) = u(0)w(1) + u(1)w(0), \quad y(2) = \sum_{k=0}^{3} u(k)w(2-k) = u(0)w(2) + u(1)w(1) + u(2)w(0),$$

$$y(3) = \sum_{k=0}^{3} u(k)w(3-k) = u(0)w(3) + u(1)w(2) + u(2)w(1) + u(3)w(0), \quad y(4) = \sum_{k=0}^{3} u(k)w(4-k) = u(1)w(3) + u(2)w(2) + u(3)w(1),$$

$$y(5) = \sum_{k=0}^{3} u(k)w(5-k) = u(2)w(3) + u(3)w(2), \quad y(6) = \sum_{k=0}^{3} u(k)w(6-k) = u(3)w(3).$$

Figure 3 illustrates the linear convolution implementation using 1D linear systolic array [8,9] where:

$$a = u_0 w_1, \ b = u_0 w_2, \ c = u_0 w_3, \ d = u_1 w_1 + u_0 w_2, \ e = u_1 w_2 + u_0 w_3, \ f = u_1 w_3, \ g = u_2 w_1 + u_1 w_2 + u_0 w_3,$$
$$h = u_2 w_2 + u_1 w_3, \ i = u_2 w_3, \ j = u_3 w_1 + u_2 w_2 + u_1 w_3, \ k = u_3 w_2 + u_2 w_3, \ l = u_3 w_3, \ m = u_3 w_2 + u_2 w_3,$$
$$n = u_3 w_3, \ p = u_3 w_3.$$

2c. Matrix - Vector Multiplication (Inner Product) Systolic Array

Matrix-vector multiplication is fundamental in linear algebraic transformations that model the operation of numerous natural and engineering systems. This type of multiplication can be viewed as the inner product between each matrix row and the transformed vector as follows:

$$\begin{bmatrix} A_{11} & A_{12} & A_{13} & A_{14} \\ A_{21} & A_{22} & A_{23} & A_{24} \\ A_{31} & A_{32} & A_{33} & A_{34} \\ A_{41} & A_{42} & A_{43} & A_{44} \end{bmatrix} \begin{bmatrix} B_1 \\ B_2 \\ B_3 \\ B_4 \end{bmatrix} = \begin{bmatrix} A_{11}B_1 + A_{12}B_2 + A_{13}B_3 + A_{14}B_4 \\ A_{21}B_1 + A_{22}B_2 + A_{23}B_3 + A_{24}B_4 \\ A_{31}B_1 + A_{32}B_2 + A_{33}B_3 + A_{34}B_4 \\ A_{41}B_1 + A_{42}B_2 + A_{43}B_3 + A_{44}B_4 \end{bmatrix}$$

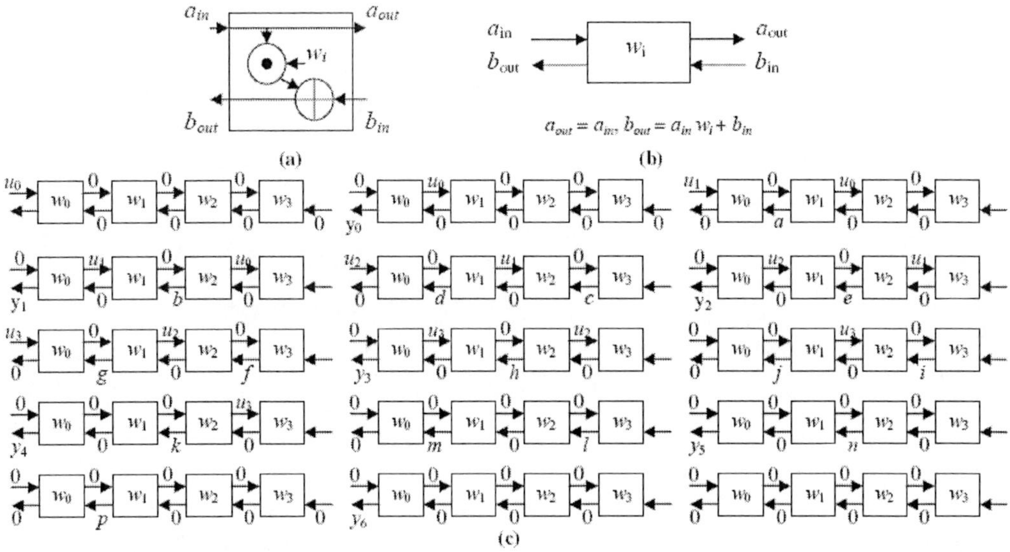

Figure 3. One-dimensional (1D) linear systolic array for linear convolution application: (a) cell, (b) cell schematic, and (c) left-to-right and top-to-down snapshots of the operation (function) of the systolic array.

Figure 4 shows the matrix-vector implementation using the illustrated 1D systolic array [8,9] where:

$$a = A_{11}B_1,\ b = A_{21}B_1,\ c = A_{11}B_1 + A_{12}B_2,\ d = A_{31}B_1,\ e = A_{21}B_1 + A_{22}B_2,\ f = A_{11}B_1 + A_{12}B_2 + A_{13}B_3,$$
$$g = A_{41}B_1,\ h = A_{31}B_1 + A_{32}B_2,\ i = A_{21}B_1 + A_{22}B_2 + A_{23}B_3,\ j = A_{11}B_1 + A_{12}B_2 + A_{13}B_3 + A_{14}B_4,$$
$$k = A_{41}B_1 + A_{42}B_2,\ l = A_{31}B_1 + A_{32}B_2 + A_{33}B_3,\ m = A_{21}B_1 + A_{22}B_2 + A_{23}B_3 + A_{24}B_4,$$
$$n = A_{41}B_1 + A_{42}B_2 + A_{43}B_3,\ o = A_{31}B_1 + A_{32}B_2 + A_{33}B_3 + A_{34}B_4,\ p = A_{41}B_1 + A_{42}B_2 + A_{43}B_3 + A_{44}B_4.$$

2d. Sorting Systolic Array

Sorting is a fundamental operation that is used in several engineering applications such as in logic synthesis. Figure 5 shows an example of a systolic sorter that is used to sort the inputs in a descending form [8].

3. Bijectivity: Reversible Logic

A (k, k) reversible circuit is a circuit that has the same number of inputs k and outputs k and is a one-to-one mapping between the vectors of inputs and the vectors of outputs, thus the vector of input states can be always uniquely reconstructed from the vector of output states [1,4,5,12]. Thus, a (k, k) reversible map is a bijective function which is both (1) injective ("one-to-one" or "(1:1)") and (2) surjective ("onto"). The auxiliary outputs and inputs that are needed only for the purpose of reversibility are called "garbage" outputs and "garbage" inputs, respectively. These are auxiliary outputs and inputs from which a reversible map is constructed.

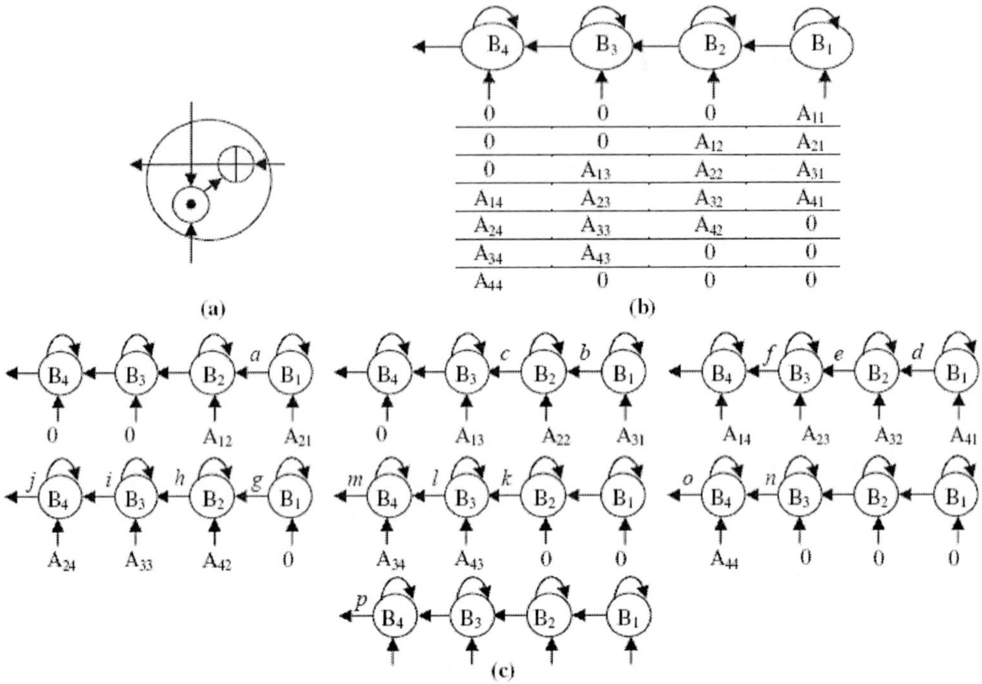

Figure 4. One-dimensional (1D) systolic array with application to the inner product: (a) cell, (b) architecture, and (c) left-to-right and top-to-down snapshots of the operation (function) of the systolic array.

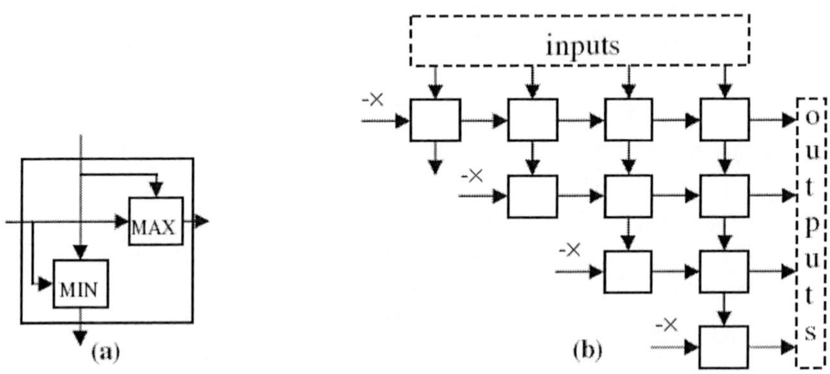

Figure 5. Two-dimensional (2D) systolic array with sorting application: (a) cell and (b) systolic architecture.

A (k, k) conservative circuit has the same number of inputs k and outputs k and has the same number of values in inputs and outputs, such as the same number of ones in inputs and outputs for binary, and the same number of ones and twos in inputs and outputs for ternary [5]. Figures 6 and 7 show important reversible gates [1,12]. These gates will be used in later sections in the reversible (bijective) implementations of the previously introduced systolic circuits in Sections 2a – 2d, and furthermore the reversible gates in Figure 6 will be used in the quantum realization and computation of the systolic systems presented in Sections 2a – 2c.

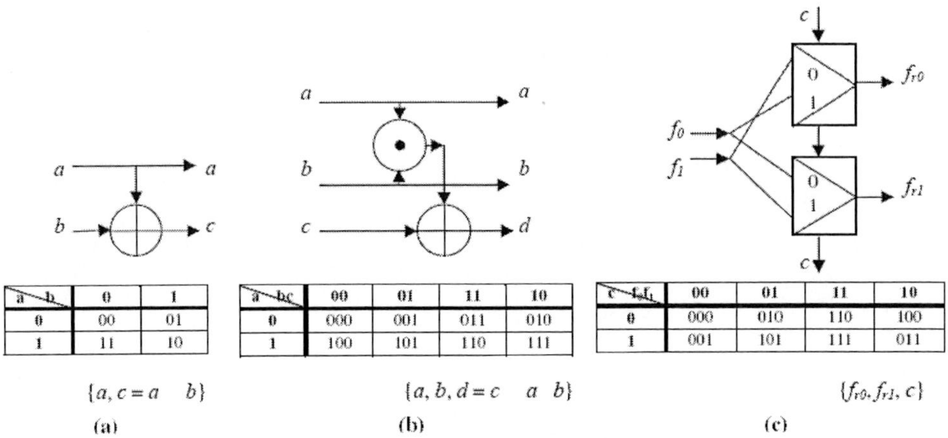

Figure 6. Fundamental binary (two-valued) reversible gates and their associated multi-input multi-output (MIMO) K-map representations: (a) (2, 2) Feynman gate, (b) (3, 3) Toffoli gate, and (c) (3, 3) Fredkin gate.

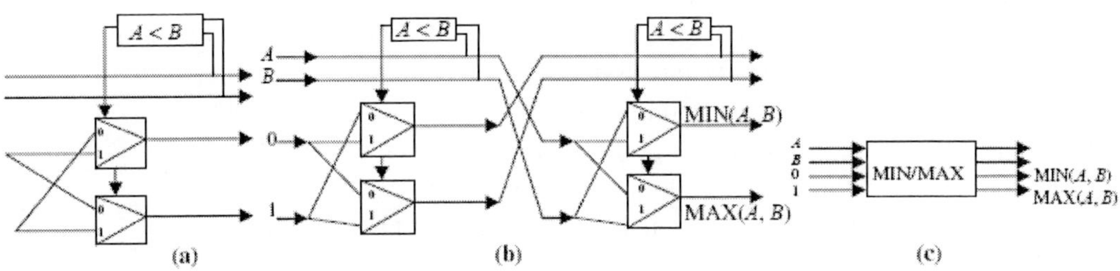

Figure 7. Reversible Picton gate and its Min/Max circuit: (a) (4, 4) reversible Picton gate, (b) (4, 4) Min/Max implementation using the Picton gate from (a), and (c) schematic block diagram for the (4, 4) reversible Min/Max circuit.

The important second radix of Galois field (GF(2)) operations of addition and multiplication are defined as shown in Table 1 [1].

Table 1. Second radix Galois field addition and multiplication

+	**0**	**1**	*****	**0**	**1**
0	0	1	**0**	0	0
1	1	0	**1**	0	1

Because Galois field (GF) proved to possess desired properties in many applications such as in testing [14], the developments of the new systolic logic circuits, in this work, will be conducted on the corresponding Galois field (GF) algebraic structures.

It has been shown in [1] that, in the binary XOR (i.e., GF(2)) logic, there are only two reversible Shannon gates as follows:

$$\vec{f} = \begin{bmatrix} \bar{e} & e \\ e & \bar{e} \end{bmatrix} \begin{bmatrix} 1 & 0 \\ 0 & 1 \end{bmatrix} \begin{bmatrix} f_0 \\ f_1 \end{bmatrix} = \begin{bmatrix} f_{r0} \\ f_{r1} \end{bmatrix}, \quad (1)$$

$$\vec{f} = \begin{bmatrix} e & \bar{e} \\ \bar{e} & e \end{bmatrix} \begin{bmatrix} 1 & 0 \\ 0 & 1 \end{bmatrix} \begin{bmatrix} f_0 \\ f_1 \end{bmatrix} = \begin{bmatrix} f_{r0} \\ f_{r1} \end{bmatrix}, \quad (2)$$

where $\bar{e}$ is the one's complement (inversion; Not) of variable e, f_0 is the cofactor of f for e = 0, and f_1 is the cofactor of f for e = 1.

4. Reversible Systolic Arrays

This section introduces new results for the synthesis of 2-valued Galois functions using reversible systolic arrays. The new synthesis method utilizes the following two methods: (1) reusing the classical add-multiply PE cells by showing their 2-valued Galois logic reversibility and thereafter reusing the whole systolic structure since the connection of reversible PEs will produce by necessity a reversible systolic circuit (cf. Figure 8), because the interconnection of reversible gates will necessarily produce a reversible circuit [1,12], and (2) direct mapping of classical irreversible systolic circuits into reversible systolic circuits by interconnecting the reversible counterpart of the irreversible PEs (cells) (cf. Figure 10). Moreover, the implementation of the 2-valued logic functions using the new reversible systolic arrays can be performed through two methods: (a) direct implementation by the substitution of the array's values using the corresponding binary functional literals, and (b) implementation using the corresponding 2-valued matrix-based elements that are obtained through the 2-valued reversible Shannon and Davio functional expansions.

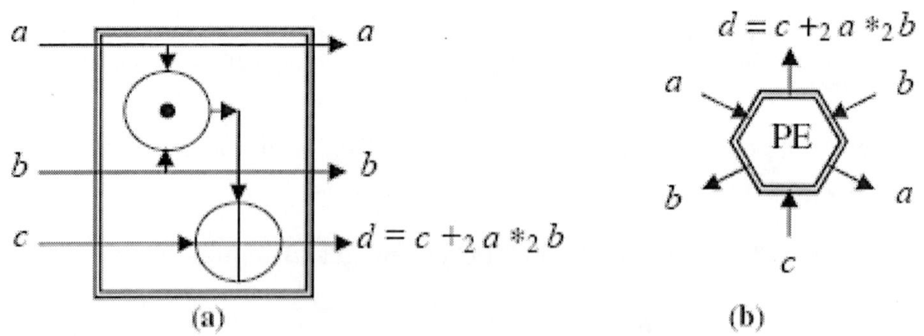

Figure 8. Reversible GF(2) Kung systolic array: (a) reversible (3, 3) Toffoli gate, and (b) reversible (3, 3) Kung cell.

Basic PEs which are used in the construction of arithmetic systolic arrays are the add-multiply cells. Figure 8a introduces the binary (two-valued) (3, 3) reversible Toffoli gate (cf. Figure 6b) that implements reversibly in GF(2) the Kung add-multiply cell as shown in Figure 8b. Since the interconnection of reversible PEs will produce by necessity a reversible systolic circuit, the hexagonal interconnects of reversible PEs such as the PE in Figure 8b will produce 2D hexagonal reversible Kung systolic array over GF(2).

For example, the 2D hexagonal systolic implementation using the corresponding GF(2) matrix-based elements that can be obtained through the GF(2) reversible Shannon functional expansions from Equation (1) is obtained as:

$$\begin{bmatrix} 0 & 0 & 0 & 0 & 0 \\ 0 & {}^{0}e & {}^{1}e & 0 & 0 \\ 0 & {}^{1}e & {}^{0}e & 0 & 0 \\ 0 & 0 & 0 & 0 & 0 \\ 0 & 0 & 0 & 0 & 0 \end{bmatrix} \cdot \begin{bmatrix} 0 & 0 & 0 & 0 & 0 \\ 0 & f_0 & 0 & 0 & 0 \\ 0 & f_1 & 0 & 0 & 0 \\ 0 & 0 & 0 & 0 & 0 \\ 0 & 0 & 0 & 0 & 0 \end{bmatrix} = \begin{bmatrix} 0 & 0 & 0 & 0 & 0 \\ 0 & {}^{0}ef_0 + {}^{1}ef_1 & 0 & 0 & 0 \\ 0 & {}^{1}ef_0 + {}^{0}ef_1 & 0 & 0 & 0 \\ 0 & 0 & 0 & 0 & 0 \\ 0 & 0 & 0 & 0 & 0 \end{bmatrix} \tag{3}$$

where: $a_{22}={}^{0}e, a_{23}={}^{1}e, a_{32}={}^{1}e, a_{33}={}^{0}e, b_{22}=f_0, b_{32}=f_1, c_{22}={}^{0}ef_0+{}^{1}ef_1, c_{32}={}^{1}ef_0+{}^{0}ef_1$.

The realization of a many-variable function using the method shown in Equation (3) follows the matrix-based expansion using the Kronecker (tensor) product [1] and the use of interconnection of Toffoli PEs (TPEs) over GF(2).

As technology mapping is important in several digital design applications, the following algorithm, which is called the Reversible Gate Mapping (RGM) algorithm, shows an XOR-based (also XNOR-based) method to map between various reversible gates over GF(2).

Algorithm RGM

1. $Map_2 = Map_1 \oplus Map_{correction}$, $Map_1 = Map_2 \oplus Map_{correction}$.
2. Using Logic Optimization technique, obtain Sum-Of-Products (SOP), or Product-Of-Sums (POS), optimized forms of the functions.
3. Synthesize the solution using the Boolean difference (XOR) between the corresponding maps.

The RGM algorithm can be used to replace reversible gates with other kind of reversible gates that are more suitable for synthesis, manufacturing, or for different types of applications. As will be shown in Section 5, that the reversible Controlled-Not-based and Controlled-Swap-based gates are essential in the quantum circuit synthesis [1,12], Figure 9 illustrates an example of the implementation of the RGM algorithm for the mapping and inverse mapping between (3, 3) Toffoli and (3, 3) Fredkin reversible gates and the resulting circuits for such mapping.

Multiple-level (N-level) reversible circuits are also possible by the iterative use (i.e., looping) of the RGM algorithm on the correction part (i.e., serial-mode RGM) or on both the correction part and the error part (which is the first part) at the same time (i.e., parallel-mode RGM). Also, the iterative use of the RGM method using a hybrid of both XOR ($\oplus$) (Boolean difference) and XNOR ($\otimes$) (Boolean equivalence) operations to decompose Boolean functions can be accomplished [2].

Although the TPE-based results are presented for the case of the 2D hexagonal systolic array, and since the add-multiply cell is the basic PE in these circuits and the TPE cell is the reversible GF counterpart of this fundamental add-multiply PE, the systolic arrays shown in Sections 2b – 2c (cf. Figures 3 – 4) can be constructed reversibly using the interconnection between TPEs as well.

Another method of producing reversible systolic circuits is by mapping the classical irreversible systolic circuits into reversible systolic circuits by interconnecting the reversible counterpart of the irreversible PEs. As an example, Figure 10 introduces the reversible Min/Max implementation for the sorting operation using the reversible counterpart of the Min/Max gate from Figure 5.

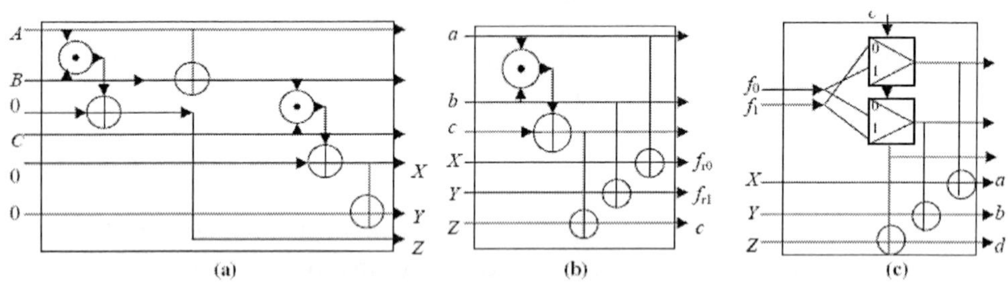

Figure 9. Mapping between reversible gates using the RGM algorithm: (a) generated mapping circuit, (b) one Toffoli gate plus three Feynman gates that when combined with (a) the result will produce one Fredkin gate, and (c) one Fredkin gate and three Feynman gates that when combined with (a) the result will produce one Toffoli gate.

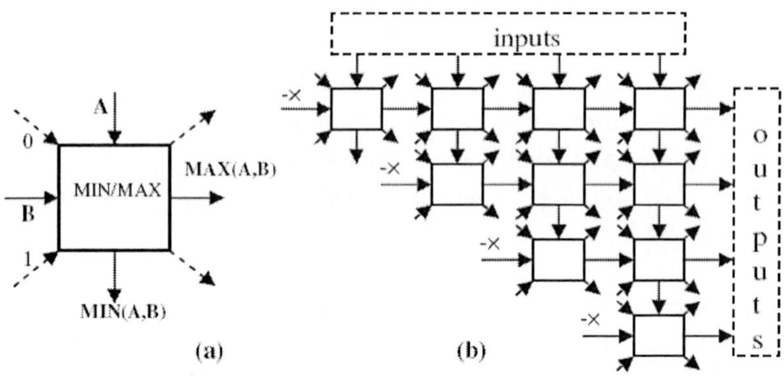

Figure 10. Reversible implementation of the Min/Max systolic array: (a) (4, 4) reversible Min/Max cell from Figure 7c, and (b) the reversible systolic Min/Max array.

5. Systolic Quantum Realizations and Computations

Quantum computing (QC) is a method of computation that uses a dynamic process governed by the Schrödinger Equation (SE) [1,12]. In the QC context, the time-independent SE (TISE) is normally used, where the solution $|\psi\rangle$ is an expansion over orthogonal basis states $|\phi_i\rangle$ defined in a linear complex vector space called Hilbert space **H** as follows $|\psi\rangle = \sum_i c_i |\phi_i\rangle$, where the coefficients c_i are called probability amplitudes, and $|c_i|^2$ is the probability that the quantum state $|\psi\rangle$ will collapse into the (eigen) state $|\phi_i\rangle$.

The probability is equal to the inner product $|\langle\phi_i \mid \psi\rangle|^2$, with the unitary condition $\sum|c_i|^2 = 1$. In QC, a linear and unitary operator $\mathfrak{I}$ is used to transform an input vector of quantum bits (qubits) into an output vector of qubits. In two-valued QC, a qubit is a vector defined as:

$$\text{qubit}_0 \equiv |0\rangle = \begin{bmatrix} 1 \\ 0 \end{bmatrix}, \text{qubit}_1 \equiv |1\rangle = \begin{bmatrix} 0 \\ 1 \end{bmatrix}. \tag{4}$$

A two-valued quantum state $|\psi\rangle$ is a superposition of quantum basis states $|\phi_i\rangle$. Thus, for the orthonormal computational basis states $\{|0\rangle,|1\rangle\}$, one has the following quantum state:

$$|\psi\rangle = \alpha|0\rangle + \beta|1\rangle, \tag{5}$$

where $\alpha\alpha^* = |\alpha|^2 = p_0 \equiv$ the probability of having state $|\psi\rangle$ in state $|0\rangle$, $\beta\beta^* = |\beta|^2 = p_1 \equiv$ the probability of having state $|\psi\rangle$ in state $|1\rangle$, and $|\alpha|^2 + |\beta|^2 = 1$. The calculation in QC for multiple systems (e.g., the equivalent of a register) follows the tensor product ($\otimes$). For example, given two states $|\psi_1\rangle$ and $|\psi_2\rangle$, one has the following:

$$|\psi_1\psi_2\rangle = |\psi_1\rangle \otimes |\psi_2\rangle = (\alpha_1|0\rangle + \beta_1|1\rangle) \otimes (\alpha_2|0\rangle + \beta_2|1\rangle) = \alpha_1\alpha_2|00\rangle + \alpha_1\beta_2|01\rangle + \beta_1\alpha_2|10\rangle + \beta_1\beta_2|11\rangle. \tag{6}$$

Figure 11 shows the fundamental binary quantum primitives of the Feynman (CN) gate, the Toffoli gate, and the Fredkin gate.

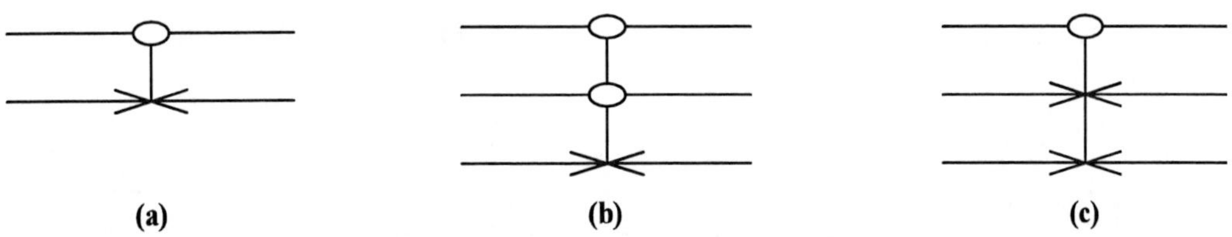

Figure 11. Binary quantum gates: (a) (2,2) Feynman (CN), (b) (3,3) Toffoli, and (c) (3,3) Fredkin.

Similarly to the reversibility introduced in the previous section, and since basic PEs used in the construction of arithmetic systolic arrays are the add-multiply cells, Figure 12a introduces the binary (3, 3) quantum Toffoli gate that implements in the Galois quantum domain the Kung add-multiply cell in Figure 12b, and Figure 12c implements the 2D quantum Kung systolic array over GF(2) by interconnecting the corresponding GF(2) quantum Toffoli gates.

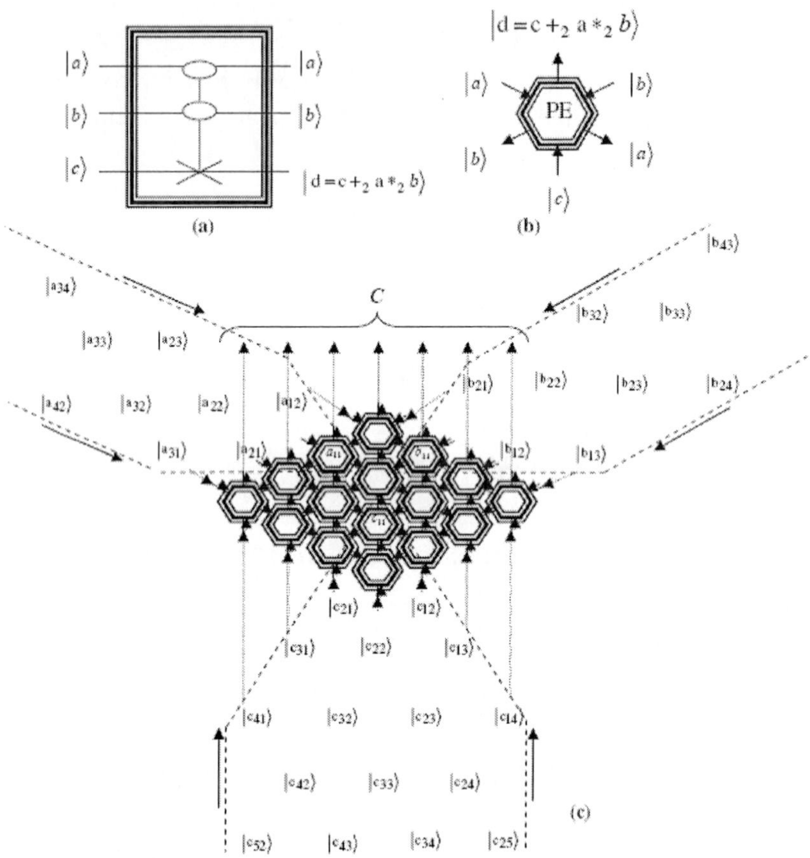

Figure 12. Quantum GF(2) Kung systolic array: (a) quantum (3, 3) Toffoli gate, (b) quantum (3, 3) Kung cell, and (c) quantum Kung systolic array.

Figure 13 shows the quantum realization for the reversible circuits in Figures 9a – 9c, respectively.

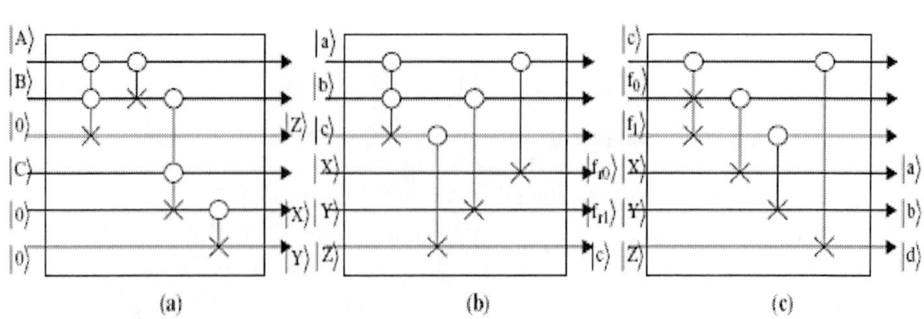

Figure 13. Quantum realization for the reversible circuits in Figures 9a – 9c, respectively.

Example 2. The evolution of quantum signals in Figure 12c is performed through the cascade (serial) evolution of input qubits using the cascading of serial binary Toffoli gates (cf. Figures 12a and 12b). Figure 14 shows the basic transformation of input qubits into output qubits through a single Toffoli cell

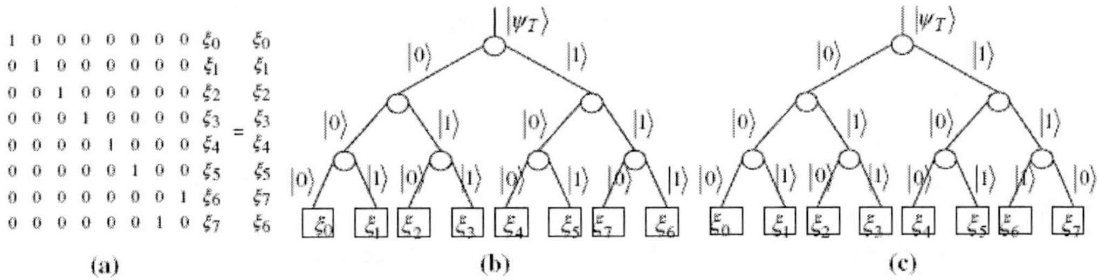

Figure 14. Three-level binary quantum decision trees (QDTs) representations for the quantum evolution of qubits through the Toffoli cell (in Figures 12a – 12b): (a) quantum evolution of input qubit using the Toffoli gate (i.e., Toffoli cell), (b) transformation **of the probabilities' vector** in the corresponding quantum space, and (c) the transformed quantum space (that is the transformed orthonormal axes of the quantum space) upon the vector of input probabilities, where $\left\|\vec{\xi}\right\| = 1$.

The state in the 2-valued quantum Toffoli-based Kung systolic array can be either: (1) decomposable into the tensor product as shown in Equation (7) for n quantum Toffoli gates, or (2) non-decomposable (that is entangled) as shown in Equation (8) for n quantum Toffoli gates.

$$|\psi_T\rangle = |\psi_{12..n}\rangle = \prod_{T=1}^{n}\left(\sum_{k=0}^{7}\xi_{kT}\left|D_{(67)}\right\rangle\right), \tag{7}$$

$$|\psi_T\rangle = |\psi_{12..n}\rangle \neq \prod_{T=1}^{n}\left(\sum_{k=0}^{7}\xi_{kT}\left|D_{(67)}\right\rangle\right), \tag{8}$$

where ξ_{kT} is the probability amplitudes and $\left|D_{(67)}\right\rangle$ is the group-theoretic representation of the Toffoli-transformed elementary basis states as shown in Figures 14 and 15. The $\left|D_{(67)}\right\rangle$ group-theoretic representation of the binary Toffoli gate stems from the fact that the TPE cell transforms the input qubit 6 into qubit 7 and input qubit 7 into qubit 6 while preserving the domain-range mapping for the rest of qubits **from 0 to 5, i.e., 0 → 0, 1 → 1, 2 → 2, 3 → 3, 4 → 4, and 5 →** 5.

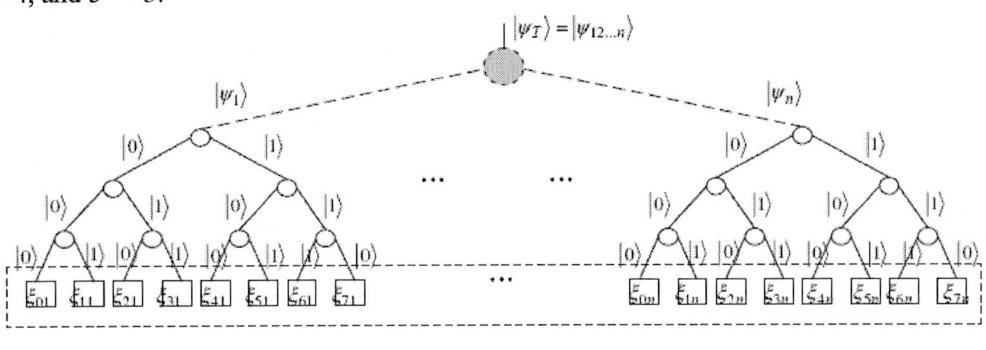

Figure 15. An n-stage Toffoli-based quantum decision tree (QDT).

Conclusion

New reversible and quantum systolic architectures for the synthesis of two-valued Galois logic functions are introduced. Since the architecture of conventional computers suffers from two inherent difficulties of (1) long communication paths and (2) the fact that the single CPU sequentially fetches and executes instructions, systolic architecture speeds up the computation through (i) cost-effectiveness through simplicity and regularity, (ii) concurrency (i.e., parallelism) through pipelining and multiprocessing, (iii) regular communication wiring occurs only between neighboring processing elements (PEs) (i.e., the elimination of global broadcasting), and (iv) I/O bandwidth-throughput improvements, where in a systolic architecture three factors are fundamental: (a) the type of the PE, (b) the systolic topology, and (c) the input/output ordering of data items in the I/O streams. The new arrays maintain the important regularity of the classical systolic arrays with the addition of preserving the reversibility (i.e., bijectivity) property in the reversible space and the superposition property in the quantum space.

Since it is estimated that at least 75 percent of all scientific applications involve some form of matrix computations which are generally expensive in terms of storage space and processing time, and since basic PEs that are used in the construction of arithmetic systolic arrays are the add-multiply cells, the new results that are introduced in this paper are general and apply to a very wide class of add-multiply-based systolic arrays and other types of systolic arrays as well. The new design method introduced in this paper can play an important role in the synthesis of circuits that consume minimal power for future circuit implementations, and the new quantum superposition property will be essential in performing super-fast arithmetic-intensive exponential-speedup computations that are fundamental in several matrix-based future applications such as in multi-dimensional quantum signal processing.

References

[1] Al-Rabadi, A. N., *Reversible Logic Synthesis: From Fundamentals to Quantum Computing*, Springer-Verlag, 2004.

[2] Al-Rabadi, A. N., "Multiple-Level Circuit Solutions to the Circuit Non-Decomposability Problem of the Set-Theoretic Modified Reconstructability Analysis (MRA)," *International Journal of General Systems (IJGS)*, Taylor & Francis, U.S.A., Vol. 35, No. 2, pp. 169-189, 2006.

[3] Barenco, A., Bennett, C. H., Cleve, R., DiVincenzo, D. P., Margolus, N., Shor, P., Sleator, T., Smolin, J. and Weinfurter, H., "Elementary Gates for Quantum Computation," *Phys. Rev. A*, 52, pp. 3457-3467, 1995.

[4] Bennett, C., "Logical Reversibility of Computation," *IBM J. of Research and Development*, 17, pp. 525-532, 1973.

[5] Fredkin, E. and Toffoli, T., "Conservative Logic," *International J. of Theoretical Physics*, 21, pp. 219-253, 1982.

[6] Guo, I. - H. and Wang, C. - L., "Hardware-Efficient Systolic Architecture for Inversion and Division in GF(2^m)," *IEEE Trans. Computers and Digital Techniques,* pp. 272-278, 1998.

[7] Huang, C. - T. and Wu, C. - W., "High-Speed C-Testable Systolic Array Design for Galois-Field Inversion," *Proc. European Design and Test Conf.,* pp. 342-346, March 1997.

[8] Hwang, K. and Briggs, F., *Computer Architecture and Parallel Processing*, McGraw-Hill, 1984.

[9] Kung, H. T., "Why Systolic Architectures?" *Computer*, Vol. 15, No.1, pp. 37-46, January 1982.

[10] Johnson, K. T., Hurson, A. R. and Shirazi, B., "General-Purpose Systolic Arrays," *Computer*, Vol. 26, No. 11, pp. 20-31, 1993.

[11] Landauer, R., "Irreversibility and Heat Generation in the Computational Process," *IBM J. of Research and Development*, 5, pp. 183-191, 1961.

[12] Nielsen, M. and Chuang, I., *Quantum Computation and Quantum Information*, Cambridge University Press, 2000.

[13] Picton, P., "Optoelectronic Multi-Valued Conservative Logic," *Int. J. of Optical Computing*, 2, pp. 19-29, 1991.

[14] Reddy, S. M., "Easily Testable Realizations of Logic Functions," *IEEE Trans. Comp.*, C-21, pp. 1183-1188, 1972.

[15] Roy, K. and Prasad, S., *Low-Power CMOS VLSI Circuit Design*, John Wiley & Sons Inc., 2000.

[16] Wang, C. - L. and Guo, J. - H., "New Systolic Arrays for C + AB^2, Inversion, and Division in GF(2^m)," *IEEE Trans. Comp.*, Vol. 49, No. 10, pp. 1120-1125, October 2000.

In: New Developments in Computer Research
Editor: Nikos E. Mastorakis
ISBN: 978-1-61470-321-1

HIGH-PERFORMANCE REVERSIBLE AND QUANTUM SYSTOLIC PARALLEL PROCESSING, PART II: GENERALIZED MULTIPLE-VALUED REALIZATIONS

Anas N. Al-Rabadi*
Department of Computer Engineering, The University of Jordan, Jordan
Office of Graduate Studies and Research (OGSR), Portland State University, US

ABSTRACT

This paper introduces a new type of multiple-valued systolic arrays, called multiple-valued reversible systolic arrays, which extends the concept of two-valued reversible systolic arrays that was introduced in the first part of my article. The multiple-valued quantum systolic architectures' computations of the new type of systolic arrays are also introduced. The new multiple-valued systolic arrays maintain the high level of regularity while exhibiting the new fundamental multiple-valued reversibility (equipollent; bijectivity) and multiple-valued quantum superposition properties. Since basic PEs that are used in the construction of arithmetic systolic arrays are the add-multiply cells, the results introduced in this paper are general and apply to a wide range of multiple-valued Galois add-multiply-based systolic arrays. The new reversibility and superposition properties will be essential in performing super-fast arithmetic-intensive computations that are fundamental in several minimal-power consuming future applications such as in multiple-valued multi-dimensional quantum signal processing.

1. INTRODUCTION

Systolic arrays are examples of single-instruction multiple-data (SIMD) machines consisting of a set of interconnected processing elements (PEs) in which a PE is only capable of performing a single simple operation [10,11,17]. In a systolic computing system, data flows from the host through the array in a rhythmic fashion and computations are synchronized by a global clock signal where data items are pumped out from a memory. The power behind the systolic arrays comes from the way in which the data flows between the processing elements [10,11,17]. Typically a systolic array is capable of performing a single operation such as matrix multiplication or inversion, and thus they are special purpose

* Email: alrabadi@yahoo.com

machines used to solve many regular problems containing repetitive operations on large arrays of data which are used for large variety of applications [4,6,8,9,10,11,12,17,20,21].

Due to the anticipated failure of Moore's law around the year 2020, quantum computing will hopefully play an increasingly crucial role in building more compact and less power consuming computers [1,2,15]. Due to this fact, and because all quantum computer gates (i.e., building blocks) should be reversible [1,2,3,5,7,13,15], reversible computing will have an increasingly more existence in the future design of regular, compact, and universal circuits and systems. For this reason, different technologies have been studied to implement reversible logic in hardware like adiabatic CMOS [19], optical [16], and quantum [1,15].

The main contribution of this paper is the new design method to implement multiple-valued logic functions bijectively through the realization of multiple-valued reversible functional expansions using multiple-valued reversible (i.e., bijective or equipollent) systolic arrays and the use of the corresponding quantum systolic arrays as illustrated in Figure 1. The new reversible logic synthesis method possesses high-level of regularity in addition to the preservation of the multiple-valued reversibility property. In addition to the multiple-valued reversibility property, the extension of the new reversible systolic arrays to the quantum domain will result in the emergence of the multiple-valued quantum superposition property which is responsible of the exponential speedups of the computational processes in the quantum domain [1,15]. One of the advantages for the use of the new families of multiple-valued quantum systolic circuits is their potential utilization in low-power circuit designs for digital signal processing applications in analogy to the role of classical systolic circuits in non-adiabatic VLSI circuits, where also the use of multiple-valued quantum circuit technology speeds up the computational process due to the existence of the multiple-valued quantum computational parallelism.

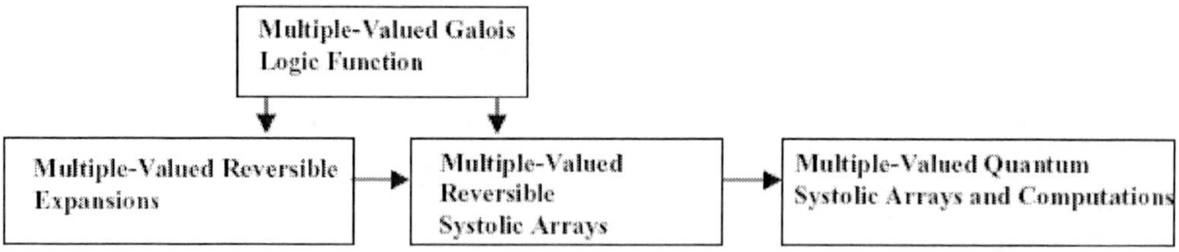

Figure 1. The implementation of a multiple-valued Galois logic function bijectively using multiple-valued reversible systolic arrays and their corresponding multiple-valued quantum systolic arrays.

Basic background on systolic arrays is given in Section 2. Multiple-valued reversible logic is presented in Section 3. The new multiple-valued reversible systolic arrays are introduced in Section 4. Quantum computations of the new multiple-valued reversible systolic architectures are introduced in Section 5. Conclusions and future work are presented in Section 6. Although the results introduced in Sections 4 and 5 are illustrated for the case of third radix of Galois field, results for higher radix Galois fields can be obtained in a similar manner as well.

2. SYSTOLIC ARRAYS

Since the architecture of conventional computers suffers from two inherent difficulties of (a) long communication paths and (b) the fact that the single CPU sequentially fetches and executes instructions, systolic architecture speeds up the computation through (1) cost-effectiveness through simplicity and regularity, (2) concurrency (that is parallelism) through pipelining and multiprocessing, (3) regular communication wiring occurs only between neighboring processing elements (PEs) (i.e., the elimination of global broadcasting), and (4) I/O bandwidth-throughput improvements. In a systolic architecture, three factors are fundamental: (i) the type of the PE, (ii) the systolic topology, and (iii) the input/output ordering of data items in the I/O streams [10,11,17].

Figure 2 shows an example of a 2D systolic array [10,11,17], where each pulsation of a systolic array consists of the following operations: (1) shift and (2) multiply and add. Basic processing cells that are used in the construction of systolic arithmetic arrays are the add-multiply cells. This kind of cells has the three inputs $\{a, b, c\}$ where the three outputs are $\{a = a, b = b, d = c + a * b\}$. One can assume six interface registers are attached at the I/O ports of a processing cell. All registers are clocked for synchronous transfer of data among adjacent cells. Hexagonally connected processors (i.e., processing elements (PEs)) can optimally perform matrix multiplication [10], where three data streams flow through the array in a pipelined fashion. One can follow the operation of the 2D hexagonal systolic array by studying the data flow by moving transparencies of the band matrices over the network (cf. Figure 2). The systolic array can finish the band matrix multiplication in T time units, where $T = 3n + \min(w_1, w_2)$ [10,11,17]. Therefore the computation time is linearly proportional to the dimension n of the matrix, and when the matrix bandwidths increase to $w_1 = w_2 = n$ (for dense matrices [**A**] and [**B**]), the time becomes $O(4n)$, neglecting the I/O time delays. If one used a single additive-multiply processor to perform the same matrix multiplication, $O(n^3)$ computation time would be needed [10,11,17]. The systolic array thus has a speed gain of $O(n^2)$, and this becomes more apparent for larger n. Multiplication of band matrices [**A**] and [**B**], [**A**] · [**B**] = [**C**], and the associated definition of bandwidth is shown as follows [10,11,17]:

$$
\begin{bmatrix} a_{11} & a_{12} & 0 & 0 & 0 \\ a_{21} & a_{22} & a_{23} & 0 & 0 \\ a_{31} & a_{32} & a_{33} & a_{34} & 0 \\ 0 & a_{42} & a_{43} & a_{44} & a_{45} \\ 0 & 0 & a_{53} & a_{54} & a_{55} \end{bmatrix} \cdot \begin{bmatrix} b_{11} & b_{12} & b_{13} & 0 & 0 \\ b_{21} & b_{22} & b_{23} & b_{24} & 0 \\ 0 & b_{32} & b_{33} & b_{34} & b_{35} \\ 0 & 0 & b_{43} & b_{44} & b_{45} \\ 0 & 0 & 0 & b_{54} & b_{55} \end{bmatrix} = \begin{bmatrix} c_{11} & c_{12} & c_{13} & c_{14} & 0 \\ c_{21} & c_{22} & c_{23} & c_{24} & c_{25} \\ c_{31} & c_{32} & c_{33} & c_{34} & c_{35} \\ c_{41} & c_{42} & c_{43} & c_{44} & c_{45} \\ 0 & c_{52} & c_{53} & c_{54} & c_{55} \end{bmatrix}
$$

Band_1 Band_2 Band_3

where bandwidth$_1$: $w_1 = 3 + 2 - 1 = 4$, bandwidth$_2$: $w_2 = 2 + 3 - 1 = 4$, and bandwidth$_3$: $w_3 = w_1 + w_2 - 1 = 4 + 4 - 1 = 7$. Figure 2 shows the two-dimensional (2D) hexagonal systolic array [10,11,17] that implements the operation of multiplying two band matrices [**A**] and [**B**].

Each propagating data level in the three data flow streams in Figure 2 is called a wave front. The initial values of the input [**C**] array elements, that are propagating from the lower side in Figure 2, are all zeros, and the final values of the output [**C**] array elements, that are propagating from the upper side in Figure 2, are obtained as follows:

$c_{11} = a_{11}b_{11} + a_{12}b_{21}$, $c_{21} = a_{21}b_{11} + a_{22}b_{21}$, $c_{31} = a_{31}b_{11} + a_{32}b_{21}$, $c_{41} = a_{42}b_{21}$, $c_{51} = 0$, $c_{12} = a_{11}b_{12} + a_{12}b_{22}$, $c_{22} = a_{21}b_{12} + a_{22}b_{22} + a_{23}b_{32}$, $c_{32} = a_{31}b_{12} + a_{32}b_{22} + a_{33}b_{32}$, $c_{42} = a_{42}b_{22} + a_{43}b_{32}$, $c_{52} = a_{53}b_{32}$, $c_{13} = a_{11}b_{13} + a_{12}b_{23}$, $c_{23} = a_{21}b_{13} + a_{22}b_{23} + a_{23}b_{33}$, $c_{33} = a_{31}b_{13} + a_{32}b_{23} + a_{33}b_{33} + a_{34}b_{43}$, $c_{43} = a_{42}b_{23} + a_{43}b_{33} + a_{44}b_{43}$, $c_{53} = a_{53}b_{33} + a_{54}b_{43}$, $c_{14} = a_{12}b_{24}$, $c_{24} = a_{22}b_{24} + a_{23}b_{34}$, $c_{34} = a_{32}b_{24} + a_{33}b_{34} + a_{34}b_{44}$, $c_{44} = a_{42}b_{24} + a_{43}b_{34} + a_{44}b_{44} + a_{45}b_{54}$, $c_{54} = a_{53}b_{34} + a_{54}b_{44} + a_{55}b_{54}$, $c_{15} = 0$, $c_{25} = a_{23}b_{35}$, $c_{35} = a_{33}b_{35} + a_{34}b_{45}$, $c_{45} = a_{43}b_{35} + a_{44}b_{45} + a_{45}b_{55}$, $c_{55} = a_{53}b_{35} + a_{54}b_{45} + a_{55}b_{55}$.

The topological distribution of the processing elements (PEs) in the systolic structure, shown in Figure 2, is obtained as follows: # PEs in top-left = $w_1 = 4$, # PEs in top-right = $w_2 = 4$, # PEs in bottom = $w_3 = 7$, and the total # PEs = $4 \cdot 4 = 16$.

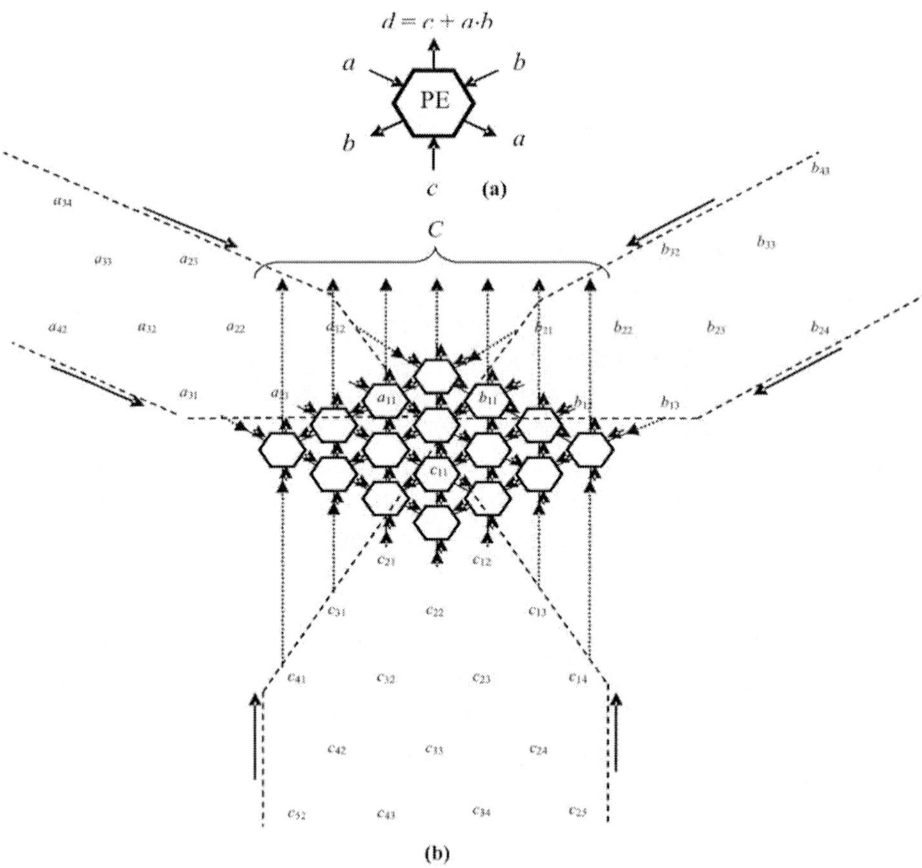

Figure 2. Two-dimensional (2D) hexagonal systolic array: (a) Kung cell, and (b) Kung systolic array.

3. Multiple-Valued Reversible Circuits

A (*k*, *k*) reversible circuit is a circuit that has the same number of inputs *k* and outputs *k* and is a one-to-one mapping between the vectors of inputs and the vectors of outputs, thus the vector of input states can be always uniquely reconstructed from the vector of output states [1,3,5,7,13,15]. Thus, a (*k*, *k*) reversible map is a bijective function which is both (1) injective ("one-to-one" or "(1:1)") and (2) surjective ("onto"). Such bijective systems are also known as "equipollent", "equipotent", and "one-to-one correspondence". The auxiliary outputs and inputs that are needed only for the purpose of reversibility are called "garbage" outputs and "garbage" inputs, respectively. These are auxiliary outputs and inputs from which a reversible map is constructed.

A (*k*, *k*) conservative circuit has the same number of inputs *k* and outputs *k* and has the same number of values in inputs and outputs (e.g., same number of ones in inputs and outputs for binary, the same number of ones and twos in inputs and outputs for ternary, etc) [1,7,15].

Because multiple-valued Galois field (GF) proved to possess desired properties in many applications such as in testing [18], the developments of the new systolic logic circuits, in this work, will be conducted on the corresponding Galois field (GF) algebraic structure. Radix three Galois field (GF(3)) addition and multiplication are defined as shown in Table 1 [1].

Table 1. Third radix Galois field addition and multiplication

+	**0**	**1**	**2**	*****	**0**	**1**	**2**
0	0	1	2	**0**	0	0	0
1	1	2	0	**1**	0	1	2
2	2	0	1	**2**	0	2	1

The 1-Reduced Post Literal (1-RPL) is a single variable function defined as [1]:

$$ {}^{i}x = \begin{cases} 1, x = i \\ 0, x \neq i \end{cases} \qquad (1)$$

For example, $\{{}^{0}x,\ {}^{1}x,\ {}^{2}x\}$ are the zero, first, and second polarities of the 1-Reduced Post Literal, respectively.

Also, let us define the ternary shifts of the variable x as $\{x, x', x''\}$ to be the zero, first, and second shifts of the variable x, respectively (i.e., $x = x + 0$, $x' = x + 1$, and $x'' = x + 2$), and the variable x can take any value in the set {0, 1, 2}.

To introduce the methodology for the creation of the reversible multiple-valued Shannon and Davio expansions, the following definitions are introduced [1].

Definition 1. The matrix that is constructed from the permutations of many basis functions of the same type of the corresponding spectral transform is called Generalized Basis Functions Matrix (GBFM).

Definition 2. From the total space of all possible Generalized Basis Function Matrices, the matrices that produce reversible expansions are called Reversible Generalized Basis Functions Matrices (RGBFM).

Example 1. The following is the ternary Shannon transform over GF(3).

$$f = \begin{bmatrix} {}^0c & {}^1c & {}^2c \end{bmatrix} \begin{bmatrix} 1 & 0 & 0 \\ 0 & 1 & 0 \\ 0 & 0 & 1 \end{bmatrix} \begin{bmatrix} f_0 \\ f_1 \\ f_2 \end{bmatrix}.$$

The following is one possible GBFM $\begin{bmatrix} {}^0c & {}^1c & {}^2c \\ {}^0c & {}^2c & {}^1c \\ {}^2c & {}^1c & {}^0c \end{bmatrix}$. Yet, as will be demonstrated in the following method, the upper GBFM is not reversible; it does not produce a reversible expansion. One possible RSGBFM that leads to a reversible expansion is as follows $\begin{bmatrix} {}^0c & {}^1c & {}^2c \\ {}^1c & {}^2c & {}^0c \\ {}^2c & {}^0c & {}^1c \end{bmatrix}$. Note that the Shannon set of basis functions $\{{}^0c, {}^1c, {}^2c\}$ will always appear in any of the rows of the corresponding RSGBFM that produces accordingly the reversible Shannon expansion (in this case, the Shannon set of basis functions $\{{}^0c, {}^1c, {}^2c\}$ appears in the first row).

A necessary and sufficient condition to generate the reversible multiple-valued Shannon expansions is that the order of the permuted basis functions in the GBFM should satisfy the following constraint [1]: in any given row or column the elements in that row or column are different than the elements in the corresponding positions of the other rows or columns. This constraint can be illustrated by means of tables as in the following: since the Shannon spectral transform matrix is orthogonal, then the following multi-input multi-output ternary Shannon expansion in the following Equation:

$$\vec{f} = [RSGBFM]\vec{f}_{in} = \begin{bmatrix} {}^2c & {}^0c & {}^1c \\ {}^1c & {}^2c & {}^0c \\ {}^0c & {}^1c & {}^2c \end{bmatrix} \begin{bmatrix} 1 & 0 & 0 \\ 0 & 1 & 0 \\ 0 & 0 & 1 \end{bmatrix} \begin{bmatrix} f_0 \\ f_1 \\ f_2 \end{bmatrix} = \begin{bmatrix} f_{r0} \\ f_{r1} \\ f_{r2} \end{bmatrix}, \tag{2}$$

is reversible. As an example, we are using in this case the Shannon set of basis functions $\{{}^0c, {}^1c, {}^2c\}$ that appear in the third row, but as discussed earlier, the Shannon set of basis functions $\{{}^0c, {}^1c, {}^2c\}$ can appear in any of the rows of the corresponding RGBFM. Equation (2) is reversible since it satisfies the following reversibility restriction: for all possible 81 input-output tuples, one can uniquely reconstruct any set of inputs from the set of outputs and vice versa. This stems from the fact that, for any reduced post literal ${}^kc$, the set of outputs is uniquely selected for the specified value of ${}^kc$ (in the corresponding ternary truth table) that corresponds to a specific set of inputs (since ${}^kc = 1$ iff $c = k$). This allows for the unique selection of inputs/outputs such that for any combination of inputs there is only one corresponding combination of outputs. For the case of the third radix, reversibility in Equation (2) appears as shown in Table 2.

Thus, as shown in Table 2, one can observe that, due to the uniqueness in the 1-RPL selection, the resulting function values (i.e., cofactors f_0, f_1, and f_2) for different 1-RPL values are always distinct (i.e., mutually exclusive). The same method can be carried out for any configuration that reflects RSGBFM for any radix.

Table 2. Reversibility proof of the reversible ternary Shannon expansion

RPL / Function	${}^{0}c$	${}^{1}c$	${}^{2}c$
Equation (2): $f=$	f_1	f_2	f_0
Equation (2): $f=$	f_2	f_0	f_1
Equation (2): $f=$	f_0	f_1	f_2

Example 2. The following are all possible permutations of the RGBFM for the Shannon transform matrix $\begin{bmatrix}1 & 0 & 0\\ 0 & 1 & 0\\ 0 & 0 & 1\end{bmatrix}$ in order to produce the corresponding reversible ternary Shannon expansions over GF(3) [1].

$$\vec{f}=\begin{bmatrix}{}^{0}c & {}^{1}c & {}^{2}c\\ {}^{1}c & {}^{2}c & {}^{0}c\\ {}^{2}c & {}^{0}c & {}^{1}c\end{bmatrix}\begin{bmatrix}1 & 0 & 0\\ 0 & 1 & 0\\ 0 & 0 & 1\end{bmatrix}\begin{bmatrix}f0\\ f1\\ f2\end{bmatrix}=\begin{bmatrix}fr0\\ fr1\\ fr2\end{bmatrix}, \tag{3}$$

$$\vec{f}=\begin{bmatrix}{}^{0}c & {}^{1}c & {}^{2}c\\ {}^{2}c & {}^{0}c & {}^{1}c\\ {}^{1}c & {}^{2}c & {}^{0}c\end{bmatrix}\begin{bmatrix}1 & 0 & 0\\ 0 & 1 & 0\\ 0 & 0 & 1\end{bmatrix}\begin{bmatrix}f0\\ f1\\ f2\end{bmatrix}=\begin{bmatrix}fr0\\ fr1\\ fr2\end{bmatrix}, \tag{4}$$

$$\vec{f}=\begin{bmatrix}{}^{1}c & {}^{2}c & {}^{0}c\\ {}^{0}c & {}^{1}c & {}^{2}c\\ {}^{2}c & {}^{0}c & {}^{1}c\end{bmatrix}\begin{bmatrix}1 & 0 & 0\\ 0 & 1 & 0\\ 0 & 0 & 1\end{bmatrix}\begin{bmatrix}f0\\ f1\\ f2\end{bmatrix}=\begin{bmatrix}fr0\\ fr1\\ fr2\end{bmatrix}, \tag{5}$$

$$\vec{f}=\begin{bmatrix}{}^{2}c & {}^{0}c & {}^{1}c\\ {}^{0}c & {}^{1}c & {}^{2}c\\ {}^{1}c & {}^{2}c & {}^{0}c\end{bmatrix}\begin{bmatrix}1 & 0 & 0\\ 0 & 1 & 0\\ 0 & 0 & 1\end{bmatrix}\begin{bmatrix}f0\\ f1\\ f2\end{bmatrix}=\begin{bmatrix}fr0\\ fr1\\ fr2\end{bmatrix}, \tag{6}$$

$$\vec{f}=\begin{bmatrix}{}^{1}c & {}^{2}c & {}^{0}c\\ {}^{2}c & {}^{0}c & {}^{1}c\\ {}^{0}c & {}^{1}c & {}^{2}c\end{bmatrix}\begin{bmatrix}1 & 0 & 0\\ 0 & 1 & 0\\ 0 & 0 & 1\end{bmatrix}\begin{bmatrix}f0\\ f1\\ f2\end{bmatrix}=\begin{bmatrix}fr0\\ fr1\\ fr2\end{bmatrix}, \tag{7}$$

$$\vec{f}=\begin{bmatrix}{}^{2}c & {}^{0}c & {}^{1}c\\ {}^{1}c & {}^{2}c & {}^{0}c\\ {}^{0}c & {}^{1}c & {}^{2}c\end{bmatrix}\begin{bmatrix}1 & 0 & 0\\ 0 & 1 & 0\\ 0 & 0 & 1\end{bmatrix}\begin{bmatrix}f0\\ f1\\ f2\end{bmatrix}=\begin{bmatrix}fr0\\ fr1\\ fr2\end{bmatrix}. \tag{8}$$

Reversible multiple-valued Davio expansions have been also created [1]. For example, for the following reversible ternary Shannon expansion:

$$\vec{f}=\begin{bmatrix} {}^0c & {}^1c & {}^2c \\ {}^1c & {}^2c & {}^0c \\ {}^2c & {}^0c & {}^1c \end{bmatrix} \begin{bmatrix} 1 & 0 & 0 \\ 0 & 1 & 0 \\ 0 & 0 & 1 \end{bmatrix} \begin{bmatrix} f_0 \\ f_1 \\ f_2 \end{bmatrix}, \tag{9}$$

It has been shown [1] that, for the above transform matrix, the following is the ternary reversible Davio$_0$ expansion:

$$\vec{f}_{D0}=\begin{bmatrix} 1 & 1+c & 1+2c+c^2 \\ 1 & c & c^2 \\ 1 & 2+c & 1+c+c^2 \end{bmatrix} \begin{bmatrix} 0 & 0 & 1 \\ 2 & 1 & 0 \\ 2 & 2 & 2 \end{bmatrix} \begin{bmatrix} f_0 \\ f_1 \\ f_2 \end{bmatrix} = \begin{bmatrix} 1 & 1+c & 1+2c+c^2 \\ 1 & c & c^2 \\ 1 & 2+c & 1+c+c^2 \end{bmatrix} \begin{bmatrix} f_2 \\ 2f_0+f_1 \\ 2f_0+2f_1+2f_2 \end{bmatrix} \tag{10a}$$

$$=\begin{bmatrix} f_2+(1+c)(2f_0+f_1)+(1+2c+c^2)(2f_0+2f_1+2f_2) \\ f_2+c(2f_0+f_1)+c^2(2f_0+2f_1+2f_2) \\ f_2+(2+c)(2f_0+f_1)+(1+c+c^2)(2f_0+2f_1+2f_2) \end{bmatrix} \tag{10b}$$

$$=\begin{bmatrix} f_0+c(2f_1+f_2)+c^2(2f_0+2f_1+2f_2) \\ f_2+c(2f_0+f_1)+c^2(2f_0+2f_1+2f_2) \\ f_1+c(2f_2+f_0)+c^2(2f_0+2f_1+2f_2) \end{bmatrix} = \begin{bmatrix} f_{r0,D0} \\ f_{r1,D0} \\ f_{r2,D0} \end{bmatrix} \tag{10c}$$

Figure 3 shows important ternary radix GF-based reversible gates [1]. These gates will be used in later sections in the ternary reversible implementation and for the extension to ternary quantum implementation, of the classical systolic arrays. For reversibility illustration, Table 3 presents reversibility proof for the ternary Toffoli gate where the inputs are in order $\{a, b, c\}$ and outputs are in order $\{a, b, d = c +_3 a *_3 b\}$.

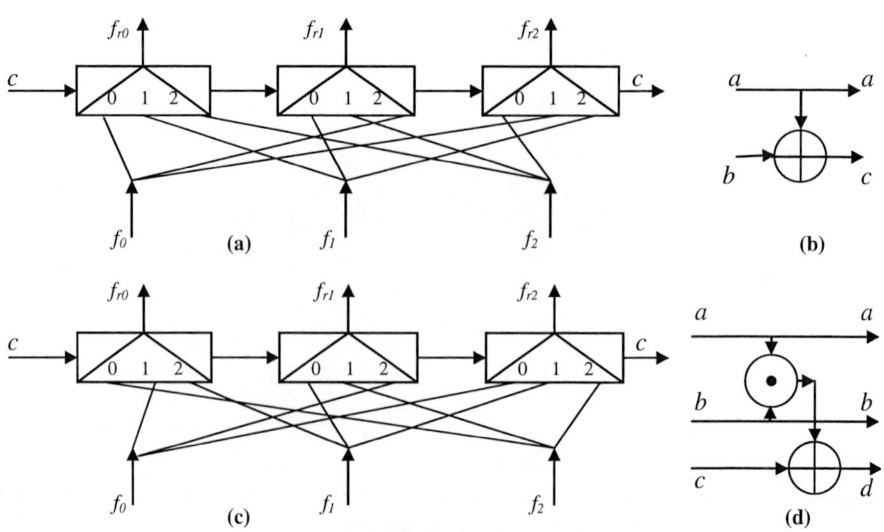

Figure 3. Ternary reversible gates: (a) ternary (4, 4) Shannon (Fredkin) gate for Equation (4), (b) ternary (2, 2) Feynman gate, (c) ternary (4, 4) Shannon (Fredkin) gate for Equation (7), and (d) ternary (3, 3) Toffoli gate.

4. MULTIPLE-VALUED REVERSIBLE SYSTOLIC ARRAYS

This section introduces new results for the synthesis of multiple-valued Galois functions using reversible systolic arrays using the following two methods: (1) reusing the classical add-multiply PE cells by showing their multiple-valued Galois logic reversibility and thereafter reusing the whole systolic structure since the connection of multiple-valued reversible PEs will produce by necessity an multiple-valued reversible systolic circuit, (since the interconnection of reversible gates will necessarily produce a reversible circuit [1]), and (2) direct mapping of classical irreversible systolic circuits into reversible systolic circuits by interconnecting the multiple-valued reversible counterpart of the multiple-valued irreversible PEs.

Moreover, the implementation of the multiple-valued logic functions using the new reversible systolic arrays is performed through two methods (cf. Example 3): (a) direct implementation by the substitution of the array's values using the corresponding multiple-valued functional literals, and (b) the implementation using the corresponding multiple-valued matrix-based elements that are obtained through the multiple-valued reversible Shannon and Davio functional expansions.

Table 3. Reversibility proof for the ternary (3, 3) Toffoli gate where the inputs are in order $\{a, b, c\}$ and the outputs are in order $\{a, b, d = c +_3 a *_3 b\}$.

000	000	100	100	200	200
001	001	101	101	201	201
002	002	102	102	202	202
010	010	110	111	210	212
011	011	111	112	211	210
012	012	112	110	212	211
020	020	120	122	220	221
021	021	121	120	221	222
022	022	122	121	222	220

Basic PEs which are used in the construction of arithmetic systolic arrays are the add-multiply cells [10,11,17]. Figure 4a introduces the ternary (3, 3) reversible Toffoli gate that implements reversibly (in the third radix Galois logic GF(3)) the classical Kung add-multiply systolic cell (cf. Figure 4b). Since the interconnection of reversible PEs will produce by necessity a reversible systolic circuit [1], the implementation of the 2D hexagonal reversible Kung systolic array over GF(3) is achieved by interconnecting the (3, 3) GF(3) reversible Toffoli PEs (cells).

For the systolic implementation of multiple-valued functions using the corresponding GF(3), as an example of a multiple-valued GF logic, the matrix-based elements that are obtained using the GF(3) reversible Shannon and Davio functional expansions from Equations (3) and (10) are obtained (in the same method the elements of {[**A**], [**B**], [**C**]} matrices were obtained in Section 2) as follows, respectively:

$$\begin{bmatrix} 0 & 0 & 0 & 0 & 0 \\ {}^0e & {}^1e & {}^2e & 0 & 0 \\ {}^1e & {}^2e & {}^0e & 0 & 0 \\ 0 & {}^0e & {}^1e & {}^2e & 0 \\ 0 & 0 & 0 & 0 & 0 \end{bmatrix} \cdot \begin{bmatrix} 0 & 0 & f_0 & 0 & 0 \\ 0 & 0 & f_1 & 0 & 0 \\ 0 & 0 & f_2 & 0 & 0 \\ 0 & 0 & f_0 & 0 & 0 \\ 0 & 0 & 0 & 0 & 0 \end{bmatrix} = \begin{bmatrix} 0 & 0 & 0 & 0 & 0 \\ 0 & 0 & {}^0ef_0 + {}^1ef_1 + {}^2ef_2 & 0 & 0 \\ 0 & 0 & {}^1ef_0 + {}^2ef_1 + {}^0ef_2 & 0 & 0 \\ 0 & 0 & {}^0ef_1 + {}^1ef_2 + {}^2ef_0 & 0 & 0 \\ 0 & 0 & 0 & 0 & 0 \end{bmatrix}, \tag{11}$$

Where:

$a_{21}={}^0e, a_{22}={}^1e, a_{23}={}^2e, a_{31}={}^1e, a_{32}={}^2e, a_{33}={}^0e, a_{42}={}^0e, a_{43}={}^1e, a_{44}={}^2e, b_{13}=f_0, b_{23}=f_1, b_{33}=f_2, b_{43}=f_0,$
$c_{23}={}^0ef_0+{}^1ef_1+{}^2ef_2, c_{33}={}^1ef_0+{}^2ef_1+{}^0ef_2, c_{43}={}^2ef_0+{}^0ef_1+{}^1ef_2.$

$$\begin{bmatrix} 0 & 0 & 0 & 0 & 0 \\ 1 & 1+e & 1+2e+e^2 & 0 & 0 \\ 1 & e & e^2 & 0 & 0 \\ 0 & 2+e & 1+e+e^2 & 1 & 0 \\ 0 & 0 & 0 & 0 & 0 \end{bmatrix} \cdot \begin{bmatrix} 0 & 0 & f_2 & 0 & 0 \\ 0 & 0 & 2f_0+f_1 & 0 & 0 \\ 0 & 0 & 2f_0+2f_1+2f_2 & 0 & 0 \\ 0 & 0 & f_2 & 0 & 0 \\ 0 & 0 & 0 & 0 & 0 \end{bmatrix} =$$
$$\begin{bmatrix} 0 & 0 & 0 & 0 & 0 \\ 0 & 0 & f_2+(1+e)(2f_0+f_1)+(1+2e+e^2)(2f_0+2f_1+2f_2) & 0 & 0 \\ 0 & 0 & f_2+e(2f_0+f_1)+e^2(2f_0+2f_1+2f_2) & 0 & 0 \\ 0 & 0 & f_2+(2+e)(2f_0+f_1)+(1+e+e^2)(2f_0+2f_1+2f_2) & 0 & 0 \\ 0 & 0 & 0 & 0 & 0 \end{bmatrix} \tag{12}$$

Where:

$a_{21}=1, a_{22}=1+e, a_{23}=1+e+e^2, a_{31}=1, a_{32}=e, a_{33}=e^2, a_{42}=2+e, a_{43}=1+e+e^2, a_{44}=1, b_{13}=f_2,$
$b_{23}=2f_0+f_1, b_{33}=(2f_0+2f_1+2f_2), b_{43}=f_2, c_{23}=f_2+(1+e)(2f_0+f_1)+(1+2e+e^2)(2f_0+2f_1+2f_2),$
$c_{33}=f_2+e(2f_0+f_1)+e^2(2f_0+2f_1+2f_2), c_{43}=f_2+(2+e)(2f_0+f_1)+(1+e+e^2)(2f_0+2f_1+2f_2).$

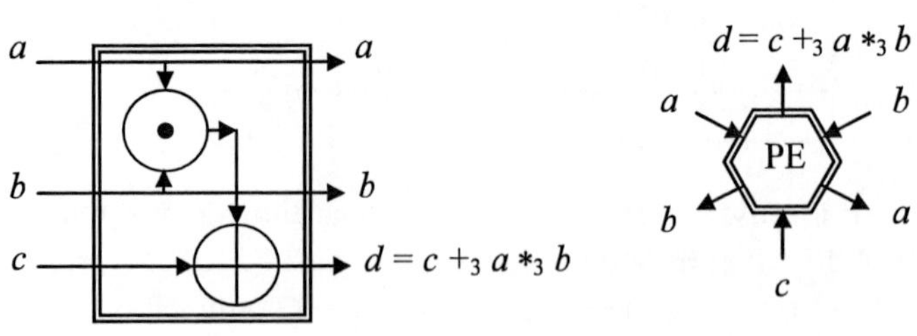

(a) (b)

Figure 4. Reversible GF(3) Kung systolic array: (a) reversible (3, 3) Toffoli PE, and (b) reversible (3, 3) Kung cell.

The realization of a many-variable function using the methods shown in Equations (11) – (12) follow the matrix-based expansion using the Kronecker (tensor) product [1] and the use of the Toffoli PE (TPE) over GF(3).

Example 3 shows the equipollent implementation, using the reversible Kung systolic array from Figure 4, of the two-digit ternary multiplication which is performed utilizing the mod-multiplication operator.

Example 3. Table 4 shows the maps for the ternary mod-multiplication (M) and the output carry (C_{out}).

Table 4. Ternary mod-multiplication for ternary 2-digit multiplier: (a) multiplication (*M*), and (b) carry out (C_{out})

(a)				(b)			
b \ a	**0**	**1**	**2**	b \ a	**0**	**1**	**2**
0	0	0	0	**0**	0	0	0
1	0	1	2	**1**	0	0	0
2	0	2	1	**2**	0	0	1

The following is a bijective implementation, using GF(3) reversible 2D hexagonal Kung systolic array from Figure 4, of the two-digit ternary multiplication which is performed using the mod-multiplication operator.

$$M={}^{1}a{}^{1}b+2\cdot{}^{2}a{}^{1}b+2\cdot{}^{1}a{}^{2}b+{}^{2}a{}^{2}b, C_{out}={}^{2}a{}^{2}b,$$
$$\rightarrow c_{33}=M, a_{31}={}^{1}a, b_{13}={}^{1}b, a_{32}=2\cdot{}^{2}a, b_{23}={}^{1}b, a_{33}=2\cdot{}^{1}a, b_{33}={}^{2}b, a_{34}={}^{2}a, b_{43}={}^{2}b.$$
$$\rightarrow c_{11}=C_{out}, a_{11}={}^{2}a, b_{11}={}^{2}b, a_{12}=0, b_{21}=0.$$

The upper implementation follows directly by the substitution of the array's values using the corresponding multiple-valued functional literals. A second way to implement the upper multiplier is by using the many-variable ternary Kronecker-based reversible Shannon and Davio expansions of Equations (3) and (10a) as:

$$\vec{f}=\begin{bmatrix} fr0\\ fr1\\ fr2\\ fr3\\ fr4\\ fr5\\ fr6\\ fr7\\ fr8 \end{bmatrix}=\left[\begin{bmatrix} {}^{0}a & {}^{1}a & {}^{2}a\\ {}^{1}a & {}^{2}a & {}^{0}a\\ {}^{2}a & {}^{0}a & {}^{1}a \end{bmatrix}\otimes\begin{bmatrix} {}^{0}b & {}^{1}b & {}^{2}b\\ {}^{1}b & {}^{2}b & {}^{0}b\\ {}^{2}b & {}^{0}b & {}^{1}b \end{bmatrix}\right]\left[\begin{bmatrix} 1&0&0\\ 0&1&0\\ 0&0&1 \end{bmatrix}\otimes\begin{bmatrix} 1&0&0\\ 0&1&0\\ 0&0&1 \end{bmatrix}\right]\left[\begin{bmatrix} fa0\\ fa1\\ fa2 \end{bmatrix}\otimes\begin{bmatrix} fb0\\ fb1\\ fb2 \end{bmatrix}\right]$$

$$=\begin{bmatrix}
{}^{0}a{}^{0}b & {}^{0}a{}^{1}b & {}^{0}a{}^{2}b & {}^{1}a{}^{0}b & {}^{1}a{}^{1}b & {}^{1}a{}^{2}b & {}^{2}a{}^{0}b & {}^{2}a{}^{1}b & {}^{2}a{}^{2}b\\
{}^{0}a{}^{1}b & {}^{0}a{}^{2}b & {}^{0}a{}^{0}b & {}^{1}a{}^{1}b & {}^{1}a{}^{2}b & {}^{1}a{}^{0}b & {}^{2}a{}^{1}b & {}^{2}a{}^{2}b & {}^{2}a{}^{0}b\\
{}^{0}a{}^{2}b & {}^{0}a{}^{0}b & {}^{0}a{}^{1}b & {}^{1}a{}^{2}b & {}^{1}a{}^{0}b & {}^{1}a{}^{1}b & {}^{2}a{}^{2}b & {}^{2}a{}^{0}b & {}^{2}a{}^{1}b\\
{}^{1}a{}^{0}b & {}^{1}a{}^{1}b & {}^{1}a{}^{2}b & {}^{2}a{}^{0}b & {}^{2}a{}^{1}b & {}^{2}a{}^{2}b & {}^{0}a{}^{0}b & {}^{0}a{}^{1}b & {}^{0}a{}^{2}b\\
{}^{1}a{}^{1}b & {}^{1}a{}^{2}b & {}^{1}a{}^{0}b & {}^{2}a{}^{1}b & {}^{2}a{}^{2}b & {}^{2}a{}^{0}b & {}^{0}a{}^{1}b & {}^{0}a{}^{2}b & {}^{0}a{}^{0}b\\
{}^{1}a{}^{2}b & {}^{1}a{}^{0}b & {}^{1}a{}^{1}b & {}^{2}a{}^{2}b & {}^{2}a{}^{0}b & {}^{2}a{}^{1}b & {}^{0}a{}^{2}b & {}^{0}a{}^{0}b & {}^{0}a{}^{1}b\\
{}^{2}a{}^{0}b & {}^{2}a{}^{1}b & {}^{2}a{}^{2}b & {}^{0}a{}^{0}b & {}^{0}a{}^{1}b & {}^{0}a{}^{2}b & {}^{1}a{}^{0}b & {}^{1}a{}^{1}b & {}^{1}a{}^{2}b\\
{}^{2}a{}^{1}b & {}^{2}a{}^{2}b & {}^{2}a{}^{0}b & {}^{0}a{}^{1}b & {}^{0}a{}^{2}b & {}^{0}a{}^{0}b & {}^{1}a{}^{1}b & {}^{1}a{}^{2}b & {}^{1}a{}^{0}b\\
{}^{2}a{}^{2}b & {}^{2}a{}^{0}b & {}^{2}a{}^{1}b & {}^{0}a{}^{2}b & {}^{0}a{}^{0}b & {}^{0}a{}^{1}b & {}^{1}a{}^{2}b & {}^{1}a{}^{0}b & {}^{1}a{}^{1}b
\end{bmatrix}\begin{bmatrix}
1&0&0&0&0&0&0&0&0\\
0&1&0&0&0&0&0&0&0\\
0&0&1&0&0&0&0&0&0\\
0&0&0&1&0&0&0&0&0\\
0&0&0&0&1&0&0&0&0\\
0&0&0&0&0&1&0&0&0\\
0&0&0&0&0&0&1&0&0\\
0&0&0&0&0&0&0&1&0\\
0&0&0&0&0&0&0&0&1
\end{bmatrix}\begin{bmatrix} fa0b0\\ fa0b1\\ fa0b2\\ fa1b0\\ fa1b1\\ fa1b2\\ fa2b0\\ fa2b1\\ fa2b2 \end{bmatrix}$$

$$\vec{f} = \begin{bmatrix} f_{r0} \\ f_{r1} \\ f_{r2} \\ f_{r3} \\ f_{r4} \\ f_{r5} \\ f_{r6} \\ f_{r7} \\ f_{r8} \end{bmatrix} = \left[\left[\begin{bmatrix} 1 & 1+a & 1+2a+a^2 \\ 1 & a & a^2 \\ 1 & 2+a & 1+a+a^2 \end{bmatrix} \otimes \begin{bmatrix} 1 & 1+b & 1+2b+b^2 \\ 1 & b & b^2 \\ 1 & 2+b & 1+b+b^2 \end{bmatrix}\right]\left[\begin{bmatrix} 0 & 0 & 1 \\ 2 & 1 & 0 \\ 2 & 2 & 2 \end{bmatrix} \otimes \begin{bmatrix} 0 & 0 & 1 \\ 2 & 1 & 0 \\ 2 & 2 & 2 \end{bmatrix}\right]\right]\left[\begin{bmatrix} f_{a0} \\ f_{a1} \\ f_{a2} \end{bmatrix} \otimes \begin{bmatrix} f_{b0} \\ f_{b1} \\ f_{b2} \end{bmatrix}\right]$$

$$= \begin{bmatrix} 1 & 1+b & 1+2b+b^2 & 1+a & (1+a)(1+b) & (1+a)(1+2b+b^2) & 1+2a+a^2 & (1+2a+a^2)(1+b) & (1+2a+a^2)(1+2b+b^2) \\ 1 & b & b^2 & 1+a & (1+a)b & (1+a)b^2 & 1+2a+a^2 & (1+2a+a^2)b & (1+2a+a^2)b^2 \\ 1 & 2+b & 1+b+b^2 & 1+a & (1+a)(2+b) & (1+a)(1+b+b^2) & 1+2a+a^2 & (1+2a+a^2)(2+b) & (1+2a+a^2)(1+b+b^2) \\ 1 & 1+b & 1+2b+b^2 & a & a(1+b) & a(1+2b+b^2) & a^2 & a^2(1+b) & a^2(1+2b+b^2) \\ 1 & b & b^2 & a & ab & ab^2 & a^2 & a^2b & a^2b^2 \\ 1 & 2+b & 1+b+b^2 & a & a(2+b) & a(1+b+b^2) & a^2 & a^2(2+b) & a^2(1+b+b^2) \\ 1 & 1+b & 1+2b+b^2 & 2+a & (2+a)(1+b) & (2+a)(1+2b+b^2) & 1+a+a^2 & (1+a+a^2)(1+b) & (1+a+a^2)(1+2b+b^2) \\ 1 & b & b^2 & 2+a & (2+a)b & (2+a)b^2 & 1+a+a^2 & (1+a+a^2)b & (1+a+a^2)b^2 \\ 1 & 2+b & 1+b+b^2 & 2+a & (2+a)(2+b) & (2+a)(1+b+b^2) & 1+a+a^2 & (1+a+a^2)(2+b) & (1+a+a^2)(1+b+b^2) \end{bmatrix} \begin{bmatrix} 0&0&0&0&0&0&0&0&1 \\ 0&0&0&0&0&0&2&1&0 \\ 0&0&0&0&0&0&2&2&2 \\ 0&0&2&0&0&1&0&0&0 \\ 1&2&0&2&1&0&0&0&0 \\ 1&1&1&2&2&2&0&0&0 \\ 0&0&2&0&0&2&0&0&2 \\ 1&2&0&1&2&0&1&2&0 \\ 1&1&1&1&1&1&1&1&1 \end{bmatrix} \begin{bmatrix} f_{a0b0} \\ f_{a0b1} \\ f_{a0b2} \\ f_{a1b0} \\ f_{a1b1} \\ f_{a1b2} \\ f_{a2b0} \\ f_{a2b1} \\ f_{a2b2} \end{bmatrix}$$

where the values of the arrays [**A**] and [**B**] (in Figure 4) are given the corresponding values from the reversible Shannon and Davio expansions in a manner similar to the method used in Equations (11) and (12).

In Example 3, the implementation of the second method (utilizing Figure 4) can be done in two ways: (1) using a single matrix-matrix multiplication systolic array that multiplies the first basis vector matrix by the second vector of weighted sum of cofactors, and (2) using two chained matrix-matrix multiplication systolic arrays where the first systolic array multiplies the spectral transform matrix [**S**] and the cofactors vector and the second systolic array multiplies the basis vector matrix and the output vector that results from the first systolic array. Although, as shown in Example 3, the second method (using the reversible expansions) is more general and more systematic than the first method, yet the second method is more expensive than the first one in terms of the number of array elements of arrays [**A**] and [**B**] that are needed to be used.

Although the TPE-based results that are presented in this section are illustrated for the case of the 2D hexagonal systolic array, and since the add-multiply cell is the basic PE in these circuits and the TPE cell is the reversible GF counterpart of this fundamental add-multiply PE, other ternary add-multiply-based systolic arrays can be constructed reversibly using the interconnection between TPEs as well. The following Section introduces the multiple-valued quantum computations of the new multiple-valued reversible systolic arrays that were introduced in this Section.

5. Multiple-Valued Quantum Systolic Realizations and Computations

Quantum computing (QC) is a method of computation that uses a dynamic process governed by the Schrödinger Equation (SE) [1,15]. In the multiple-valued quantum computing context, the *time-independent* SE (TISE) is normally used, where the solution $|\psi\rangle$

is an expansion over orthogonal basis states $|\phi_i\rangle$ defined in a linear complex vector space called Hilbert space **H** as follows:

$$|\psi\rangle = \sum_i c_i |\phi_i\rangle, \tag{13}$$

where the coefficients c_i are called *probability amplitudes*, and $|c_i|^2$ is the *probability* that the quantum state $|\psi\rangle$ will collapse into the (eigen) state $|\phi_i\rangle$. The probability is equal to the inner product $|\langle\phi_i | \psi\rangle|^2$, with the unitary condition $\sum|c_i|^2 = 1$. In QC, a linear and unitary operator $\mathfrak{I}$ is used to transform an input vector of quantum bits (qubits) into an output vector of qubits.

Multiple-valued QC can also be accomplished [1,14]. For the three-valued QC, the qubit becomes a 3-dimensional vector quantum discrete digit (qudit), and in general, for multiple-valued QC (MVQC) the qudit is of dimension "many". For example, one has for 3-state QC (in Hilbert space **H**) the following qudits:

$$\text{qudit}_0 \equiv |0\rangle = \begin{bmatrix}1\\0\\0\end{bmatrix}, \text{qudit}_1 \equiv |1\rangle = \begin{bmatrix}0\\1\\0\end{bmatrix}, \text{qudit}_2 \equiv |2\rangle = \begin{bmatrix}0\\0\\1\end{bmatrix}. \tag{14}$$

A three-valued quantum state is a superposition of three quantum orthonormal basis states (i.e., vectors). Thus, for the orthonormal computational basis states $\{|0\rangle,|1\rangle,|2\rangle\}$, one has the following quantum state:

$$|\psi\rangle = \alpha|0\rangle + \beta|1\rangle + \gamma|2\rangle,$$

where $\alpha\alpha^* = |\alpha|^2 = p_0 \equiv$ the probability of having state $|\psi\rangle$ in state $|0\rangle$, $\beta\beta^* = |\beta|^2 = p_1 \equiv$ the probability of having state $|\psi\rangle$ in state $|1\rangle$, $\gamma\gamma^* = |\gamma|^2 = p_2 \equiv$ the probability of having state $|\psi\rangle$ in state $|2\rangle$, and $|\alpha|^2 + |\beta|^2 + |\gamma|^2 = 1$. The calculation in QC for multiple-valued multiple-systems follows the tensor product in a manner similar to the one demonstrated for the higher-dimensional qubit in two-valued QC. Figure 5 shows important Galois-based multiple-valued quantum gates [1].

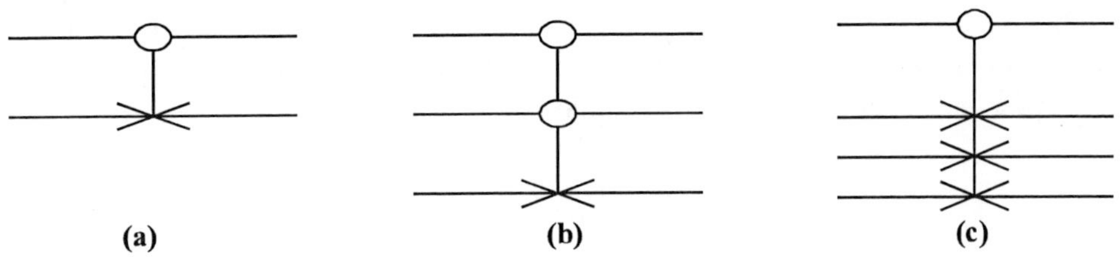

Figure 5. Fundamental GF(3) quantum gates: (a) ternary Feynman, (b) ternary Toffoli, and (c) ternary Fredkin gates.

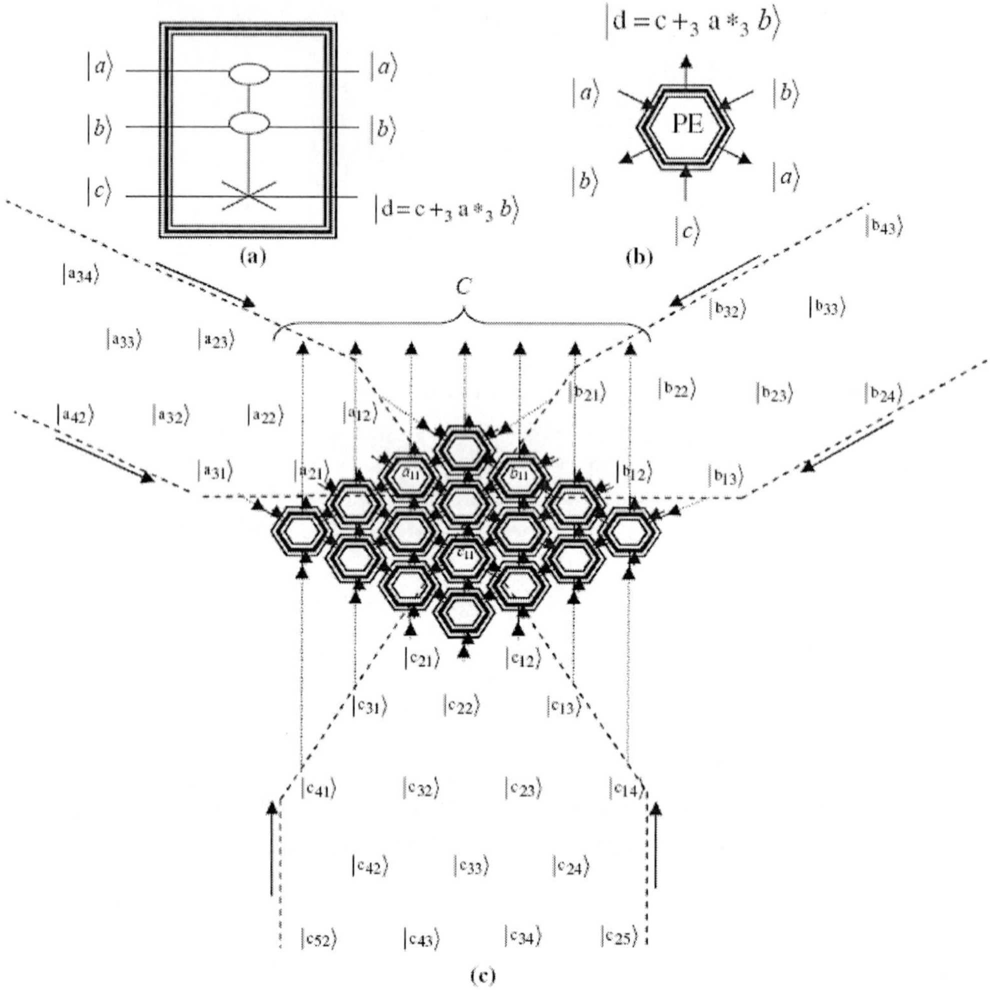

Figure 6. Quantum GF(3) systolic array: (a) quantum (3, 3) Toffoli PE, (b) quantum (3, 3) Kung cell, and (c) quantum Kung systolic array.

Similarly to the reversibility introduced in the previous section, and since basic PEs used in the construction of arithmetic systolic arrays are the add-multiply cells, Figure 6a introduces the ternary (3, 3) quantum Toffoli gate that implements, in the Galois quantum domain, the Kung add-multiply cell (in Figure 6b), and Figure 6c implements the 2D hexagonal quantum Kung systolic array over GF(3) by interconnecting the general GF(3) quantum Toffoli PEs (i.e., Toffoli cells). In Figure 6, the state in the ternary quantum Toffoli-based 2D hexagonal systolic array for n quantum Toffoli gates can be either: (1) decomposable into the tensor product as shown in Equation (15), or (2) non-decomposable (also known as entangled) as shown in Equation (16).

$$|\psi_T\rangle = |\psi_{12..n}\rangle = \prod_{T=1}^{n}\left(\sum_{k=0}^{26}\xi_{kT}\left|D_{(121314)(151716)(212322)(242526)}\right\rangle\right), \tag{15}$$

$$|\psi_T\rangle = |\psi_{12..n}\rangle \neq \prod_{T=1}^{n}\left(\sum_{k=0}^{26} \xi_{kT} \left| D_{(121314)(151716)(212322)(242526)} \right\rangle\right), \tag{16}$$

where ξ_{kT} is the probability amplitudes, and $|D_{(121314)(151716)(212322)(242526)}\rangle$ is the group-theoretic representation of the Toffoli-transformed fundamental basis states, where the $|D_{(121314)(151716)(212322)(242526)}\rangle$ group-theoretic representation of the ternary Toffoli cell stems from the fact that the ternary TPE cell transforms the input qudits as 12→13→14→12, 15→17→16→15, 21→23→22→21, 24→25→26→24, while preserving the domain-range mapping for the rest of the qudits.

CONCLUSION

New multiple-valued reversible and quantum systolic architectures for the synthesis of general multiple-valued Galois-based logic functions are introduced in the paper. The new arrays maintain regularity while preserving the reversibility (equipollent; bijectivity) property in the reversible space and the superposition property in the quantum space. Since it is estimated that at least 75% of all scientific applications involve matrix computations which are generally expensive in terms of storage space and processing time, and since basic PEs used in the construction of arithmetic systolic arrays are the add-multiply cells, the results introduced in this paper are general and apply, among others, to a wide class of add-multiply-based multiple-valued systolic arrays.

Since reversibility will reduce the power consumption in several future technologies, the new multiple-valued design method introduced in this paper can play an important role in the synthesis of circuits and systems that consume minimal power for future circuit implementations, and the new multiple-valued quantum superposition property will be essential in performing super-fast arithmetic-intensive computations that are fundamental in matrix-based future applications such as in multiple-valued multi-dimensional quantum signal processing (QSP) implementations.

REFERENCES

[1] Al-Rabadi, A. N., *Reversible Logic Synthesis: From Fundamentals to Quantum Computing*, Springer-Verlag, 2004.

[2] Barenco, A., Bennett, C. H., Cleve, R., DiVincenzo, D. P., Margolus, N., Shor, P., Sleator, T., Smolin, J. and Weinfurter, H., "Elementary Gates for Quantum Computation," *Phys. Rev. A*, 52, pp. 3457-3467, 1995.

[3] Bennett, C., "Logical Reversibility of Computation," *IBM J. of Research and Development*, 17, pp. 525-532, 1973.

[4] Brent, R. P. and Kung, H. T., "Systolic VLSI Arrays for Polynomial GCD Computation," *IEEE Trans. Comp.*, Vol. 13, pp. 731-736, 1984.

[5] DeVos, A., "Reversible Computing," *Progress in Quantum Electronics*, 23, pp. 1-49, 1999.
[6] Fortes, J. and Wah, B., "Systolic Arrays--From Concept to Implementation," *IEEE Comp. Mag.*, 20, pp. 12-17, 1987.
[7] Fredkin, E. and Toffoli, T., "Conservative Logic," *International J. of Theoretical Physics*, 21, pp. 219-253, 1982.
[8] Guo, I. - H. and Wang, C. - L., "Hardware-Efficient Systolic Architecture for Inversion and Division in GF(2^m)," *IEEE trans. Computers and Digital Techniques,* pp. 272-278, 1998.
[9] Huang, C. - T. and Wu, C. - W., "High-Speed C-Testable Systolic Array Design for Galois-Field Inversion," *Proc. European Design and Test Conf.*, pp. 342-346, March 1997.
[10] Kung, H. T., "Why Systolic Architectures?" *Computer*, Vol. 15, No.1, pp. 37-46, January 1982.
[11] Kung, S. Y., *VLSI Array Processors*, Prentice-Hall, 1988.
[12] Johnson, K., Hurson, A. and Shirazi, B., "General-Purpose Systolic Arrays," *Computer*, 26 (11), pp. 20-31, 1993.
[13] Landauer, R., "Irreversibility and Heat Generation in the Computational Process," *IBM J. Research and Development*, 5, pp.183-191, 1961.
[14] Muthukrishnan, A. and Stroud, C., "Multi-Valued Logic Gates for Quantum Computation," *Phy. Rev. A*, 62, 052309, 2000.
[15] Nielsen, M. and Chuang, I. L., *Quantum Computation and Quantum Information*, Cambridge University Press (CUP), 2000.
[16] Picton, P., "Optoelectronic Multi-Valued Conservative Logic," *Int. J. of Optical Computing,* 2, pp. 19-29, 1991.
[17] Quinton, P. and Robert, Y., *Systolic Algorithms & Architectures*, Prentice-Hall,
[18] N. J., 1991.
[19] Reddy, S. M., "Easily Testable Realizations of Logic Functions," *IEEE Trans. Comp.*, C-21, pp. 1183-1188, 1972.
[20] Roy, K. and Prasad, S., *Low-Power CMOS VLSI Circuit Design*, John Wiley & Sons Inc., 2000.
[21] Wang, C. - L. and Guo, J. - H., "New Systolic Arrays for C + AB^2, Inversion, and Division in GF(2^m)," *IEEE Trans. Comp.*, Vol. 49, No. 10, pp. 1120-1125, October 2000.
[22] Yan, Z. and Sarwate, D. V., "New Systolic Architectures for Inversion and Division in GF(2^m)," *IEEE Trans. Comp.*, Vol. 52, No. 11, pp. 1514-1519, 2003.

In: New Developments in Computer Research
Editor: Nikos E. Mastorakis
ISBN: 978-1-61470-321-1

10 YEARS OF SOFTWARE DEVELOPMENT FOR APPROXIMATE BAYESIAN COMPUTATION

Joao Sollari Lopes*
CCMAR, Faculdade de Ciências e Tecnologia, Ed.7, Universidade do Algarve, Campus de Gambelas, Faro, Portugal

ABSTRACT

Approximate Bayesian computation (ABC) is a recent developed statistical methodology that allows one to apply likelihood-free Bayesian statistics to complex models. This method relies on two main approximations: the use of Monte Carlo simulations, that avoid the need to use explicit likelihood functions; and the use of summary statistics to summarize data, which significantly reduces the amount of data to handle. The first approximation is particularly interesting in that it allows researchers to perform Bayesian inference provided they can generate simulations from the models of interest. Furthermore, one is not bound to a particular model. In fact one can assess the relative fit of different models just by evaluating the fit of the simulated data for all of them. These properties make ABC a powerful tool for statistical inference, which can be applied to many different fields. This method can be particularly attractive for computer scientists since their know-how in software development can be of great value. ABC can also be a very "democratic" method in the sense that, as long as computer packages are available, even researchers with just standard statistical knowledge can perform complex Bayesian inferences.

ABC has been developed in the late 90's in population genetics. Early work aimed to estimate demographic parameters using different population models. For this reason, the existing computer packages that perform ABC (e.g. SerialSimCoal, msBayes, DIY-ABC, popABC) were developed mostly to be applied to population biology. As ABC matured and its efficiency and robustness were recognized its popularity increased and the usage of the method expanded greatly. At first, ABC spread mostly to fields related to population genetics, such as, phylogeography, conservation genetics and epidemiologic studies. At present, only 10 years since its first application, the method has already spread to a vaster variety of fields, for example, theoretical statistics, protein structure evolution, stereology, chromosomal evolution, biochemical signaling pathways, meteorology and hatching management.

Despite the intensification of its usage, the statistical potential of this method is far from being reached. Indeed, although the core algorithm of ABC methods is fairly well established, modifications to widening its application and increase its efficiency have been proposed. Researchers have suggested sophisticated methodologies such as

* Correspondong author: Phone: +351 28 9800909 Fax: +351 28 9800051 Email: j.sollari.lopes@gmail.com

sequential approaches and hierarchical Bayesian methods, as well as, improvements on conditional density estimations, making ABC one of the most promising and fast-developing statistical techniques of the moment. The possibilities of ABC usage are also far from being fulfilled. Until now most of ABC applications have been in Natural Science, whereas fields that commonly use Bayesian applications, for example Finance, Health and Social sciences or Engineering, are yet to get the most out of this novel method. In order to bridge such gap and to increase the use of ABC there is a need for computer scientists to get more involved and to use their expertise to produce flexible user-friendly computer packages allowing more researchers from a wide variety of fields to use this recently developed statistical tool.

INTRODUCTION

The approximate Bayesian computation (ABC) algorithm is a fairly new technique with its origin in the field of population genetics about 10 years ago [1-3]. Despite the considerable developments of this still young statistical method [4-6], there are quite a few questions remaining unanswered regarding its core algorithm, in particular, the selection of summary statistics, the choice of the tolerance interval and the determination of the needed number of simulations. Nevertheless, the use of this Bayesian method verified an exponential expansion since its development till the end of 2009 (see figure 1; for the detailed list of publications contact the author).

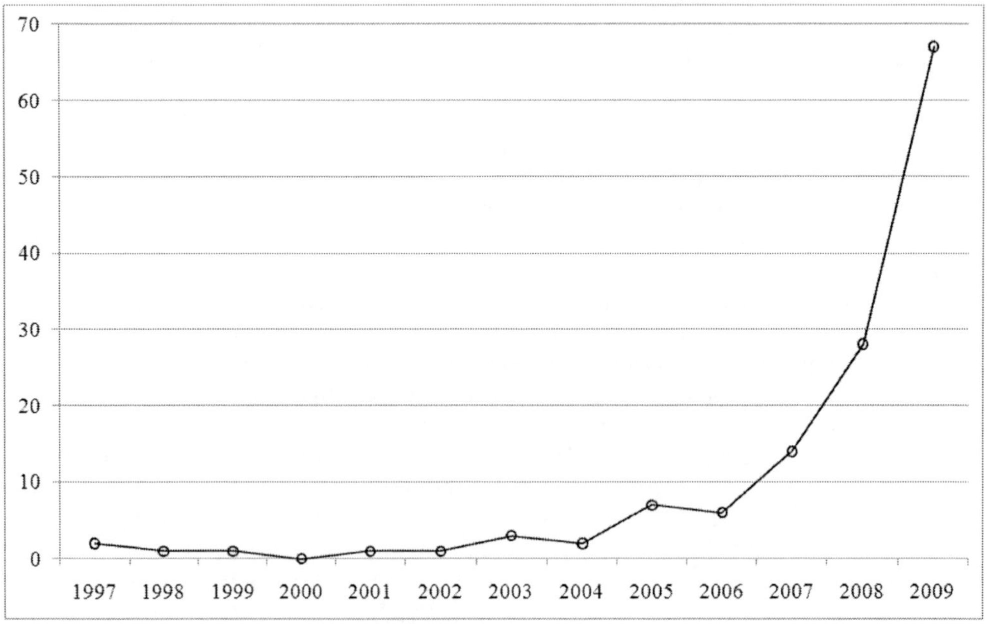

Figure 1. Number of papers using ABC methods since its introduction till the end of 2009.

ABC is characterized by two main features: the use of summary statistics to summarize data, which significantly reduces the amount of data to handle; and the use of Monte Carlo simulations that avoid the need to use explicit likelihood functions. These characteristics confer great flexibility to this statistical approach allowing for: analysis of complex models; use of large data sets; and estimation of parameters that would otherwise be intractable.

Numerous packages have been developed to be used within this framework [7-9]. As ABC methods started to be applied to a wider variety of fields (e.g. phylogeography [10]; conservation [11]; epidemiology [12]) and its robustness and flexibility were demonstrated [10, 13-15] there was a need for the development of more user-friendly software. As a consequence, some packages have been developed targeting empiricists [16-18]. With the growing ambition of using more complex models, the need for such software continued to increase. The characteristics of an ABC method, however, depend mainly on the model and the parameter values assumed. For this reason, each ABC procedure is commonly treated as an isolated study requiring some testing and tuning. Thus, newly developed software to be applied to other fields/models need to be rigorously tested and its efficiency assessed.

Quick Introduction to Bayesian Inference

The fundamentals of Bayesian statistics are very simple. The Bayesian paradigm is one of learning from data. The function of data is to add some information to our knowledge and, in this way, to update what we can say about the relevant parameters and hypotheses. As such, when wanting to learn from a new set of data, there is a need to identify what is known before the observation of those data. This is commonly called prior information. According to O'Hagan [19], it is through the incorporation of prior information that the Bayesian approach uses more information than the frequentist approach. The prior information is then synthesized with the information extracted from the new data to produce the posterior distribution. This will then express what we know about the parameters after seeing the data [19].

From a historical perspective, the name originated from the Reverend Thomas Bayes, an 18th century minister who first showed the use of the theorem in this way and gave rise to Bayesian statistics. The mathematical mechanisms for this synthesis come from the Bayes' theorem:

$$p(D,\Phi) = p(D|\Phi) \times p(\Phi), \tag{1}$$

where $p(\Phi)$ is the prior distribution, which is where our background knowledge is inputted; $p(D|\Phi)$ is the likelihood, which is the conditional distribution that specifies the probability of the observed data given any particular parameter set, and it is commonly obtained from a statistical model in which it is necessary to consider how the data can be "explained" by the parameters; $p(D,\Phi)$ is the joint distribution, which is the joint probability of a particular data and a parameter sets. With the joint distribution it is possible to calculate the posterior distribution, $p(\Phi|D)$, which is the aim of the Bayesian theorem:

$$p(\Phi|D) = \frac{p(D,\Phi)}{p(D)}, \qquad (2)$$

where $p(D)$ is the marginal distribution to the data and is characteristic of the data set in use. This distribution is often the central problem of the Bayesian analyses.

Although straightforward in principle, exact applications of the Bayesian paradigm are virtually impossible for very large data sets and complex models since their application often requires a considerable amount of computation power. For this reason, at the moment, the computational and technical details of different approaches to inference tend to take over of much of the research on this field. Presently, there are two main interrelated computer-intensive methods to statistical inference, Markov Chain Monte Carlo (MCMC) and importance sampling (IS). MCMC is a method for generating autocorrelated random samples from probability distributions. IS is generally used to approximate likelihoods based on independent samples [20].

Origin of Approximate Bayesian Computation

In the past decades, there has been a great increase in the use of Bayesian statistics in very many different fields. The practical advantages of such methods are well-known: they can easily accommodate unobserved data and latent variables; they provide an explicit mechanism for incorporating previous information via prior probability distributions; the resulting posterior probabilities are intuitively interpreted in contrast to the results from classic statistics; and they allow for analyses of complex data sets while assuming complicated models.

The aim of Bayesian inference is to calculate the probability distribution of the (typically vector-valued) parameter, Φ, given some empirical data, D, i.e. the posterior distribution $p(\Phi|D)$. This distribution can be obtained as the product of the prior distribution $p(\Phi)$, representing prior knowledge of the parameters, with the probability of observing particular values of the empirical data given particular values of the parameters, the likelihood $p(D|\Phi)$ (equation 1).

$$p(\Phi|D) \propto p(\Phi) \cdot p(D|\Phi), \qquad (3)$$

In the context of population genetics, coalescent theory [21-23] has provided a useful modeling framework for describing genetic data. This theory has revolutionized the field by forming the basis for likelihood calculations in genealogical models [24]. Fields such as molecular ecology, phylogeography, the study of human origins and evolutionary genetics also underwent considerable advances as a consequence of these developments [1, 25-27].

In the early 1990s the use of likelihood-based statistical methods, such as MCMC, to perform accurate statistical inferences from molecular genetic data increased in popularity [28]. However these methods have some limitations, in particular the need to use explicit likelihood calculations. Even when such calculations are possible, the application of MCMC methods can be computationally prohibitive and lead to convergence problems. Attempts to use increasing amounts of data and models of greater complexity led to the development of ABC methods [29].

When writing about ABC methods three papers should be mentioned: the first description of a true ABC method in population genetics by Pritchard and co-workers [1] and two papers that extended the approach and gave the technique its name: the study by Beaumont et al. [6] that explicitly recognized the technique as a method of conditional density estimation and provided refinements based on local linear regression; and the embedding of the ABC method within MCMC by Marjoram et al. [30]. However, the path to these methods as a simulation based approach had been laid down previously by other papers, particularly Tavaré et al. [2] and Weiss and von Haeseler [3] who actually used a non-Bayesian approach. The initial development of ABC depended also on the ability to rapidly simulate genetic data from different demographic scenarios based on coalescent theory.

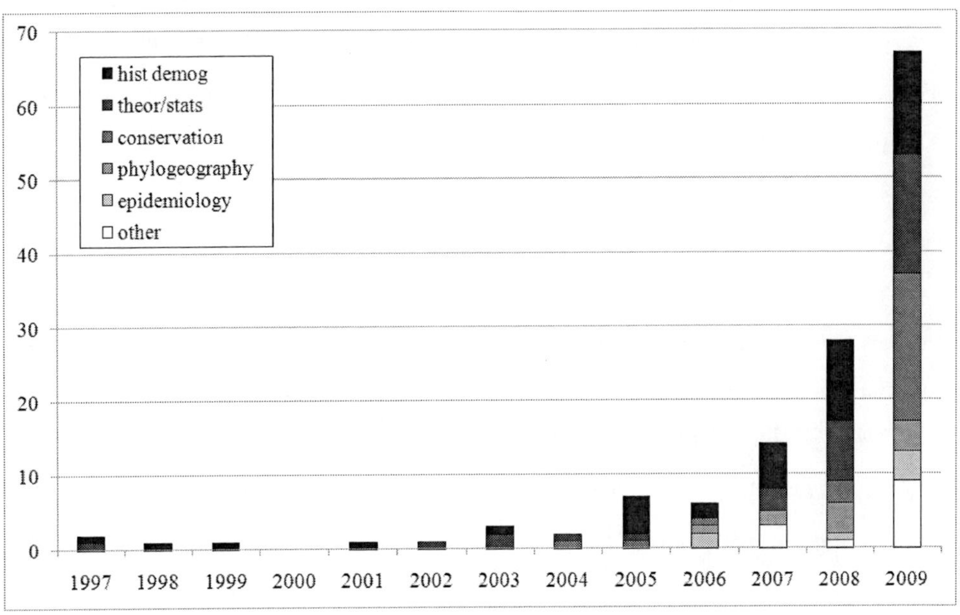

Figure 2. The use of ABC since its development in 5 main fields: historical demography (hist demog); theoretical or statistics studies (theor/stats); conservation genetics (conservation); phylogeography; and epidemiology.

Early uses of the method were primarily in population genetics, for inferring demographic history [1, 14, 31-33]. As its efficiency and robustness were recognized its popularity increased and the method has started to be used in a wide variety of fields [34]. The usage of ABC in fields related to population genetics occurred early on (see figure 2). For example: phylogeographic studies [10, 35, 36]; conservation studies [11, 37, 38] (for a review see [39]); epidemiologic studies [12, 40, 41] (for a review see [34]); and studies in ecology [42]. The method has also been applied to other fields, such as, theoretical statistics [43], protein structure evolution [44], stereology [45], chromosomal evolution [46], biochemical signaling pathways [47], and hatching management [48].

ABC Algorithms

The ABC-rejection and ABC-regression methods appear to have been the most widely used ABC "flavors" in population genetics [6, 49, 50].

ABC-Rejection

The basic algorithm, as introduced by Pritchard and co-workers [1] can be written as following:

(1) Sample (vector valued) parameter, Φ, from the prior: $\Phi_i \sim p(\Phi)$;

(2) Simulate data, D, given Φ_i: $D_i \sim p(D|\Phi_i)$;

(3) Summarize D_i with a set of chosen summary statistics to obtain S_i; go to (1) until N sample points from the joint distribution $p(S,\Phi)$ have been created;

(4) Accept the points whose S_i is within a distance δ from s', the real data summarized by the same set of summary statistics, $|S_i - s'| < \delta$.

In steps (1) to (3) one simulates independent pairs (Φ_i, S_i), $i = 1, 2, \ldots, N$, where each Φ_i is an independent draw from the prior distribution of Φ, and S_i are values that summarize simulated values of D with $\Phi = \Phi_i$. The (Φ_i, S_i) are then random draws from the joint density. Step (4), the rejection-step, provides an estimate of the conditional density, when $S = s'$, that is, the posterior distribution $p(\Phi|S = s')$. The idea is that the Φ_i for which $|S_i - s'|$ is small forms an approximation of a random sample from the desired posterior distribution $p(\Phi|D = d')$ [6].

ABC-Regression

In the regression method two innovations are proposed at step (4): smooth weighting and regression adjustment. The aim is to improve the sampling of the posterior density by weighting the Φ_i according to its distance from the real data by evaluating $|S_i - s'|$ and to adjust the Φ_i using local-linear regression to weaken the effect of that discrepancy [6].

The proposed algorithm [6] can be described as:

(4) Apply a weighting scheme to the points according to their distance to the s'. And then perform a weighted linear multiple regression with points assigned non-zero

weight. Adjust them according to $\Phi_i^* = \Phi_i + R_i$, where R_i is the residual of the ith point.

As noted by Beaumont and co-workers the rejection method can be viewed as a special case of the local-linear regression approach when using a uniform kernel and a local-constant regression. Furthermore, as δ tends to zero, the regression and rejection methods become equivalent.

RECENT DEVELOPMENTS IN ABC

Although the core algorithm of ABC methods is fairly well established, modifications to improve it have been proposed (see figure 3 for the use of the main ABC algorithms across time). Both the capabilities and the limitations of the standard ABC algorithm have been extensively studied [15, 49-52]. Recently, there have been some attempts to overcome the latter by proposing modifications at different stages of this Bayesian framework [4, 5, 53].

Efficient Sampling from the Priors

As mentioned before, one advantage of using Bayesian approaches is to be able to use previously available information in the studies through prior distributions. In the absence of information, however, a broad, flat distribution should be used. Analysis using these vague priors can be rather inefficient when using a standard rejection- or regression-based ABC approach.

MCMC-ABC methods

Marjoram and co-workers [30] proposed a method that came to be known as MCMC-ABC. This algorithm has the same properties as the standard ABC approach in the sense that it also relies on the use of summary statistics to summarize data and uses Monte Carlo simulations to avoid the need to use explicit likelihood functions. However, as in a standard MCMC approach, the sampling is performed via a transition kernel method and the new states are accepted via a Metropolis-Hasting algorithm [30]. The motivation behind this method was also to be able to apply a Bayesian analysis without having to treat the likelihood analytically. Despite these changes the MCMC-ABC approach can still present typical full-likelihood problems such as difficulties on the convergence and mixing of the chain and the demand for prohibitive computation times due to low acceptance rate [54]. Furthermore, as pointed out by Wegmann and co-workers [54], this approach is particularly sensitive to the tolerance interval. Truly, small tolerance intervals may lead to very long burn-in periods, since a very large number of simulations may be requested to have the first step accepted if the starting point is in a region with low likelihood. Nevertheless, this method has been recently given special attention because it allows a more efficient sampling than the standard ABC "blind" simulations, e.g. [54, 55].

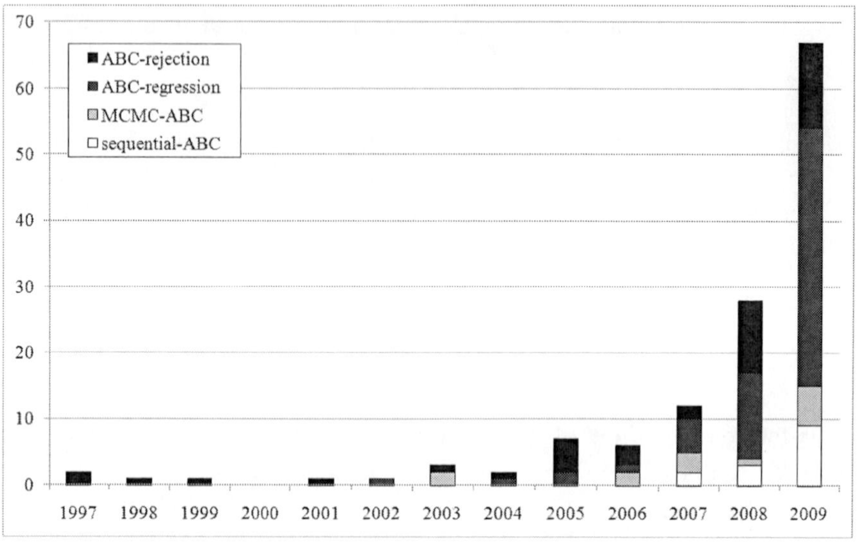

Figure 3. The use of 4 of the main ABC algorithms since its development: ABC-rejection; ABC-regression; MCMC-ABC; and sequential-ABC.

Sequential methods

One other way to improve the efficiency of vague prior distributions is to use sequential algorithms [4, 41, 56]. A basic example of such algorithms, based on standard rejection, is:

(1) Run the standard ABC algorithm once:

(1.1) Sample parameters, Φ, from the prior: $\Phi \sim p(\Phi)_1$;

(1.2) Obtain the first posterior, through rejection-based ABC procedure; $p(\Phi|D = d')_1$

(2) Run the ABC method n times (i = 1, 2, 3, … n), using a rough estimate of the ith posterior as the $i+1^{th}$ prior, but with a weight that corrects for not using the true prior:

(2.1) Sample, parameters, Φ, from the $i+1^{th}$ prior: $\Phi \sim p(\Phi)_{i+1}$;

(2.2) Weight the sampled value Φ with: $p(\Phi)_1 / p(\Phi)_{i+1}$;

(2.3) Obtain samples from the $i+1^{th}$ posterior, through standard ABC Procedures: $p(\Phi|D = d')_i$.

Note that in step (2.2) of this algorithm, we require an analytical expression for $p(\Phi)_{i+1}$, which is provided by fitting a kernel density. Note that this does not need to be an accurate density. This description of the sequential procedure in terms of importance sampling [step (2.2)] is quite intuitive. A more general description, based on theory in Del Moral et al. [57], which is rather less intuitive, is used in Sisson et al. [4], but this can lead to some problems, highlighted in Beaumont et al. [56]. When using a sequential algorithm the ABC method can be rerun as much as it is necessary in order to sharpen the posterior distribution

Hierarchical Bayesian methods

Hierarchical Bayesian models are based on the use of a hierarchical scheme for the prior distribution [58, 59]. In these models the values that characterize the prior distribution of its parameters, rather than being fixed and chosen by the modeler, may themselves be drawn from another prior distribution (the hyperprior). This hierarchy can be extended indefinitely. As an example one can consider two marginal prior distributions defining the mean, Π_{μ}, and the standard deviation, Π_{σ}, of a third distribution, $\Pi(\mu,\sigma)$, the former two are hyper priors of the latter. These approaches can be especially useful when analyzing parameter-rich models that consist of groups of parameters related to each other. For example, in population genetics rather than modeling mutation rate independently for each locus, or assuming that mutation rate is the same, one can model an intermediate stage in which the standard deviation and mean mutation rate across loci can also be inferred. Examples of ABC applications in hierarchical Bayesian models are given in Excoffier et al. [14], Hickerson et al. [10], Beaumont [60] and Cornuet et al. [16].

Conditional Density Estimation

The main approximation of the ABC algorithm concerns the final step, i.e. when attempting to sample from the posterior distribution. It is essentially a problem in conditional density estimation. In the standard algorithm instead of recovering samples corresponding to the exact posterior distribution, $p(\Phi|D=d')$, samples are taken from an approximation of that distribution using summary statistics, $p(\Phi|S=s')$. Additionally, in order to make the sampling more efficient, that approximation is further relaxed with the use of the rejection step [1], $p(\Phi\|S-s'|<\lambda)$. As seen before, the regression step [6] allows the use of larger values of δ by correcting the sampled values according to their distance from the real data set. We can interpret this as an improvement in conditional density estimation.

The regression step proposed by Beaumont and co-authors uses a linear regression to study the variation of the expected value of the summary statistics within the local interval of points with a non-zero weight. This method makes two assumptions: a linear relation between the variables in study; and that only the first moment of the distribution, the expected value, is varying within the accepted interval. Both assumptions should hold when dealing with small values of δ. However, methods that use non-linear regression and relax the assumption of constancy of all but the first moment of the sampled points have been explored, and found to produce some improvements on the ABC analyses [5].

Optimizing a Standard ABC Method

As seen before, ABC relies on a couple of approximations: the use of summary statistics to summarize the data, and the use of Monte Carlo simulations to avoid working with explicit likelihood functions. For this reason the conditional density estimates obtained by such methods should not be as accurate as the ones obtained from a full-likelihood method. Because of this, a fairly common procedure is to compare a standard ABC and the correspondent full-likelihood method [4, 6, 10, 60-65], when it exists. Following such comparison or using the ABC method alone, researchers can suggest updates and changes in order to optimize and tune ABC algorithms. Investigators often use synthetic data (i.e. generated data for which the parameter values are known) to test ABC efficiency. The comparison between tests can be performed by calculating the relative mean integrated square error (RMISE):

$$\frac{1}{n}\sum_{i=1}^{n}\left(\frac{(\phi_i - \phi')^2}{(\phi')^2}\right), \tag{5}$$

where n is the number of points sampled from the posterior distribution, ϕ_i is the parameter value of the ith accepted simulated data and ϕ' is the true value of the parameter under consideration. The advantage of the relative errors is to allow for the comparison of errors between parameters measured in different units.

Choosing the Number of Iterations and the Tolerance Interval

Ideally, when performing the rejection step, one would want to simulate an infinite number of realizations. If this was possible, one would then select a proportion of these simulations that matched exactly the data being analyzed, thus, obtaining the posterior distribution. The only concern would be to select a large enough proportion to estimate the posterior distribution accurately. Since it is not possible to simulate infinite amounts of data, one can set a tolerance interval to accept the simulated data that are "close enough" to the analyzed data. This approach has, however, the downside of aiming only for an approximation of the posterior distribution. It also raises a couple of important questions: How many simulations should be performed? And what value should one assume for the tolerance? These two questions are fundamentally connected.

There are two main approaches to set the tolerance value, either by establishing an absolute distance and accepting only the simulated data that are within that distance [1] or by setting a proportion of simulations to be accepted according to their "closeness" to the analyzed data [6]. Either way the main goal remains to obtain a good characterization of the simulated data distribution in the vicinity of the analyzed data. The advantage of the latter approach is to allow for a fast and simple sampling while guaranteeing a clear separation between the simulation and the rejection steps. In such approach the risk of setting a small proportion of accepted points is to obtain a poor or even biased sample of that distribution. The problem of setting a proportion too large is to sample simulated data that are very distant from the analyzed data, thus, obtaining a poor approximation of the posterior distribution.

The use of the regression and weighting step introduces some efficiency on sampling but adds a new complication. The aim of this step is to correct the sampled simulated data according to their distance from the data being analyzed. This allows sampling distant simulated data without decreasing the level of approximation of the posterior distribution, drastically reducing the total required number of simulations. However, the use of a small number of accepted simulated data, can introduce typical regression errors which often lead to erroneous posterior distributions. The final goal then is to choose a range of simulated data that, in one hand, is large enough to take into account the inherent stochasticity of the analyzed data, do not lead to a poor approximation of the posterior distribution and do not lead to regression problems, and in the other, do not accept simulated data that are too distant which cannot be corrected via the local linear regression step.

Unfortunately there is no general rule to calculate either the optimum range of tolerance intervals or the minimum needed simulations. Often such numbers are chosen by performing empirical studies, which provide guidelines solely for the analyzed problems [32, 33].

Choosing the Summary Statistics Set

The choice of the most suitable summary statistics is still a problematic area for ABC researchers [60]. Several attempts to provide a methodology for such choice have been proposed [15, 52], but there is little general consensus on the approach to take. This choice, however, is of great importance. The motivation behind using summary statistics is to reduce the dimensionality of the data (D) and to allow to easily calculate distances between data. Ideally one wants to use a set of statistics $S = \{S_1, \ldots, S_p\}$ sufficient for D, in that the posterior distribution $p(\Phi|S)$ is similar to the posterior distribution $p(\Phi|D)$[30]. The general rule is then to choose enough summary statistics, so that S is close to sufficient for D, while at the same time taking in account the dimensionality problems that arise with the increasing number of summary statistics, in particular the poor sampling of the joint distribution $p(\Phi, S)$ [60].

In order to choose summary statistics to estimate parameters using ABC one should be aware of their sensitivity to variation in such parameters. Ideally, the summary statistics should be highly correlated with the parameters in study. A simple linear correlation can provide a first insight into the relationship between one parameter and one particular summary statistic. This single value, however, fails to provide insights into the nature of the relationship. The simplest way to attain a better knowledge is from visual plots as in Hickerson et al. [51].

However, the correlation between a parameter and a summary statistic can lead to an erroneous choice of the summary statistics because it does not take into account the correlation between different summary statistics. Ideally, the summary statistics should be weakly correlated with each other, so that the extraction of information from the data is optimized. One way to deal with this problem is to calculate a multiple correlation coefficient between a parameter and different sets of summary statistics [e.g. R^2, Akaike's information criterion (AIC [66]), Mallow's Cp [67]]. One should be aware, however, that most of the available statistical tools for such calculations can only deal with linear relations. Another problem is that this approach does not consider all the parameters jointly. So far, the most useful method described in the literature to take all the information in consideration is to run

ABC analysis on synthetic data, in which the true parameter values are known, and compare the errors obtained from the use of different sets of summary statistics [10, 68].

Performing a Model-Choice Test with ABC

In order to perform model selection several methods have been proposed. Two of the most frequently used methods are likelihood ratio tests and the Akaike information criterion (AIC). Bayesian methods offer alternatives to such methods, in particular through the computation of Bayes factors [69] or less frequently through the use of Bayesian information criterion (BIC [70]). ABC offers yet another simpler but powerful method.

Within the ABC framework a model choice can be performed by considering the model itself as an additional parameter to infer. It is possible to sample a model indicator $x = 1, 2, \ldots, m$ for m models ($M_1, M_2, \ldots, M_m$) from a prior and treat this as a categorical random variable, X, in the ABC simulations [as suggested by 1]. In the beginning this was the standard use for performing model selection using ABC methods [10, 13, 71]. Beaumont [60] proposed to estimate the posterior probability of each candidate model using an approach based on a weighted multinomial logistic regression procedure. This approach is of the same nature of the regression step used for estimating parameters. After the ABC-rejection procedure one can then apply a categorical regression to estimate the posterior distribution $p(X = x_1 | S = s')$, where S is the summary statistic set and s' is the vector of the summary statistics that summarize the observed data. A scheme of weighting, as done in a standard regression procedure, can also be used. Since being proposed this step has been used fairly frequently [16, 63, 72, 73].

Existing Packages to Perform ABC

As stated above, the first application of ABC studies was on the estimation of historical demographic parameters. In these studies it was essential to use software to simulate genetic trees using the coalescence. Table 1 summarizes the main software (up to the end of 2009) developed to apply ABC methods. All these packages were developed to study population genetics related problems. In this table I also present the "flavor" of the ABC algorithm provided and whether the software has an interface, graphical or of other sort, to guide the user through its use.

In 2002, Richard Hudson published an extremely flexible coalescence simulator called ms. In 2005 the use of ABC analysis increased considerably and many studies used ms [51, 79-84]. The ms software has been pipelined in the msBayes package [8]. This package comprises several scripts that allow the user to run a complete ABC analysis. It has been used mainly in phylogeographic studies [10, 85-87].

In 2004 Laval and Excoffier released the coalescent simulator SIMCOAL2.0. This software simulates genetic trees using the discrete-generation coalescent approach. Although this approach involves slow simulations, it allows greater flexibility when defining demographic models. This software has been applied to ABC studies fairly frequently [14, 63,

88, 89]. A user-friendly interface for SIMCOAL to perform ABC analysis has also been developed [Serial SimCoal, 9]. This interface has also been used in a few ABC studies [11, 90].

Table 1. Available software to help users perform ABC analysis

	Algorithm	Interface	Reference
ms	Simulator	-	[7]
SIMCOAL 2.0	Simulator	-	[74]
SPLATCHE	Simulator	yes	[75]
SPAms	Simulator	yes	[76]
Serial SimCoal	ABC-regression	-	[9]
MIMAR	MCMC-ABC	-	[55]
msBayes	ABC-regression	-	[8]
DIY ABC	ABC-regression	yes	[16]
Rejector	ABC-rejection	-	[77]
ONeSAMP	ABC-rejection	yes	[17]
popABC	ABC-rejection	yes	[18]
2BAD	ABC-rejection	-	[78]

More recently two other packages have been developed: DIY ABC [16] and popABC [18]. These programs have been developed mainly to provide a fast and user-friendly way to run ABC studies, in particular for model-choice inferences. DIY ABC has been shown to be of importance when analyzing microsatellite data [73]. popABC is particularly useful for multilocus phylogeographic approaches with both STR and SNP data [39, 91].

Another program that was recently developed and had been used fairly frequently is ONeSAMP [17]. This software can only deal with a single Wright-Fisher population but has a very friendly web-based interface. For this reason it has already been extensively used to calculate effective population sizes [38, 48, 92, 93].

One cam also mention 2BAD a program developed to use an ABC approach around models of admixture or divergence. The number of models that can be analyzed is relatively limited, but the program is user-friendly and allows the comparison between models. It is possible for instance to determine whether genetic data can better be explained by one or two admixture events. The SPAms software was also developed to simulated data using ms as an engine but in a user-friendly environment. It is limited to a relatively small family of models, but computes many statistics for several types of markers.

Figure 4 present the uses of seven of the main existing ABC packages. One observation that is particularly striking is the high use of ONeSAMP package immediately after its release in 2008 (see table 1). On the other hand one can also observe the relatively low frequency of use of ms and SIMCOAL packages in 2009, even though these have been released much earlier (table 1) and can be applied to a wider range of problems. These observations can be explained by the easiness of use of ONeSAMP. Indeed, biologists with little expertise in statistics or computation can adopt the method in their analysis just by uploading their data to a webpage. In contrast, in order to use ms or SIMCOAL they require some programming knowledge to pipeline the ABC algorithm through the use of computer scripts. Software like popABC, 2BAD, SPAms and DIYABC provide menus to guide the user through the simulation or ABC procedures. Nevertheless, the increase of their use is not comparable to the one of ONeSAMP. This seems to indicate that in order to increase the use of ABC packages it is more important to invest in its interface and portability than to invest in the complexity and flexibility of the implemented models. As for the more theoretical and statistical works, researchers tend to use their own developed software.

WHAT OTHER FIELDS COULD BENEFIT FROM ABC?

In order to use ABC one has only to have a simulator machine capable of generating data under an assumed model. For this reason such technique can be applied to a wide range of fields. Such use is particularly interesting when other Bayesian models are hard to apply, for example, in complex models with untreatable likelihood functions or in analysis presenting convergence or mixing problems.

Allingham et al [94] demonstrated the application of ABC to complex data sets that often comprise skew and kurtotic data. Such data have rarely analytical defined likelihood functions, which makes ABC a good alternative to full-likelihood methods. According to the authors this modeling platform has strong potential in a wide range of disciplines, such as finance, psychology, astronomy and epidemiology, in which such data is commonplace [94].

Toni et al [41] studied the application of ABC to ordinary, delay and stochastic differential equations, in particular, to systems lacking reliable information and with several competing models for the structure of the underlying equations. In such studies the likelihood surfaces are often complex, hence, the advantage of using ABC. According to the authors the study of these dynamical systems has often application in physical, life and social sciences and engineering. Parameter estimation for stochastic models, in particular, has been extensively explored in financial mathematics [41].

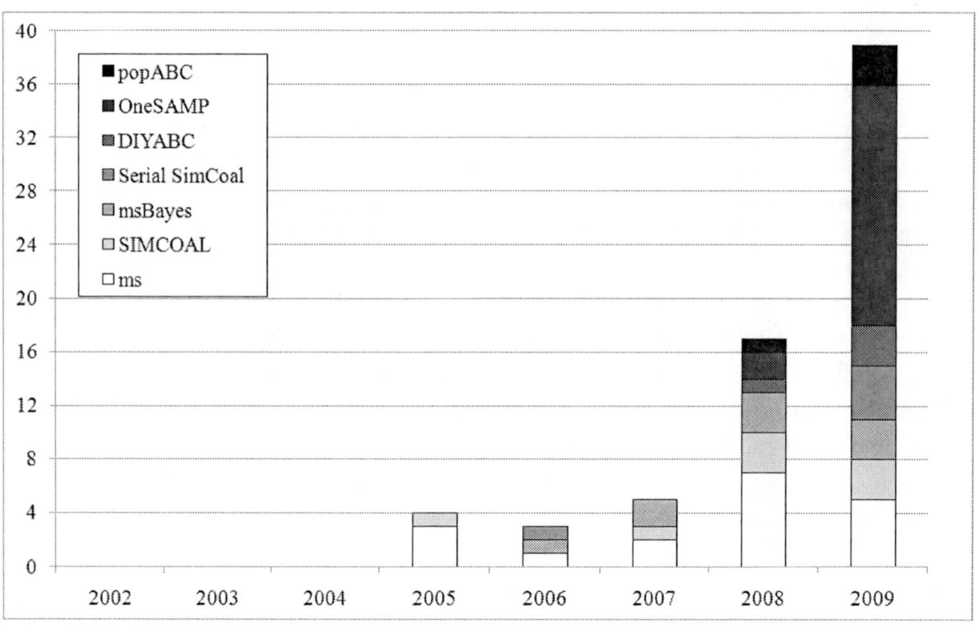

Figure 4. The use of 7 of the main ABC packages through time.

Blum and Tran [95] underline the importance of ABC in epidemiology, in particular in the role for understanding and predicting the spread of diseases. Luciani et al [96] demonstrate the importance of ABC to estimates the cost of resistance. Both aspects are highly important subjects for defining public health policies.

Blum and Francois [5] emphasize the ability of ABC to combine the power of simulating from stochastic individual based models with Bayesian theory, which potentiate the application of complex models to the field of social science, as well as the already mentioned areas of ecology, evolution and epidemiology.

Finally, Peters and co-authors [97] call attention to the fact that sequential Monte Carlo algorithms have been developed mostly in the fields of engineering, probability and statistics suggesting the use of sequential ABC-like algorithms in such fields.

CONCLUSION

There are a number of advantages in using likelihood-free methods such as ABC. In particular, this class of methods allows researchers to assume complex models, to analyze large amounts of data, compare different models easily, and produce estimations of parameters that would otherwise be intractable. Furthermore, despite the layers of approximation in ABC, several studies show that this general approach can obtain results very close to the correspondent full-likelihood approach. Moreover, frequent statistical research aiming to improve this Bayesian method seems to suggest a bright future for the increasing development of ABC. Recent advances include a better exploration of the prior space through a sequential approach, and the use of nonlinear conditional heteroscedastic regression to improve the conditional density estimation. These should lead to more efficient algorithms able to deal with more complex problems.

Early studies using ABC were applied to the field of population genetics. As this method became more popular and its flexibility and robustness were recognized, its application started spreading to other fields. At first researchers used ABC to study problems in fields related to population genetics (e.g. phylogeography, conservation genetics, epidemiologic studies and ecology), later on, however, this method started to be applied to fields unrelated to that area (e.g. theoretical statistics, stereology, biochemistry, meteorology and hatching management). The fast expansion of ABC can be explained in part by the numerous packages that have been developed to help researchers using the statistical method. In fact, at the moment there are several software that can lead researchers through the steps of the algorithm and that allow the use of several different models. Nevertheless there is still a need for tools for inferences based on complex models that can be easily used by empiricists [98]. In fact, packages that invest in more user-friendly interfaces register the largest number of uses, whereas more flexible software (i.e. that allows applications to wider range of problems) which often are not as user-friendly, do not have as many users. This suggests a strong demand for easy to use programs and the need for expertise in human-machine interface. Thus, there seem to be a clear niche for computer scientists in the development of ABC software.

At the moment, for historical reasons, available computer packages can only deal with population genetics related problems. The successful application of ABC to other fields, however, shows that the development of software in such areas would be most advantageous. Indeed, the rapid spread of this statistical method in the past suggests a similar success for new software applied to these other areas of research. Researchers have also shown that ABC methods can have a great potential on whole new fields, namely, engineering, finance, public health and social sciences. Moreover, some studies consider ABC methods ideal for models and types of problems characteristic of these new areas, such as, presence of complex data sets, solving problems involving differential equations and dynamical systems and considering stochastic agent-based models [99]. In this scenario the involvement of computer scientist to the development of software can again be essential.

REFERENCES

[1] Pritchard, J.K., et al., Population growth of human Y chromosomes: a study of Y chromosome microsatellites. Mol. Biol. Evol., 1999. 16(12): p. 1791-8.

[2] Tavare, S., et al., Inferring coalescence times from DNA sequence data. Genetics, 1997. 145(2): p. 505-18.

[3] Weiss, G. and A. von Haeseler, Inference of population history using a likelihood approach. Genetics., 1998. 149(3): p. 1539-46.

[4] Sisson, S.A., Y. Fan, and M.M. Tanaka, Sequential Monte Carlo without likelihoods. Proc. Natl. Acad. Sci. U.S.A., 2007. 104(6): p. 1760.

[5] Blum, M.G.B. and O. François, Non-linear regression models for Approximate Bayesian Computation. Stat. Comput., 2009. 20(1): p. 63-73.

[6] Beaumont, M.A., W. Zhang, and D.J. Balding, Approximate Bayesian computation in population genetics. Genetics, 2002. 162(4): p. 2025-35.

[7] Hudson, R.R., Generating samples under a Wright-Fisher neutral model of genetic variation. Bioinformatics, 2002. 18(2): p. 337-8.

[8] Hickerson, M.J., E. Stahl, and N. Takebayashi, msBayes: Pipeline for testing comparative phylogeographic histories using hierarchical approximate Bayesian computation. BMC Bioinformatics, 2007. 8: p. 268.

[9] Anderson, C.N.K., et al., Serial SimCoal: A population genetics model for data from multiple populations and points in time. Bioinformatics, 2005. 21(8): p. 1733-1734.

[10] Hickerson, M.J., E.A. Stahl, and H.A. Lessios, Test for simultaneous divergence using approximate bayesian computation. Evolution, 2006. 60(12): p. 2435-2453.

[11] Chan, Y.L., C.N.K. Anderson, and E.A. Hadly, Bayesian estimation of the timing and severity of a population bottleneck from ancient DNA. PLoS Genet., 2006. 2(4): p. e59.

[12] Tanaka, M.M., et al., Using Approximate Bayesian Computation to Estimate Tuberculosis Transmission Parameters From Genotype Data. Genetics, 2006. 173(3): p. 1511-1520.

[13] Estoup, A., et al., Genetic analysis of complex demographic scenarios: spatially expanding populations of the cane toad, Bufo marinus. Evolution, 2004. 58(9): p. 2021-36.

[14] Excoffier, L., A. Estoup, and J.M. Cornuet, Bayesian analysis of an admixture model with mutations and arbitrarily linked markers. Genetics, 2005. 169(3): p. 1727-38.

[15] Hamilton, G., et al., Bayesian estimation of recent migration rates after a spatial expansion. Genetics, 2005. 170(1): p. 409-17.

[16] Cornuet, J.M., et al., Inferring population history with DIY ABC: a user-friendly approach to approximate Bayesian computation. Bioinformatics, 2008. 24(23): p. 2713.

[17] Tallmon, D.A., et al., onesamp: a program to estimate effective population size using approximate Bayesian computation. Mol. Ecol. Resourc., 2008. 8(2): p. 299-301.

[18] Lopes, J., D. Balding, and M. Beaumont, PopABC: a program to infer historical demographic parameters. Bioinformatics, 2009. 25: p. 2747 - 2749.

[19] O'Hagan, A. and B.R. Luce, A Primer on Bayesian Statistics in Health Economics and Outcomes Research. 2003, London: Medtap International Inc. 72.

[20] Beaumont, M.A., Estimation of population growth or decline in genetically monitored populations. Genetics, 2003. 164(3): p. 1139-60.

[21] Kingman, J.F., The coalescent. Stoch. Proc. Appl., 1982. 13: p. 235-248.

[22] Hudson, R.R., Properties of a neutral allele model with intragenic recombination. Theor. Popul. Biol., 1983. 23: p. 183-201.

[23] Tajima, F., Evolutionary relationship of DNA sequences in finite populations. Genetics, 1983. 105(2): p. 437-60.

[24] Felsenstein, J., Estimating effective population size from samples of sequences: inefficiency of pairwise and segregating sites as compared to phylogenetic estimates. Genet. Res., 1992. 59(2): p. 139.

[25] Takahata, N., S.H. Lee, and Y. Satta, Testing multiregionality of modern human origins. Mol. Biol. Evol., 2001. 18(2): p. 172-183.

[26] Ford, M.J., Testing models of migration and isolation among populations of chinook salmon (Oncorhynchus tschawytscha). Evolution, 1998. 52: p. 539-557.

[27] Edwards, S.V. and P. Beerli, Perspective: gene divergence, population divergence, and the variance in coalescence time in phylogeographic studies. Evolution, 2000. 54(6): p. 1839-54.

[28] Wilson, I.J. and D.J. Balding, Genealogical inference from microsatellite data. Genetics, 1998. 150(1): p. 499-510.

[29] Marjoram, P. and S. Tavare, Modern computational approaches for analysing molecular genetic variation data. Nat. Rev. Genet., 2006. 7(10): p. 759-70.

[30] Marjoram, P., et al., Markov chain Monte Carlo without likelihoods. Proc. Natl. Acad. Sci. U.S.A., 2003. 100(26): p. 15324-8.

[31] Bonhomme, M., et al., Origin and number of founders in an introduced insular primate: estimation from nuclear genetic data. Mol. Ecol., 2008. 17(4): p. 1009-1019.

[32] Estoup, A., et al., Inferring population history from microsatellite and enzyme data in serially introduced cane toads, Bufo marinus. Genetics, 2001. 159(4): p. 1671-87.

[33] Estoup, A. and S.M. Clegg, Bayesian inferences on the recent island colonization history by the bird Zosterops lateralis lateralis. Mol. Ecol., 2003. 12(3): p. 657-74.

[34] Lopes, J.S. and M. Beaumont, ABC: a useful Bayesian tool for the analysis of population data. Infect. Genet. Evol., 2010. 10(6): p. 825-832.

[35] Leaché, A.D., S.C. Crews, and M.J. Hickerson, Two waves of diversification in mammals and reptiles of Baja California revealed by hierarchical Bayesian analysis. Biol. Lett., 2007. 3(6): p. 646.

[36] Legras, J., et al., Bread, beer and wine: Saccharomyces cerevisiae diversity reflects human history. Mol. Ecol., 2007. 16(10): p. 2091-2102.

[37] Evans, B.J., et al., A coalescent framework for comparing alternative models of population structure with genetic data: evolution of Celebes toads. Biol. Lett., 2008. 4(4): p. 430.

[38] Aspi, J., et al., Genetic structure of the northwestern Russian wolf populations and gene flow between Russia and Finland. Conservat. Genet., 2009. 10(4): p. 815-826.

[39] Lopes, J.S. and S. Boessenkool, The use of approximate Bayesian computation in conservation genetics and its application in a case study on yellow-eyed penguins. Conservat. Biol., 2009. 11(2): p. 421-433.

[40] Shriner, D., et al., Evolution of intrahost HIV-1 genetic diversity during chronic infection. Evolution, 2006. 60(6): p. 1165-1176.

[41] Toni, T., et al., Approximate Bayesian computation scheme for parameter inference and model selection in dynamical systems. J. R. Soc. Interface, 2009. 6(31): p. 187-202.

[42] Jabot, F. and J. Chave, Inferring the parameters of the neutral theory of biodiversity using phylogenetic information and implications for tropical forests. Ecol. Lett., 2009. 12(3): p. 239-248.

[43] Grelaud, A., C.P. Robert, and J.M. Marin, ABC methods for model choice in Gibbs random fields. Comptes rendus-Mathématique, 2009.

[44] Ratmann, O., et al., Using Likelihood-Free Inference to Compare Evolutionary Dynamics of the Protein Networks of H. pylori and P. falciparum. PLoS Comput. Biol., 2007. 3(11): p. e230.

[45] Bortot, P., S.G. Coles, and S.A. Sisson, Inference for stereological extremes. J. Am. Stat. Assoc., 2007. 102(477): p. 84-92.

[46] Koerich, L.B., et al., Low conservation of gene content in the Drosophila Y chromosome. Nature, 2008. 456: p. 949-51.

[47] Toni, T. and M.P.H. Stumpf (2009) Parameter inference and model selection in signaling pathway models. Volume,

[48] Slabbert, R., A.E. Bester, and M.E. D'Amato, Analyses of Genetic Diversity and Parentage Within a South African Hatchery of the Abalone Haliotis midae Linnaeus Using Microsatellite Markers. J. Shellfish Res., 2009. 28(2): p. 369-375.

[49] Wilkinson, R.D. (2008) Approximate Bayesian computation (ABC) gives exact results under the assumption of model error. Arvix preprint arXiv:0811.3355 Volume,

[50] Blum, M. (2009) Approximate Bayesian Computation: a non-parametric perspective. Arxiv preprint arXiv:0904.0635 Volume,

[51] Hickerson, M.J., G. Dolman, and C. Moritz, Comparative phylogeographic summary statistics for testing simultaneous vicariance. Mol. Ecol., 2005. 15(1): p. 209-223.

[52] Joyce, P. and P. Marjoram, Approximately sufficient statistics and Bayesian computation. Stat. Appl. Genet. Mol. Biol., 2008. 7(1): p. 26.

[53] Leuenberger, C., D. Wegmann, and L. Excoffier (2009) Bayesian Computation and Model Selection in Population Genetics. Arxiv preprint arXiv:0901.2231v1 Volume,

[54] Wegmann, D., C. Leuenberger, and L. Excoffier, Efficient Approximate Bayesian Computation Coupled With Markov Chain Monte Carlo Without Likelihood. Genetics, 2009. 182: p. 1207-1218.

[55] Becquet, C. and M. Przeworski, A new approach to estimate parameters of speciation models with application to apes. Genome Res., 2007. 17(10): p. 1505.

[56] Beaumont, M., et al., Adaptivity for ABC algorithms: the ABC-PMC scheme. Biometrika, 2009. 96: p. 983 - 990.

[57] Del Moral, P., A. Doucet, and A. Jasra, Sequential Monte Carlo samplers. J. Roy. Stat. Soc. B, 2006. 68(3): p. 411-436.
[58] Storz, J.F. and M.A. Beaumont, Testing for genetic evidence of population expansion and contraction: an empirical analysis of microsatellite DNA variation using a hierarchical Bayesian model. Evolution, 2002. 56(1): p. 154-66.
[59] Storz, J.F., M.A. Beaumont, and S.C. Alberts, Genetic evidence for long-term population decline in a savannah-dwelling primate: inferences from a hierarchical bayesian model. Mol. Biol. Evol., 2002. 19(11): p. 1981-90.
[60] Beaumont, M., Joint determination of topology, divergence time, and immigration in population trees., in Simulations, Genetics, and Human Prehistory, S. Matsumura, P. Forster, and C. Renfrew, Editors. 2008, McDonald Institute for Archaeological Research: Cambridge. p. 135-154.
[61] Sousa, V.M.C., et al., Approximate Bayesian Computation (ABC) Without Summary Statistics: The Case of Admixture. Genetics, 2009. 181: p. 1507-1519.
[62] Becquet, C., et al., Genomic analysis of chimpanzee population structure. PLoS Genetics, 2007. 3(2007): p. e66.
[63] Fagundes, N.J.R., et al., Statistical evaluation of alternative models of human evolution. Proc. Natl. Acad. Sci. U.S.A., 2007. 104(45): p. 17614.
[64] Foll, M., M.A. Beaumont, and O.E. Gaggiotti, An approximate Bayesian computation approach to overcome biases that arise when using AFLP markers to study population structure. Genetics, 2008. 179: p. 927-939.
[65] Plagnol, V. and S. Tavare, Approximate Bayesian computation and MCMC, in Monte Carlo and Quasi-Monte Carlo Methods 2002, H. Niederreiter, Editor. 2003, Springer-Verlag: Heidelberg. p. 99-113.
[66] Akaike, H., A new look at the statistical model identification. IEEE Transactions on Automatic Control, 1974. 19(6): p. 716–723.
[67] Mallows, C.L., Some Comments on Cp. Technometrics, 1973. 15: p. 661-675.
[68] Neuenschwander, S., et al., Colonization history of the Swiss Rhine basin by the bullhead (Cottus gobio): inference under a Bayesian spatially explicit framework. Mol. Ecol., 2008. 17(3): p. 757-772.
[69] Gelman, A., et al., Bayesian Data Analysis. 1995, London: Chapman & Hall. 696.
[70] Schwarz, G., Estimating the dimension of a model. Ann. Stat., 1978. 6(2): p. 461-464.
[71] Miller, N., et al., Multiple Transatlantic Introductions of the Western Corn Rootworm. Science, 2005. 310(5750): p. 992-.
[72] Ingvarsson, P.K., Multilocus patterns of nucleotide polymorphism and the demographic history of Populus tremula. Genetics, 2008. 180(1): p. 329.
[73] Verdu, P., et al., Origins and genetic diversity of Pygmy hunter-gatherers from western Central Africa. Curr. Biol., 2009. 19(4): p. 312-318.
[74] Laval, G. and L. Excoffier, SIMCOAL 2.0: a program to simulate genomic diversity over large recombining regions in a subdivided population with a complex history. 2004. 20(15): p. 2485-2487.
[75] Currat, M., N. Ray, and L. Excoffier, SPLATCHE: a program to simulate genetic diversity taking into account environmental heterogeneity. Mol. Ecol. Notes, 2004. 4(1): p. 139-142.
[76] Parreira, B., et al., SPAms: A user-friendly software to simulate population genetics data under complex demographic models. Mol. Ecol. Resour., 2009. 9(3): p. 749-753.

[77] Jobin, M.J. and J.L. Mountain, REJECTOR: software for population history inference from genetic data via a rejection algorithm. Bioinformatics, 2008. 24(24): p. 2936.

[78] Bray, T.C., et al., 2BAD: an application to estimate the parental contributions during two independent admixture events. Mol. Ecol. Resour., 2009. 10(3): p. 538-541.

[79] Haddrill, P.R., et al., Multilocus patterns of nucleotide variability and the demographic and selection history of Drosophila melanogaster populations. Genome Res., 2005. 15(6): p. 790-799.

[80] Wright, S.I., et al., The effects of artificial selection on the maize genome. Science, 2005. 308(5726): p. 1310-1314.

[81] Thornton, K. and P. Andolfatto, Approximate Bayesian inference reveals evidence for a recent, severe bottleneck in a Netherlands population of Drosophila melanogaster. Genetics, 2006. 172(3): p. 1607-1619.

[82] De Mita, S., et al., Investigation of the demographic and selective forces shaping the nucleotide diversity of genes involved in nod factor signaling in Medicago truncatula. Genetics, 2007. 177(4): p. 2123.

[83] François, O., et al., Demographic history of European populations of Arabidopsis thaliana. PLoS Genet., 2008. 4(5): p. e1000075.

[84] Legrand, D., et al., Species-wide Genetic Variation and Demographic History of Drosophila sechellia, a Species Lacking Population Structure. Genetics, 2009. 182: p. 1197-1206.

[85] Rosenblum, E.B., M.J. Hickerson, and C. Moritz, A multilocus perspective on colonization accompanied by selection and gene flow. Int. J. Organ. Evol., 2007. 61(12): p. 2971-2985.

[86] Hickerson, M.J. and C.P. Meyer, Testing comparative phylogeographic models of marine vicariance and dispersal using a hierarchical Bayesian approach. BMC Evol. Biol., 2008. 8(1): p. 322.

[87] Carnaval, A.C., et al., Stability predicts genetic diversity in the Brazilian Atlantic Forest hotspot. Science, 2009. 323(5915): p. 785.

[88] Kayser, M., et al., Genome-wide analysis indicates more Asian than Melanesian ancestry of Polynesians. Am. J. Hum. Genet., 2008. 82(1): p. 194-198.

[89] Patin, E., et al., Inferring the Demographic History of African Farmers and Pygmy Hunter–Gatherers Using a Multilocus Resequencing Data Set. PLoS Genet., 2009. 5(4): p. e1000448.

[90] Fabre, V., S. Condemi, and A. Degioanni, Genetic Evidence of Geographical Groups among Neanderthals. PLoS ONE, 2009. 4(4): p. e5151.

[91] Palero, F., et al., Rapid radiation in spiny lobsters (Palinurus spp) as revealed by classic and ABC methods using mtDNA and microsatellite data. BMC Evol. Biol., 2009. 9(1): p. 263.

[92] Witzenberger, K.A. and A. Hochkirch, Genetic consequences of animal translocations: A case study using the field cricket, Gryllus campestris L. Biol. Conservat., 2008. 141(12): p. 3059-3068.

[93] Johnson, J.A., et al., Long-term survival despite low genetic diversity in the critically endangered Madagascar fish-eagle. Mol. Ecol., 2009. 18(1): p. 54-63.

[94] Allingham, D., R.A.R. King, and K.L. Mengersen, Bayesian estimation of quantile distributions. Statistics and Computing, 2009. 19(2): p. 189-201.

[95] Blum, M.G.B. and V.C. Tran (2010) HIV with contact tracing: a case study in approximate Bayesian computation. Biostatistics Volume, DOI: 10.1093/biostatistics/kxq022

[96] Luciani, F., et al., The epidemiological fitness cost of drug resistance in Mycobacterium tuberculosis. Proc. Natl. Acad. Sci. U.S.A., 2009. 106(34): p. 14711.

[97] Peters, G.W., Y. Fan, and S.A. Sisson (2010) On sequential Monte Carlo, partial rejection control and approximate Bayesian computation. Arxiv preprint arXiv:0808.3466v2 Volume,

[98] Hickerson, M.J., et al., Phylogeography's past, present, and future: 10 years after. Molecular Phylogenetics and Evolution, 2009.

[99] Beaumont, M., Approximate Bayesian Computation in Evolution and Ecology. Annu. Rev. Ecol. Systemat., 2010. 41.

In: New Developments in Computer Research
Editor: Nikos E. Mastorakis

ISBN: 978-1-61470-321-1

BROADBAND INFRASTRUCTURE PROGRAMS IN THE AMERICAN RECOVERY AND REINVESTMENT ACT

Lennard G. Kruger*
Science and Technology Policy

SUMMARY

The American Recovery and Reinvestment Act (ARRA, P.L. 111-5) provided $7.2 billion primarily for broadband grant programs to be administered by two separate agencies: the National Telecommunications and Information Administration (NTIA) of the Department of Commerce (DOC) and the Rural Utilities Service (RUS) of the U.S. Department of Agriculture (USDA). Of the $7.2 billion total, the ARRA provided $4.7 billion to establish a Broadband Technology Opportunities Program (BTOP) at NTIA, and $2.5 billion as funding for broadband grant, loan, and loan/grant combination programs at RUS. Broadband grants and loans funded by the ARRA are competitive and applicants must apply directly to NTIA and RUS. The NTIA appropriation also included $350 million for a national broadband inventory map, funding for the Broadband Data Improvement Act (P.L. 110-385), and funding to be transferred to the Federal Communications Commission (FCC) to develop a national broadband plan.

The unprecedented scale and scope of the ARRA broadband programs, coupled with the short time frame for awarding grants, presents daunting challenges with respect to program implementation as well as Congressional oversight. Congress is closely monitoring how equitably and effectively broadband grants are allocated among states and the various stakeholders, and to what extent the programs fulfill the goals of short term job creation and the longer term economic benefits anticipated from improved broadband availability, access, and adoption. A continuing issue is how to strike a balance between providing federal assistance for unserved and underserved areas where the private sector may not be providing acceptable levels of broadband service, while at the same time minimizing any deleterious effects that government intervention in the marketplace may have on competition and private sector investment.

The first round of funding for broadband grants, loans, and loan/grant combinations was announced with the release of a Notice of Funds Availability (NOFA) on July 1, 2009. The NOFA contains eligibility requirements, application rules and procedures, and evaluation criteria for BTOP at NTIA and for the Broadband Initiatives Program (BIP) at RUS. Program

* Email: lkruger@crs.loc.gov, 7-7070

implementation decisions made by NTIA and RUS could have a significant impact on how the program is shaped and targeted, and the extent to which the program meets the goals and purposes set forth by the ARRA. Implementation issues include defining "underserved" and "unserved" areas with respect to broadband service, defining "nondiscrimination and network interconnection obligations," defining "broadband," the role of the states, broadband data collection, and evaluation and transparency.

NTIA and RUS received over 2,200 applications requesting nearly $28 billion in funding. While initially NTIA and RUS had expected to begin announcing awards in November, because of the volume and complexity of the applications received, award announcements are expected to begin by December 15, 2009. Meanwhile, the second funding round will likely open in early 2010. Prior to the second round, NTIA and RUS will collect public comment on "lessons learned" and on what changes should be reflected in the second round NOFA. Controversial issues, such as the RUS definition of "remote unserved areas," will likely be reexamined as part of the second NOFA process.

INTRODUCTION

Broadband infrastructure refers to networks of deployed telecommunications equipment and technologies necessary to provide high-speed Internet access and other advanced telecommunications services for private homes, businesses, commercial establishments, schools, and public institutions. In the United States, broadband infrastructure is constructed, operated, and maintained primarily by the private sector, including telephone, cable, satellite, wireless, and other information technology companies. Currently deployed broadband technologies include cable modem, DSL (copper wire), wireless systems (mobile and fixed), fiber, and satellite. Although broadband is deployed by private sector providers, federal and state regulation of the telecommunications industry as well as government financial assistance programs can have a significant impact on private sector decisions to invest in and deploy broadband infrastructure, particularly in underserved and unserved areas of the nation.

The American Recovery and Reinvestment Act (ARRA, P.L. 111-5) provided $7.2 billion primarily for broadband grant programs to be administered by two separate agencies: the National Telecommunications and Information Administration (NTIA) of the Department of Commerce (DOC) and the Rural Utilities Service (RUS) of the U.S. Department of Agriculture (USDA). Of the $7.2 billion total, the ARRA provided $4.7 billion to establish a Broadband Technology Opportunities Program (BTOP) at NTIA, and $2.5 billion for broadband grant, loan, and loan/grant combination programs at RUS. The ARRA also directed the Federal Communications Commission (FCC) to develop a national broadband strategy. In comparison with previously existing federal broadband programs in the United States,[16] the broadband grant and loan programs established and funded by P.L. 111-5 are unprecedented in scale and scope.

The impetus behind broadband provisions in the ARRA was two-fold: in the short term, to create jobs through the construction and deployment of broadband infrastructure, and in the long term, to address concerns over economic and societal impacts of inadequate broadband

[16] See CRS Report RL30719, Broadband Internet Access and the Digital Divide: Federal Assistance Programs, by Lennard G. Kruger and Angele A. Gilroy.

availability, access, and adoption, particularly in rural and lower-income areas of the nation.[17] The unprecedented scale and scope of the ARRA broadband programs, coupled with the short time frame for awarding grants, presents daunting challenges with respect to program implementation as well as Congressional oversight.

AMERICAN RECOVERY AND REINVESTMENT ACT OF 2009, P.L. 111-5

In December 2008, leadership in the House and Senate, as well as the Obama transition team, announced their intention to include a broadband component in the infrastructure portion of the economic stimulus package. At the same time, numerous interested parties, including broadband equipment manufacturers; large, mid-sized, and small wireline and wireless service providers; satellite operators; telecommunications unions; consumer groups; education groups; public safety organizations; think tanks; and others unveiled a multitude of specific proposals for government support of broadband infrastructure.[18]

The House and Senate approved the Conference Report on H.R. 1 (H.Rept. 111-16) on February 13, 2009. On February 17, 2009, President Obama signed P.L. 111-5, the American Recovery and Reinvestment Act (ARRA). Broadband provisions of the ARRA provided a total of $7.2 billion, primarily for broadband grants. The total consists of $4.7 billion to NTIA/DOC for a newly established Broadband Technology Opportunities Program (BTOP) and $2.5 billion to RUS/USDA broadband grant, loan, and loan/grant combination programs.[19]

NTIA/DOC

Of the $4.7 billion appropriated to NTIA:

- $4.35 billion was directed to a competitive broadband grant program, of which not less than $200 million shall be available for competitive grants for expanding public computer center capacity (including at community colleges and public libraries); not less than $250 million to encourage sustainable adoption of broadband service; and $10 million transferred to the DOC Office of Inspector General for audits and oversight;
- $350 million was directed for funding the Broadband Data Improvement Act (P.L. 110-385) and for the purpose of developing and maintaining a broadband inventory map, which shall be made accessible to the public no later than two years after enactment; and

[17] See ibid., pp. 1-4.

[18] See CRS Report R40 149, Infrastructure Programs: What's Different About Broadband?, by Charles B. Goldfarb and Lennard G. Kruger.

[19] For information on stimulus funding directed to the existing broadband programs at RUS, see CRS Report RL33816, Broadband Loan and Grant Programs in the USDA's Rural Utilities Service, by Lennard G. Kruger.

- Funds deemed necessary and appropriate by the Secretary of Commerce, in consultation with the FCC, may be transferred to the FCC for the purposes of developing a national broadband plan, which shall be completed one year after enactment.

The Broadband Technology Opportunities Program within NTIA is authorized by Division B, Title VI of the ARRA. Specific implementation requirements and guidelines for the new NTIA broadband grants are as follows:

- Established a "national broadband service development and expansion program" with purposes to include providing access to broadband service to consumers residing in unserved and underserved areas; providing broadband education, awareness, training, access, equipment and support to various institutions; improving access to, and use of, broadband service by public safety agencies; and stimulating demand for broadband, economic growth, and job creation.
- Directed NTIA to consult with each state to identify unserved and underserved areas (with respect to access to broadband service) as well as the appropriate allocation of grant funds within that state.
- Directed NTIA, to the extent practical, to award not less than one grant in each state.
- Did not define "unserved area," "underserved area," and "broadband." The Conferees instructed NTIA to coordinate its understanding of these terms with the FCC, and in defining "broadband service" to take into consideration technical differences between wireless and wireline networks and to consider the actual speeds these networks are able to deliver to consumers under a variety of circumstances.
- Directed NTIA, in coordination with the FCC, to publish "non-discrimination and network interconnection obligations" that shall be contractual conditions of awarded grants, and specifies that these obligations should adhere, at a minimum, to the FCC's broadband principles to promote the openness and interconnected nature of the Internet (FCC 05-151, adopted August 5, 2005).[20]
- Directed NTIA, when considering applications for grants, to consider whether the project will provide the greatest broadband speed possible to the greatest population of users in the area. There are no specific speed thresholds that applicants must meet to be eligible for a grant. The Conferees acknowledged that while speed thresholds could have the unintended effect of thwarting broadband deployment in some areas, deploying next-generation speeds would likely result in greater job creation and job preservation. NTIA is instructed to "seek to fund, to the extent practicable, projects that provide the highest possible, next-generation broadband speeds to consumers."

[20] See CRS Report R40616, Access to Broadband Networks: The Net Neutrality Debate , by Angele A. Gilroy

- Defined entities eligible for grants as: a state or political division thereof; the District of Columbia; a territory or possession of the United States; an Indian tribe or native Hawaiian organization; a nonprofit foundation, corporation, institution or association; or any other entity, including a broadband service or infrastructure provider, that NTIA finds by rule to be in the public interest.
- Required NTIA to consider whether a grant applicant is a socially and economically disadvantaged small business as defined under the Small Business Act.
- Directed NTIA to ensure that all awards are made before the end of FY20 10. Grantees will be required to substantially complete projects within two years after the grant is awarded.
- Directed that the federal share of any project cannot exceed 80% unless the applicant petitions NTIA and demonstrates financial need.
- Directed that grant applicants must demonstrate that the grant project would not have been implemented during the grant period without federal grant assistance.

RUS/USDA

The $2.5 billion appropriated to RUS was designated as additional amounts for RUS grant and loan programs. The ARRA did not specify how the $2.5 billion is to be divided between grants and loans. Regarding projects applying for ARRA funding, the law stated that:

- at least 75% of the area to be served by a project receiving these funds shall be in a rural area without sufficient access to high-speed broadband service to facilitate economic development, as determined by the Secretary of Agriculture;
- priority shall be given to projects that will deliver end users a choice of more than one broadband service provider;
- priority shall be given to projects that provide service to the highest proportion of rural residents that do not have access to broadband service;
- priority shall be given to borrowers and former borrowers of rural telephone loans;
- priority shall be given to projects demonstrating that all project elements will be fully funded, that can commence promptly, and that can be completed; and
- no area of a project may receive funding to provide broadband service under the Broadband Technology Opportunities Program at NTIA/DOC.

IMPLEMENTATION OF ARRA BROADBAND PROGRAMS

ARRA broadband programs encompass three distinct programs or activities: (1) grants, loans, and loan/grant combinations to expand broadband services and infrastructure (NTIA and RUS); (2) the State Broadband Data and Development Grant Program (NTIA); and (3) development of a national broadband plan (FCC). "Broadband USA," the official web portal to apply for ARRA broadband funding, is located at http://broadbandusa.sc.egov.usda.gov/. Agency websites tracking the latest ARRA broadband program developments are located at NTIA,[21] RUS,[22] and the FCC.[23]

Table 1. Selected Comparison of BIP and BTOP Provisions in NOFA

Broadband Initiatives Program (BIP), Rural Utilities Service	Broadband Technology Opportunities Program (BTOP), National Telecommunications and Information Administration
Funding	
$2.4 billion total for first round (program level), includes up to: • $1.2 billion for Last Mile projects ($400 million in grants for Remote Area projects, $800 million in loans and loan/grant combinations for Non-Remote projects); • $800 million in loans and loan/grant combinations for Middle Mile projects; and • $325 million for reserve fund.	$1.6 billion for first round (budget authority), includes up to: • $1.2 billion for broadband infrastructure grants (Last Mile and Middle Mile projects); • $50 million for Public Computer Center grants; • $150 million for Sustainable Broadband Adoption grants; and • $200 million for reserve fund.
Definition of "Unserved" and "Underserved"	
Same as NTIA/BTOP definition. Additionally defines "Remote Area" as an unserved, rural area 50 miles from the limits of a non-rural area.	Eligible "unserved areas" defined as where at least 90% of households lack access to terrestrial broadband service. Eligible "underserved areas" for last mile projects if at least one of the following factors is met: (1) no more than 50% of the households in the proposed funded service area have access to facilities-based, terrestrial broadband service at greater than the minimum broadband transmission speed; (2) no broadband service provider advertises broadband transmission speeds of at least 3 megabits per second (Mbps) downstream; or (3) the rate of broadband subscribership for the proposed funded service area is 40% of households or less. A proposed funded service area may qualify as underserved for middle mile projects if one interconnection point terminates in a proposed funded service area that qualifies as unserved or underserved for last mile projects.

[21] http://www.ntia.doc.gov/broadbandgrants.

[22] http://www.usda.gov/rus/telecom/index.htm.

[23] http://www.fcc.gov/recovery/broadband/.

Definition of "Broadband"	
Same as NTIA/BTOP definition.	Two-way data transmission with advertised speeds of at least 768 kbps downstream and at least 200 kbps upstream to end users, or providing sufficient capacity in a middle mile project to support the provision of broadband service to end users.
Definition of "Rural Area"	
Any area, as confirmed by the latest decennial census of the Bureau of the Census, which is not located within: (1) a city, town, or incorporated area that has a population of greater than 20,000 inhabitants or (2) an urbanized area contiguous and adjacent to a city or town that has a population of greater than 50,000 inhabitants. For purposes of the definition of rural area, an urbanized area means a densely populated territory as defined in the latest decennial census of the U.S. Census Bureau.	Same definition as used by BIP/RUS. Applications to fund broadband infrastructure projects in areas which are at least 75% rural are required to be submitted to BIP. BTOP may make awards to such applications NTIA determines to be meritorious after RUS has reviewed the application and determined not to fund it. All other applications for Broadband Infrastructure projects, as well as applications for Public Computer Centers or Sustainable Broadband Adoption projects, must be submitted to BTOP.
Financial Obligation of Applicant	
For grants (Last Mile Remote Area projects): funding up to 100%. For grants receiving greater than 80% of eligible costs, the Administrator must determine that the awardee has a specific financial need that justifies funding greater than 80%; all applicants must be able to generate a minimum current ratioa of one by the end of the forecast period and demonstrate a positive cash balance for each year of the forecast period. For loans: the applicant must be able to generate sufficient revenues to cover expenses, have sufficient cash flow to service debts and obligations as they come due, and meet the minimum Times Interest Earned Ratio (TIER)[b] requirement of one by the end of the forecast period, as determined by RUS.	Required to provide matching funds of at least 20% toward the total eligible project cost. Applicants must document their capacity to provide matching funds. NTIA will provide up to 80% of total eligible project costs, unless the applicant petitions the Assistant Secretary for a waiver of the matching requirement and that waiver is granted by the Assistant Secretary based on the applicant's demonstration of financial need. In- kind contributions, including third party in-kind contributions, are non-cash donations to a project that may count toward satisfying the non-federal matching requirement of a project's total budget. In-kind contributions must be allowable project expenses.

a. "Current ratio" is defined as the applicant's current assets divided by the current liabilities.

b. TIER is defined as the ratio of an applicant's net income (after taxes) plus (adding back) interest expense, all divided by interest expense (existing and any new interest expense including the interest expense associated with the proposed loan).

Grants, Loans and Loan/Grant Combinations for Broadband Expansion

On July 1, 2009, NTIA and RUS jointly released the first Notice of Funds Availability (NOFA) detailing requirements, rules, and procedures for applying for ARRA grants, loans, and loan grant combinations.[24] The total amount available in this first funding round is $4 billion. This total consists of $2.4 billion (program level) under the RUS Broadband Initiatives Program (BIP), which will extend loans, grants, and loan/grant combinations to facilitate broadband deployment in rural areas; and $1.6 billion (budget authority) under the NTIA Broadband Technology Opportunities Program (BTOP), which will make available grants for deploying broadband infrastructure in unserved and underserved areas, enhance broadband capacity at public computer centers, and promote sustainable broadband adoption projects. **Table 1** compares the NOFA provisions for BTOP and BIP with respect to funding; definitions of "unserved," "underserved," and "broadband;" definitions of "rural area;" and financial obligations of applicants.

BIP Grants, Loans and Grant/Loan Combinations

The ARRA requires that areas served by BIP-funded projects be at least 75% rural.

Predominantly non-rural areas are therefore *not* eligible for BIP funding. A rural area is defined as any area not located within a city, town, or incorporated area that has a population of greater than 20,000 inhabitants; or not located within an urbanized area contiguous and adjacent to a city or town that has a population of greater than 50,000 inhabitants.

Grants under BIP can only be used to fund applications proposing to exclusively serve remote, unserved, rural areas. Terms are defined as follows:

- "Remote area" is a rural unserved area at least 50 miles from a non-rural area;
- "Unserved area" is an area where at least 90% percent of households lack access to terrestrial (non-satellite) broadband service; and
- "Broadband" means two-way data transmission with advertised speeds of at least 768 kbps downstream and at least 200 kbps upstream to end users. According to the NOFA, this speed encompasses all current major wired and wireless technologies and is sufficient for applications such as voice service over the Internet (VOIP), web browsing, and one way video.

Loans and loan/grant combinations are available for applications proposing to serve non-remote and underserved rural areas. Loan/grant combinations can consist of up to 50% grant money. For an area to be considered "underserved," at least one of the following three statements must be true:

- 50% or more of households don't have any terrestrial broadband access;
- No provider in the area is advertising broadband speeds of at least 3 or more megabits per second (Mbps); or
- Broadband subscribership is 40% or less.

---

[24] Available at http://www.ntia.doc.gov/frnotices/2009/FR_BBNOFA_090702.pdf.

Available first round funding for BIP grants, loans, and loan/grant combinations is $2.5 billion.[25] Funding is available for Last Mile Projects[26] and Middle Mile Projects.[27] Last Mile Projects ($1.2 billion available) include:

- Up to $400 million in grants for projects exclusively serving remote unserved rural areas.
- Up to $800 million in loans and loan/grant combinations for projects serving non-remote rural areas (both unserved and underserved).

Up to $800 million in loans and loan/grant combinations are available for Middle Mile Projects. Additionally, $325 million is directed to a reserve fund, which may be used to either augment the above categories or be carried over to the next funding round.

BTOP Grants

BTOP grant funds are available through three categories of eligible projects:

- Broadband Infrastructure ($1.2 billion available);
- Public Computer Centers ($50 million available); and
- Sustainable Broadband Adoption ($150 million available).

Additionally, $200 million is directed to a reserve fund, which may be used to either augment the above categories or be carried over to the next funding round.

Broadband Infrastructure grants are available for both Last Mile and Middle Mile projects, and must support projects that serve either unserved or underserved areas (see above definitions). The Public Computer Center category funds projects that expand public access to broadband service and enhance broadband capacity at entities, such as community colleges and public libraries, that permit the public to use these computing centers. The Sustainable Broadband Adoption category funds innovative projects that promote broadband demand, including projects focused on providing broadband education, awareness, training, access, equipment or support, particularly among vulnerable population groups where broadband technology has traditionally been underutilized.

BIP and BTOP Application and Evaluation Process

All applications for projects serving areas that are at least 75% rural are *required* to be submitted to the Broadband Initiatives Program at RUS. Those applications may subsequently be considered by NTIA if RUS decides not to fund them. Thus for broadband infrastructure project applications proposing to serve rural areas, applicants have the choice of either applying to BIP only, or to BIP and BTOP simultaneously. All other applications –

[25] The $2.5 billion represents program level. Corresponding budget authority is $1.3 billion. Program level exceeds budget authority because a portion of budget authority goes towards subsidizing loans.

[26] Last Mile project means any infrastructure project the predominant purpose of which is to provide broadband service to end users or end-user devices.

[27] Middle Mile project means a broadband infrastructure project that does not predominantly provide broadband service to end users or to end-user devices, and may include interoffice transport, backhaul, Internet connectivity, or special access.

broadband infrastructure for non-rural areas, public computer centers, and sustainable broadband adoption projects – are submitted directly to the Broadband Technology Opportunities Program at NTIA.

Both NTIA and RUS are evaluating and scoring each application based on the proposed project's purpose, benefits, viability, and budget and sustainability. Both agencies employ a two-stage application evaluation process in which lower scoring applications are eliminated after stage one, and further documentation is required from applications reaching the second stage. Additionally, each state and territory has the opportunity to provide recommendations on which projects they feel are most deserving of funding.

NTIA is utilizing volunteer "expert reviewers" to rate applications during the first phase, while RUS is relying solely on staff and contractors for its review process. On September 28, NTIA and RUS posted online service area maps for proposed projects. During the 30-day period after those maps were posted, existing service providers and the public had the opportunity to inform the agencies if they believe those proposed service areas are not unserved or underserved. RUS and NTIA will make the final decision as to whether those applications are genuinely seeking to serve unserved or underserved areas.

First Funding Round

Applications for the first funding round were accepted between July 14 and August 20, 2009. While initially NTIA and RUS had expected to begin announcing awards in November, because of the volume and complexity of the applications received, award announcements are expected to begin by December 15, 2009.

On September 9, NTIA and RUS released preliminary data on applications received during the first round application period. In total, over 2,200 applications requested nearly $28 billion in funding for proposed projects reaching all 50 states, five territories, and the District of Columbia. The total amount of federal funding requested is seven times the amount available ($4 billion) in the first funding round. **Table 2** summarizes preliminary application data.[28]

Second Funding Round

The second funding round will likely open in early 2010. NTIA and RUS are considering whether to eliminate the third round altogether, and award the remainder of funds in the second round. The rationale behind combining the second and third rounds is reduced administrative costs, completion of the awards process by summer 2010, additional time for applicants to provide input on first round experiences, and additional time for applicants to prepare their applications. Prior to the second round, NTIA and RUS will collect public comment on "lessons learned" and on what changes should be reflected in the second round NOFA. Controversial issues, such as the RUS definition of "remote unserved areas," will likely be reexamined as part of the second NOFA process.

---

[28] A searchable database is available at http://www.ntia.doc.gov/broadbandgrants/applications/search.cfm.

Table 2. First Round Applications to BTOP and BIP

Submitted to	Number of Applications	Federal Funding Requested
Infrastructure (grants, loans, and grant/loan combos)		
BTOP solely	260	$5.4 billion
BIP solely	400	$5 billion
Both BTOP and BIP	830	$12.8 billion
Sustainable Broadband Adoption (grants)		
BTOP	320	$2.5 billion
Public Computer Centers (grants)		
BTOP	360	$1.9 billion

Source: NTIA. Preliminary data as of 9/9/2009.

State Broadband Data and Development Grant Program

On July 2, 2009, NTIA released a NOFA and solicitation of applications for the State Broadband Data and Development Grant Program.[29] The program will provide approximately $240 million in grants to assist states or their designees to develop state-specific data on the deployment levels and adoption rates of broadband services. These data, including publicly available state-wide broadband maps, will also be used to develop the comprehensive, interactive national broadband map that NTIA is required by the ARRA to create and make publicly available by February 17, 2011.

Grant awards will also include funding for state broadband planning. Up to $500,000 may be awarded for the planning portion of each project. Planning projects may include, for example, efforts to identify barriers to broadband adoption in a state and creation of local technology planning teams. Awardees will be required to provide at least 20% non-federal matching funds toward project costs, either cash or in-kind contributions. Applications were accepted from July 14 through August 14, 2009.

On September 9, 2009, NTIA announced that it had received applications representing all 50 states, 5 territories, and the District of Columbia. NTIA also announced that it had decided to initially fund state mapping and data collection efforts for a two-year period, rather than the five- year period originally intended. This will allow NTIA to assess lessons learned and best practices prior to awarding funds for subsequent years. Applications requested totals of approximately $100 million for mapping and $26 million for state broadband planning. On October 5, 2009, NTIA announced its first four awards. Subsequent awards are being announced throughout the fall. **Table 3** provides a listing of announced state broadband data and development grants.

---

[29] Department of Commerce, National Telecommunications and Information Administration, "State Broadband Data and Development Grant Program," 74 *Federal Register* 32545-32565, July 8, 2009.

Table 3. State Broadband Data and Development Grant Awards $millions

State	Applicant	Data Collection and Mapping Grant	Planning Grant	Total
AR	Connect Arkansas	1.6	0.5	2.1
CA	California Public Utilities Commission	1.8	0.5	2.3
DC	District of Columbia Office of the Chief Technology Officer	1.0	0.5	1.5
IN	Indiana Office of Technology	1.3	—	1.3
NC	Rural Economic Development Center, The e-NC Authority	1.6	0.4	2.0
NY	New York State Office of Cyber Security & Critical Infrastructure	2.0	0.5	2.5
VT	Vermont Center for Geographic Information	1.2	—	1.2
WV	West Virginia Geologic and Economic Survey	1.2	0.2	1.4

Source: Compiled by CRS from NTIA press announcements.

Note: Current as of November 5, 2009. More state grants will be announced in subsequent weeks.

Development of National Broadband Plan

On April 8, 2009, the FCC adopted and released a Notice of Inquiry[30] to gather data, expertise, and public input in preparation for its effort to develop a national broadband plan by February 17, 2010, as mandated by the ARRA. As part of this process, the FCC is collecting comments on a wide range of issues including:

- the most effective and efficient ways to ensure broadband access for all Americans;
- strategies for achieving affordability and maximum utilization of broadband infrastructure and services;
- evaluation of the status of broadband deployment, including the progress of related grant programs; and
- how to use broadband to advance consumer welfare, civic participation, public safety and homeland security, community development, health care delivery, energy independence and efficiency, education, worker training, private sector investment, entrepreneurial activity, job creation, and economic growth, and other national purposes.[31]

In an effort to gather further data, information, and perspectives on a national broadband plan, the FCC held a series of public workshops on a variety of broadband-related topics

[30] Available at http://hraunfoss.fcc.gov/edocs_public/attachmatch/FCC-09-31A1.pdf.

[31] FCC, News Release, "FCC Launches Development of National Broadband Plan," April 8, 2009, available at http://hraunfoss.fcc.gov/edocs_public/attachmatch/DOC-289900A1.pdf.

during August and September of 2009. The FCC has established a website on the national broadband plan at http://www.broadband.gov.

Issues Related to Implementation

The Broadband Technology Opportunities Program (BTOP) is newly authorized and established at NTIA, while the Broadband Initiatives Program (BIP) significantly expands the scope and size of RUS broadband loan and grant programs. The ARRA gives NTIA and RUS considerable flexibility to implement the BTOP and BIP. According to the Conference Report:

> The Conferees intend that the NTIA has discretion in selecting the grant recipients that will best achieve the broad objectives of the program. The Conferees also intend that the NTIA select grant recipients that it judges will best meet the broadband access needs of the area to be served, whether by a wireless provider, a wireline provider, or any provider offering to construct last-mile, middle-mile, or long haul facilities.

Implementation decisions made by NTIA and RUS have a significant impact on how the program is shaped and targeted, and the extent to which the program meets the goals and purposes set forth by the ARRA. On March 12, 2009, NTIA and RUS released a joint request for information (RFI) and notice of public meetings designed to gather public input into many of the implementation decisions which the agencies make as they develop rules and regulations for the program.[32] A series of public meetings were held in March 2009. The RFI solicited public comments from all interested parties on the following topics:

- the purposes of the BTOP program;
- the role of the states;
- eligible grant recipients;
- the establishment of selection criteria for grant awards;
- grant mechanics;
- grants for expanding public computer center capacity;
- grants for innovative programs to encourage sustainable adoption of broadband service;
- broadband mapping;
- financial contributions by grant applicants;
- timely completion of proposals;
- coordination between BTOP and the RUS grant program;
- how terms set out in relevant sections of the ARRA should be defined;
- how the success of the BTOP program should be measured;
- any other issues NTIA should consider in creating the BTOP;

[32] Department of Commerce, National Telecommunications and Information Administration, and Department of Agriculture, Rural Utilities Service "American Recovery and Reinvestment Act of 2009 Broadband Initiatives," 74 *Federal Register* 10716-10721, March 12, 2009.

- the most effective ways RUS could offer broadband funds;
- how RUS and NTIA can best align their activities;
- how RUS can evaluate whether a particular level of broadband access and service is needed to facilitate economic development;
- how RUS should consider priorities set out in the ARRA in selecting applications; and
- what benchmarks should be used to determine the success of RUS ARRA broadband activities.

Below is a discussion of selected issues that were ultimately addressed in the NOFA that was released on July 1, 2009.

Defining "Underserved" and "Unserved"

As specified in the ARRA, the purpose of BTOP is to provide broadband service to consumers residing in unserved and underserved areas of the United States. The issue of which areas should be defined as "underserved" with respect to broadband service has long been controversial. There is no generally accepted definition of "underserved." Factors such as a minimal number of existing providers, a lack of adequate market competition, unaffordable consumer prices for existing broadband service, or substandard download and upload available speeds may singularly or in combination lead some to define an area as "underserved." The definition of "unserved" is also not uniformly accepted. For example, should unserved be defined only as an area with no terrestrial (nonsatellite) broadband service, or should areas with some terrestrial but no mobile wireless service also be considered "unserved?"

The ARRA does not define either "unserved" or "underserved." The law directs NTIA to consider whether a grant application would increase broadband affordability and subscribership, and provide the greatest broadband speeds possible to the greatest population of users in the area served. The ARRA directs NTIA to consult with the states (plus the District of Columbia and the territories) to identify unserved and underserved areas within that state. The Conferees instructed NTIA to coordinate its understanding of the terms "unserved area" and "underserved area" with the FCC.

In approaching an understanding of these terms, the NTIA (and the states with which the NTIA will consult on this issue) must balance competing policy concerns, particularly when developing or embracing a definition of "underserved." For example, too narrow a definition may make it more difficult for rural areas in need of adequate broadband service to receive grants. On the other hand, too broad a definition of "underserved" may inappropriately confront existing broadband providers with government-funded competitors and may divert funding from projects in unserved areas with no broadband service whatsoever.

In the NOFA, both BTOP and BIP use identical definitions of "unserved" and "underserved." "Unserved" includes areas with a very small number of households served by terrestrial (non- satellite) broadband (10% or less). RUS and NTIA stated their belief that "a definition requiring that 100 percent of households lack access to broadband service could prove overly restrictive and risk inadvertently excluding populations," and that "establishing a

90 percent threshold acknowledges that a *de minimis* level of broadband service may exist in portions of the area, while also seeking to minimize the risk of unintentionally excluding an entire area from funding."[33]

RUS also designated separate categories of "remote" and "non-remote" areas. A remote area is defined as an unserved rural area at least 50 miles from the limits of a non-rural area. For Last Mile projects, only remote unserved rural areas are eligible for BIP grants.

The NOFA's definition of "underserved" encompasses not only relatively low broadband availability (no more than 5 0%), but also low adoption (40% or less) and the lack of available higher-end advertised broadband speeds (3 Mbps or more). NTIA and RUS pointed out that the underserved definition "includes a broadband speed criterion to recognize that a proposed funded service area can have the minimum level of broadband service available (defined as 768 kbps downstream and 200 kbps upstream), but still be considered 'underserved.'"[34] NTIA and RUS declined to define "underserved" in terms of pricing, median income, or demographic characteristics, arguing that the broadband adoption threshold would encompass those factors.

Defining Broadband

The term "broadband" is typically characterized or defined by minimum download and upload speeds, specific technologies (i.e., cable modem, fiber-to-the-home, wifi), or specific applications (e.g., telemedicine, distance learning). The ARRA broadband provisions do not specify minimum download/upload speed thresholds, are technology neutral, and cite a wide variety of applications eligible for funding.

The issue of speed thresholds is particularly controversial. While a high speed threshold has the benefit of encouraging the construction of next generation networks (such as fiber or next generation cable systems), it also runs the risk of excluding current generation technologies that may be uniquely suitable for some unserved or underserved areas. The Conferees acknowledged this dilemma, stating in the Conference Report that while speed thresholds could have the unintended effect of thwarting broadband deployment in some areas, deploying next-generation speeds would likely result in greater job creation and job preservation. The Conferees instructed NTIA to "seek to fund, to the extent practicable, projects that provide the highest possible, next- generation broadband speeds to consumers."[35] Thus, NTIA has the flexibility to balance the sometimes competing goals of constructing next generation networks with providing broadband to unserved and underserved areas.

In the NOFA, RUS and NTIA concluded that "broadband service" should be defined as the provision of two-way data transmission with advertised speeds of at least 768 kbps downstream and 200 kbps upstream to end users, or providing sufficient capacity in a Middle Mile project to support the provision of broadband service to end users. RUS and NTIA favor this broadband speed threshold because it conforms with the established FCC standard for

---

[33] Rural Utilities Service and National Telecommunications and Information Administration, Notice of Funds Availability (NOFA) and Solicitation of Applications, Online Version, July 1, 2009, p. 106.

[34] Ibid., p. 109.

[35] U.S. Congress, Conference Report to Accompany H.R. 1, 111th Cong., 1st sess., February 12, 2009, H.Rept. 111-16 (Washington: GPO, 2009), p. 775.

minimum broadband speed, allows the use of currently common broadband applications, allows for consideration of cost-effective solutions for difficult-to-serve areas, and is the most technology-neutral option because it encompasses all major wired and wireless technologies. In evaluating applications, RUS and NTIA intend to provide additional consideration to applications exceeding the minimum speed threshold or offering superior upgradeability.

Defining "Non-Discrimination and Network Interconnection Obligations"

Congressional policymakers continue to debate and consider whether laws or regulations are needed to ensure the "openness" of the Internet with respect to both content and access.[36] The debate over nondiscrimination (also commonly referred to as "net neutrality," "open access," and "network management") has shifted to a debate over the extent to which nondiscrimination requirements or standards should be imposed on broadband networks funded by BTOP and BIP. The ARRA directed NTIA, in coordination with the FCC, to publish "non-discrimination and network interconnection obligations that shall be contractual conditions of grants awarded." The ARRA says that these obligations, at a minimum, should adhere to the principles contained in the FCC's broadband policy statement (FCC 05-15, adopted August 5, 2005) as follows:

> To encourage broadband deployment and preserve and promote the open and interconnected nature of the public Internet, consumers are entitled to access the lawful Internet content of their choice.
>
> To encourage broadband deployment and preserve and promote the open and interconnected nature of the public Internet, consumers are entitled to run applications and use services of their choice, subject to the needs of law enforcement.
>
> To encourage broadband deployment and preserve and promote the open and interconnected nature of the public Internet, consumers are entitled to connect their choice of legal devices that do not harm the network.
>
> To encourage broadband deployment and preserve and promote the open and interconnected nature of the public Internet, consumers are entitled to competition among network providers, application and service providers, and content providers.[37]

In developing nondiscrimination and interconnection obligations for funded projects, NTIA, RUS, and the FCC face the challenge of ensuring the "openness" of federally funded broadband networks, while at the same time minimizing regulatory burdens on prospective grantees that, some say,[38] may constitute a disincentive for some entities to apply.

According to the NOFA, both BTOP and BIP require all applicants to commit to nondiscrimination and interconnection obligations. BTOP applications are scored on the extent to which the applicant exceeds the minimum requirements for interconnection and nondiscrimination. At a minimum all applicants (both BTOP and BIP) are required to adhere

---

36 See CRS Report RS22444, *Net Neutrality: Background and Issues*, by Angele A. Gilroy.

37 FCC, Policy Statement on Broadband Internet Access, FCC 05-151, adopted August 5, 2005, available at http://hraunfoss.fcc.gov/edocs_public/attachmatch/FCC-05-151A1.pdf. The FCC principles are not rules – rather they are intended as general principles to be incorporated in FCC's ongoing policymaking activities.

38 Stephanie Condon, "Telecoms Oppose Tighter Net Neutrality Rules for Stimulus Funds," *CNET News*, February 26, 2009.

to the principles contained in the FCC's Internet Policy Statement; not favor any lawful Internet applications and content over others; display any network management policies in a prominent location on the service provider's web page and provide notice to customers of changes to these policies; connect to the public Internet directly or indirectly, such that the project is not an entirely private closed network; and offer interconnection, where technically feasible without exceeding current or reasonably anticipated capacity limitations, on reasonable rates and terms to be negotiated with requesting parties (this includes both the ability to connect to the public Internet and physical interconnection for the exchange of traffic).

Role of the States

While the BTOP grants are competitive and will be awarded directly by NTIA, the states are expected to play a significant role. The ARRA directs NTIA to consult with each state to identify unserved and underserved areas (with respect to access to broadband service) as well as the appropriate allocation of grant funds within that state. States themselves (as well as municipalities) are eligible to apply for broadband grants, and the ARRA specifies that NTIA, to the extent practical, shall award not less than one grant to an entity within each state.

Regarding NTIA consultation with the states, the Conferees expressed the following:

> The Conferees recognize that States have resources and a familiarity with local economic, demographic, and market conditions that could contribute to the success of the broadband grant program. States are encouraged to coalesce stakeholders and partners, assess community needs, aggregate demand for services, and evaluate demand for technical assistance. The Conferees therefore expect and intend that the NTIA, at its discretion, will seek advice and assistance from the States in reviewing grant applications, as long as the NTIA retains the sole authority to approve the awards. The Conferees further intend that the NTIA will, in its discretion, assist the States in post-grant monitoring to ensure that recipients comply fully with the terms and conditions of their grants.[39]

An issue will likely be to what extent the NTIA follows the recommendations of the states with respect to award decisions.[40] States vary widely with respect to their own broadband programs and initiatives. Some states have embarked on state-wide broadband strategies and have been extremely active in mapping broadband availability and identifying unserved and underserved areas, while other states have not yet begun such an effort.[41]

According to the NOFA, for BTOP only, the states will receive a list of applications under consideration during the second stage of the application evaluation process. States may provide NTIA with a list and prioritization of recommended projects, along with an

[39] Ibid.

[40] Some states have already set up their own ARRA websites and have begun soliciting proposals for grant funding, including broadband projects. See http://www.recovery.gov/?q=content/state-recovery-page.

[41] For more information, see *State Broadband Initiatives: A Summary of State Programs Designed to Stimulate Broadband Deployment and Adoption*, A Joint Report of the Alliance for Public Technology and the Communications Workers of America, July 2008, 54 pages. State program database available at http://www.speedmatters.org/ statepolicy.

explanation of why the selected proposals meet the greatest needs of the state. The final decision on whether the application will or will not be funded rests with NTIA.

Eligible Entities

The ARRA defines eligible entities for BTOP grants as a state or political division thereof; the District of Columbia; a territory or possession of the United States; an Indian tribe or native Hawaiian organization; a nonprofit foundation, corporation, institution or association; or any other entity, including a broadband service or infrastructure provider, that NTIA finds by rule (required to be technologically neutral) to be in the public interest.

NTIA was thus directed to set the parameters of eligibility beyond states, political subdivisions, and nonprofit organizations. The issue was the extent to which eligibility would be extended to private sector for-profit broadband providers, be they large or small, incumbents or new entrants. According to the ARRA Conference Report, it was the intent of the Conferees that as many entities as possible be eligible to apply for a grant, including wireless carriers, wireline carriers, backhaul providers, satellite carriers, public-private partnerships, and tower companies.

Through the NOFA, NTIA found it to be in the public interest to permit for-profit corporations and non-profit entities (not otherwise encompassed by the ARRA statute) to be eligible for BTOP grants. According to NTIA, "many for-profit corporations have expertise in deployment and sustainable operation of telecommunications facilities, which may lead to the creation of more efficient and sophisticated broadband networks that consumers will be able to access in a shorter period of time. In some cases, for-profit corporations also may have the resources to deploy new infrastructure more quickly or efficiently than other types of entities."[42] For-profit corporations are also eligible for RUS grants, loans and loan/grant combinations.

Broadband Data Gathering

There is widespread agreement that data regarding broadband deployment in the United States are inadequate and that policymakers have an incomplete picture of where broadband service is available (and at what speeds and prices). Broadband data are important, because the more detailed and granular broadband data are, the more effectively government can direct broadband assistance to areas with the greatest need.

The ARRA addressed broadband data by designating $350 million for funding the Broadband Data Improvement Act (P.L. 110-385) and for the purpose of developing and maintaining a national broadband inventory map. The Broadband Data Improvement Act (P.L. 110-385) was signed into law on October 10, 2008, and requires the FCC to collect demographic information on unserved areas, data comparing broadband service with 75 communities in at least 25 nations abroad, and data on consumer use of broadband. The act also directs the Census Bureau to collect broadband data, the Government Accountability

[42] NOFA, p. 121.

Office to study broadband data metrics and standards, and the Department of Commerce to provide grants supporting state broadband data, mapping, and planning initiatives.

Regarding the inventory map, the ARRA directed NTIA to develop and maintain a comprehensive nationwide inventory map of existing broadband service capability and availability in the United States that depicts the geographic extent to which broadband service capability is deployed and available from a commercial provider or public provider throughout each state. Not later than two years after enactment of the ARRA, the NTIA is directed to make the national inventory map available online to the public in a form that is interactive and searchable.

A continuing and controversial issue related to broadband data is striking a balance between making available broadband deployment data to the public that is sufficiently detailed to be useful, without revealing what some providers may consider to be proprietary information.

According to the State Broadband Data and Development Grant program NOFA, entities receiving grants must agree to protect sensitive commercial and financial information from public disclosure except as otherwise mutually agreed to by the entity and the broadband service provider. Grant recipients may execute nondisclosure agreements to ensure confidentiality, but such agreements may not restrict a grant recipient from providing collected data to NTIA.

Evaluation and Transparency

Given the large amounts of grant money to be awarded within tight deadlines (by September 30, 2010, for the BTOP grants), there is considerable interest in the issue of transparency and how the programs will be evaluated and monitored in order to avoid waste, fraud, and abuse. To address this issue, the ARRA:

- required the Secretary of Agriculture to submit a report to the House and Senate Appropriations Committees on planned spending and actual obligations describing the use of ARRA funds ($2.5 billion) for the RUS broadband programs not later than 90 days after enactment, and quarterly thereafter until all funds are obligated;
- transferred $10 million to the Department of Commerce Office of Inspector General for audits and oversight of funds provided for the Broadband Technology Opportunities Program;
- directed NTIA to report every 90 days on the status of BTOP to the House and Senate Appropriations Committees, the House Committee on Energy and Commerce, and the Senate Committee on Commerce, Science and Transportation;
- directed NTIA to require grant recipients to file quarterly reports (which will be publicly available) on the grantee's use of the grant money and progress on fulfilling the objectives for which the funds were granted;
- authorized NTIA, if it chooses, to establish additional reporting and information requirements for any grant recipient;

- authorized NTIA, in addition to other authority under applicable law, to deobligate awards to grantees that demonstrate an insufficient level of performance, or wasteful or fraudulent spending, as defined in advance by NTIA, and award these funds competitively to new or existing applicants; and
- directed NTIA to create and maintain a fully searchable database, accessible on the Internet at no cost to the public, that contains at least a list of each entity that has applied for a grant, a description of each application, the status of each application, the name of each entity receiving funds, the purpose for which the entity is receiving funds, each quarterly report submitted by the entity, and other information sufficient to allow the public to understand and monitor grants awarded under the program.

The NOFA implements the ARRA requirements with respect to transparency and program evaluation. According to the NOFA, while RUS and NTIA will protect confidential and proprietary information from public disclosure to the fullest extent authorized by applicable law, the ARRA requires RUS and NTIA to make publicly available on the Internet a list of each entity that has applied for a grant, a description of each application, the status of each application, the name of each entity receiving funds, the purpose for which the entity is receiving the funds, each quarterly report, and other information.

CONCLUSION

The broadband programs in the ARRA, funded at $7.2 billion, are unprecedented in scope and scale compared with previously existing federal broadband assistance programs. Policy decisions made by NTIA, RUS, and the FCC could have major impacts on the implementation of the program and the extent to which it meets the goals set by Congress for short-term job creation and long-term improvement of the nation's broadband infrastructure.

The NOFA released on July 1, 2009, sets forth eligibility requirements, application rules and procedures, and evaluation criteria for broadband grants, loans, and loan/grant combinations offered by NTIA and RUS. Depending on the agencies' experience in the first funding round, rules, regulations, and funding allocations developed for the second and third rounds could be modified as long as they remain consistent with the statutory requirements in the ARRA.

The ARRA broadband provisions are only one component in the nation's overall broadband strategy. Among other issues which may be addressed as part of a national broadband policy (likely to be formulated by the Administration and the FCC) are universal service reform, tax incentives to encourage private sector broadband rollout, and spectrum policy to spur roll-out of wireless broadband services. As Congress continues to monitor broadband stimulus programs, while considering various additional options for encouraging broadband deployment and adoption, a key issue is how to strike a balance between providing federal assistance for unserved and underserved areas where the private sector may not be providing acceptable levels of broadband service, while at the same time minimizing any deleterious effects that government intervention in the marketplace may have on competition and private sector investment.

In: New Developments in Computer Research
Editor: Nikos E. Mastorakis
ISBN: 978-1-61470-321-1

SPECTRUM POLICY IN THE AGE OF BROADBAND: ISSUES FOR CONGRESS

Linda K. Moore
Telecommunications Policy

SUMMARY

The convergence of wireless telecommunications technology with the Internet Protocol (IP) is fostering new generations of mobile technologies. This transformation has created new demands for advanced communications infrastructure and radio frequency spectrum capacity that can support high-speed, content-rich uses. Furthermore, a number of services, in addition to consumer and business communications, rely at least in part on wireless links to broadband backbones. Wireless technologies support public safety communications, sensors, smart grids, medicine and public health, intelligent transportation systems, and many other vital communications.

Existing policies for allocating and assigning spectrum rights may not be sufficient to meet the future needs of wireless broadband. A challenge for Congress is to provide decisive policies in an environment where there are many choices but little consensus. In formulating spectrum policy, mainstream viewpoints generally diverge on whether to give priority to market economics or social goals. Regarding access to spectrum, economic policy looks to harness market forces to allocate spectrum efficiently, with spectrum license auctions as the driver. Social policy favors ensuring wireless access to support a variety of social objectives where economic return is not easily quantified, such as improving education, health services, and public safety. Both approaches can stimulate economic growth and job creation.

Deciding what weight to give to specific goals and setting priorities to meet those goals pose difficult tasks for federal administrators and regulators and for Congress. Meaningful oversight or legislation may require making choices about what goals will best serve the public interest. Relying on market forces to make those decisions may be the most efficient and effective way to serve the public but, to achieve this, policy makers may need to broaden the concept of what constitutes competition in wireless markets.

The National Broadband Plan (NBP), a report on broadband policy mandated by Congress, has provided descriptions of perceived issues to be addressed by a combination of regulatory changes and the development of new policies at the Federal Communications Commission, with recommendations for legislative actions that Congress might take.

Among the spectrum policy initiatives that have been proposed in Congress in recent years are: allocating more spectrum for unlicensed use; auctioning airwaves currently allocated for federal use; and devising new fees on spectrum use, notably those collected by the FCC's statutory authority to implement these measures is limited. The NBP reiterates these proposals and adds several more.

Substantive modifications in spectrum policy would almost surely require congressional action. The Radio Spectrum Inventory Act introduced in the Senate (S. 649, Kerry) and the similar House-introduced Radio Spectrum Inventory Act (H.R. 3125, Waxman) would require an inventory of existing users on prime radio frequencies, a preliminary step in evaluating policy changes. The Spectrum Relocation and Improvement Act of 2009 (H.R. 3019, Inslee) and the Spectrum Relocation Act of 2010 (S. 3490, Warner) would amend the Commercial Spectrum Enhancement Act of 2004 (P.L. 108-494, Title II). The Broadband for First Responders Act (H.R. 5081, King) would allocate additional radio frequencies for public safety use.

The Role of Spectrum Policy

Wireless broadband[43] can play a key role in the deployment of broadband services. Because of the importance of wireless connectivity, radio frequency spectrum policy is deemed by the National Broadband Plan[44] (NBP) to be a critical factor in national broadband policy and planning. Wireless broadband, with its rich array of services and content, requires new spectrum capacity to accommodate growth. Spectrum capacity is necessary to deliver mobile broadband to consumers and businesses and also to support the communications needs of industries that use fixed wireless broadband to transmit large quantities of information quickly and reliably.

The purpose of spectrum policy, law, and regulation is to manage a natural resource[45] for the maximum possible benefit of the public. Radio frequency spectrum is managed by the Federal Communications Commission (FCC) for commercial and other non-federal uses and by the National Telecommunications and Information Administration (NTIA) for federal government use. International use is facilitated by numerous bilateral and multilateral agreements covering many aspects of usage, including mobile telephony.[46]

Although radio frequency spectrum is abundant, usable spectrum is currently limited by the constraints of applied technology. Spectrum policy therefore requires making decisions about how radio frequencies will be allocated and who will have access to them.[47] Spectrum policy also entails encouraging innovation in wireless technologies and their applications. Arguably, the role of technology policy in crafting spectrum policy has increased with the

---

[43] Broadband refers here to the capacity of the radio frequency channel. A broadband channel can quickly transmit live video, complex graphics, and other data-rich information as well as voice and text messages, whereas a narrowband channel might be limited to handling voice, text, and some graphics.

[44] Federal Communications Commission, *Connecting America: The National Broadband Plan*, March 17, 2010, at http://download.broadband.gov/plan/national-broadband-plan.pdf.

[45] The Code of Federal Regulations defines natural resources as "land, fish, wildlife, biota, air, water, ground water, drinking water supplies and other such resources belonging to, managed by, held in trust by, appertaining to, or otherwise controlled by the United States.... " (15 CFR 990, Section 990.30).

[46] The International Telecommunication Union (ITU), an agency of the United Nations, is the primary organization for coordinating global telecommunications and spectrum management.

[47] Spectrum allocation and assignment is addressed in **Appendix B**, Competition.

need to reduce or eliminate capacity constraints that may deter the expansion of broadband mobile services. The adoption of spectrum-efficient technologies is likely to require a rethinking of spectrum management policies and tools. Policies for channel management to control interference might be superseded by managing interference through guidelines for networks and devices. The assignment and supervision of licenses might give way to policies and procedures for managing pooled resources. Auctioning licenses might be replaced by auctioning access; the static event of selling a license replaced by the dynamic auctioning of spectrum access on a moment-by-moment basis.

Current spectrum policy relies heavily on auctions to assign spectrum rights through licensing. Economy of scale in wireless communications has become an important determinant in the outcome of these auctions. Companies that have already made substantial investments in infrastructure have been well placed to maximize the value of new spectrum acquisitions. Corporate mergers and acquisitions represent another way to improve scale economies. Efficiencies through economy of scale have contributed to creating a market for wireless services where four companies—Verizon Wireless LLC, AT&T Inc., Sprint Nextel Corporation, and T- Mobile USA Inc.—had approximately 90% of the customer base of subscribers at the end of 2009.[48] These companies also own significant numbers of spectrum licenses covering major markets nationwide.

The leading position of these few companies in providing a critical distribution channel—wireless—for information and services may need to be considered in plans for national broadband deployment. One approach to ensuring wireless access to meet national broadband goals might be to tighten the regulatory structure under which wireless communications are managed. Other approaches might seek ways to modify spectrum policies to increase market competition and to accommodate the age of broadband. In the NBP, the FCC has emphasized the latter course and committed to a number of actions intended to increase opportunities for competition and innovation in mobile broadband.

Competition

With the introduction of auctions for spectrum licenses in 1994, the United States began to shift away from assigning spectrum licenses based on regulatory decisions and toward competitive market mechanisms. One objective of the Telecommunications Act of 1996 was to open up the communications industry to greater competition among different sectors. One outcome of the growth of competition was the establishment of different regulatory regimes for information networks and for telecommunications.[49] As a consequence of these and other legislative and regulatory changes, the wireless industry has areas of competition, e.g. for spectrum licenses, within a regulatory shell, such as the rules governing the Public Switched

[48] Subscribers are customers who have signed up for a plan, including those with more than one plan subscription; prepaid and pay-as-you go customers may not be included in reported totals. FCC, *Fourteenth Report; annual report and analysis of competitive market conditions with respect to commercial mobile services*, FCC, WT Docket No. 09- 66, released May 20, 2010, Table 3, p. 31, reported for second Quarter 2009.

[49] For a discussion of policy issues, see CRS Report R40234, ***The FCC's Authority to Regulate Net Neutrality after*** *Comcast v. FCC* , by Kathleen Ann Ruane, and CRS Report R40616, *Access to Broadband Networks: The Net Neutrality Debate* , by Angele A. Gilroy.

Telephone Network (PSTN).[50] As the bulk of wireless communications traffic moves from voice to data, companies will likely modify their business plans in order to remain competitive in the new environment. A shift in infrastructure technology and regulatory environment[51] might open wireless competition to companies with business plans that are not modeled on pre-existing telecommunications industry formulae. Future providers of wireless broadband might include any company with a robust network for carrying data and a business case for serving broadband consumers. Potential new entrants, however, may lack access to radio frequency spectrum, the essential resource for wireless broadband.

The FCC, in the NBP, has concluded that an effective way to improve competition among wireless broadband providers is to increase the amount of spectrum available. This approach was validated by a number of filings with the FCC; for example, the Department of Justice provided arguments as to why the "primary tool for promoting broadband competition should be freeing up spectrum."[52] Policy tools that might be used to increase the availability of radio frequency spectrum for wireless broadband include allocating additional spectrum, reassigning spectrum to new users, requiring that wireless network infrastructure be shared, pooling radio frequency channels, moving to more spectrum-efficient technologies, and changing the cost structure of spectrum access.

Innovation

From a policy perspective, actions to speed the arrival of new, spectrally efficient technologies might have significant impact on achieving broadband policy goals over the long term. In particular, support for technologies that enable sharing could pave the way for dramatically different ways of managing the nation's spectrum resources. The NBP has laid out several opportunities for the FCC, the NTIA, and other government agencies to contribute to and encourage the development of new technologies for more efficient spectrum access.[53] Among the technologies that facilitate spectrum sharing are cognitive radio and Dynamic Spectrum Access (DSA).[54] Enabling technologies such as these allow communications to switch instantly among network frequencies that are not in use and therefore available to any radio device equipped with cognitive technology. Among the steps that might be taken to

50 PSTN is a global system; rights of access and usage in the United States are regulated by the FCC.

51 On December 1, 2009, the FCC published a public notice seeking comments on the "appropriate policy framework to facilitate and respond to the market-led transition in technology and services, from the circuit-switched PSTN system to an IP-based communications world." "Comment Sought on Transition from Circuit-Switched Network to All-IP Network," NBP Public Notice #25, DA 09-2517 at http://hraunfoss.fcc.gov/edocs_public/attachmatch/DA-09- 2517A1.pdf.

52 *Ex Parte* Submission of the United States Department of Justice, In the matter of Economic Issues in Broadband Competition: A National Broadband Plan for Our Future, GN Docket 09-51, January 4, 2010, p. 21 at http://fjallfoss.fcc.gov/ecfs/document/view?id=7020355122.

53 *Connecting America*, Recommendations 5.13 and 5.14. The NBP proposed that the National Science Foundation "should fund wireless research and development that will advance the science of spectrum access." p. 96.

54 Dynamic Spectrum Access, Content-Based Networking, and Delay and Disruption Technology Networking, along with cognitive radio, and decision-making software, are examples of technologies that can enable Internet-like management of spectrum resources. DSA is part of the neXt Generation program, or XG, a technology development project sponsored by the Strategic Technology Office of the Defense Advanced Research Projects Agency (DARPA). The main goals of the program include developing both the enabling technologies and system concepts that dynamically redistribute allocated spectrum.

encourage spectrum-efficient technologies, the NBP has recommended that the FCC identify and free up a "new, contiguous nationwide band for unlicensed use"[55] and provide spectrum and take other steps to "further development and deployment"of new technologies that facilitate sharing.[56]

The NTIA has recommended exploring "ways to create incentives for more efficient use of limited spectrum resources, such as dynamic or opportunistic frequency sharing arrangements in both licensed and unlicensed uses."[57] This suggestion was incorporated into the 2011 Budget prepared by the Office of Management and Budget. The budget document directed the NTIA to collaborate with the FCC "to develop a plan to make available significant spectrum suitable for both mobile and fixed wireless broadband use over the next ten years. The plan is to focus on making spectrum available for exclusive use by commercial broadband providers or technologies, or for dynamic, shared access by commercial and government users."[58]

A Presidential Memorandum[59] has directed the NTIA to take a number of actions in support of NBP goals, including taking the lead in creating and implementing a plan that will facilitate the exploration of "innovative spectrum-sharing technologies."

The NTIA's Commercial Spectrum Management Advisory Committee is actively looking at policy and technology issues in a series of subcommittee reports. The reports are addressing spectrum inventory, transparency, dynamic spectrum access, incentives, unlicensed spectrum, and sharing.[60]

THE NATIONAL BROADBAND PLAN AND SPECTRUM POLICY

In the American Recovery and Reinvestment Act of 2009 (ARRA), Congress required the FCC to prepare a national broadband plan, to be delivered not later than February 17, 2010 (later extended to mid-March). The primary objective of the plan is "to ensure that all people of the United States have access to broadband capability...." The plan is to include "an analysis of the most effective and efficient mechanisms for ensuring broadband access...." and "a plan for use of broadband infrastructure and services in advancing consumer welfare...."[61]

On March 16, 2010, the FCC publically released its report, *Connecting America: The National Broadband Plan.*[62] The National Broadband Plan is presented as three major policy areas.

---

55 *Connecting America,* Recommendation 5.11.

56 *Connecting America*, Recommendation 5.13.

57 Letter to the FCC, Re: National Broadband Plan, GN Doc. No. 09-5 1, January 4, 2010 at http://www.ntia.doc.gov/ filings/2009/FCCLetter_Docket09-5 1_20100104.pdf.

58 Office of Management and Budget, *Budget of the U.S. Government, Fiscal Year 2011, Appendix*, "Other Independent Agencies," p. 1263. See also, FCC, *Fiscal Year 2011 Budget Estimates Submitted to Congress,* February 2010 at http://hraunfoss.fcc.gov/edocs_public/attachmatch/DOC-296111A1.pdf.

59 The White House, *Presidential Memorandum: Unleashing the Wireless Broadband Revolution*, June 28, 2010, at http://www.whitehouse.gov/the-press-office/presidential-memorandum-unleashing-wireless-broadband-revolution.

60 See Spectrum Management Advisory Committee website at http://www.ntia.doc.gov/advisory/spectrum/.

61 P.L. 111-5, Division B, Title VI, Sec. 6001 (k); 123 Stat. 515.

62 Available at http://www.broadband.gov/plan/.

- *Innovation and Investment* "discusses recommendations to maximize innovation, investment and consumer welfare, primarily through competition. It then recommends more efficient allocation and management of assets government controls or influences." The recommendations address a number of issues, including spectrum policy.
- *Inclusion* "makes recommendations to promote inclusion—to ensure that all Americans have access to the opportunities broadband can provide."
- *National Purposes* "makes recommendations to maximize the use of broadband to address national priorities. This includes reforming laws, policies and incentives to maximize the benefits of broadband in areas where government plays a significant role." National purposes include health care, education, energy and the environment, government performance, civic engagement, and public safety.

Spectrum Policy Recommendations

The section in the NBP on spectrum policy (Chapter 5) has taken particular note of the convergence of the Internet with mobile devices and the resulting increased demand for spectrum capacity to support mobile broadband services.

The NBP has proposed to increase spectrum capacity by

- Making more spectrum licenses available for mobile broadband.
- Increasing the amount of spectrum available for shared use.
- Encouraging and supporting the development of spectrum-efficient technologies, particularly those that facilitate sharing spectrum bands.
- Instituting new policies for spectrum management, such as assessing fees on some spectrum licenses, to encourage more efficient use.

To facilitate the deployment of broadband in rural areas, the NBP also has proposed

- Improving the environment for providing wireless components to build out infrastructure.

Many of the NBP proposals for wireless broadband may be achieved through changes in FCC regulations governing spectrum allocation and assignment. Other actions may require changes by federal agencies, state authorities, and commercial owners of spectrum licenses. To assist the implementation of the NBP there are also a number of areas where congressional action might be required to change existing statutes or to give the FCC new powers. Legislation has been proposed that would create an inventory of existing users on prime radio frequencies, a preliminary step in evaluating policy changes.[63] The NBP included the

---

[63] Radio Spectrum Inventory Act introduced in the Senate (S. 649, Kerry) and the similar House-introduced Radio Spectrum Inventory Act (H.R. 3125, Waxman).

announcement of plans for the FCC to create what it refers to as a Spectrum Dashboard.[64] The initial release of the FCC's Spectrum Dashboard provided an interactive tool to search for information about how some nonfederal frequency assignments are being used.[65] The dashboard could be expanded to meet requirements set by Congress for a spectrum inventory. In addition to the dashboard, the NBP has proposed that the FCC and the NTIA should create methods for recovering spectrum[66] and that the FCC maintain an ongoing spectrum strategy plan.[67] All of these steps will facilitate decisions about spectrum management by providing detailed information about the current and potential use of spectrum resources.

The Administration has supported the FCC's recommendations regarding means to increase the amount of spectrum capacity for wireless broadband.[68] In particular, the NTIA has been directed to collaborate with the FCC to identify spectrum holdings that can be made available for wireless broadband use. A deadline of October 1, 2010, has been set for the completion of a plan and timetable for releasing a total of 500 MHz of spectrum by 2020.

Spectrum Licenses

One of the management tools available to the FCC is its power to assign spectrum licenses through auctions. Auctions are regarded as a market-based mechanism for rationing spectrum rights. Before auctions became the primary method for distributing spectrum licenses the FCC used a number of different approaches, primarily based on perceived merit, to select license- holders. The FCC was authorized to organize auctions to award spectrum licenses for certain wireless communications services in the Omnibus Budget Reconciliation Act of 1993 (P.L. 103- 66). Following passage of the act, subsequent laws that dealt with spectrum policy and auctions included the Balanced Budget Act of 1997 (P.L. 105-33), the Auction Reform Act of 2002 (P.L. 107-195), the Commercial Spectrum Enhancement Act of 2004 (P.L. 108-494, Title II), and the Deficit Reduction Act of 2005 (P.L. 109-171). The Balanced Budget Act of 1997 gave the FCC auction authority until September 30, 2007. This authority was extended to September 30, 2011, by the Deficit Reduction Act of 2005 and to 2012 by the DTV Delay Act (P.L. 111-4).

In the NBP, the FCC has proposed taking steps to add 300 MHz of licensed spectrum for broadband within five years and a total of 500 MHz of new frequencies in ten years.[69] Approximately 50 MHz would be released in the immediate future by the completion of existing auction plans. An additional 20 MHz might be reassigned from federal to commercial use and made available for auction. Reallocating some spectrum from over-the-air broadcasting to commercial spectrum might provide an additional 120 MHz of spectrum. Final rulings on existing proceedings would release 110 MHz, of which 90 MHz would be for

---

[64] *Connecting America*, Recommendation 5.1.

[65] For more information on the Spectrum Dashboard, go to http://reboot.fcc.gov/reform/systems/spectrum-dashboard/ about.

[66] *Connecting America*, Recommendation 5.2.

[67] *Connecting America*, Recommendation 5.3.

[68] The White House, *Presidential Memorandum: Unleashing the Wireless Broadband Revolution*, June 28, 2010, at http://www.whitehouse.gov/the-press-office/presidential-memorandum-unleashing-wireless-broadband-revolution.

[69] *Connecting America*, Recommendation 5.8.

Mobile Satellite Services (MSS); resolution of interference issues between Wireless Communications Services (WCS) and satellite radio would free up 20 MHz of new capacity.

The spectrum assignment proposals put forth in the NBP are contentious in that the various parties affected by the decisions have diverging views on how technology should be used to provide access to these frequencies. Although Congress has shown interest in all of these debates, three proposals that are the most likely to generate pressure for congressional action are the plans for: repurposing and auctioning an estimated 120 MHz of airwaves assigned to over-the-air digital television broadcasting; auctioning the D Block (10 MHz in the 700 MHz band); and auctioning up to 60 MHz of spectrum for Advanced Wireless Services.

Television Broadcast Spectrum

The Balanced Budget Act of 1997, which mandated the eventual transition to digital television, represented the legislative culmination of over a decade of policy debates and negotiations between the FCC and the television broadcast industry on how to move the industry from analog to digital broadcasting technologies. To facilitate the transition, the FCC provided each qualified broadcaster with 6 MHz of spectrum for digital broadcasting to replace licenses of 6 MHz that were used for analog broadcasting. The analog licenses would be yielded back when the transition to digital television was concluded. The completed transition freed up the 700 MHz band for commercial and public safety communications in 2009.

The FCC has revisited the assumptions reflected in the 1997 act and has made new proposals, and decisions based on, among other factors, changes in technology and consumer habits. The NBP announced that a new proceeding would be initiated to recapture up to 120 MHz of spectrum from broadcast TV allocations for reassignment to broadband communications. This proceeding would propose four sets of actions to achieve the goal; a fifth set of actions to increase efficiency would be pursued separately.[70] The FCC stipulated in the NBP that its recommendations "seek to preserve [over-the-air television] as a healthy, viable medium going forward, in a way that would not harm consumers overall, while establishing mechanisms to make available additional spectrum for flexible broadband uses."[71]

Many of the proposals for redirecting TV broadcast capacity are based on refinements in the way frequencies are managed and are procedural in nature. Because over-the-air digital broadcasting does not necessarily require 6 MHz of spectrum, the NBP has proposed that some stations could share a single 6 MHz band without significantly reducing service to over-the-air TV viewers. Among the proposals for how broadcasters might make better use of their TV licenses, the NBP has raised the possibility of auctioning unneeded spectrum and sharing the proceeds between the TV license-holder and the U.S. Treasury. The FCC has called on Congress to provide new legislation that would allow these "incentive auctions."

D Block

The D Block refers to a set of frequencies within the 700 MHz band that were among the frequencies made available after the transition from analog to digital television in 2009. In

---

[70] *Connecting America*, Recommendation 5.8.5.

[71] *Connecting America*, p. 89.

compliance with instructions from Congress to auction all unallocated spectrum in this band, the FCC conducted an auction, which concluded on March 18, 2008. As part of its preparation for the auction (Auction 73), the FCC sought to increase the amount of spectrum available to public safety users in the 700 MHz band. Congress had previously designated 24 MHz of radio frequencies in the 700 MHz band for public safety channels. In 2007, the FCC proposed to designate 10 MHz – part of the original 24 MHz designated for public safety use – specifically for public safety broadband communications. Of the balance, 12 MHz were designated for mission critical voice communications on narrowband networks and 2 MHz were set aside as a guard band to protect against interference. In the FCC plan for Auction 73, the Public Safety Broadband License would be matched with a commercial license for 10 MHz, known as the D Block. The D Block was to be auctioned under rules that would require the creation of a public- private partnership to develop the two 10-MHz assignments as a single broadband network, available to both public safety users and commercial customers. The D Block license was offered for sale in 2008 but did not find a buyer. The FCC then set about the task of writing new service rules for a reauction of the D Block. [72]

In the NBP, the FCC announced its decision to auction the D Block under rules that would not require a partnership with public safety but would establish a framework for priority access to the D Block network by public safety users.[73] Based mainly on FCC efforts to create a public-private partnership, public safety officials have, by and large, anticipated that the D Block would be an integral part of a public safety broadband network. Since the failed D Block auction of 2008, there has also been growing pressure on the FCC and on Congress to take the steps necessary to reallocate the D Block from commercial to public safety use.[74] The NBP announcement regarding the D Block is considered by many to be a reversal of announced policy, creating controversy and renewed calls for Congress to take action to release the D Block to public safety. Although funding and control are critical elements of the debate, the controversy is rooted in contradictory assumptions about the level of service and reliability that new, largely untried, and in some cases undeveloped technology will be able to deliver for public safety broadband communications.

The FCC would address public safety needs such as developing standards and establishing procedures through the newly established Emergency Response Interoperability Center (ERIC).[75] ERIC would work closely with the Public Safety Communications Research program, jointly managed by the National Institute of Standards and Technology (NIST) and the NTIA, to develop and test the technological solutions needed for public safety broadband communications.[76] The Department of Homeland Security will participate in the areas of

---

[72] Background information regarding the D Block is provided in CRS Report R40859, *Public Safety Communications and Spectrum Resources: Policy Issues for Congress*, by Linda K. Moore

[73] *Connecting America*, Recommendation 5.8.2.

[74] A bill that would assign the D Block for public safety communications has been introduced (Broadband for First Responders Act of 2010, H.R. 5081, King).

[75] FCC News, "The Federal Communications Commission Establishes New Emergency Response Interoperability Center," April 23, 2010 at http://hraunfoss.fcc.gov/edocs_public/attachmatch/DOC-297707A1.pdf.

[76] NIST, "Demonstration Network Planned for Public Safety 700 MHz Broadband," December 15, 2009 at http://www.nist.gov/eeel/oles/network_121509.cfm.

public safety outreach and technical assistance, as well as best practices development.[77]

ERIC would take on the role of creating and implementing a federal plan to assist in building a nationwide, interoperable network for public safety. As the lead agency, the FCC would rely on its authority to require the D Block and other commercial license-holders in the 700 MHz band to accommodate public safety needs. Although public safety users would be charged for access to commercial networks, proponents of the plan have argued that overall costs would be less than if a network were built primarily or exclusively for public safety use, because of greater economies of scale. One of the expectations is that ERIC will be able to guide the development of standards for crucial radio components, with the participation of commercial providers and public safety representatives. The participation of commercial carriers in developing and deploying, for example, a common radio interface, is expected to put the cost of public safety radios in the same price range as commercial high-end mobile devices ($500). By contrast, interoperable radios for the narrowband networks at 700 MHz cost $3,000 and up, each.

Advanced Wireless Service Auctions

During 2007, the FCC was petitioned by several companies, led by M2Z Networks Inc., to release 20 MHz of spectrum licenses at 2155-2175 MHz for a national broadband network. M2Z offered to provide free basic service to consumers and public safety and to offer content filtering for family-friendly access. In return for the grant of the license, which would be assigned without auction, M2Z offered to pay a percentage of gross revenues to the U.S. Treasury. In September 2007, the FCC issued a Notice of Proposed Rulemaking to establish service rules for the auction of a license or licenses at 2155-2175 MHz, designated as Auction AWS-3.[78] Proposed provisions for the auction included obligations to offer free broadband service similar to that proposed by M2Z and family-friendly access. The proposed spectrum band is adjacent to bands previously auctioned in the Advanced Wireless Service (AWS-1) auction that concluded in 2006. T-Mobile, a major winner in the AWS-1 auction, has stated to the FCC that the network proposed by M2Z would cause "pervasive harmful interference" to licensees of the AWS-1 frequencies.[79]

The FCC did not act on the AWS-3 auction proposal but announced new plans in the NBP that included the 2155-2175 MHz frequencies.[80] As outlined in the NBP, the FCC would seek to pair the AWS-3 frequencies with an additional 20 MHz of frequencies reassigned from federal use. The plan has recommended that the NTIA, in consultation with the FCC, assess the possibility of such a reallocation and, if the reallocation appears feasible, that they move ahead with plans to organize an auction. If reallocation and auction is not deemed feasible, the FCC would proceed "promptly" to auction the AWS-3 frequencies, according to the plan. The plan had proposed using frequencies in the 1755-1780 MHz range, but the NTIA has instead offered to assess the feasibility of using frequencies in the 1675-

---

[77] FCC News, "The Federal Communications Commission Establishes New Emergency Response Interoperability Center," April 23, 2010.

[78] FCC, *Notice of Proposed Rulemaking*, WT Docket No. 07-195, released September 19, 2007.

[79] See for example, comments by T-Mobile USA, Inc. filed July 25, 2008, FCC, Docket No. 07-195.

[80] *Connecting America*, Recommendation 5.8.3.

1710 MHz band.[81] The FCC subsequently requested comments to evaluate approaches to making this band available for shared use that would include wireless broadband services.[82]

In addition to the AWS-3 frequencies, there are two blocks of spectrum under the designation of AWS-2 "H" and "J" that have been under consideration for auction since 2004. The AWS-2 "J" band, with paired frequency assignment at 2020-2025 MHZ and 2175-2180 MHz, might be paired with AWS-3 or with an adjacent Mobile Satellite Service band.

The process of finalizing auction plans for licenses to use the AWS-2 and AWS-3 frequencies might renew the debate over interference. FCC proceedings also might provide an opportunity to revisit the possibility of including a requirement for auction winners to offer basic broadband service at no cost to the consumer. The concept of a lifeline broadband service has received support from many policy makers in Congress.

Shared Resources

The FCC has stated in the NBP that it would facilitate sharing resources through a number of regulatory means.[83] Among the methods of sharing wireless connectivity currently practiced in the United States are sharing network facilities, sharing network operations, and sharing spectrum. Examples of sharing include nationwide roaming,[84] selling packages of minutes purchased from a facilities-based network, leasing network capacity and spectrum access from a facilities-based network to create a new service provider—known as a Virtual Mobile Network Operator—and spectrum sharing. In general, access is leased from an owner—of a tower, a network, or a spectrum license. Another option is to allocate spectrum for unlicensed use; any device authorized by the FCC may operate on the designated frequencies.

The primary difficulty for regulators in overseeing the sharing of spectrum is to minimize interference among devices operating on the same or nearby frequencies. It was primarily to prevent interference to wireless messages that spectrum licensing was first instituted. Today, a number of administrative and technological methods are available to minimize interference of wireless transmissions. In theory, all spectrum bands can be shared if interference can be managed.

Open Access

In the 2008 auction of spectrum licenses at 700 MHz,[85] several companies associated with Silicon Valley and Internet ventures petitioned the FCC to set aside a block of spectrum as a national license with a requirement that the network be available—open—to all. Open

---

[81] Remarks of Lawrence E. Strickling, June 3, 2010 at http://www.ntia.doc.gov/presentations/2010/PublicKnowledge_Spectrum_06032010.html.

[82] FCC, Public Notice, "Office of Engineering and Technology Requests Information on Use of 1675-17 10 MHz Band," DA 10-1035, released June 4, 2010, Docket No. 10-123 at http://fjallfoss.fcc.gov/edocs_public/attachmatch/ DA-10-1035A1.pdf.

[83] Connecting America, p. 79 and Recommendation 5.7.

[84] The practice of transferring a wireless call from one network to another—or roaming—is described in *Understanding Wireless Telephone Coverage Areas,* FCC Consumer Facts at http://www.ifap.ru/library/book385.pdf.

[85] For information, see Auction 73 at http://wireless.fcc.gov/auctions/default.htm?job=auction_summary&id=73.

access was defined as open devices, open applications, open services, and open networks.[86] The position put forward by these companies was that access of unlicensed airwaves was not enough to stimulate innovation and competition for new devices, services, and applications. They argued that innovators, especially start-up companies, were often closed out of markets unless they could convince a wireless network operator to accept and market their inventions.[87] The FCC subsequently ruled to auction licenses for 22 MHz of spectrum (designated as the C Block) with service rules requiring the first two criteria: open devices and open applications. The winning bidders, most notably Verizon Wireless,[88] are required to allow their customers to choose their own handsets and download programs of their choice, subject to reasonable conditions needed to protect the network from harm.

Wholesale Networks

The FCC was also petitioned to designate spectrum licenses at 700 MHz for networks that would operate on a wholesale business model. It was argued that the wholesale business model would be the most viable for a small business new entrant and that the auction rules and conditions adopted by the FCC were prejudicial to small business.[89] Wireless incumbents, in particular, have challenged the concepts of open access and wholesaling. They have claimed that the unproven nature of a wholesale business model makes it risky and that therefore the auction value of licenses with a wholesaling requirement would be diminished. They have argued that imposing requirements that would create a wholesale network introduces an extra level of regulatory oversight, covering such areas as handset compatibility, applications standards, market access regulation, and interconnection rules.[90]

Proponents of open access argue that only an open network that anyone can use—not just subscribers of one wireless company—can provide consumer choice. From this perspective, a wholesale network could provide more market opportunities for new wireless devices, especially wireless devices that could provide unrestricted access to the Internet. A wholesale network would allow customers to choose their own wireless devices without necessarily committing to a service plan from a single provider. The network owner would operate along the same principles used for shopping malls, providing the infrastructure for others to retail their own products and services.

Unlicensed Use

Unlicensed spectrum is not sold to the highest bidder and used for the services chosen by the license-holder but is instead accessible to anyone using wireless equipment certified by the FCC for those frequencies. Both commercial and non-commercial entities use unlicensed spectrum to meet a wide variety of monitoring and communications needs. Suppliers of

---

[86] FCC filings, WT Docket No. 96-86, by Frontline Wireless, LCC, Google, Inc., the 4G Coalition, and the Public Interest Spectrum Coalition.

[87] Comments, for example, made by Ram Shriram and Vanu Bose at the Frontline Town Hall, July 12, 2007, Washington, DC, and by Jason Devitt at a panel discussion during the State of the Net conference, January 30, 2008, Washington, DC.

[88] Of the 10 licenses of the C Block, seven were auctioned to Verizon Wireless: all six licenses covering the continental United States and a seventh license for Hawaii. Licenses providing coverage for Alaska, Puerto Rico, and the Gulf of Mexico were won by other bidders. See "FCC 700 MHz Band Auction, Auction ID:73, Winning Bids," attachment A, p. 63, at http://hraunfoss.fcc.gov/edocs_public/attachmatch/DA-08-595A2.pdf.

[89] Petition for Reconsideration of Frontline Wireless, LLC, WT Docket No. 96-86.

[90] FCC filings, WT Docket No. 96-86, by CTIA-The Wireless Association, AT&T, and others.

wireless devices must meet requirements for certification to operate on frequency bands designated for unlicensed use. Examples of unlicensed use include garage door openers and Wi-Fi communications.

New technologies that can use unlicensed spectrum without causing interference are being developed for vacant spectrum designated to provide space between the broadcasting signals of digital television, known as white spaces. On September 11, 2006, the FCC announced a timetable for allowing access to the spectrum so that devices could be developed.[91] Devices using the white-space frequencies would be required to incorporate geolocation technology to signal when and where potential interference was detected.[92] A geolocation database would be created and maintained to facilitate sharing of the white space by authorized devices. The design and operation of this database is being studied by the FCC.[93] The National Association of Broadcasters (NAB), and others, have protested the use of white space for consumer devices on the grounds that they could interfere with digital broadcasting and with microphones used for a variety of purposes.[94] Companies such as Microsoft, Dell, and Motorola, however, have stated the belief that solutions can be found to prevent interference. In November 2008, the FCC established rules that permit the unlicensed use of the white spaces, with special provisions to protect microphone use.[95] One of the recommendations of the NBP is that the FCC complete the proceeding that would allow use of the white spaces for unlicensed devices.[96]

Spectrum-Efficient Technology

Mobile communications became generally available to businesses and consumers in the 1980s. The pioneering cell phone technologies were analog.[97] Second-generation (2G) wireless devices were characterized by digitized delivery systems. Third-generation (3G) wireless technology represents significant advances in the ability to deliver data and images. The first commercial release of 3G was in Japan in 2001; the technology successfully debuted in the United States in 2003. 3G technologies can support multi-function devices, such as the BlackBerry and the iPhone. Successor technologies, often referred to as 4G, are expected to

---

91 FCC, *First Report and Order and Further Notice of Proposed Rule Making*, ET Docket No. 04-186, released October 18, 2006, at http://fjallfoss.fcc.gov/edocs_public/attachmatch/FCC-06-156A1.pdf.

92 Geolocation associates a geographic location with a device using embedded information such as an IP address, Wi-Fi address, GPS coordinates, or other, perhaps self-disclosed information. Geolocation usually works by automatically looking up an IP address.

93 FCC, Public Notice, "Office of Engineering and Technology Invites Proposals from Entities Seeking to be Designated TV Band Device Database Managers," ET Docket No. 04-186, released November 25, 2009 at http://fjallfoss.fcc.gov/edocs_public/attachmatch/DA-09-2479A1.pdf.

94 In addition to filed comments with the FCC. NAB, the Association for Maximum Service Television, and a coalition of theater groups, sports leagues, and TV networks have challenged the FCC white spaces order in the U.S. Court of Appeals for the District of Columbia. Requirements intended to protect microphone use in the white spaces are proposed in the Wireless Microphone Users Interference Protection Act (H.R. 4353, Representative Rush).

95 FCC, *Second Report and Order and Memorandum Opinion and Order*, ET Docket No. 04-185, released November 14, 2008 at http://fjallfoss.fcc.gov/edocs_public/attachmatch/FCC-08-260A1.pdf.

96 *Connecting America*, Recommendation 5.12.

97 A wireless analog signal uses a continuous transmission form. Digital signals are discontinuous (discrete) transmissions.

support broadband speeds that will rival wireline connections such as fiber optic cable, with the advantage of complete mobility. 4G wireless broadband technologies include WiMAX[98] and Long Term Evolution (LTE) networks. Both are based on TCP/IP, the core protocol of the Internet.[99]

Wireless technologies to facilitate broadband deployment for which spectrum may need to be allocated that were identified by the NBP include 4G networks; fixed wireless as an alternative to fiber optic cable; and broadband on unlicensed frequencies.

The NBP spectrum assignment proposals are based on managing radio channels as the way to maximize spectral efficiency while meeting common goals such as minimizing interference among devices operating on the same or nearby frequencies. Today, channel management is a significant part of spectrum management; many of the FCC dockets deal with assigning channels and resolving the issues raised by these decisions. In the future, channel management is likely to be replaced by technologies that operate without the need for designated channels. In the NBP, the FCC refers to these spectrum-seeking technologies as opportunistic. Identifying an opportunity to move to an open radio frequency is more flexible—and therefore more productive—than operating on a set of pre-determined frequencies. The primary benefit from these new technologies will be the significant increase in available spectrum but new efficiencies in operational and regulatory costs will also be realized.

The concept of channel management dates to the development of the radio telegraph by Guglielmo Marconi and his contemporaries. In the age of the Internet, however, channel management is an inefficient way to provide spectrum capacity for mobile broadband. Innovation points to network-centric spectrum management as an effective way to provide spectrum capacity to meet the bandwidth needs of fourth-generation wireless devices.[100] Network-centric technologies organize the transmission of radio signals along the same principle as the Internet. A transmission moves from origination to destination not along a fixed path but by passing from one available node to the next. Pooling resources, one of the concepts that powers the Internet now, is likely to become the dominant principle for spectrum management in the future.

New Technologies

The iPhone 3G and 3GS provide early examples of how the Internet is likely to change wireless communications as more and more of the underlying network infrastructure is converted to IPbased standards. The iPhone uses the Internet Protocol to perform many of its functions; these require time and space—spectrum capacity—to operate. The next generation of wireless networks, 4G, for Fourth Generation, will be supported by technologies structured and managed to emulate the Internet. The wireless devices that operate on these new, IP-powered networks will be able to share spectrum capacity in ways not currently used on commercial networks, greatly increasing network availability on licensed bandwidths. Another technological boost will come from improved ways to use unlicensed spectrum.

---

98 WiMAX stands for Worldwide Interoperability for Microwave Access.

99 Key technologies for mobile broadband are summarized in **Appendix A**, Spectrum-Hungry Technologies.

100 A leading advocate for replacing channel management of radio frequency with network-centric management is Preston Marshall, the source for much of the information about network-centric technologies in this report. Mr. Marshall is Director, Information Sciences Institute, University of Southern California, Viterbi School of Engineering, Arlington, Virginia.

Unlicensed spectrum refers to bands of spectrum designated for multiple providers, multiple uses, and multiple types of devices that have met operational requirements set by the FCC. Wi-Fi is an example of a current use of unlicensed spectrum.

More efficient spectrum use can be realized by integrating adaptive networking technologies, such as DSA, with IP-based, 4G commercial network technologies such as LTE. Adaptive networking has the potential to organize wireless communications to achieve the same kinds of benefits that have been seen to accrue with the transition from proprietary data networks to the Internet. These enabling technologies allow communications to switch instantly among network frequencies that are not in use and therefore available to any wireless device equipped with cognitive technology. Adaptive technologies are designed to use pooled spectrum resources. Pooling spectrum licenses goes beyond sharing. Licenses are aggregated and specific ownership of channels becomes secondary to the common goal of maximizing network performance.

New Policies

Among the steps that might be taken to encourage "opportunistic" technologies, the NBP recommends that the FCC identify and free up a "new, contiguous nationwide band for unlicensed use" by 2020;[101] and provide spectrum and take other steps to "further development and deployment" of new technologies that facilitate sharing.[102] Unlike its recommendations for auctioning spectrum licenses in the near future, the FCC's plans for bringing new technologies into play provide few details. The NBP provides a glimpse through the keyhole of the horizons beyond, but not the key that might open the door.

The testing of new technologies that increase spectrum capacity, and the policy changes they are likely to bring, has been designated by the NBP as a future event. Its immediate plans for spectrum policy are to fine-tune existing spectrum assignments to increase the availability of licensed capacity. The level of opposition to most of these spectrum assignment plans might suggest that current spectrum management practices have reached the point of diminishing returns. The FCC might consider first identifying the new technologies mobile broadband will require before it begins the hunt for more spectrum.

Management Tools

In the NBP, the FCC has asked Congress to consider granting it authority to impose spectrum fees on license holders as a means of addressing inefficient use.[103] The report has presented the hypothesis that "Fees may help to free spectrum for new uses such as broadband, since licensees who use spectrum inefficiently may reduce their holdings once they bear the opportunity cost" of holding the spectrum.[104]

---

[101] *Connecting America,* Recommendation 5.11.

[102] *Connecting America,* Recommendation 5.13.

[103] *Connecting America,* Recommendation 5.6.

[104] *Connecting America,* p. 82.

The Obama Administration also has proposed that the FCC be given the authority to levy fees, and to use other economic mechanisms, as a spectrum management tool.[105] The 2011 fiscal year budget prepared by the Office of Management and Budget projects new revenue from spectrum license user fees of $4.775 billion for fiscal years 2011 through 2020.[106] Similar projections were made in the 2010 budget[107] and in budget proposals during the administration of President George W. Bush.[108]

Although Congress never took up legislation in response to the Bush Administration proposals, the 108th Congress instructed the GAO to take note of the possible impact of changing the spectrum license fee structure. In the Commercial Spectrum Enhancement Act, the GAO was instructed to examine "national commercial spectrum policy as implemented by the Federal Communications Commission" and report on its findings in 2005.[109] The GAO was to examine the impact of auctioning licenses on the economic climate for broadcast and wireless technologies and to assess whether the holders of spectrum licenses received before the auction process was instituted (i.e., largely for free) have an economic advantage over license holders that purchased spectrum through the auction process. The GAO was also to evaluate whether the disparate methods of allocating spectrum had an adverse impact on the introduction of new services. The conclusions of the study were to be reviewed in the context of an Administration proposal to introduce license user fees on licenses that had not been auctioned. The GAO was also to provide an evaluation for Congress regarding the impact of assessing license fees on the competitive climate in the wireless and broadcast industries.

After consultation with the committees of jurisdiction, the GAO did not include an analysis of license fees in its report. Instead it focused on the impact of auctions on factors such as end-user prices, investment in infrastructure, and competition. One of the report's conclusions was that the cost of purchasing licenses did not affect price and competition in the long run because the cost was a one-time, sunk cost.[110] New licensing regimes were mentioned in the report as a possible means of increasing spectral efficiency but the suggestion received no discussion in the report.[111]

The FCC's statutory authority to impose new spectrum user fees is limited. The FCC was authorized by Congress to set license application fees[112] and regulatory fees to recover

---

[105] Office of Management and Budget, *Budget of the U.S. Government, Fiscal Year 2011, Appendix*, "Other Independent Agencies," p. 1263. See also, FCC, *Fiscal Year 2011 Budget Estimates Submitted to Congress,* February 2010 at http://hraunfoss.fcc.gov/edocs_public/attachmatch/DOC-296111A1.pdf.

[106] Office of Management and Budget, *Budget of the U.S. Government, Fiscal Year 2011,* Summary Tables, Table S-8, p. 169.

[107] Office of Management and Budget, *A New Era of Responsibility: Renewing America's Promise,* Table S-6, p. 126.

[108] For example, the President's budget for FY2004 and again for 2006 proposed that (1) the FCC's authority to conduct auctions be extended indefinitely; (2) user fees be levied on unauctioned licensed spectrum; and (3) broadcasters pay an annual lease fee on analog TV spectrum that they are holding as part of the Congressionally-mandated transition to digital television. In his budget for 2005, the President supported proposals for indefinitely extending the FCC's auction authority and giving the FCC the authority to set user fees on unauctioned spectrum.

[109] P.L. 108-494, Title II, Sec. 209 (a).

[110] GAO, *Telecommunications: Strong Support for Extending FCC's Auction Authority Exists, but Little Agreement on Other Options to Improve Efficient Use of Spectrum*," December 20, 2005, GAO-06-236, p. 2.

[111] *Ibid.*, p. 10, footnote 15.

[112] 47 USC § 158 (a).

costs.[113] A new fee structure seeking recovery beyond costs would require Congressional authorization, either through an appropriations bill or new legislation. New fees could be difficult to devise as many of the licenses originally assigned at little cost to the acquirer were subsequently sold to other carriers.

Wireless Backhaul

Most mobile communications depend on fixed infrastructure to relay calls to and from wireless networks. The infrastructure that links wireless communications to the wired world is commonly referred to as backhaul. In situations where installing communications cables is impractical, fixed wireless infrastructure may be used to provide the needed backhaul. Microwave technologies, for example, are used in a number of applications to extend coverage to areas not served by fiber- optic or other wire links.

The NBP has predicted that the importance of backhaul will increase with the implementation of 4G technologies, as mobile access to the Internet and other wired networks becomes increasingly prevalent.[114] The FCC therefore has proposed to take a number of procedural steps to increase the flexibility and capacity for point-to-point wireless backhaul technologies.[115] On June 7, 2010, the FCC adopted an order intended to "enhance the flexibility and speed" of acquiring spectrum for wireless backhaul.[116]

NATIONAL PURPOSES

Among the requirements for the National Broadband Plan, Congress specified that it should include

> a plan for use of broadband infrastructure and services in advancing consumer welfare, civic participation, public safety and homeland security, community development, health care delivery, energy independence and efficiency, education, worker training, private sector investment, entrepreneurial activity, job creation and economic growth, and other national purposes.[117]

In the plan, the Federal Communications Commission (FCC) has made recommendations that might fulfill both social and economic goals. In the section of the plan titled "National Purposes," it has focused on social goals with an agenda of actions for federal, state, and local agencies. The areas covered in this section are

---

[113] 47 USC § 159 (a).

[114] *Connecting America*, p. 93.

[115] *Connecting America*, Recommendations 5.9 and 5.10.

[116] FCC, *Report and Order*, released June 8, 2010, Docket No. 09-114 at http://fjallfoss.fcc.gov/edocs_public/attachmatch/FCC-10-109A1 .pdf.

[117] P.L. 111-5, § 6001 (k) (2) (D); 123 Stat. 516.

- Health care. The NBP has identified stated goals of the Department of Health and Human Services that might be effectively supported with technologies that are enhanced by access to broadband communications.
- Education. The NBP has proposed that broadband can provide an effective tool for meeting the educational needs and ambitions of educators, students, and parents of young children as well as support the Department of Education's strategies to improve educational achievement.
- Energy and the Environment. Broadband has multiple applications in the field of energy, conservation, and environmental protection. For example, SmartGrid goals set by Congress[118] might not be achievable without broadband communications.
- Economic Opportunity. Actions proposed in the NBP to further economic opportunity are centered on increasing access to Information Technology for small and medium-sized businesses. The role of broadband in providing job training and employment services and supporting telework are also addressed in recommendations.
- Government Performance. The recommendations for federal government actions encompassed both ways that broadband might improve the effectiveness of government and also steps the federal government might take to increase the availability of broadband networks. The latter included federal actions to improve cybersecurity and ways that federal agencies might assist communities and state and local governments in building broadband infrastructure.
- Civic Engagement. The NBP has described concepts such as government transparency that can lead to greater participation by all in the democratic process. Broadband access has been described in the plan as a useful tool for encouraging civic engagement because of the part it plays in interactive communication and providing information.
- Public Safety. The NBP recommendations dealt primarily with delivering wireless broadband to the radios of first responder. It also considered the role of broadband in upgrading the nation's 911 services and emergency alert systems.

Meeting Policy Goals

Each of the sections on national purposes has mentioned the existing legislative and regulatory framework and trends in the field that might benefit from better broadband access and services. Although each sector serves different needs and goals, the NBP recommendations are fairly similar for each. In general, stakeholders have been encouraged to

Create incentives to achieve broadband goals.

- Leverage broadband technology, including wireless broadband.
- Encourage innovation and improved productivity.

[118] P.L. 110-140, Sec. 1301; 123 Stat. 1783.

- Provide or increase funding for programs that support broadband policy goals.
- Modify regulations.

The NBP has recommended that the Executive Branch create a Broadband Strategy Council.[119] This council would coordinate efforts by the many agencies that the FCC has identified as having a role in the plan's implementation. The NBP has suggested that the President could require that federal departments and agencies submit broadband implementation plans to the council. The council could also act as an intermediary between the agencies and Congress regarding legislation that might facilitate meeting the NBP 's goals. Another recommendation of the NBP would require the FCC to track progress in meeting the plan's goals.[120]

Community Broadband

Rural communities have on occasion used their resources to install fiber-optic networks in part because they were too small a market to interest for-profit companies. Networks that depend on a fiber-optic cable backbone are capital-intensive and usually more profitable in high-density urban areas. Increasingly, communities of all sizes are looking at wireless technologies to support their networks. Municipalities, for example, are installing free Wi-Fi zones. Among the reasons often cited for installing wireless facilities are that generally available access to the Internet through wireless connections has become an urban amenity, a necessity in sustaining and developing the local economy, and a part of essential infrastructure with many public benefits.[121]

Opponents to community-owned networks contend that they provide unfair competition, distorting the marketplace and discouraging commercial companies from investing in broadband technologies. In particular, the fact that urban areas are creating Wi-Fi networks and providing, among other services, free wireless links to the Internet is viewed as a threat to commercial companies.

Several states have passed laws prohibiting or limiting local governments' ability to provide telecommunications services. An effort to challenge such a law in Missouri by municipalities offering local communications services in the state was heard before the U.S. Supreme Court in 2004.[122] In the Telecommunications Act of 1996, Congress barred states from "prohibiting the ability of any entity to provide any interstate or intrastate telecommunications service."[123] The Court ruled that "entity" was not specific enough to include state political divisions; if Congress wished specifically to protect both public and private entities, they could do so by amending the language of the law. This Court decision and the steady improvement in broadband communications technologies that municipalities

---

[119] *Connecting America*, Recommendation 17.1.

[120] *Connecting America*, Recommendation 17.2.

[121] The Federal Trade Commissions' Internet Access Task Force has published a report discussing many aspects of municipal broadband implementation and related issues, at http://www.ftc.gov/opa/2006/10/muniwireless.htm.

[122] U.S. Supreme Court, Docket Number 02-1238.

[123] 47 U.S.C. 253 (a).

wish to have available in their communities have provided fuel for a policy debate about access to broadband services.

Because community broadband networks can help with NBP goals for inclusion and national purposes, the NBP has considered the possibility that federal investment in broadband infrastructure might be leveraged for community and state broadband services. For example, the NBP has recommended that federal agencies could open their broadband networks to state and local agencies and to unserved and underserved areas.[124] It has also made recommendations to help reduce costs and improve funding to community broadband programs.[125]

ISSUES FOR THE 111TH CONGRESS

The NBP has made a number of recommendations for Congressional action to grant new authorities to the FCC, including several related to spectrum policy and auctions. The Radio Spectrum Inventory bills being considered by the 111th Congress parallel NBP recommendations. The NBP has recommended changes to the Commercial Spectrum Enhancement Act; not all of these recommendations are included in the bill that would amend that act, H.R. 3019, the Spectrum Relocation and Improvement Act of 2009. Congress may decide to consider NBP recommendations for legislation that would permit incentive auctions, particularly as they apply to recommended reassignments of digital TV broadcast frequencies. H.R. 5081, the Broadband for First Responders Act of 2010, would require the reallocation of 700 MHz D Block frequencies, contrary to announced plans to auction the frequencies.

Spectrum Inventory

Similar versions of a Radio Spectrum Inventory Act (S. 649, Senator Kerry and H.R. 3125, Representative Waxman) would require the FCC and NTIA to prepare an inventory of spectrum allocations and assignments in prime radio frequency bands. The information from the detailed report on users and uses would help policy makers evaluate whether spectrum is being allocated and used effectively. The bills would require an accounting of spectrum allocation in the designated bands that would identify commercial license-holders, government agency spectrum allocations, and the number of devices deployed in those bands. If available, information would be provided on the types of wireless devices used on licensed frequencies and on unlicensed frequencies within each band. Contour maps and information on the location of base stations and other fixed transmitters might also be included in the inventory. The inventory results would be available over the Internet. Exemptions from public access to some information may be granted for reasons of national security, although the two

[124] *Connecting America*, Recommendation 14.1.

[125] *Connecting America*, Recommendation 14.2, 14.3, and 14.4.

bills vary on terms for these exemptions. The inventory is to be completed and submitted in reports to Congress within 180 days of passage into law.[126]

The Commercial Spectrum Enhancement Act and Federal Relocation

The Spectrum Relocation and Improvement Act of 2009 (H.R. 3019, Representative Inslee) and the similarly worded Spectrum Relocation and Improvement Act of 2010 (S. 3490, Senator Warner) would address issues arising from current experiences in relocating federal users to clear space for commercial license-holders. The bills would define the rights and responsibilities of federal entities in the spectrum relocation process, especially obligations for sharing, and their eligibility for payments from the Spectrum Relocation Fund. The NBP has recommended that Congress consider improvements to the Commercial Spectrum Enhancement Act (CSEA) to provide "adequate incentives and assistance" to support relocation. The NBP has further recommended that the compensation to federal agencies be structured to provide additional incentives "for using commercial services and non-spectrum based operations." In particular, the NBP has recommended that "Congress revise the CSEA to provide for payments of relocation funds to federal users that vacate spectrum and make use of commercial networks instead...."[127]

The Spectrum Relocation Fund was created by the Commercial Spectrum Enhancement Act in 2004, to provide a mechanism whereby federal agencies could recover the costs of moving from one spectrum band to another. The fund is administered by the Office of Management and Budget. Following procedures required by the act, the FCC scheduled an auction of designated federal frequencies for commercial use as Advanced Wireless Services (AWS). The AWS auction was completed on September 18, 2006, attracting nearly $13.9 billion in completed bids.[128] The FCC ruled that auction winners wishing to put acquired licenses to immediate use would in most cases be able to share with current federal users under guidance from the FCC.[129] The act was written to be applied to most transfers of spectrum from federal to commercial use.

Incentive Auctions

The NBP has asked Congress to consider expanding the FCC's auction authority to permit incentive auctions.[130] As outlined in the NBP, such authority would enable spectrum license- holders to return spectrum for auction, with the expectation of receiving part of the proceeds as compensation for the costs associated with relinquishing the asset. Although most

---

126 The status of the bills can be monitored through the Legislative Information System (LIS) at http://www.congress.gov.

127 *Connecting America*, Recommendation 5.5.

128 FCC News, "FCC's Advanced Wireless Services (AWS) Spectrum Auction Concludes," September 18, 2006.

129 FCC Public Notice "Coordination Procedures in the 1710-1755 MHz Band," FCC 06-50, April 20, 2006 (WTB Docket No. 02-353).

130 *Connecting America*, Recommendation 5.4.

spectrum license auction revenues are deposited as general funds,[131] Congress has passed laws, such as the Commercial Spectrum Enhancement Act, that permit the proceeds to be used for other purposes.

Broadband for First Responders Act

The Broadband for First Responders Act of 2010 (H.R. 5081, Representative King) would amend the Communications Act of 1934 by requiring the FCC to allocate an additional 10 MHz of spectrum, known at the D Block, at 758-763 MHz and 788-793 MHz, for public safety services and assign these paired bands for public safety broadband use. The bill would require the FCC to establish rules to encourage the rapid deployment of an interoperable national wireless broadband network.

Service rules would provide priority access to mission critical public safety applications; provide for roaming on public safety spectrum by authorized users; encourage public-private partnerships by requiring consideration of the use of existing or planned commercial infrastructure; meet technical and operational standards for interoperability and roaming; require that networks are built to survive most large scale disasters; ensure networks have the appropriate level of cyber security; and facilitate the shared use of the public safety broadband spectrum and infrastructure with commercial and other entities.

Standards would be set in consultation with the National Institute of Standards and Technology (NIST) and others to enable nationwide interoperability and roaming across any communications system using public safety broadband spectrum.

CONCLUSION

Telephone service was once considered a natural monopoly, and regulated accordingly. The presumption was that redundant telephone infrastructure was inefficient and not in the public interest. State and federal regulators favored granting operating rights to a single company, within a specific facilities territory, to benefit from economies of scale, facilitate interoperability, and maximize other benefits. In return for the monopoly position, the selected provider was expected to fulfill a number of requirements intended to benefit society. Thus, for decades, the regulated monopoly was seen by most policy-makers as (1) ensuring that costly infrastructure was put in place and (2) meeting society's needs, as interpreted by regulations and the law.[132] Past policies to regulate a monopolistic market may have influenced current policies for promoting competition. The FCC's emphasis on efficiency for delivering services to a pre-determined market could be leading wireless competition toward monopoly; new regulatory regimes might be a consequence of this trend, if it continues.

---

[131] As required by the Communications Act of 1934, 47 U.S.C. 309 j (8).

[132] The original Communications Act of 1934 codified many regulations for monopolies as practiced at the time.

Current spectrum policy seeks to maximize the value of spectrum by encouraging economies of scale and appears to treat spectrum assets as an extension of existing infrastructure (spectrum license ownership and network management, for example) instead of an alternative infrastructure (Wi-Fi and wireless backhaul are examples). This policy course has provided a form of workable competition that has brought wireless services (until 2006, almost exclusively voice) at affordable prices to most of the country. However, wireless technology has reached an inflection point and is shifting from voice to data. Some argue that wireless policy should also shift, placing a greater value on innovation to achieve goals deemed to be in the public interest. A policy that prioritizes providing spectrum to spur innovation, for example, could create new markets, new models for competition, and new competitors. If spectrum policy serves broadband policy and broadband policy serves multiple sectors of the economy, then perhaps spectrum should be more readily available for a wider pool of economic participants.

The amount of spectrum needed for fully realized wireless access to broadband is such that meeting the needs of broadband policy goals could be difficult to achieve through the market-driven auction process unless large amounts of new radio frequencies can be identified and released for that purpose.[133] Without abandoning competitive auctions, spectrum policy could benefit from including additional ways to assign or manage spectrum that might better serve the deployment of wireless broadband and the implementation of a national broadband policy.

Legislation geared to improve auction mechanisms might benefit from the consideration of measures that would use technology to increase the amount of spectrum available, thereby opening the field to new players, fostering competition, and spurring innovation.

To further the transition to new technologies, Congress might choose to require performance goals for improved spectrum efficiency, not unlike the way federal goals have been set for energy conservation or transportation safety.

Appendix A. Spectrum-Hungry Technologies

Enabling technologies that are fueling both the demand for mobile broadband services and the need for radio frequency spectrum include Long Term Evolution, WiMAX; fixed wireless; Wi-Fi; high performance mobile devices such as smartphones and netbooks; and cloud computing. Fixed wireless and Wi-Fi are not new technologies but mobile broadband has given them new roles in meeting consumer demand. Future technologies include network-centric technologies, which include opportunistic solutions such as Dynamic Spectrum Access (DSA).

---

[133] International Telecommunications Union projects an estimated need for additional spectrum capacity that could reach nearly 1,000 MHz in the United States, as reported in "Summary of Results of ITU-R Report M. 2079," p. 13, presented by Cengiz Evci, Chief Frequency Officer, Wireless Business Group, Alcatel-Lucent, August 28, 2007. Available at http://standards.nortel.com/spectrum4IMT/Geneva/R03-WRCAFR07-C-0024.pdf. See also CTIA-The Wireless Association, *Written Ex Parte Communication,* FCC, GN Docket No. 09-5 1, September 29, 2009, which suggests a goal of at least 800 MHz, based on extrapolations from the ITU research.

Long Term Evolution (LTE)

LTE is the projected development of existing 3G networks built on Universal Mobile Telephone System (UMTS) standards.[134] Like all fourth-generation wireless technologies, LTE's core network uses Internet protocols. The network architecture is intended to facilitate mobile broadband deployment with capabilities that can deliver large amounts of data, quickly and efficiently, to large numbers of simultaneous users. LTE will likely be implemented in stages through modifications to networks using frequencies in bands already allocated for commercial wireless networks.[135] LTE might operate on spectrum bands at 700 MHz, 1.7 GHz, 2.3 GHz, 2.5 GHz, and 3.4 GHz.[136]

WiMAX

WiMAX provides mobile broadband but its earliest applications were for fixed wireless services. WiMAX (Worldwide Interoperability for Microwave Access) refers to both a technology and an industry standard, the work of an industry coalition of network and equipment suppliers.[137] WiMAX uses multiple frequencies around the world in ranges from 700 MHz to 66 GHz. In the United States, available frequencies include 700 MHz, 1.9 GHz, 2.3 GHz, 2.5 GHz and 2.7 GHz. The introduction of WiMAX in the United States is being jointly led by Sprint Nextel Corporation and Clearwire Corporation under the name Clearwire. Clearwire Wi-MAX, branded CLEAR, plans to serve 80 markets by the end of 2010.[138]

Fixed Wireless Services

Fixed wireless services have taken on new importance as a "backhaul" link for 4G. Backhaul is the telecommunications industry term that refers to connections between a core system and a subsidiary node. An example of backhaul is the link between a network—which could be the Internet or an internetwork that can connect to the Internet—and the cell tower base stations that route traffic from wireless to wired systems. Two backhaul technologies well-suited for mobile Internet access are fiber optic cable and point-to-point microwave radio relay transmissions.[139] Network expansion plans for WiMAX and LTE include

---

134 See, for example, "Mobile Broadband Evolution: the roadmap from HSPA to LTE," UMTS Forum, February 2009, Universal Mobile Telephone System Forum at http://www.umts-forum.org/.

135 Implementation summarized in *Connecting America*, Exhibit 5-B, p. 77.

136 Spectrum is segmented into bands of radio frequencies and typically measured in cycles per second, or hertz. Standard abbreviations for measuring frequencies include kHz—kilohertz or thousands of hertz; MHz—megahertz, or millions of hertz; and GHz—gigahertz, or billions of hertz.

137 Founding members of the WiMAX Forum include Airspan, Alvarion, Analog Devices, Aperto Networks, Ensemble Communications, Fujitsu, Intel, Nokia, Proxim, and Wi-LAN. For additional information, see http://www.wimaxforum.org/.

138 Implementation summarized in *Connecting America*, Exhibit 5-B, p. 77.

139 A discussion of backhaul technology is part of the testimony of Ravi Potharlanka, Chief Operating Officer, Fiber Tower Corp., at House of Representatives, Committee on Energy and Commerce, Subcommittee on

microwave links as a cost-effective substitute for fiber optic wire under certain conditions. Radio frequencies available in the United States for microwave technologies of different types start in the 930 MHz band and range as high as the 90 GHz band.

Wi-Fi

The popularity of Wi-Fi is often cited as a successful innovation that was implemented using unlicensed frequencies.[140] Wi-Fi provides wireless Internet access for personal computers and handheld devices and is also used by businesses to link computer-based communications within a local area. Links are connected to a high-speed landline either at a business location or through hotspots. Hotspots are typically located in homes or convenient public locations, including airports and café environments such as Starbucks. Wi-Fi uses radio frequencies in the free 2.4 GHz and 5.4/5.7GHz spectrum bands. Many 3G and 4G wireless devices that operate on licensed frequencies can also use the unlicensed frequencies set aside for Wi-Fi.[141]

Smartphones and Netbooks

Two of the fastest growing segments in the category of mobile Internet devices are smartphones and netbooks. The introduction of Apple Inc.'s iPhone, in 2007, is widely viewed as heralding a new era in wireless smartphones. The smartphone market is predicted to thrive on growing demand for downloadable applications,[142] interactive web sites, and imaginative videos—all delivered wirelessly. A parallel development has been the accelerating use of netbooks. These book-sized laptop computers are designed to provide broadband wireless access to the Internet. The line between smartphone and netbook technologies is fading as the newer generations of these devices provide many of the same features. The iPad, introduced by Apple Inc. in 2010, provides an example of the interchangeability of features across different platforms. The majority of these devices can operate on Wi-Fi as well as over 3G and 4G networks using licensed frequencies.

Cloud Computing

Cloud computing is a catch-all term that is popularly used to describe a range of information technology resources that are separately stored for access through a network, including the Internet. An Internet search on Google, for example, is using cloud computing

Communications, Technology, and the Internet, "An Examination of Competition in the Wireless Industry," May 7, 2009.

140 Unlicensed frequencies are bands set aside for devices approved by the FCC. The frequencies are effectively managed by the FCC instead of by a license-holder.

141 "Wi-Fi Popular Now in Smartphones, Set to Boom," by Matt Hamblen, Computerworld, April 1, 2009.

142 See, for example, "Smart Phones are Edging Out Other Gadgets," by Christopher Lawton and Sara Silver, The Wall Street Journal, March 25, 2009, for a discussion of how "beefed up cellphones" are replacing some electronic devices as their functions are incorporated into smart phones.

to access a rich resource of data and information processing. Network connectivity to services is another resource provided by cloud computing. Google Inc. also offers word processing, e-mail and other services through Google Docs. Although off-site data processing and information storage are not new concepts, cloud computing benefits from the significant advances in network technology and capacity that are hallmarks of the broadband era. Cloud computing can provide economies of scale to businesses of all sizes. Small businesses in particular can benefit from forgoing the costs of installing and managing hardware and software by buying what they need from the cloud. Consumers also can benefit because they no longer need to buy personal computers in order to run complex programs or store large amounts of data. The convergence of 4G wireless technology—with its smartphones and netbooks—and the growing accessibility of cloud computing to businesses and consumers alike will contribute to the predicted explosive growth in demand for wireless bandwidth.[143]

Network-Centric Technologies

More efficient spectrum use can be realized by integrating adaptive networking technologies, such as dynamic spectrum access, with IP-based commercial network technologies such as LTE. Radios using DSA chipsets are more effective at managing interference and congestion than the channel management techniques currently in use. If a channel's link fails, the radio is cut off. When radios are networked using DSA, individual communications nodes continue to operate and can compensate for failed links. The effects of interference are manageable rather than catastrophic. The network is used to overcome radio limitations.

Adaptive networking has the potential to organize radio communications to achieve the same kinds of benefits that have been seen to accrue with the transition from proprietary data networks to the Internet. Adaptive technologies are designed to use pooled spectrum resources. Pooling spectrum licenses goes beyond sharing. Licenses are aggregated and specific ownership of channels becomes secondary to the common goal of maximizing network performance.

The Department of Defense (DOD) is working to implement network-centric operations (NCO) through a number of initiatives.[144] Leadership and support to achieve DOD goals in the crucial area of spectrum management is provided by the Defense Spectrum Organization (DSO) created in 2006 within the Defense Information Systems Agency (DISA). The DSO is leading DOD efforts to transform spectrum management in support of future net-centric operations and warfare, and to meet military needs for dynamic, agile, and adaptive access to spectrum. The DSO is guiding DOD spectrum management along a path that envisions moving away from stove-piped systems to network-centric spectrum management and, ideally, to bandwidth on demand and cognitive self-synching spectrum use.

---

[143] The many factors driving demand for mobile broadband and the impact of growth in data and video services on demand for spectrum are reviewed in *Mobile Spectrum Broadband Demand*, Rysavy Research, December 2008.

[144] A discussion of the goals of NCO is included in CRS Report RL3241 1, *Network Centric Operations: Background and Oversight Issues for Congress*, by Clay Wilson.

Among the steps to advance toward the goal of spectrum access that is fully adaptable to any situation is the testing of network-centric technologies developed by the Defense Advanced Research Projects Agency (DARPA) within the Wireless Network After Next (WNaN) program.

WNaN is evaluating DSA, Disruptive Tolerant Networking, and other tools, possibly to replace the existing Joint Tactical Radio System (JTRS) now in use. JTRS uses software-programmable radios to provide interoperability, among other features.[145] WNaN's testing and evaluation of network-centric technologies is expected to lead to a decisison in late 2010. WNAN technology is planned for transition to the Army in 2010.[146]

APPENDIX B. COMPETITION

A combination of policy and market forces has divided the commercial wireless market into sharply different tiers. Policies that have encouraged economies of scale have favored mergers and acquisitions of wireless companies. There are now four facilities-based[147] wireless companies in the United States that the FCC describes as nationwide: AT&T, Verizon Wireless, Sprint Nextel, and T-Mobile,[148] which had approximately 90% of the subscriber market at the beginning of 2010. Another four providers had subscriber bases of between 1 million and 15 million Over one hundred smaller carriers serve niche markets.[149]

Barriers to Competition

In evaluating competition within an industry, economists and policy makers examine barriers to entry, among other factors.[150] Barriers might come from high costs for market entry such as investment in infrastructure or there might be legal and regulatory barriers to entry. As part of its evaluation of competition for mobile services, the FCC has identified three factors that could constitute barriers to entry to the commercial mobile communications industry. These barriers affect not only competitiveness but also access to networks and investment in new technology. The factors are: "first-mover advantages, large sunk costs, and access to spectrum."[151] All three of these factors are subject to regulations that have been influenced by past or existing policies regarding spectrum allocation and assignment.

---

145 Information at http://jpeojtrs.mil/.

146 Information about the WNaN program is based on comments by Bob Wilson, Deputy Program Manager for Army WNaN program, Communications-Electronics Command at DoD Spectrum Symposium, Arlington, VA, October 14- 15, 2009.

147 Facilities-based mobile telephone operators own and operate their network facilities.

148 *Fourteenth Report,* paragraph 27.

149 *Fourteenth Report,* paragraph 29.

150 For example, U.S. Department of Justice and the Federal Trade Commission, "Horizontal Merger Guidelines," Jointly issued April 2, 1992, revised April 8, 1997.

151 FCC, "Wireless Telecommunications Bureau Seeks Comment on Commercial Mobile Radio Services Market Competition," Public Notice, February 25, 2008, DA 08-453, WT Docket No. 08-27 at http://hraunfoss.fcc.gov/ edocs_public/attachmatch/DA-08-453A1.pdf. Earlier annual reports have also cited these barriers.

First-mover advantages[152] have accrued primarily to the early entrants in the wireless industry. Early in the development of the cell phone industry, the FCC created cellular markets and assigned two spectrum licenses to each market; one license went automatically to the incumbent provider in that market. The second license was made available to a competing service provider (not the market incumbent); the difficulties in choosing the competitors that would receive licenses contributed to the subsequent move to auctions as a means for assigning spectrum rights.[153] These early entrants, and the successor companies that acquired them and their licenses, have maintained their core customer base and benefit from early investments in infrastructure. Many first movers into the wireless market, therefore, acquired their market-leader status through regulatory decisions that provided them with spectrum licenses, not through market competition.

Large sunk costs refer to the high levels of investment needed to enter the wireless market. Not including the price of purchasing spectrum, billions of dollars are required to build new infrastructure. The sunk costs of incumbent wireless service providers set a high bar for new entrants to match if they are to compete effectively in major markets. In the mobile telephone industry, the FCC has observed that most capital expenditures are spent on existing networks: to expand and improve geographic coverage; to increase capacity of existing networks; and to improve network capabilities. Performance requirements for spectrum license-holders, such as the size of a market that must be served or deadlines for completing infrastructure build-outs, are some of the policy decisions that can add to the cost of entry.

Spectrum Auctions and Competition

The FCC, acting on the statutory authority given to it by Congress, has broad regulatory powers for spectrum management. The FCC was created as part of the Communications Act of 1934[154] as the successor to the Federal Radio Commission, which was formed under the Radio Act of 1927.[155] The first statute covering the regulation of airwaves in the United States was the Radio Act of 1912, which gave the authority to assign usage rights (licenses) to the Secretary of the Department of Commerce and Labor.[156] Licensing was necessary in part because, as radio communications grew, it became crucial that frequencies be reserved for specific uses or users, to minimize interference among wireless transmissions.[157]

---

152 The initial occupant of a market segment may benefit from a number of advantages such as preemption of resources, advantageous relationships with customers and suppliers, and early profits for reinvestment in infrastructure.

153 The distribution of licenses for cell phone networks from the early days of the technology until the introduction of auctions is described in *Wireless Nation: The Frenzied Launch of the Cellular Revolution in America*, by James B. Murray, Jr., Perseus Press, 2001, 2002.

154 47 U.S.C. § 151.

155 P.L. 632, Sec. 3.

156 P.L. 264, "License."

157 An "Act to regulate radio communications," usually referred to as the Radio Act of 1912, was passed partly in response to radio problems—including interference—associated with the sinking of the *Titanic*. Hearings Before a Subcommittee of the Committee on Commerce, 62nd Congress, 2nd Session, pursuant to S. Res. 283, "Directing the Committee on Commerce to Investigate the Cause Leading to the Wreck of the White Star Liner 'Titanic,'" testimony of Guglielmo Marconi, et al.

A key component of spectrum policy is the allocation of bands of frequencies for specific uses and the assignment of licenses within those bands. Allocation refers to the decisions, sometimes reached at the international level, that set aside bands of frequencies for categories of uses or users; assignment refers to the transfer of spectrum rights to specific license-holders. Radio frequency spectrum is treated as a natural resource that belongs to the American people. The FCC, therefore, licenses spectrum but does not convey ownership. Before auctions became the primary method for assigning spectrum licenses the FCC used a number of different approaches, primarily based on perceived merit, to select license-holders.

Auctions are regarded as a market-based mechanism for assigning spectrum. The FCC was authorized to organize auctions to award spectrum licenses for certain wireless communications services in the Omnibus Budget Reconciliation Act of 1993 (P.L. 103-66). The act amended the Communications Act of 1934 with a number of important provisions affecting the availability of spectrum. The Licensing Improvement section[158] of the act laid out the general requirements for the FCC to establish a competitive bidding methodology and consider, in the process, objectives such as the development and rapid deployment of new technologies.[159] The law prohibited the FCC from making spectrum allocation decisions based "solely or predominately on the expectation of Federal revenues...."[160] The Emerging Telecommunications Technologies section[161] directed the NTIA to identify not less than 200 MHz of radio frequencies used by the federal government that could be transferred to the commercial sector through auctions.[162] The FCC was directed to allocate and assign these released frequencies over a period of at least ten years, and to reserve a significant portion of the frequencies for allocation after the ten-year time span.[163] Similar to the requirements for competitive bidding, the FCC was instructed to ensure the availability of frequencies for new technologies and services, and also the availability of frequencies to stimulate the development of wireless technologies.[164] The FCC was further required to address "the feasibility of reallocating portions of the spectrum from current commercial and other non-federal uses to provide for more efficient use of spectrum" and for "innovation and marketplace developments that may affect the relative efficiencies of different spectrum allocations."[165] Over time, auction rules have been modified in accordance with the changing policy goals of the FCC and Congress but subsequent amendments to the Communications Act of 1934 have not substantively changed the above-noted provisions regarding spectrum allocation.[166]

The rules set by the FCC for using spectrum licenses (service rules) may have been oriented toward the concepts of building and managing networks that were formed in the days of the telephone, favoring traditional telecommunications business plans over those of companies with different business models. Some companies that might be well suited to meet

158 P.L. 103-66 Title III, Subtitle C, Chapter 1.

159 47 U.S.C. § 309 (j), especially (1), (3), and (4).

160 47 U.S.C. § 309 (j) (7) (A).

161 P.L. 103-66 Title III, Subtitle C, Chapter 2.

162 47 U.S.C. § 923 (b) (1).

163 47 U.S.C. § 925 (b) (1).

164 47 U.S.C. § 925 (b) (2).

165 47 U.S.C. § 925 (b) (3).

166 See United States Code Annotated, Title 47, sections as footnoted, WEST Group, 2001 and the 2007 Cumulative Annual Pocket Part.

social goals, such as access in rural areas, might have been precluded from bidding at all because of constraints not considered relevant to market-driven allocations. For example, public utilities, municipal cooperatives, commuter railroads, and other public or quasi-public entities face a variety of legal, regulatory, and structural constraints that limit or prohibit their ability to participate in an auction or buy spectrum licenses. Many of these constraints exist at the state level but federal spectrum policy plays a role in perpetuating the status quo.

Auction winners are deemed to be the companies that can maximize the value of the spectrum to society by maximizing its value as a corporate asset. However, auction-centric spectrum policies appear to have generally focused on assigning licenses to commercial competitors in traditional markets that serve consumers and businesses. Auctioning spectrum licenses may direct assets to end-use customers instead of providing wireless services where the consumer may be the beneficiary but not the customer. Wireless networks are an important component of smart grid communications. Spectrum resources are also needed for railroad safety,[167] for water conservation,[168] for the safe maintenance of critical infrastructure industries,[169] and for many other applications that may not have an immediate commercial value but can provide long-lasting value to society as a whole.

Spectrum Caps

As part of its preparations for the first spectrum license auctions, the FCC decided to set caps on the amount of spectrum any one company could control in any geographically designated market.[170] The theory behind spectrum capping is that each license has an economic value and a foreclosure value. The economic value is derived from the return on investment in spectrum licenses and network infrastructure. The foreclosure value is the value to a wireless company that already has substantial market share and wants to keep its dominant position by precluding competition. Spectrum caps were chosen as the method to prevent foreclosure bidding. The intent was to ensure multiple competitors in each market and to restrict bidding to only the licenses that could be used in the near term.

Beginning in 2001, spectrum policy placed increased emphasis on promoting spectrum and market efficiency through consolidation. The FCC ruled to end spectrum caps, citing greater spectral efficiency from larger networks as one benefit of the ruling. Spectrum caps were seen as barriers to mergers within the wireless industry, to the growth of existing wireless companies, and to the benefits of scale economies. The spectrum caps were eliminated on January 1, 2003.[171] Auction rules requiring the timely build-out of networks

---

[167] The railroad industry uses wireless communications as part of their information networks to monitor activity.

[168] For example, sensors buried at the level of plant roots recognize when watering is needed and communicate this information over wireless networks.

[169] In general, critical infrastructure industries facilitate the production of critical goods and services such as safe drinking water, fuel, telecommunications, financial services, and emergency response. A discussion of key issues appears in CRS Report RL30153, *Critical Infrastructures: Background, Policy, and Implementation*, by John D. Moteff.

[170] Licenses are designated for a specific geographic area, such as rural areas, metropolitan areas, regions, or the entire nation.

[171] FCC News, "FCC Announces Wireless Spectrum Cap to Sunset Effective January 1, 2003," November 8, 2001. Report and Order FCC-01-328. See Docket No. 01-14, *Notice of Proposed Rulemaking*, released January 23, 2001 at http://hraunfoss.fcc.gov/edocs_public/attachmatch/FCC-01-28A1.pdf.

became a key policy tool to deter hoarding. The FCC instituted a policy for evaluating spectrum holdings on a market-by-market, case-by-case basis—a practice referred to as spectrum screening—as a measure of competitiveness.

In 2008, the Rural Telecommunications Group, Inc. (RTG) petitioned the FCC to impose a spectrum cap of 110 MHz for holdings below 2.3 GHz. In October 2008, the FCC sought comments on the RTG petition for rulemaking.[172] RTG argued that competition in the industry was declining as it became more concentrated. It claimed that the larger carriers were warehousing their spectrum holdings in rural areas while rural carriers were struggling to acquire spectrum capacity for mobile broadband and expansion. Rural carriers, RTG reported, were being shut out of opportunities to acquire new spectrum holdings and were being outbid in spectrum auctions.[173] Opponents to the spectrum cap cited data to support their claims that the wireless communications market is competitive. They argued that additional amounts of spectrum are needed to support the growth in mobile broadband and that a spectrum cap could cut off growth and innovation.[174] Implementing spectrum caps as a tool for regulating competition would represent a significant shift in policy for the FCC, were it to take that course.

In comments filed regarding the National Broadband Plan, the Department of Justice considered the possibility that "the foreclosure value for incumbents in a given locale could be very high."[175] Although it recognized some form of spectrum caps as an option for assuring new market entrants, it observed that "there are substantial advantages to deploying newly available spectrum in order to enable additional providers to mount stronger challenges to broadband incumbents."[176]

Market Competition

There are many ways to view competition. Although competitiveness may be evaluated by factors such as barriers to entry or number of market participants, a key measure of whether market competition is working is an assessment of the dynamic of a specific market: its prices, variety, level of service, and other indicators that are considered hallmarks of competitive behavior. The Federal Trade Commission, for example, promotes competition as "the best way to reduce costs, encourage innovation, and expand choices for consumers."[177] Viewpoints about the level of competitiveness in providing wireless services to the U.S.

---

[172] FCC RM No. 11498, October 10, 2008. Comments supporting and opposing the petition are published in this proceeding.

[173] Those supporting the RTG petition included the Organization for the Promotion and Advancement of Small Telecommunications Companies (OPASTCO), the National Telecommunications Cooperative Association, the Public Interest Spectrum Coalition, and a number of smaller (non-dominant) wireless carriers.

[174] Opponents to spectrum caps that filed comments were AT&T Inc., Verizon Wireless, CTIA – The Wireless Association, the Telecommunications Industry Association, and the Wireless Communications Association International.

[175] *Ex Parte* Submission of the United States Department of Justice, In the matter of Economic Issues in Broadband Competition: A National Broadband Plan for Our Future, GN Docket 09-51, January 4, 2010, p. 23 at http://fjallfoss.fcc.gov/ecfs/document/view?id=7020355122.

[176] Ibid., p. 24.

[177] "Competition in the Technology Marketplace" at http://www.ftc.gov/bc/tech/index.htm.

market differ. [178] However, telecommunications business analysts generally describe the U.S. market for wireless services as competitive because consumers benefit in many ways from competition on price, service, coverage, and the availability of new devices.

Both the wireless industry and its regulator have focused on "wireless consumer welfare"[179] in evaluating competition and the effectiveness of spectrum policies for assigning spectrum licenses. Auctions are judged to be an efficient way of assigning spectrum for commercial uses that adhere to traditional business plans.[180]

Competition in Rural Markets

Over the years, various legislative and policy initiatives have created a number of requirements to help small and rural carriers acquire spectrum licenses.[181] Some of the FCC's efforts to encourage spectrum license ownership for small, rural, or entrepreneurial businesses are in response to Congressional mandates.[182] These and other statutory and regulatory programs may have allowed many small carriers to remain in business even though many others have been absorbed by larger carriers.[183] As wireless traffic, revenue, and profits migrate to broadband, business models that were effective for voice traffic may no longer be viable, especially for companies that have relied on the regulatory environment to protect their markets. This change in operating environment may have disproportionately affected the ability of rural wireless carriers, in particular, to compete effectively.[184] A study of how new technologies might be affecting the competitiveness of small and rural carriers might be useful in reviewing the effectiveness of policies intended to aid them.[185]

---

[178] Different assessments of competition in the wireless market have been filed as comments in FCC Docket No. 09-66, part of the process for the preparation of the FCC's *Fourteenth Report; annual report and analysis of competitive market conditions with respect to commercial mobile services.*

[179] This phrase is used in the written statement of AT&T Inc. submitted for a hearing before the House of Representatives, Committee on Energy and Commerce, Subcommittee on Communications, Technology, and the Internet, "An Examination of Competition in the Wireless Industry," May 7, 2009. In written testimony submitted by Verizon Wireless for the same hearing, comments stated that wireless providers need suitable and sufficient spectrum because of "consumers' reliance on broadband services."

[180] The GAO has reported this viewpoint in several reports, including *Telecommunications: Strong Support for Extending FCC's Auction Authority Exists, but Little Agreement on Other Options to Improve Efficient Use of Spectrum,*" December 20, 2005, GAO-06-236 and *Telecommunications: Options for and Barriers to Spectrum Reform,* March 14, 2006, GAO-06-526T.

[181] For example, most auctions have provided bidding credits for small businesses.

[182] In 47 USC § 309 (j) (3) (B), the FCC is instructed to promote "economic opportunity and competition and ensuring that new and innovative technologies are readily available to the American people by avoiding excessive concentration of licenses and by disseminating licenses among a wide variety of applicants...."

[183] The Congressional Budget Office (CBO) reported in a 2005 study that a significant number of small companies that acquired spectrum licenses through preferential programs later transferred the licenses to larger companies: *Small Businesses in License Auctions for Wireless Personal Communications Services*, A CBO Paper, October 2005, at http://www.cbo.gov/ftpdocs/68xx/doc6808/10-24-FCC.pdf.

[184] A number of rural wireless carriers and their associations have filed comments on the increasing difficulties they face in competing for wireless customers. Comments are in a number of FCC dockets, such as RM1 1498, regarding spectrum caps, and WT Docket No. 09-66, on the state of wireless competition.

[185] The CBO study cited above was prepared at the request of the Senate Budget Committee to examine the impact of small-bidder preferences on federal revenue and was completed before data traffic became a significant factor in providing wireless services.

Appendix C. International Policies for Spectrum Management

Wireless companies also compete as providers in global markets. Although international traffic may be a small part of wireless voice communications, competition in providing services is global.[186] AT&T, Verizon, and T-Mobile are major players internationally as well as in the United States.[187] Corporate decisions such as the introduction of new technologies and services are made for both the United States and international markets. Actions taken for domestic markets may influence decisions made to enhance global competition and vice versa. Therefore, policies for assigning spectrum assets might incorporate U.S. goals for global competiveness.

Spectrum allocation is not a uniquely domestic process. Some spectrum allocations are governed by international treaty. Additionally, there is a trend to harmonize spectrum allocations for commercial use across countries through international agreements. Harmonization of radio frequencies is achieved by designating specific bands for the same category of use worldwide. With harmonization, consumers and businesses are able to benefit from the convenience and efficiency of having common frequencies for similar uses, thus promoting development of a seamless, global communications market. Spectrum allocation at the national level, therefore, is sometimes coordinated with international spectrum allocation agreements. The Advanced Wireless Services (AWS) auction in the United States, completed in 2006,[188] was the conclusion of a process initiated by an agreement for international harmonization of spectrum bands.[189] At this auction, T-Mobile was able to acquire new spectrum licenses that improved its competitiveness in the United States[190] and, consequently, the worldwide competiveness of its owner, Deutsche Telekom.[191]

The International Telecommunications Union (ITU), the lead United Nations agency for information and communication technologies, has been vested with responsibility to ensure interference-free operations of wireless communication through implementation of international agreements.[192] The ITU adopts a Table of Frequency Allocations in conjunction with International Radio Regulations. This International Table allocates spectrum for various

[186] The international framework for spectrum management and wireless competition is summarized in **Appendix C**, International Policies for Spectrum Management.

[187] Verizon Wireless is 45% owned by the British telecommunications giant Vodafone, PLC. T-Mobile is 100% owned by Deutsche Telecom.

[188] FCC News, "FCC's Advanced Wireless Services (AWS) Spectrum Auction Concludes," September 18, 2006.

[189] The WRC-2000 agreed on spectrum bands to be harmonized for advanced wireless services, referred to as IMT 2000. See FCC News, "International Bureau Reports on Success of the 2000 World Radio Communications Conference," June 8, 2000, http://www.fcc.gov/Bureaus/International/News_Releases/2000/nrin0009.html.

[190] FCC, *Twelfth Report; annual report and analysis of competitive market conditions with respect to commercial mobile services*, Docket No. 07-71, released February 4, 2008, p. 9 and paragraph 75, at http://hraunfoss.fcc.gov/ edocs_public/attachmatch/DA-08-453A1 .pdf.

[191] Deutsche Telekom owns 100% of T-Mobile International, which includes T-Mobile USA. For information see "Global Player on the Mobile Communications Market" at http://www.telekom.com/dtag/cms/content/dt/en/530494.

[192] The GAO notes that "The federal government considers ITU the principal, competent, and appropriate international organization for the purpose of formulating international treaties and understandings regarding certain telecommunications matters." *Better Coordination and Enhanced Accountability Needed to Improve Spectrum Management*, GAO-02-906, September 2003, p. 19, fn. 26.

radio services and includes, directly or indirectly, conditions for the use of the allocated spectrum.[193] There is also a domestic table for each country. The United States Table of Allocations is maintained by the National Telecommunications and Information Administration (NTIA). The U.S. Table of Allocations is modified to correspond with changes in international spectrum allocations agreed to under the auspices of the ITU. These agreements are reached through processes such as the World Radiocommunications Conferences (WRC). Each WRC provides an opportunity to revise the International Radio Regulations and International Table of Frequency Allocations in response to changes in technology and other factors. Modifications to rules from one WRC to the next are part of an ongoing process of technical review and negotiations. WRC meetings are held approximately every two years. Provisions that require changes in frequency allocation to accommodate new technology will typically take effect 10 to 15 years after agreement is reached. These delays give time to phase out older technologies and to formulate new investment strategies.

The possibility of allocating additional spectrum for mobile broadband was among the deliberations of WRC-07 (October 22-November 16, 2007) and may be considered at the next WRC, scheduled to be held in January 2012.[194] Future decisions about spectrum allocation for broadband in the United States might be influenced by international agreements. Worldwide harmonization of frequencies for mobile broadband may be sought in bands at 3 GHz and higher.

In the NBP, the FCC has briefly discussed its participation in world forums and the role of the ITU in the development of new wireless technologies and services.[195] The NBP has recommended that the FCC should work within the ITU to promote innovative and flexible approaches to global spectrum allocation.[196]

[193] There are 39 internationally defined wireless services, including broadcasting, meteorological satellite, and mobile services. Description of ITU-R functions are at http://www.itu.int/ITU-/index.asp?category=information&rlink= rhome&lang=en.

[194] The NTIA and FCC websites carry information about planning for WRC 2012. For FCC, see IB Docket No. 04-286, Public Notice at http://hraunfoss.fcc.gov/edocs_public/attachmatch/DA-09-763A1.pdf. An NTIA overview is at http://www.ntia.doc.gov/osmhome/wrc/ntia.html. The ITU site is at http://www.itu.int/ITU-R/index.asp?category= conferences&rlink=wrc-1 1 &lang=en.

[195] The International Telecommunications Union (ITU) is considering how policies and regulations may need to be changed in response to new technologies. A World Telecommunication Policy Forum in April 2009, organized by the ITU, addressed these and other topics. See http://www.itu.int/osg/csd/wtpf/wtpf2009/about.html.

[196] *Connecting America,* Recommendation 5.16.

INDEX

C

G

H

I

J

Q

R

S

T

U

V

W

X